SETTING THE AGENDA

Jean Royce and the Shaping of Queen's University

STUDIES IN GENDER AND HISTORY

General editors: Franca Iacovetta and Karen Dubinsky

SETTING THE AGENDA

Jean Royce and the Shaping of Queen's University

ROBERTA HAMILTON

UNIVERSITY OF TORONTO PRESS
Toronto Buffalo London

Toronto Buffalo London

Printed in Canada

ISBN 0-8020-3671-6 (cloth)

Printed on acid-free paper

National Library of Canada Cataloguing in Publication

Hamilton, Roberta
Setting the agenda : Jean Royce and the shaping of Queen's University / Roberta Hamilton.

(Studies in gender and history)
Includes bibliographical references and index.
ISBN 0-8020-3671-6

1. Royce, Jean, 1904–1982. 2. College registrars – Canada – Biography. 3. Queen's University (Kingston, Ont.) – Biography. I. Title. II. Series.

LE3.Q318R69 2002 378.713'72'092 C2002-901377-1

University of Toronto Press acknowledges the financial assistance to its publishing program of the Canada Council for the Arts and the Ontario Arts Council.

This book has been published with the help of a grant from the Humanities and Social Sciences Federation of Canada, using funds provided by the Social Sciences and Humanities Research Council of Canada.

University of Toronto Press acknowledges the financial support for its publishing activities of the Government of Canada through the Book Publishing Industry Development Program (BPIDP).

In memory of my mother
Elizabeth Russell
22 November 1919–3 January 2002

Contents

SETTING THE AGENDA

Jean Royce and the Shaping of Queen's University

Introduction

In fall 1963, a don in the residence at Carleton University in Ottawa announced to our group: 'My cousin has just received a "Miss Royce letter."' This was my introduction to the registrar at Queen's University, who, it seemed, embodied the university itself, and whose letters were awaited eagerly by all who coveted entrance. All the students at Queen's knew her: some sought her out, others had been summoned. All the faculty and staff remembered her, and almost everyone who knew her had an opinion of her. For the most part, they admired her. After she received an honorary degree from Queen's in 1968, one of her fellow graduands turned to Chancellor Stirling: '[Today] you installed a new principal [and] gave honorary degrees to your very distinguished prime minister and to us. [But] the *only* person who got a standing ovation was [a] little lady. Now what had she done?'[1]

The lady was Jean Isobel Royce, whose association with Queen's began in 1925, when, through correspondence courses, she began working toward an Honours BA, which she completed in 1930. A year after graduation she became assistant to the registrar; in 1933, six months after the death of the incumbent, she became registrar. She was twenty-nine. Principal William Hamilton Fyfe hastened to reassure 'those who detect in this succession an omen of matriarchy [that] Miss Royce's imperturbable efficiency made the appointment inevitable, and indeed would go far to justify any system of government.'[2]

In the second volume of the university's official history, Frederick W. Gibson provides a succinct account of Jean Royce's subsequent career at Queen's: 'Miss Royce served as registrar for thirty-five years, to the immeasurable benefit of several generations of Queen's students and faculty.'[3] Gibson might have said more, yet my sympathies are with him. His is an institutional history, written mainly from the record – minutes, correspondence, principals' reports. The registrar was usually present, setting agendas, doing minutes, providing information, and so on. But Jean Royce doesn't leap off the page to beckon researchers. Often her name doesn't even appear in the list of those present: most often she is simply 'Registrar' or 'Secretary.' Years after retirement she asked a friend: 'Is it enough that you do these things, or do you need recognition?'[4] My guess is that at the time it was enough merely to do these things. Recognition came during the interactions of daily life. Perhaps unaware that a 'Miss Royce letter' was a hallmark of Queen's, she conducted herself as the university's servant and persona. Take her response, written two years after her retirement, to a request by the Dean of Arts and Science for her reflections on student grievances: The Registrar's Office, once a 'central directory of information ... is now a series of autonomous activities.' As a result, 'a common complaint' of today's student is that 'he [*sic*] is given the "run-around," he knows ... no-one who gives evidence of concern for him ... who can give a true assessment of his quality [or] to whom he can appeal in circumstances that may seem unfair.'[5]

For decades, the small size of Queen's, along with its small-town location, its administrative and academic structure, and the loyalty of its alumni – who sent their sons and daughters there, and their grandsons and granddaughters after them – made it possible for a single person to embody the whole institution. For many students an invitation to Jean Royce's office was tantamount to a summons by the university. By their accounts (and hers), she became 'a central directory of information [giving] evidence of concern ... and true assessments of [their] qualities,' and a court of appeal 'in circumstances that [seemed] unfair.' Jean's life provided plenty of recognition, albeit not of the neon-lights variety, and not even of the sort to make it into an institutional history. What she *did* enjoy was the daily acknowledgment of all who crossed her path. Yet in the years after her retirement, perhaps she reconsidered: Hence, her question – 'Is it enough that you do these things or do you need recognition?'[6]

In February 1968, Principal James Corry informed her that he had selected her successor and that she should prepare to retire.[7] When she remonstrated – her sixty-fifth birthday was a year away and she had unfinished projects – he dissimulated. He had thought she was older and told her he couldn't renege on his commitment to his friend, the registrar-elect. That Jean was unhinged by this decision is borne out by subsequent events, which I will describe later. My point in mentioning this now is to highlight this question: How was it possible for someone so centrally located to be so apparently invisible to the principal of the university? How, after thirty-five years in the same position, could a successor be chosen 'too soon,' without warning to the incumbent?

Until 1992, a decade after her death, only a handful of people knew that her resignation had in fact been a dismissal. That year, Margaret Hooey, the Secretary of the Senate and Jean's closest friend, revealed the actual circumstances in a presentation for the Ban Righ Foundation's conference, 'Sisters in the Old Boys Network.'[8] The revelation reverberated through generations of Queen's students, faculty, and staff, and was for some a stark reminder of how women in general were treated at the university. The dismissal set Jean herself to speculating about the need for recognition.

During the period in which Jean was formulating her views on recognition, a new generation of historians intent on resurrecting the history of women was hard at work, revisiting Clio's vineyards with a view to illuminating the lives of women whose contributions had gone unmarked. My interest in Jean Royce's 'benefit to countless generations of Queen's students and faculty' is informed by this movement. What did she do? What was 'immeasurable' about this benefit, so much so that it could not be mentioned again? In reviewing Gibson's book, historian and Queen's alumnus Royce MacGillivray observed that 'the late Miss Royce seemed in the 1950s almost to be Queen's. [Yet] [i]ncredibly, in this volume she is not mentioned later than the year 1933.' Though Principal William Mackintosh was 'much involved in university finance and expansion,' he seems to have been 'curiously remote from other aspects of the University, including students and the courses of study.' MacGillivray asks: 'What about the people who seemed to rule the University in his place, particularly the registrar, Miss Jean I. Royce?'[9] What about her?

Like the historians of women to whom I am indebted, however, my interest lies not merely in providing recognition to a particular person, however egregious the oversight may be. Jean Royce's life, which spanned the first eight decades of this century, provides an opportunity to look at working-class family life before the Great Depression, to examine social mobility through education, and to chart the development of middle-class English Canada through another lens. As Paul Axelrod's study of the links between university education and class formation reveals, most students in the 1930s were from the middle class, and most were male.[10] Only a handful of women from poor, working-class families – like Jean and her sister Marion – went to university and set out to develop lifelong careers. Economically, Jean barely made it into the middle class, but by making careful choices she was able to enjoy considerable discretionary income. She never owned a house or a car – those two pillars of the middle-class lifestyle – but she was able to satisfy her yearnings to travel, to see beautiful paintings, to enjoy good music and theatre, and to immerse herself in other worlds. As soon as she gained permanent employment, she began visiting New York, London, and beyond. Little has been written about the Canadian contingent of newly mobile and educated international travellers in the middle decades of the twentieth century,[11] and Jean provides a vibrant example.

Her life story also provides evidence for those historians who argue that feminism was present in Canadian society throughout the twentieth century.[12] It also reveals the constraints facing women who did not marry or have children, and the possibilities open to them, and shows how occupational spaces for women appeared and disappeared. Jean's later years in particular direct our attention to forms of family and intimacy that went unheralded in the past and that continue to be occluded by the current mania for 'family values.'

More than anything else, her life permits a close look at the development of a good – sometimes very good – Canadian university. By focusing on Jean Royce as registrar, I develop an interpretation of the history of Queen's University that challenges past accounts in several ways. As I moved through the Royce years at Queen's, my understanding of what went on there – and what might have gone on there – shifts, and destabilizes home truths even as the possibility of replacing those truths grows dim.

Frederick Gibson noted that he faced no 'serious obstacle' to preparing a 'candid portrait' of the history of Queen's.[13] I offer no such assurance. Like other feminist historians who challenge those institutional histories that focus on leaders and great men, I acknowledge the inevitable partiality of vision. Networks of power relations, whether bureaucratic or informed by racism, personal talent and proclivities, or gender, ethnic, and cultural valuations, not only shape institutional events but also do a great deal to dictate what qualifies as significant. Put another way, writing history delineates the events and people who qualify as history.[14]

Hence, I approach my subject in two ways. First, I attempt to understand the person who took the position of registrar in 1933. This quest took me to St Thomas, Ontario, where Jeanette Isabella – shortened immediately to the more serviceable Jean Isobel – was born in 1904, the third child and second daughter of a cooper at the Empire Flour Mills and a seamstress/homemaker, both parents active members of the Church of Christ (Disciples). What was it like to grow up her?

I walked the streets of her childhood, from home to school to church to the library to the mill where her father worked. All this within a few blocks, in a railway town still in its heyday. Alma College, the private girls' school, built as a gothic castle, stood close by, and the town council occasionally contributed to the school's periodic fundraising. In the year of Jean's birth, news of the Russo-Japanese War provided the headlines for the *St Thomas Times-Journal*. And in 1908 the newspaper carried the notice of the funeral procession of fifteen-month-old James Henry (Harry) Royce from his home at 45 Catharine Street to the cemetery. Baby deaths did not often appear in the newspaper, and Harry was the child of a poor working family. I wondered how this notice came to appear, even if the family name was misspelled – 'Royee' – and his father's middle initial was inaccurate. Jean was four when Harry died, her sister Marion was six, and her brother Stewart five. A year later her second sister, Catherine, was born, and in 1912 Donald's appearance completed the family.

The question of who Jean Royce was when she left town sixteen years later, and who she was becoming, is more complicated and leads to my second theme. Current scholarship rightly contests the notion that it is possible to discover who someone 'really is.' First, one encounters the practical problem that we have access to people only through what is said or written about them, and through what remains of what they said or wrote themselves. Even what they 'do' is not indisputable, for the doing is committed to language even as the action takes place. This raises a second dilemma – one posed by the structuring of language. If, for example, someone described Jean Royce as 'formal' in manner, the meaning may seem quite straightforward. Yet language works by setting up distinctions that are actually far from self-evident. 'Formal' relies on some notion of 'informal,' and this dichotomy in turn depends on the customs of the time, of the speaker, and of those who heard or read the comment. The meanings of formal and informal shift, and certainly during the decades during which Jean was registrar, what passed for formal and informal scarcely remained static. But let us say we settle on the word 'formal' as a descriptor of her demeanour in her role as registrar. Does the word mean something different when applied to a woman than to a man? To a registrar rather than to a professor or custodian? Did a formal demeanour make it possible for a woman still in her twenties to be taken seriously in her new position and to sustain authority in the succeeding decades? Did certain behaviours, deliberate or not, make it possible, in an institution governed by men, for a woman to be treated seriously yet remain unthreatening?

These reflections suggest a second limitation to the notion that there was a 'real' Jean Royce who left St Thomas in 1928, and that delineating that person will help us understand her career. What might be more telling is not who she was but who she could become, and be seen to become, in the position she came to occupy. What did convention make possible? What does the language of her era tell us about what a woman could do and could not do – or be seen to do and not to do? Given the gendered practices of the time, how did Jean negotiate that thicket of possibilities and restraints? Here I reverse my earlier question about her premature dismissal and ask instead: How did she last all those decades, how did she come 'almost to be Queen's'? For the moment, two illustrations may help ease the reader's suspicion that I may have made this story from whole cloth. On 24 November 1995, Muriel Uprichard died, leaving Queen's University a bequest of $5,000 'in gratitude for ... encouragement when I was young and poor and to replace the moneys given me as scholarships when I graduated.' The rest of the pertinent clause from her will reads: 'If a memorial is set up to Jean Royce I would like this to be added to the fund. Otherwise Queen's may use this money for any promising young woman whose studies are hindered for lack of funds. No strings are attached to the way Queen's will use this small token of my love for Jean Royce and my high regard for the institution itself.'[15]

Clearly Muriel was under no illusions: the institution did exist apart from Jean Royce. Yet these carefully chosen words suggest that her 'love' for Jean Royce and her 'high regard for the institution *itself*' were not discrete, and that for her, Jean personified this place. Another Queen's graduate and benefactor, Alfred Bader – whose gifts to the university run to the millions of dollars – made a similar point in this recollection of his admission to the university: 'I had been in an internment camp on the Ile aux Noix in Quebec. The International Student Service had helped some of us to pass the McGill junior and senior matriculation in June and September of 1941, and when I was released into the care of a family in Westmount I had hoped that McGill would accept me. But my application was turned down both by McGill and the University of Toronto, and one of the daughters of that family, Rosetta Wolff Elkin who had gone to Queen's, suggested Queen's. And – *mirabile dictu* – Queen's, that is, Jean Royce, accepted me.'[16]

In this book I look at how Jean Royce came to personify Queen's University. I tell the story of how she came by the position of registrar, and I assess the role she played in the university's development. For at least two reasons, this is a difficult task. First, Jean was the secretary of many of the university bodies on which she served, among them the Senate, the Faculty Board of Arts and Science, the Board of Library Curators, and the School of Graduate Studies. Secretaries may well speak at meetings – and there is evidence that she did – but they are unlikely to put their own names in the minutes, and Jean did not. After perusing these minutes, one might conclude that whenever the minutes read 'it was suggested ...,' that 'it' was herself.[17] This seems a reasonable supposition, since other suggestions came with names attached. But I cannot build a whole case on speculation.

Second, Jean Royce was always a woman in a man's world. There is now a good deal of scholarly evidence that women's suggestions often go unremarked. Yet once stated, these ideas may be echoed by others, who then receive credit for contributing them.[18] Though former administrators and professors quickly acknowledged Jean Royce's impact on students, most weren't sure what contributions she might have made to programs and policies. Of course, this could mean that she contributed little. However, my hypothesis is that she contributed heavily, even if the evidence is less than conclusive. This hypothesis is based on the literature on bureaucracy. Jean Royce served under four principals: William Hamilton Fyfe (1930–6), Robert Charles Wallace (1936–51), William Archibald Mackintosh (1951–61), and James Alexander Corry (1961–8). She had the advantage of being there, while her bosses came and went. For example, she missed only one meeting of the Queen's University Board of Graduate Studies from its establishment in 1943 until it was reconstituted as the School of Graduate Studies in 1963. And in the years between 1943 and 1966, no member of the powerful Board of Library Curators attended as consistently as Jean. Her knowledge of past and present practice was unparalleled, and we know from her speeches and papers that she had views. In fact, I contend that she possessed the influence of a loyal and trusted civil servant, though it remains for us to figure out how and when she used this influence.[19]

Contemporary research on bureaucracies also indicates that it would be surprising if a Jean Royce did not play an active role in the university's development. Anthropologists as contemporary ethnographers have shown that ideas are mobilized and carried forward in complex ways; it is not simply a trickle-down process.[20] Indeed, my respondents from the Registrar's Office indicated that I should be focusing on Jean's assistant and secretaries as much as on Jean herself. How did subalterns affect admissions and programs, passes and failures? Did they contribute to the perception that Jean Royce *was* Queen's University? This question reinforces my point that historical events are constructed, and are worth interrogating for that reason.

As registrar, Jean had contact with virtually every applicant and student, even if just through a letter dictated to her secretary. She was the university's main gatekeeper, especially for the Faculty of Arts (renamed the Faculty of Arts and Science in 1959).[21] In the early years, entrance to the faculty was easy: Principal Fyfe was heard to say that 'a student seeking a pass BA degree need do little more than register and grow older,'[22] while Chancellor Richardson once referred to Queen's as a 'glorified high school.'[23] Standards rose over time, and Jean Royce played a role, however difficult to specify precisely. Certainly she had the authority to admit or reject, and Kingstonians remember her for this warmly, or with anger, as many of my casual conversations about town attest. Once admitted, students counted on the registrar to ensure they chose courses that would result in the awarding of a degree. Many alumni described to me – in interviews, letters, e-mails, and phone calls – how closely she tracked their programs, and how willing she was to act as a mother of invention when she deemed a course to be in their best interests, and sometimes – with dismay – how arbitrary her decisions could be. Much of the time, this uncommon registrar honoured the spirit rather than the letter of the very regulations that she had been instrumental in formalizing.

Those who remember Jean Royce most vividly recall her as a superb talent scout. Without any question, she considered herself a strong judge of student ability and potential, especially when it came to singling out students for graduate scholarships and fellowships. She kept one eye on the calendar and scholarship deadlines and another on the unassuming but gifted and overworked students – many of them women without other mentors – who had not yet thought to apply. And when she brought them together her advice was simple: 'You had *better* go for it.' Nor did she fail to inform students of her disappointment when their performance did not measure up to her estimate of their potential. Most of the students she encouraged and chastised later reported that she got it right, and they were grateful to her for perceiving qualities and ambitions they had not fully recognized themselves. But some note – with a glint – that she got it wrong: whomever she saw, it wasn't them.

Yet she harboured no disappointment when her advice went unheeded: after all, the revolving door brought an endless supply of recruits, many of whom could be counted on to need help plotting their future. With so many stories – none of which detract from or trump any other – we see that Jean Royce was not all of a piece, but rather a complicated and engaged woman, mistress of the one-liner that could amuse or sting, as well as a thoughtful confidante and advisor, remembered decades later with appreciation if not adoration.

My assumption that Jean Royce was involved not only in implementing programs and policies, but also in their development, rests on my understanding of bureaucracies and on the knowledge that near the end of her career the principal fired her. Logic argues that had she been *only* a servant of the people, she would have survived. In Chapter 4 I reconstruct the events of the 1960s that led to her removal.

Some observers suggest that, however valuable Jean's past contributions, by the 1960s she was caught in a time warp, insisting on outmoded practices, refusing to delegate, losing perspective. Thus, she had to go if the university was to strengthen itself in an era of higher enrolments, increased government involvement, technological progress, and changing student expectations. What did Jean think during this period of unprecedented university expansion? Was she in fact a relic, or were there other reasons for wanting her off the lot? Perhaps Principal Corry merely wanted to give his good friend a sinecure. Perhaps he and others perceived her as an obstacle to progress. Whatever the reasons, Chapter 4 ends on a high note, with the university awarding her an honorary degree at fall convocation in 1968.

Queen's did not use up all of Jean's energies and talents – far from it. Her life while registrar included wide-ranging travel, deep relationships with friends and family, meaningful intellectual engagements, and many commitments to organizations, including the Student Christian Movement and later the International Federation of University Women. For Jean, there was no sharp border between work and home, public and private, professional and intimate life.[24]

In the language of her era, she remained a single lady. Her small apartments on the upper floor of three successive houses on the Queen's campus were comfortable but no refuge. When her young niece and nephews, Lyn, Stewart, and Dave, visited with their parents one afternoon in 1967, she suggested that they alleviate their boredom by counting the books. 'It took a long time for a ten, an eight, and a six-year-old, but when we were finished we had reached 3,000. And then our aunt said, "But you still haven't counted the books in the bathroom and basement!"'[25] Jean was an eclectic reader from early childhood, and one strains to find a part of the world or a topic to which she had not turned her attention at some point. Her collection of papers includes an assortment of contributions from faculty who sent her their scholarly work, confirming that she was, for many, a colleague and peer.

From the time she was appointed registrar she spent nearly all of her holiday time travelling, mostly in England and Europe. Nieces and nephews confirm that they rarely saw her, even at family gatherings. She was often out of the country, and her conversations with students, friends, and colleagues attest to her wide range of interests and enthusiasms. As registrar, she felt the need to prepare students for life in the world; in this sense, she needed to know that world. Her interest in opening Queen's to students from all countries and backgrounds was as apparent to everyone then as it is now to the researcher revisiting the scene. One wonders how the girl from St Thomas came by her easy acceptance of the diverse band that she encouraged to come to Queen's.

Above all, Jean Royce was a cosmopolitan – a woman who saw herself as citizen of the world and who never tired of educating herself about it. While registrar, in many small acts, she showed herself quietly but firmly out of sympathy with those who wanted to preserve Queen's as a Protestant men's club or an English-Canadian enclave. She shared these views with her older sister, Marion, with whom she had a relationship that lasted almost all her life. Her relationships with Marion, their sister, Catherine, and their brothers, Stewart and Donald, remained important all her life. Marion is the more famous sister – according to their brother Donald, deservedly so. Indeed, he was amazed when I told him I was writing a book about Jean rather than

Marion, who received the Order of Canada in 1971. One can see his point.[26] Born in 1901, Marion Victoria was the editor of the St Thomas Collegiate Institute magazine *The Collegian.* She won a full scholarship to McMaster in 1918. After graduating, she worked for the All-Canada Committee of the Church of Christ and later for the YWCA in Geneva. Perhaps most compelling from a feminist perspective, from 1954 until her retirement in 1966, she served as first director of the Women's Bureau of the federal Department of Labour. After retiring, she held a small, salaried post at the Ontario Institute of Higher Education, writing about women's education. Four years before her death in 1987, she published a biography of Eunice Dyke, a leader in the field of public health.[27]

The two sisters remained in close touch all their lives. Many of their letters were written when one or the other was out of the country. These letters reveal some of their joint interests – in the status of women, in international affairs, in the prospects for peace and order, and in the well-being of their brothers, nieces, and nephews, and especially in Catherine, their younger sister and the family favourite. The complex family life of the Royces of St Thomas leads one to wonder which part of family worked for Jean, and which part didn't, for in the end she helped create an alternative family, not through marriage or partnering, but rather at Queen's University, through a cross-generational network of support and friendship.

Jean Royce had an intriguing personal life, especially in two of her close relationships, which continued until her death. By his own admission, Robert Legget was her closest male friend. They met in 1937, having passed each other often enough walking through City Park to venture an exchange of greetings. She was the young lady registrar, he a new engineering professor with a wife and son at home.[28] Marion Royce told her sister-in-law that Robert had been in love with Jean ever since. An affair, had one become public, would have ended her career (and possibly his). Perhaps they never entertained the thought.

On her closest later-life relationship, less speculation is necessary. In 1962 Jean hired Margaret Hooey to replace Jean Richardson, who had been her assistant since 1939. Twenty-eight-year-old Margaret was a graduate of the University of Toronto and Bryn Mawr, and at the time of their meeting held an internship with the federal government. Like many, Margaret was intimidated on first meeting Jean Royce. But by 1966 they were good friends, travelling together and sharing much of their leisure time. Their friendship provides an opportunity for us to explore the families that people create – families that often don't correspond to those recognized in obituaries, hospital regulations, party invitations, or public policy.

Jean's wide interests provided a broad bridge to her retirement years, as did her connection with Queen's. Despite increasingly debilitating illnesses, the story of her last years is primarily a story of a love affair with the world, of an active woman engaged on many fronts, thoroughly immersed in a range of commitments and pleasures. In the spring of 1969 she was elected by the alumni to the Board of Trustees, on which she served actively until 1975. During her years as a trustee she made one of her most notable contributions to the women of Queen's. Her friendships, professionalism, knowledge of the university, and continuing personal authority helped create the Ban Righ Foundation to facilitate the entry of mature women into the university as students. In this effort, Jean was indicating her empathy with a central concern of the women's movement: namely, how to expand the options of women who unlike herself had left the labour force to marry and raise children.

This book reflects a broad chronology: the first chapter covers Jean's early years, the last treats her retirement. However, my approach remains thematic. This allows me to analyze relationships, topics, and hunches with little interruption. Equally important, this allows Jean Royce to emerge in all her many incarnations. Indeed, the variation in perceptions among those who knew her in different contexts – and sometimes in similar contexts – is often arresting.

As we know, the discourses of professional life, of women in professional life, of friendship, of same-sex and cross-sex friendship, of the university, of family and kinship, while not discrete, have their own shifting axioms, constraints, openings, and silences. Who Jean Royce was, who she could be, and who she was perceived to be are shaped – some would say enabled – by these differing discourses. We must remember that discourses both permit and restrain. They allow some things to be said but leave much unspoken and perhaps unthought. Moreover, what is said or not said can be analysed in multifarious ways.

I seek to honour the record here – the inconsistencies produced by competing discourses and perceptions. Though I don't embrace wholly the contemporary theoretical view that insists on the fragmented, contingent, discursive self,[29] I am enough persuaded by it that

I have not asked the 'real' Jean Royce to stand up. I have not tried to find unity, an essential self, a person who might be summed up in a few words. I like to think that Jean Royce appears in each of these narratives in ways she would recognize, as would those who shared some part of those stories with her and with me. Let us return to St Thomas, Ontario, in 1904.

Chapter One

'The Girls Got All the Charisma'

In a letter to Marion in 1972, four days after the death of their sister, Catherine, on 16 October, Jean wrote: 'She will always be with us. We have so many memories of her ... she brought so much into our rather arid household.' Marion agreed with her that Catherine was much less inhibited 'than the rest of us and so full of imagination'; however, she did not acknowledge Jean's assessment of the general atmosphere.[1]

That Jean chose the word 'household' rather than the more ideologically loaded 'home' or 'family' suggests a dearth of fun and affection. In the Royce household, daily life was a serious undertaking, economically and spiritually. Jean's father, David, toiled long hours at the flour mill, known variously as Erie Mills, Empire Mills, or the John Campbell Company. The first mention of him in the St Thomas City Directory was in 1891. In various editions of the directory he is listed sometimes as a foreman at the mill, sometimes as a cooper or miller, once as fireman.[2] Perhaps his dexterity helped him secure stable employment. Housing was a big problem for him, first as a single man and later as a husband and father. In his early years in St Thomas he boarded in a succession of small, unprepossessing houses, close by his workplace, sometimes with fellow labourers.

When the children arrived, moving house remained a ritual occasioned, no doubt, by a search for accommodation for the growing family, within easy walking distance of the mill. The year Jean was born the family moved from Erie Street to First Avenue and Elm, just around the corner. After that, they moved every year until 1907. Finally, in 1908, they found 47 Catharine Street, a small house 'with a little yard and picket fence,' attached to and behind Mr Corduroy's corner store, where neighbourhood children bought their penny candies.[3] Here the family lived until David died in 1928. Across the street was the gas works, which a neighbour, Flossie Snell, remembered mainly for its smell of rotten eggs – which 'we took for granted' – and for its subsidiary role in putting old and unwanted animals to sleep.[4] Just around the corner stood St Thomas Public Library, without which, Katherine Royce claimed, she would not have been able to raise her family. From here, for the first time since he became a father, David could walk quickly to work. His children could walk to school in minutes.

The Royce children had to walk much farther, four times a day, when they began attending St Thomas Collegiate. Only the handful of pupils from out of town were permitted to bring lunch. The school provided a 90-minute lunch break for city children – so they could go home – rather than a supervised lunch period. When she was five, Helen Babe's family had moved from 'unfashionable' Catharine Street to 'near the doctors and lawyers.' Helen's walk to high school was quite short, and she remembered bringing home a classmate for lunch who didn't take off her galoshes. No time for that, her friend explained when she went home.[5]

At the time of Jean's birth, Katherine Royce was working hard, making ends meet, keeping house, cooking, and raising three-year-old Marion and two-year-old Stewart. How much attention could the third of three closely spaced children command in such a labour-intensive household in turn-of-the-century Ontario? As Jean's maternal aunt Nettie discovered soon after Jean's birth, very little. 'Doesn't that baby ever cry?' she asked tellingly, after she arrived on an errand of mercy when Katherine contracted measles. Even as a child of three-and-a-half, Marion noticed 'the pall of fear for mother's life,' and concluded that 'a small infant, herself a victim of the disease, certainly would have lacked the cuddling love that is so essential to well-being.' No wonder, she mused, that 'Jean became a literary person. From her earliest years books were her solace and joy.' Family members dodged her as she sat 'on the front stairs reading in peace.' Marion, meanwhile, 'was frequently admonished for not taking things more calmly, like Jean.'[6] Jean clocked in nearly two years as the family's youngest. Then the birth of James Henry (Harry) on 28 December 1906 further diverted her mother's attention, completely capturing it for at least some time. On 28 March 1908 the *St Thomas Daily Times* carried notice of Harry's death: 'Royee – In this city on the 27th inst., James Henry, youngest son of Mr. and Mrs. David T. Royee, aged 15 months. The funeral will take place on Sunday, March 29, at 2:15 p.m., from the residence 45 1-2 Catharine street, to St. Thomas cemetery. Friends kindly accept this intimation.'[7] Seventy years later, Jean remembered 'his beautiful blue eyes [and] his passionate fondness for men – he had no use for women at all.' An interesting construction, which she based on her memory of her little brother racing 'to catch father as he came in [,calling] "daddy, daddy."'[8]

Jean was barely four when Harry died. He must have been a competitor for parental attention, and like any child she must have harboured a wish to banish him. That being said, she may well have retreated into herself long before his birth. As the second daughter it is likely that she was spared much of the responsibility for her younger siblings, unlike Marion, who cared for (and bossed around) her brothers and sisters all her life. But in fact, neither Marion nor Jean took to nurturing; no nephew or niece remembers an indulgent auntie. In the Royce household all the children learned to develop autonomy, inner strength, and emotional distance from themselves and others – a lesson that lasted all their lives.

The Royce household soldiered on after Harry's death. The Honour Role for the City Public Schools, published in the *St Thomas Daily Times* on 1 April 1908, less than a week later, listed seven-year-old Marion as fourth in her Senior First class at Scott Street School. (Perhaps this was a slip – she was usually first.) More remarkably, during the first week of June, only two months after Harry's death, the Royce family billeted three delegates to the week-long Church of Christ (Disciples) convention, which was being held in St Thomas. Their small home, recently the site of Harry's funeral, was stretched to accommodate the Reverends J. Munro from Grand Valley and J.D. Stephens from Winger, and Ida M. Royce – David's much younger sister – from Everton.[9]

This church connection went back to David Royce's great-grandfather, Josiah, who came to Canada from England in 1816 with his wife, Mary Curtis, and their children, Robert, Josiah, and Alice, and settled in Dundas, Ontario. According to John Clendenning, 'the Royces were pious Baptists who liked to remember that an ancestor had stood guard over the execution of Charles I.'[10] In 1834, Josiah started a Baptist Church in his home.

The Scottish Baptist tradition in Canada proved to be fertile soil for the made-in-America Church of Christ (Disciples).[11] In the late 1840s, Josiah's son Robert (David's grandfather), a Wellington County farmer, joined the fledgling church, followed in 1857 by his second son, Josiah, who was unsuccessfully seeking his fortune in California.[12] This church, which was established in the 1830s through the merger of Barton W. Stone's twenty-five-year-old Christians and Thomas and Alexander Campbell's more recent Disciples of Christ,[13] offered itself as a direct route to Jesus Christ. The founders hoped to unite all Christians by rejecting creeds and relying instead on direct oral interpretations of the New Testament. No one was entitled to trump another's version of the scripture: there would be no theology.[14] Such a church seemed to spurn dogmatism, yet controversies and schisms remained endemic to it. Even the church's unusual name – Church of Christ (Disciples) – reflected the unresolved conflict between Stone and Campbell over whether the word *Christian* or *Disciple* more accurately portrayed the movement.[15]

David Royce and Katherine Jeffrey joined the St Thomas church in 1894 and 1893 respectively.[16] Like David, Katherine had been affiliated with the Church of Christ before arriving in St Thomas; she had been a member of its large Hillcrest congregation in Toronto.[17] The St Thomas church welcomed both of them by appointing David secretary and Katherine librarian of the Sunday school at the annual meeting in January 1894. David and Katherine had ample time to observe each other; they did not marry until 1899. She was almost thirty, he was almost fourteen years her senior. By then David had been elected a deacon. He would serve on the church board as secretary and (after 10 January 1917) as elder until his death.

David's sincerity as a 'good Christian gentleman'[18] was never in doubt. However, according to his obituary, more than his spiritual well-being was served by his 'unremitting and unswerving' dedication to his church. 'Inculcated with those qualities which typify the finest Canadian [and] Christian character, [his loyalty] to his fellow men and to his employer [was] indicated by the fact that, although during his long employment by Empire Mills, workmen had sometimes to be suspended or placed on short time, he was never laid off for a single day.[19] This passage makes clear the link between the qualities of a Canadian and Christian character and those of an exemplary worker.

The mill on Moore Street provided an unobstructed view of the Church of Christ (Disciples), just a block to the west. This arrangement made tangible the connection between mill worker and congregant and expressed more clearly than words could the interest that John Campbell – mill owner and church founder – took in loyal workers and good Christians.

As a church member, Campbell had spearheaded the congregation's move from Yarmouth Township to St Thomas, where the new building on Railway Street was dedicated in 1879.[20] At that time 'the church served a lot of substantial people and prospered.' The expanding railway town turned out to be fertile ground for those key members of the congregation who were 'possessed of a business conscience.'[21] Four years later, in 1883, Campbell built his mill on Moore Avenue.[22] When David Royce walked his family the few blocks to church on Sunday mornings, he passed within a stone's throw of the mill where he worked the other six days of the week.

For nearly three decades David Royce lived, worked, and prayed within an area six blocks square. That his routine suited his employers is incontrovertible. But consider also this arrangement from David's perspective. He had spent the first decades of his adult life trying unsuccessfully to find a niche. When he found a place in the mill some eight years after it opened, he must have been benefitting from Campbell's search for good Disciples. David's first cousin, Reuben Butchart, has provided the most detailed history of the Disciples in Canada.[23] He writes that by the time David found a job at the mill, the Royce and Campbell families had been intertwined for decades. David's grandfather, Robert – 'one of Everton's root and branch men as elder, teacher, and lay preacher' – received a warm acknowledgment in Butchart's book on the Disciples in Eramosa Township.[24]

Robert's oldest son, Josiah, David's father, was a deacon, but his main contribution to the church was to provide it with new members. Alone among Robert's children, Josiah had a huge family. While his six siblings contented themselves with three to five children each, Josiah and his wife Janet (Stewart) had thirteen. Janet gave birth to her first child when she was twenty, her last, Jennie, when she was forty-three. Perhaps Janet's daughters, if not her sons, took a certain message from their mother's experience: Mary died when she was ten; Lizzie married at forty-seven and had no children; Ida and Jennie both married 'in time' for children but, intentionally or not, never had any. Only Jessie had children – two sons, born ten years apart. Josiah and Janet could not provide much for their children, and their reticent second-oldest child, David, was obviously going to have to make his own way in the world. His obituary notes that he had been 'in business in Harriston' in early life and afterwards had 'resided at Paisley and Ingersoll.' Although the family tree is silent on the subject, Katherine was his second wife. There had been no children in his first marriage. Just after Jean's birth, while retaining his job in the mill, he had tried farming,[25] and the story that came down to Donald held 'that he had almost gone out of his mind' from the experience.[26] David's first child, Marion, was not born until he was forty-five, and when his youngest child, Donald, was born he was fifty-six. None of his brothers sired children this late in life: the runner-up was Josiah Jr, who called it a day when he was thirty-nine, six years before David even began. David was old enough to be his children's grandfather, and the economic responsibility must have weighed on him heavily.

A year after Harry's death, Jean returned home from school to find 'a crying baby, so pretty, beautiful hands and fingers.' She was 'enthralled' – and surprised. No one had told this five-year-old 'that a baby was coming.'[27] Three years later, pregnant with her last child, Katherine wondered how they would manage but comforted herself with the notion that 'babies bring their own love.'[28] Donald's birth came after the only existing formal family photograph, which was taken shortly after Catherine's birth. The photograph suggests a christening; however, the Church of Christ (Disciples) practised believer, total immersion baptism. (This explains why Harry's name does not appear on the church membership list, which includes the names of his brothers and sisters, all of whom were baptized in adolescence.) The occasion for the picture, then, might well have been simply the picture, thereby speaking not only to the ability of David Royce to provide for his wife and children, but also to the symbolic importance of family among those for whom such an expenditure would count as luxury. The immediate motivation to spend scarce resources was surely the death of Harry, baby without a picture.

Katherine's comment that babies bring their own love made an impression on her neighbour, who repeated it to her young daughter, Helen. Seventy-five years later, Helen explained that she took the phrase to be about 'finances – my impression then and now was that they were very poor and this was quite a family, four or five children, on a dollar an hour or whatever they paid.' Helen's father, in contrast, was a railway worker, 'a union man – most of them were Americans and well paid.'[29] But David Royce had his own form of job security. The Disciples' connection paid off for him and his family – not well but steadily. Empire Mills provided him with steady employment until he died at seventy-two.

David's heavy involvement with the church may have had little to do with his desire to keep his job. It may have been a happy coincidence. He was a devout Christian born and raised and he continued the traditions of his childhood with his own family. But John Campbell's Disciples had not left this to chance. In 1889 the church had formed committees 'to look after families coming into the city' as well as 'those who absented themselves from meetings.'[30] The minutes of the church board during David's employment also raise questions. It was one thing to attend church regularly, another to help run it. What was the nature of David's involvement? Did he want to be there? Did he have a choice?

David was named deacon in 1895. The board minutes record that though he attended all special meetings – usually after Sunday service – he was often absent from regular meetings. For example, he was present on 29 June 1908 at the first meeting held after Baby Harry's death. In those days he worked long hours at Campbell's mill[31] and had a growing family to tend to, so his absences might be explained by a conflicting work schedule, or by overwork and fatigue – or, perhaps, by enough being enough. How did he experience the interlacing of economic, spiritual, and family pressures? A biographer, revisiting the scene nearly a century later, is not the only one who can never hope to answer these questions. Most likely no one could at the time.

For David Royce was a man of few words. From 1895 until his death thirty-three years later, he seconded only two motions and moved one – and this singular event not until 18 January 1920. Three years earlier, almost to the day, he had been elected a church elder. No longer was he expected to be concerned merely with the church's practical concerns. Now he was one of the congregation's spiritual leaders, distinguished from the pastor only by the fact that the latter was salaried. By then David was sixty-one, a family man and a diligent worker, and a man of 'unimpeachable integrity.'[32] He had earned the respect of the congregation – a respect clearly predicated, however, on his stalwart character, not on any contribution that he made with words to communal life and church governance.

David Royce was among the first in his family's history to join the industrial labour force. His father had been a farmer and had been a far more physical presence in the lives of his thirteen children than any of his wage-earning sons managed to be with theirs. David's physical absence from home – mainly for work but also for church obligations – was underscored by his reticence. To his children he was a shadowy figure. His son Stewart was taken aback when as a young man of twenty-six he arrived at his father's funeral to find a full church and a big black limousine parked out front. As he confided to his children, he was impressed with his father as he had never been during his life.[33] Donald's memory of his father was detached but respectful: 'He was a very hard worker. He worked until a few days before he died of cancer of the liver, not from drinking because he was a teetotaller. My father was a good Christian gentleman and quite wise but he lacked the background of our mother.'[34]

Understandably, as he entered his sixties, David Royce must have craved peace at the end of his long day. But when asked whether his father's injunction to 'go to bed' meant that he was the family disciplinarian, Donald replied simply, 'He was just sort of there.' Donald didn't remember his father playing cards or reading, but he clearly recalled that 'we had to go to church every Sunday morning [where] I remember sitting on dad's knee playing with his watch when I could hardly walk around.'

'On your father's knee? Was your father affectionate?'

'Well he's the only one who had a pocket watch. He was kind of stiff, actually.'

As a child, Helen Babe was surprised when after dinner the Royces gathered around the stove and David read from the Bible. Her household ran differently: 'They used to take my brother to Sunday School [but] we used to get up late ... on Sundays.' As a result they would have only 'two meals. My brother told us that "the Royces say we are not Christian because we only have two meals on Sunday"!'[35]

Almost nothing is known of Katherine's family. Apparently, she and her two sisters left home in their early to mid-teens to make their living as milliners. It is too late to know what provoked them to this early departure, but Katherine was clearly committed to educating her daughters for a life of economic independence. According to Donald, she backed the right horses: 'The girls in our family got the brains.' Donald's nephew Stewart explained that 'everyone seemed to know my Aunt Jean and Aunt Marion but no one knew my father.'[36] School records indicate that Stewart and Donald had a rocky time in school. Stewart passed his high school entrance exams at the same time as Jean, although he was a year and a half older.

There are no existing high school records for him, and I had thought, along with his children, that he had gone directly to work from public school. However, the May 1917 issue of the high school magazine *The Collegian* is full of awful jokes, two of which indicate that Stewart had had a presence in Form 1C, however dubious in nature, for at least most of grade nine. 'Mr. Stewart Royce has recently been presented with an alarm clock' by his classmates, intoned the first. 'It is hoped that he will use it to the best advantage for the remaining months of the school year.' The second was no less edifying: 'Royce (in Algebra period) – where shall I go when I finish Exercise 32? Teacher – You will probably be going away for your summer holidays by that time.'

Surely it was adding insult to injury to have a joke from the same class submitted by 'L. Rinn and J. Royce'[37] ridiculing a fellow classmate. Before an exam, the teacher 'had ordered the books ... placed in the aisle.' One benighted student 'placed his books beside the wall about 3 feet away [and upon] finishing his examinations ... proceeded to [retrieve them by] slowly extending [his feet] towards the black board' and drawing them in 'with the aid of his lower extremities. The teacher saw him – "Bridgeman, your feet are of more use to you than your head" – Yes, said Bridgeman (under his breath), for they are not quite so light.' In the same year Jean served on the editorial staff of *The Collegian* and joined the General Literary Society. Marion, in Form III, published an impressive short story called *A Sense of Duty*.[38] It must have been painful for Stewart. Donald, for his part, failed grade eleven and left school.

Growing up, Marion was the star sibling – 'the scholar of the family,' according to Jean.[39] 'Marion was brilliant; everyone in the family looked up to her,'[40] her younger brother recalled. Marion made her mark early and sustained the promise. By twelve she had a namesake, who tells the tale: 'We lived on the same street as the Royces and my mother named me after her because she hoped some of Marion's smarts would rub off on me!' So explained Dorothy Marion Scram with a laugh, some eighty-five years after her birth.[41] By then, Marion Royce had tied for first place in the city in the high school entrance exams.

Halfway through her final year of high school, and in trying circumstances, Marion took over as editor of *The Collegian*. At the end of a glowing tribute to her under the masthead in June 1918, the staff predicted accurately that she would 'secure the honours for which she is striving this year.' Marion won the Wheeler scholarship to McMaster University, which paid full tuition for four years and provided $100 a year 'in cash,' as the *St Thomas Times-Journal* put it.[42]

Jean was the more pedestrian sister. Her early difficulties at school cleared up after she was prescribed thick glasses, but not before some labelling had gone on, especially within the family. She passed her high school entrance exams when she was just twelve, but while Marion completed high school in four years, Jean took six. She did well in her final year, finishing second in her class with 75 per cent average.[43] Her highest mark – 95 – came in English composition. (Generations of secretaries in the Registrar's Office at Queen's would remark on her diligence in correcting any errors that crept into letters and documents.) Catherine's school record is patchy, as a result of fairly long periods of illness.[44] She passed her entrance exams just as she turned thirteen – the only student to graduate with honours from Scott Street School.[45] She came first in her class in the first term of high school and third at the end of the year. In grade ten she ranked ninth in first term, dropped to twenty-fourth in second term, and did well at the end of the year. Although she remained in the top ten in grade eleven, she fell to the bottom of her class in grade twelve, receiving a graduation diploma but failing to matriculate.

Jean, Marion, and even the frail Catherine did better in school than their brothers, which seems to bear out Donald's verdict that the girls got the brains – and, he added later, all the charisma.[46] But this comparison passes over the specifically gendered messages in the Royce household. Katherine Royce did not share the societal view that sons need and deserve more education than daughters. Indeed, all indications point to her unswerving belief that girls had to be educated and prepared to earn their own living.[47] 'Your mother was ahead of her time,' Katherine's friend, Florence Campbell, wrote in a letter congratulating Jean on her honourary degree. 'In her day ... most people did not realize ... what a fine education meant to people, and especially to women.'[48] As it turned out, two of Katherine's daughters graduated from university and went on to support themselves their whole life through. Both Marion and Jean set out on rewarding careers at a time when women's opportunities for paid work waxed and waned with war and peace. Katherine's youngest daughter, the 'artistic one,' also had strong interests and talents. Catherine married when she was twenty-seven, and continued afterwards to teach children with disabilities and English as a second language.

The Royce sisters did better than their brothers. Did the girls stay in school because Katherine knew that without an education any wage they might earn would consign them to a life of poverty? Marion and Jean clearly found time for school activities as well, while Catherine, as Donald relates, became an accomplished violinist, 'not a concert musician but very good.'[49] Katherine prepared the girls carefully to succeed in the world. If boys are supposed to grow up to be like their fathers, this must have been a household of mixed messages. David's example did not invite emulation – as Donald put it, 'he didn't have the background of our mother.' And it is hard to imagine this man of few words, who supported his family in such an exemplary fashion, having much implicit or explicit advice for his sons. Certainly they didn't repeat any words of wisdom from their father.

I am not suggesting that the boys had no chances. Stewart played in a bugle band as a young boy, to the friendly consternation of his neighbour, who worked shifts on the railway and did not always appreciate an early wake-up call.[50] And Donald took piano lessons for a while: 'I had to cart my little music case down to the Alma College with all the other kids laughing at me because it was a girls' school.' But his main extracurricular activity, 'from day one' as Donald's wife, Celia, put it, was part-time work. 'I delivered the *Times-Journal* when I was seven years old,' Donald recalled. 'Later I had a morning paper route. I worked in the drug store after school and delivered the *Detroit Free Press*. I had three jobs at the same time. In those years when my father was alive, the jobs were for spending money, not family support.' But Celia thought it telling that his mother allowed him to work so many hours.[51]

Being a female child in the Royce household paid off, although both Stewart and Donald, without university education, went on to successful careers in banking and business.[52] But when it came to her daughters, Katherine turned out to be right: What would their chances have been had they left school early, like their brothers?

There is a another possible reason why the Royce girls did better in school. The socialization that prepares girls for subordinate roles also prepares them for the quiet and obedient behaviour that schools promote and that teachers appreciate. Girls get less attention from teachers, but they are also more likely to get on with their work, to refrain from boisterous and obnoxious behaviour in class, and to arrive on time with their homework done. Perhaps the Royce girls simply sat still long enough to learn something, even if that learning came mostly by rote.[53]

Marion and Jean look for all the world like goody-two-shoes. Stewart, judging from his behaviour, was more relaxed about expectations than his sisters. 'My dad didn't tell us much about the past, but he had some stories,' his son Stewart recalled. 'When he worked at the Canadian Imperial Bank of Commerce in St Thomas he and another guy were wrestling in the bank. He banged a glass window and broke it and had to work for nothing for a week or two to pay for it.'[54] One imagines some especially quiet nights in the Royce household. Yet Stewart did well with the bank, and soon afterwards he was transferred to Winnipeg. While he was there his parents called on him to help deal with his brother. Donald by then was spending summers with Stewart. Then, when he was fifteen, his father died and his mother, in Celia's words, couldn't 'cope with a boy.'[55] The main problem was that he preferred pool to school. So the summer arrangement became year-round. 'I wasn't wild,' Donald observed, 'but the pool rooms didn't have the same aura of respectability that they do now.'[56] Stewart told his son that 'Uncle Donald was a real terror,' and that he was shipped out to Winnipeg to live with him even before their father died.[57] Donald had failed grade eleven, and was now listed in the City Directory as a messenger for Mr E.C. Harvey's hardware store, and by his own admission played a good game of snooker. These were not capital offences.

One can well imagine David Royce, by then seventy-one and in poor health, having little patience with his younger son's behaviour. Indeed, it seems unlikely that Katherine ever had her husband's help or companionship in raising their children. 'In a sense,' Jean mused, 'she brought us all up.'[58] Katherine seems to have been the undisputed centre of hearth and home. Ultimately she must have been pleased with her decision to send Donald to Winnipeg. In 1931, when Stewart moved to Toronto, Donald came too, moved back in with her, and completed high school.

Katherine Royce was not a cozy mum; her upright posture in photographs serves as metaphor for her behaviour and her expectations. Donald had no memory of being held or hugged, and agreed with his wife, Celia, that his mother was not 'very demonstrative.' But when Celia added that 'the Royce family was rather stiff and formal and reserved,' Donald responded, 'You never even *knew* them' – forty-nine years of marriage notwithstanding.

Donald's respect and love for his wife shone through the interviews with them. What was reflected in his refrain – 'You didn't even *know* them' – was not only the conviction that one doesn't talk about feelings, family, and people, but also a lack of experience in doing so. For example, he did not know where in the family order Baby Harry stood, though he knew there had been a baby. Even more extraordinary, he discovered that he had had polio as a child only when he tried to enlist in the services at the beginning of the Second World War. 'His left leg was shorter than the other one,' Celia told me. 'He knew that but he didn't know why.' Small wonder that those who married into the Royce clan, or who had some opportunity to observe them, were quite astounded at the level of discretion. Celia told me that Stewart's (first) mother-in-law 'used to laugh about the Royces, and she'd say, "You can't pry anything out of them." They were always the type of people who didn't want to get involved with anything, didn't want to talk about anything too personal.'[59]

Donald and Celia agreed that Stewart had been the most relaxed of the Royces and that Jean had been the most tense.[60] Their opinion differs sharply from that of Jean's friends who knew Marion, and from that of most of their nieces and nephews, who saw Marion as the more proper. 'Her name was Marion Victoria and she was born in 1901,' her niece Lyn told me, drawing herself up to her full height and speaking primly. 'Now what does that tell you?'

In contrast, when you walked into Catherine's apartment, Lyn recalled, 'you had your corset laces undone.' From her father's stories, she divined that 'she must have been like that' from childhood. One fall day, en route to church, 'my dad and Catherine load[ed] their pockets ... with chestnuts.' During the service Catherine 'dropped them, and ... the church floor sloped down to the front and those chestnuts made that noise all the way down ... She started to giggle, though she knew they'd be in dreadful trouble ... when they got home.'[61]

Clearly, for Catherine – the family called her Skitty – life was not as continuously serious an affair as it was for her older sisters. Born only a year after Harry's death, and lacking the robust health of her siblings, she probably had an easier time. A grieving family needed a light-hearted child, and she seemed to be that. As an adult she knew how to indulge and amuse children, and in this she stood apart from her sisters.

Katherine Royce is crucial for understanding the family, but her story proves elusive. Certainly her children spoke well of her. 'Our mother was a terrific person,' Donald reported, pride evident in his voice. 'She had a very modest education. I couldn't say [how much]. But she could hold her own in any company, believe me.'[62] 'We all owe her a great deal,' Jean reflected. 'She was sympathetic and kind and generous.' She also wanted her children 'to cling closely to the church. She was a great church woman and would have liked us all to be missionaries.'[63]

Though the Church of Christ (Disciples) shared the patriarchal practices common in more established Christian churches of the time,[64] Katherine was more active than other female members of her congregation. According to the record, she was the first woman to make a motion at an annual meeting, in 1920. In March of that year she was elected one of the first two deaconesses by the congregation.[65]

Jessie (Mackinnon) Reid knew Katherine Royce as a den mother at the church's camp on Lake Erie, and remembers her as 'a lovely person, kindly, interested in the people.' After becoming a teacher, Jessie earned a Queen's degree extramurally, except for summer sessions when she lived in residence, taking her meals in the big dining hall. One night, as the head table filed out – the students stood for this ritual – Jessie 'wasn't paying much attention and the line stopped. It was Jean's mother. "Oh, it's Jessie Mackinnon!"' A couple of days later she was invited to Jean's house for tea.[66] Jessie's story provides the only sighting we have of Katherine visiting Jean in Kingston, but she may well have visited her busy daughter regularly.[67]

Katherine was left destitute after her husband's death. None of her children had much income, and Jean was scraping money together to continue her degree at Queen's. Yet she landed on her feet. In 1929, soon after she moved to Toronto, she became residence mother for the Church of Christ (Disciples) College, then attached to McMaster University. The *Canadian Disciple* carried the news, assuring readers that she would 'bring to this new responsibility the same wise motherly spirit that has characterized the life of her home through the years and made it a place of good cheer and inspiration to many others.'[68]

Clearly, Katherine had the characteristics necessary for this position, but she was also well connected. In early 1928 her daughter Marion was serving alongside Hugh Kilgour (whose family intertwined with the Royces in Erosma and whose wife, Frances, was residence mother) and John H. Wells (who became pastor in St Thomas three months before David Royce's death) as a field worker for the All-Canada Committee of the Churches of Christ (Disciples).[69] To Katherine's children, who were troubled about their mother's future, Frances Kilgour's resignation as residence mother was a godsend.

Marion's success at helping place her widowed mother in an appropriate position revealed the wisdom of Katherine's earlier sacrifices to help finance her daughter's university education.[70] As Donald recalled, 'Marion got some help from mother.[71] Jean did it all herself. She was always independent. She was one of those types who set a goal and then damned well met it. Jean did everything on her own, with no financial support whatsoever.' 'Probably,' he added, 'she was too independent to worry about that.'[72] But more than fifty years after those events, hospitalized, critically ill and disoriented, Jean revealed her disappointment. Those present assumed that she was speaking to Marion.

> 'Mother never complained, never complained. [sobbing] Mother made a lot of plans and it was too much. Mother promised to support *you* throughout. I guess I'll go to Library School instead.'
>
> 'Instead of what?'
>
> 'Instead of going to university.'
>
> 'Why not university?'
>
> 'I can't afford it. Don't most families help each other?'

And later the same day with her doctor:

> '[Sobbing] I am so disappointed.'
>
> 'Why?'
>
> 'Because I can't go to university.'[73]

Both Jean and Donald believed that their parents had helped Marion through university. This set me to thinking about Jean's desperately unhappy memory that her family had not helped her the way they had apparently helped Marion. What had happened, and why?

As I pondered this question I listened to a program on Gracie Fields, England's darling wartime singer. Gracie's brother recounted how his mother had raised four children alone, in poverty and hardship. From the time it became clear that Gracie had a talent, their mother spared no effort in furthering her career. All resources that could be scraped together went into Gracie, as the family's most likely route to something better. It paid off, too, said her brother. Perhaps, when Katherine Royce realized that she had in her family what they call in Britain 'a little brainbox' – who was, incidentally, born the same year as Gracie – she made a similar calculation.

But perhaps more important, Marion's scholarship to McMaster covered tuition and some living expenses. Helping Marion seemed doable: the gap between what she had won and what she needed could be closed – though barely. Helen Bythell remembered that when

Marion went to university 'they wore gowns and for the first few days she skulked about' until she received hers, so that no one could see her clothes.[74]

Still, imagine Jean's feelings when the month before she completed high school, Marion – from her new promontory as a university graduate – published a column in *The Collegian* called 'University Life.' The tone was alternatively sophomoric, jubilant, and exhortatory. The closing words must have thrilled her younger sister, who so wanted to follow in her footsteps: 'Remember, then, that your country, indeed, society as a whole, needs your best, and do not pass lightly by the privilege of a university education.'[75] Marion's university record was, 'if possible, more brilliant than that of her collegiate days,' as *The Collegian* bragged in its accompanying 'Alumni' column. 'Some bring honor to the school through brain, others through brawn. Marion Royce was a student whose brain gave her school fame, and whose personality was as charming as her head was clever.'[76]

Jean's grades easily qualified her for admittance to university but were insufficient to win a coveted scholarship[77] – a double heartbreak, in light of Marion's success. The amount she needed was far beyond the family means. Perhaps the help she lamented not getting from family was not only financial but also the help that encourages, that shows confidence in abilities, that indeed discerns and nurtures those abilities. Generations of students insisted that as registrar, Jean saw in them possibilities that otherwise would have remained dormant. She had learned to give what she had not received. Indeed, her disappointment, perhaps resentment, must have found creative expression whenever she summoned a student to her office, to express satisfaction at achievements or chagrin that potential remained in the wings.

Before I went to St Thomas I had the impression that Jean was an isolated child whose main solace came from reading. But church and school records offer glimpses that she was more social, more a participant, than I had thought. The church's young people's group, Junior Christian Endeavour, met once a week. All the Royce children attended for several years, and when Jean was thirteen she was a very conscientious president, never missing a meeting. At high school she was active in the Literary Society, and as a contributor to *The Collegian* she wrote poetry, short stories, and reports of meetings. Mostly her work sounds earnest but there is whimsy too, as in the following poem, from May 1921:

THE JUNIORS

A group of aimless wanderers from afar,
They come, a timid crowd of modest mien,
With carefree laugh and glad triumphant paean,
Gaze fixed apparently upon their star,
Youthful ambition! Surely now they're nigh
To Wisdom's boundless stores! And yet 'twould seem
That though there be somewhat of self esteem
On those first mornings in the S.T.C.I.,
Fate lurks hard by, and dreadful dooms await
The lazy youth, gathered with noisesome pen
In quiet rooms where dread 'exams' do hold
The sway. Slowly the heavy hand of Fate
Descends. They sink beneath its force, and then –
Emerge as Seniors!

Jean and Marion each published a 'war story' in *The Collegian*. In December 1914, Marion's first year in high school, the St Thomas Collegiate Institute sent its first soldier to the front. Before leaving, Lieutenant Beeson (as described in *The Collegian*) was honoured by a throng of citizens gathered in the auditorium. 'From the school he received a purse of $50.00, and from the Board of Education an automatic revolver.'[78] That war meant death had not yet dawned on anyone. After Lieut. Beeson had offered his thanks, 'the students joined in singing "For He's a Jolly Good Fellow."' The unrestrained exuberance in this report isn't repeated. Just before that issue went to press, news came 'of the death of the first ex-cadet of the St Thomas Collegiate Institute in action in Flanders, as far as is now known, namely, Major Ed. C. Norsworthy.' A picture of Major Norsworthy accompanied the story, which went on to reveal that 'his name appears in the list of those killed in the fighting at Langemarck, on Saturday, April 24, when the Canadians won world-wide admiration for their gallant conduct.'

Two months later, *The Collegian*, reported the ecstatic departure of the 91st Battalion: 'Our own boys swung into line and marched down Talbot Street to the station ... Little did we think that inside of five months the 91st would cease to exist, and that many of the men drafted into other Battalions, would find their way to the firing line, one to make the great sacrifice and several wounded.' It was Private Kenneth Davidson who made 'the great sacrifice ... He was of magnificent physique and did good work for the Collegiate Institute Rugby team at centre scrimmage in 1914 and 1915.' But he received no false praise from his former schoolmates: 'Although his course in school was not brilliant, it was successful.'[79] Little more than a year after graduating, he was dead. Jean had just started high school.

Like students across Canada, the pupils of St Thomas Collegiate – under the guidance of Miss Palmer, Miss Cook, and Mr Grey – 'undertook to do their part towards supplying comforts for the soldiers.' In October 1916 they sent 48 trench towels, 9 pairs of socks, 1 scarf, 8 news from home, and 17 dozen fruit cookies. This was followed in November by 64 towels, 31 handkerchiefs, 5 pairs of socks, 1 pair of kneecaps, and 8 news from home. On 23 April 1917 the students decorated the marble memorial tablets in the lower hall in honour of Norsworthy and three others who died in the fighting at Ypres. In November a similar ceremony honoured those who died at the Somme. By the end of the war, twenty-six ex-cadets from STCI had been added to the honour role. The war had claimed thousands of Canadian men, and thereby drastically reduced the cohort from which the same generation's women might draw friends, lovers, and husbands.

That Jean and Marion both wrote war stories – what we now would call women's war stories – is not surprising. They wrote about those left behind, about the home front – though not specifically about what they knew. Jean's story, published in December 1920, when she was sixteen, is about an old woman, a grandmother living in Brittany just before the Germans march into Belgium. All her love is centred on her young grandson, but once war is declared she tells him with great agony: 'You will have to fight too, Jacques. Remember that it is for France.' Not wanting to fight, but knowing that he must, he gives up his dreams and leaves his grandmother, who prays 'unceasingly that this war of pitiless destruction might soon be over.' His death leaves her reminding herself that this sacrifice was 'for France.' Yet there is nothing triumphal in the story's tone, nothing to suggest that any comfort can be taken.

Marion's story, *A Sense of Duty,* appeared in December 1916, in the same issue that reported the death of Ken Davidson and those of two older former students, Private George Sutherland Foster at Ypres and Lieutenant William Bell at the Somme. Yet her story is neither contaminated by death (though her two protagonists are injured) nor marred by any geographical specificity: her hero fights in the trenches 'somewhere in France.' Hers is a story of high idealism. It is about duty, about love conquering all, about learning to 'love your enemy.' The hero is a young Scottish Canadian, Duncan Anderson, a farmer in northern Manitoba who falls in love with 'the pretty little German girl,' Freida Shreck, from the next farm. The two families are oblivious to the approaching war until Freida's father, Fritz, returns from town with the *Globe* and its blazing headline: 'Britain declares war on Germany.' Fritz's respect for Duncan is transmogrified instantly into hostility; Freida and Duncan are devastated, although they secretly agree to resume their love after the war, in words that could have come directly from *Cement*, Fedor Vasil'evich Gladkov's novel of Soviet realism:

> 'Oh, Duncan! What shall we do? Must the war make any difference?'
>
> 'No, Freida ... But we must wait. My country needs me now, and I will go to Winnipeg to enlist for services right away. Remember me, Freida, I'll be back soon and then everything will be alright.'

Duncan enlists immediately, stopping only long enough to line up a friend to harvest his grain.

More incredibly, Freida's father, Fritz, also finds himself in the trenches, but on the other side: 'Fritz received an order from his Fatherland to go back to do "his bit" in defeating the Allies. He left his family and his home, not because he wished to do so, but because he had received a command which must be obeyed. So he, too, was fighting, and a brave soldier he was.'

Marion stretches credulity even farther, and forgoes all historical accuracy, when she places Duncan and Fritz in face-to-face combat in the trenches, and later in adjoining beds in hospital. This unlikely story reflects Marion's high romantic idealism – an idealism that became, in more sophisticated form, the basis for much of her life's work in the international arena. After recognizing Freida's father, Duncan 'conquered his obstinate Scottish will' and delivered the author's message: 'I've been thinking a whole lot since I've been here and I realize now that it's the awful war we hate and not each other.'

On returning to Canada, Duncan receives Freida 'with a fuller more beautiful love than before.' But the real drama involves Duncan and Fritz: 'A common love united their feelings, and their thoughts ... It was no trouble for either to "love his enemies" now.'

Marion's attitude might well have been grounded in the unspoken stance on the war taken by the Church of Christ in St Thomas. Between

1914 and 1918 the war is mentioned only twice in the church minutes. One entry reports the sending of delicacies to the soldiers. The other, on 12 November 1918, relates to a motion by Pastor L.C. Hammond 'thanking God that the war is over and [extending] sympathy to relatives.' There is no mention of victory, and no jingoism, just as there is none in Marion's story.

In December 1921, for a theme issue of *The Collegian* on 'Sports,' Jean produced a piece very different from either *For France* or *A Sense of Duty.* Jean was a major presence in this issue, contributing a poem, a short story, a report on the Girls' Club, and a 'think piece' called 'Athletics' that is as bizarre in its content as it is conventional in message. The message of this piece is clear: athletic competition is preparation for courage in war. Launching herself with a verse from Rudyard Kipling – 'Oh, it ain't the individual, / Nor the army as a whole, / But the everlastin' teamwork / Of every blooming soul' – she declares that 'we feel a bond of sympathy with the man who saw so clearly what is necessary to insure success in any undertaking – the steady, united efforts of us who are "behind the man behind the gun," as it were.' Without stopping to take a breath, she then swoops her readers back to ancient Greece, lauding the Athenians and the Spartans, 'whose severe training ... seems to us almost brutal' for developing 'men of splendid physique.' In a robust description of the Olympian games, in which she reproduces the inner feelings of the competitors, she locates the spirit 'which we are trying to make manifest in our present-day sports.' She then returns explicitly to her theme of athletics and war.

Was it not just a few short years ago, she writes, that 'the boys who maintained the honour of their schools on the rugby fields' marched 'to the trenches, to go over the top in the morning?' In her description of these events she displays a good if not reckless imagination: 'Full well they know that ere to-morrow's sun will set they may be laid to rest; yet they meet it all with a calm, confident smile.' Here, clearly, she is recalling the playing fields of Eton, not those of the St Thomas Collegiate: 'Our hearts swell with pride that we belong to the same Empire.' Nearly sixty years later, in declining health, she would suddenly be moved to declare to an interviewer: 'Oh my dear, the flower of England was lost in the first war and again ...' – rhetoric, learned as a schoolgirl, returning undefiled.

Continuing with her paean to athletics and war, Jean turns explicitly to the Canadians. She was certainly aware of the huge number of Canadian casualties. She recalls the second Battle of Ypres and the 1st

Canadian Division, which brought glory to Canada. Here 'the Huns committed that dastardly outrage which will forever be a blot upon their name. They poisoned the atmosphere.' One can share her sentiments about poison gas without failing to notice that the 'Germans and the Fatherland' portrayed by Marion in 1916, had been replaced by the Huns – 'the enemy of civilization and humanity.'

Given the reckless jingoism of the times, we can understand her thinking so far in this piece. It is more difficult to conjure with the next bit, when she imagines the reaction of the 'brawny Canadian Highlanders [as they lay] gasping and dying.' What did the stretcher bearers hear when 'they stooped down to catch the last whisper'? 'Did those men curse the day they left the shores of Canada, and all that was near and dear to them, or did they curse the day that had brought them into this terrible plight? No! The question asked by those dying heroes was: Did the Huns get through?'

After a maudlin look at Flanders Field, 'where the silence reigns and all nature seems to harmonize ... and the pale moon pours down her benediction,' she quotes the third verse of John McCrae's poem – 'To you, with failing hands, we throw The Torch ...' – before rehearsing for the last time the moral of her tale. 'This challenge [means] that we must foster that "spirit of athletics," that we must help in the anti-cigarette campaigns, that we must ... advance the standard of the past, so that ... our men ... may meet unflinchingly [any] trial ... so that we, too, may say that we ... played the game.' And so she returns to Kipling.

It is tempting to speculate about such passions. How much were they wartime militarism? Girlish romanticism? Repressed sexuality? She is drawn to 'the splendid physique' of the Greek men, 'the brawny Canadian Highlanders,' and 'the deeds of heroism and chivalry [that] make those of the "Round Table" pale in significance.' Passions abound, but how is she to direct them, except toward encouraging the exploits of brave young men and the stiff resolve of their female compatriots?

Two of Jean's contributions to the same issue of *The Collegian* suggest that she was already developing the world view that would inform her life as a working woman and make sense of the encouragement she gave to female students. In 1919 there had been, as reported in the Victory issue, a Great Event at St Thomas Collegiate Institute: the girls in the school 'resolving to be no longer onlookers but rather doers called a meeting of all the girls in the school ... and there and then, organized a society which promises to be the most enthusiastic and energetic society ever formed in the school.'

The rhetoric describing the formation of the Girls' Club was charged: '"The old order changeth yielding place to new." How true this has been in the past few years in which woman has proved her ability to retain her own inalienable right of being the homemaker and yet to interest herself in the affairs of the world at large and to take part in work hitherto considered outside her realm.'

Three years later, in her account of the Girls' Club's activities, Jean describes a nature walk, complete with a hot dog roast. The rhetoric for such a simple story seems overblown, designed to inject more meaning than it could possibly have for the reader (and perhaps for the participants). But the rhetoric has its purposes. At the beginning of the article our girl reporter hearkens back to 'what seems like ancient history' to remind her readers of the Great Event, the founding of the Girls' Club, 'with Doris Hammond at the helm.' This event, Jean assures her readers, marked 'a new era in the lives of the girls of S.T.C.I.'[80]

More telling, perhaps, is a short story, *She's Some Spunky Kid.* As far as I could establish, Jean did not play sports, then or later, though her heroine carries a shortened version of her own middle name. Isobel Fields, the star of the basketball team, has a serious ankle sprain and the doctor 'forbade her to even think of playing.' The game is carried by Marge Kennedy, who strikes this reader as the *real* spunky kid, but no matter. Marge plays a superb game but loses her verve just before the last free throw, on which victory depends. In that second, Isobel convinces her coach that she is ready to play and, surprise of surprises, she enters the court and makes the shot.

Framing this epic tale is a conversation between two boys. Jack wants Bill to accompany him to the game, but Jack's answer says it all: 'No; it's only a girls' game.' Jack works on Bill's school spirit, and he enters the gymnasium that night 'with a bored grin on his face,' comforting himself with this thought: 'It wouldn't last long, anyway. Girls couldn't play basketball.' The game constitutes Bill's trip to Damascus, and along with the others he pays 'husky tribute to Isobel' after her inspired winning shot. On the way home, 'after a long silence,' Bill asks: 'I say, Jack, where does Isobel Fields live? She's some spunky kid.'

At Queen's, no bravado, no ringing statements, no defensiveness would ever surface in Jean's sustained support for women students who worked hard and did well. I think this was part of her girlhood legacy, part of her mother's inheritance, part of the world of women's suffrage, part of how these thoughts were expressed in the Girls' Club. Girls could do what boys can do and should have the chance to prove it. Yet one never gets any sense that Jean supported female more than male students. Indeed, any resentment she felt stemmed from what she saw as her family's favouritism toward Marion. Her affection for her brothers and for Catherine always seemed less ambivalent than her feelings for Marion. In her family, the competition didn't come from brothers.

After graduating from high school, Jean took a course at the Ontario Library School and then accepted a position at the public library in St Thomas.[81] Florence Snell, a decade her junior, remembers 'Jean the librarian, short with glasses.'[82] Jean's high school classmates dispersed themselves, a few heading to university, some going into banking or entering local businesses, often family owned.[83] But Jean was determined to go to university. In April 1925 she enrolled in an extramural course in biology at Queen's. She followed this up by attending the university in July for the summer school session.[84] It wasn't easy sledding. She passed Latin with a 69, and she passed the written exam in French (though not the oral one). She didn't complete the extramural course in biology until April 1926 – though, interestingly, with a mark of 80. In 1925–6 she took an extramural course in English, but managed only a 55. Her progress the following year was no more auspicious: 57 in French, also taken extramurally.

Until 1927, except for library school and the Queen's summer session, she had lived at home with her parents and younger siblings. But by the time she left high school – indeed, long before – she had distanced herself from them. Donald had more memory of Marion at home – even though she had left for university in 1918 – than he did of Jean, who lived in the same house until 1927. Jean's years as an extramural student at Queen's were tough. She was working full-time at the library, it seemed to be taking forever to get a degree, her marks weren't great, and the Royce house was small. She felt cramped in every way. Then she made her move: in the fall of 1927 she abandoned her secure job and entered Queen's as a full-time student. She was proud of having been out in the world before coming to university, and would continue to see this as a good option for 'a great many people who ... just lose their way because they don't have any sense of study, scholarship.' In her view, staying out brought 'a kind of maturity and particularly if you've been a librarian you know how to read.'

When she remembered the experience, Jean was always excited and vibrant.[85] None of the difficulties, then or later, suppressed her determination to enter Queen's or the many pleasures to be had. She recalled that 'there was quite a formality about residence in those days. We didn't dress for dinner but we always put on a sort of afternoon dress [and] tidied ourselves up to make ourselves civilized.' This suited her well, but having been on her own for some time, she was shocked by some of the regimentation. 'A rather stern looking girl paraded up and down the line going into dinner and if people fell out of line she would pull them in; she was elected to do it.'

Although she had to work to support herself, her graduation profile declared her a 'Student Mover.'[86] She participated actively in extracurricular activities (and would urge later generations of students to do the same). Two months after she arrived, the *Queen's Journal* ran a front-page story: 'Co-Eds Break Even with Win over Varsity Debaters, Misses Erma Beach and Jean Royce on Top at Trinity.' The two women had defeated the motion that 'the present system of education affords adequate preparation for modern life.'

As the second speaker for the negative, Jean 'outlined the many demands' that modern life was making 'upon the individual' and declared that the antiquated educational system was unable to keep pace: 'The increased speed of living means a greater tax on health which must be met. In the present day, leisure is an important part of ... life, and the modern system of education must [help graduates] make use of it.' The speaker, the *Queen's Journal* reported, 'presented [her arguments] confidently and clearly.'[87] Although this was a debate – these women would have cheerfully presented the other side – one can easily hear the Miss Royce of later years making similar points – with gusto.

Facing the debaters that day, from Varsity, was Mary Winspear, whom Jean would know all her life in the Canadian and International Federations of Women. The following March, Jean was elected president of the Debating Society, and thereby became an officer on the Levana Society executive. During those years, women were excluded from student government and it was Levana that organized their extracurricular life – and their general decorum.

In March 1928, at a mass meeting, Queen's students voted to strike to protest the suspensions of students who had organized a post-Frolic, off-campus dance. The Frolic was the students' annual fling, and many members of Senate took a jaundiced view of the event itself for 'wasting' students' time, and more specifically of the excesses that followed it – a dance, intoxication, even female intoxication. According to Frederick Gibson, half the members of Levana opposed the strike.[88] In an address to the Alumnae in 1972, Jean recalled more categorically that 'this was a male initiative; the women had no part in it. It was a short-lived protest but an unpleasant one – the women were labelled as scabs and in the New Arts Building particularly were subjected to unpleasant altercations.'[89] Arthur L. Davies's thinly disguised fictional rendition of the strike in *Sketches, Scholars and Scandals of a Quiet College Town* supports Jean's account. From the promontory of his Convocation, the book's protagonist, Bob Prentice, 'hazily ... recalled The Big Strike.' Though he couldn't 'remember exactly the *cause celebre* that triggered the decision to strike [he retained] a vivid recollection of the excitement that morning when most of the male students stayed away from classes. The girls wanted no part of a strike and boldly crossed our picket lines to go to lectures.'[90]

Jean always spoke warmly of Levana and regretted its passing from the scene when co-ed student government rendered it redundant. In the fall of 1929 the elected vice-president of Levana did not return to university, and Jean was elected as her successor.[91] President that year was Mary White, Jean's best friend. At the end of the year Mary won a scholarship from the Canadian Federation of University Women (CFUW). The *Queen's Journal* proudly announced: 'When interviewed, she stated that she intended to go to Oxford with her scholarship.' This she proceeded to do. Jean must have been wistful about this. Mary's success didn't make her feel deprived and excluded the way Marion's scholarship had; even so, Jean was an intellectual and longed for educational opportunities.

Jean's main affiliation was the Student Christian Movement. This brought her into contact with the Reverend Nathanial Micklem, who came to Queen's in 1927 as Professor of New Testament Literature in the Theological College.[92] He and his wife Agatha stayed only a brief time, leaving in 1931 for Oxford, where he had been offered a chair. Nearly fifty years later, Jean recalled 'delightful Sunday evening parties at their house where we sat around the fire and talked of many things.' Later she told Marion that it was from him that she learned the following 'delicious' limerick:

There was a young lady named Bright
Who travelled much faster than light
She set out one day in a relative way
And came back on the previous night.

The Micklems, she recalled, 'were very dear people, with well stored minds and subtle wit and wisdom.'[93]

Academically, her first full-time year was hard. She finally passed the oral exam in French, along with four other courses – English, Latin, and two in history – all with marks in the sixties. The notation beside her fifth course – Philosophy 1 – was '40dnw' [did not write]. That spring her father had been ill. In July, he died – a fact recorded at the bottom of her transcript, and no doubt the reason why she was granted permission to proceed directly to Philosophy 2, in which she earned a 71. For whatever reason – more settled family circumstances, gaining confidence, learning the ropes, finally hitting her stride – her last two years as an undergraduate were an improvement, academically speaking. She managed only a 56 and a 50 in geology and mathematics respectively, but her other grades were in the high 70s and earned her a first-class degree.

Her graduation profile presages the future: 'She does things about college, which is quite natural when one likes a place as well as she likes Queen's ... There is about her an eagerness, something of the gay, adventurous search for beauty and truth, and the swift "evanescent gleam."'[94] Mary White's profile reveals something of the gleam: 'Among her friends, [Mary] answers to "Christopher Robin" and we are not surprised to find "Pooh" and "Piglet" in the company. Their exploitations bring them such fun and their quiet times such Grand Thoughts about Nothing.'[95] Four years later, after she was appointed registrar, Jean received a letter from Pooh Bear. 'Dear Piglet,' wrote Pooh, "Oh to be in Ban Righ again and be able to go to your room and read you my thesis in-the-raw as I did parts of that first Shelley paper! Your attentive ear and appreciative comments were a real inspiration.'[96] Such naming – whatever its particular meaning – set them apart from the rest as a coterie of whimsical young intellectual women. They intended to make a mark.

During summers, including the summer after graduation, Jean worked in the university library. Fifty years later, she recalled: 'We got all the documents from the government and other agencies and when we moved from the old library in the Theological Hall they were just dumped on the basement floor. And I remember that summer that I graduated, I spent day after day after day, sorting this material and getting it together. A lot of this material hadn't been touched for a long time.' She added, with a little laugh: 'I always said that *that* was my greatest contribution to Queen's.' It was also how she got a foot in the door of the Registrar's Office, as she explained to an interviewer:

> I graduated in '30 and went to the Ontario Ladies College in Whitby and I taught there; I got an invitation during the year to come back to Queen's to the registrar's office.
> *That must have been an extraordinary offer.*
> Well I don't know that it was an extraordinary offer. The pressure of work was very heavy; Miss King was very – getting very old and she had a breakdown just before ...
> *What was your position when you came back?*
> I was the assistant registrar when I first came.
> *That was quite a notable position to be offered at that time in your career.*
> Well, that's quite an amusing tale. I worked for Miss Rayson as an undergraduate in the reference department. And Miss King was the first woman registrar at Queen's and was ... on the verge of a nervous breakdown and Miss Rayson came in to see her one day and said, 'Well, I know a good worker. We worked together on some project in reference. And she really gets a lot done. And I'd recommend her to you. And,' she added, 'she's not particularly interested in men.'
> [laughs]
> *Was that accurate?*
> Well, I think she thought I wasn't particularly interested in marriage, I don't know. After I was appointed registrar she came to see me one day and she said, 'I can tell you how you got into Miss King's office.'[97]

No woman at Queen's University before or after Jean Royce commanded anything approaching her influence. Power at the institution has remained unalterably in male hands, and the jobs held by women have been effectively constrained. Yet the conditions permitting the emergence of a Jean Royce at Queen's might well have existed at other institutions. When I spoke about this research at Dalhousie University, one of my colleagues, there since the 1960s, responded: 'I'm feeling guilty. I can't remember her name but there was a 'Miss Royce' at Dalhousie when I first came here. She did everything. You should look for her.'

That comment resonates. What was it about universities in those decades, from the end of the First World War to the mid-1960s, that permitted some women to create the space from which they could wield influence and power in such deeply patriarchal institutions? What did they have to do to be there, to survive, to navigate change? And what happened, by the end of the 1960s, to bring closure to that era? In the next chapter I interrogate the institutional history of Queen's through the lens of the registrar and her office, and follow Jean Royce through the changing practices and policies of the institution.

Chapter Two

Did She Run the Place?

After Alice King died in 1933 and Jean Royce was promoted to registrar, the principal assured the trustees that she would do her work 'very well.'[1] It is easy to assume that Queen's was so small and simple that securing the position of registrar – in a two-bit university[2] in an even less prepossessing town – had been a small matter. Jean's own story, related in bits and pieces during six interviews some forty-five years later, deals only with the university's offer to appoint her as Alice King's assistant and the immediate aftermath.[3] The second instalment – how she was, in Frederick Gibson's words, 'promoted to be registrar' – she saw as a natural progression, and gave no details.

After graduating, Jean once again took a summer job in the Queen's Library, where she clearly made an impression on 'the old lady who recommended me to Ali King.'[4] Perhaps Jean was unaware that Miss Rayson's excellent impression of her found its way to the university librarian, E.C. Kyte, who praised her 'great contribution [in] reorganizing the mass [of Parliamentary Papers] and making them readily available.' No longer, he added, was there any 'need to blush when asked to give assistance to inquirers.'[5]

However, Jean saw her position in the library as only an interim job. Right afterwards she went to the Ontario Ladies College in Whitby to teach English and history, although she believed that she was 'really appointed as director of religious knowledge.' After a year as teacher and den mother, she rejected this second women's job. The many 'weekend excursions' had made the school 'a fun place,' but they had also led her to decide she didn't want to go on 'living with' her job.[6]

This explanation sounds plausible: perhaps she decided against a job that didn't carry normal working hours. Yet when she came to Queen's and found that she couldn't live on the salary, she became a warden in successive residence annexes until 1936. More likely she spurned teaching itself: 'It was a very worthwhile experience' (for Jean, *all* experiences were worthwhile) 'but I didn't think that I wanted to teach endlessly.' Clearly, her forte was not adolescent girls, except in their most academic (and often unlikely) incarnation. Yet fifty years later, Jean's 'most responsive' student,[7] Alice Carscallen, still recalled that her religious knowledge classes constituted 'a real challenge to explore ideas and think about the meaning of life. She was a stimulating and fine teacher.'[8]

During her year at Whitby, in the winter of 1931, Jean received a letter from that 'power in the land,'[9] Dr William Everett McNeill, the treasurer and vice-principal of Queen's University, informing her that 'they were planning to make another appointment in the Registrar's Office' and offering her the post. In the same letter, he explained to her how ill Miss King was. It isn't clear whether he came clean at that point, that is, whether he revealed the full implications of Alice King's health for Jean if she should accept the offer. Perhaps he did, for only 'after considerable agitation'[10] did she accept, taking up the newly created post of assistant to the registrar 'in the last week of June ... at a salary of $1200.00 a year.'[11] Her responsibilities soon mushroomed: within days 'Ali took sick [and] went off on holidays almost immediately.'[12]

Lord knows that Alice King needed to get away. Still, let us detain her briefly. When she was appointed in 1930, *The Tricolour* declared that it was 'not only fitting but inevitable that Miss King should become in name what she had long been in fact.' Alice King, 'the first woman to become registrar of a Canadian University'[13] and the unacknowledged registrar for the preceding twenty-three years, helps explain Jean's succession to the post.

The *Queen's Review* reported in October 1931 that 'when Miss King returned from a month's holiday on September 1, her doctors insisted that she have several additional months of rest. The Registrar's work is temporarily being done by Miss Jean Royce, Arts '30, and others of the administration staff under the supervision of Dr McNeill.' Jean recalled that no one 'expected that Ali would live very long. [She was] too overworked.' Jean's conception of overwork is interesting: 'I think every registrar is perhaps overworked.'[14] Indeed, though Jean herself used the words 'ill,' 'sick,' and 'breakdown' to describe Alice King's condition,[15] when her interviewer asked, 'She was ill at the time?' Jean replied emphatically: 'She was just *worked out*, really she was just exhausted from the pressure of work.'[16] It seems unsurprising that Alice King checked out immediately after Jean arrived. Like loyal employees everywhere, she waited for assurance that her work would get done.

Imagine McNeill's sigh of relief when the young woman, highly recommended by a trusted librarian, accepted his offer. In the summer of 1930, just before he was named vice-principal and Alice King registrar, the Board of Trustees, 'having in mind [his] heavy and increasing burden carried for years,' basically ordered him 'to take a [paid] holiday of not less than two months.'[17] When Alice King faltered less than a year later, her responsibilities fell squarely on his shoulders and multiplied his own heavy mandate. Moreover, as William Hamilton Fyfe, invested as principal the year before, had discovered, McNeill was 'firmly in control' of the university.[18] Clearly, with one man responsible for – if not actually executing – every important administrative job, the university was poised for turmoil during the period of Alice King's breakdown.

No one in Alice King's domain possessed the capacity to keep the Registrar's Office on course in her absence. Jean herself walked in cold. Only once before had she been in the Registrar's Office 'with a change of address [after her father died]; it wasn't familiar ground at all.' Within days of her arrival she had moved into Alice King's office and was learning the ropes from Dr McNeill, whose office adjoined hers. Her library training stood her in good stead: 'When I got to that point in my career – if you could call it a career,' she said laughingly, 'there was a good deal of similarity; I was dealing with books and people at the library and with students and staff at the university.'[19]

Still, the learning curve must have been steep, and she had to have been very quick, though she didn't put it quite that way: 'We used to register people up in the Reading Room in the Douglas Library.' At first,

> Dr. McNeill sat with me but pretty soon he found [the students] coming to me instead of him [probably because] he was testy.
> *He didn't mind that the students preferred going to you?*
> He was just glad to be able to have somebody whom he thought could handle what was needed.

In those early days, in contrast to McNeill, she gave 'an immense amount of time to every student. This wasn't good either [but] there was nobody else.'[20] One gets the sense that the university was plummeting into the Great Depression, hanging on by its administrative fingernails.

When Alice King returned to her office early in 1932, makeshift arrangements had to be made for her assistant: 'I took a little office that had been set up for professors to come in and mark their papers and so on.'[21] Obviously, no arrangements had been made for the registrar to have a permanent assistant, even though this had been the ostensible reason for Jean's appointment. In fact, Jean had been hired to take over for Miss King – at least in the short run – and to prop her up for the duration of her employment, which was expected to be short, and was short.[22] Alice King died on 1 April 1933. In her obituary, Professor May Macdonnell wrote: 'Her many friends feared that the exacting work and increased responsibility might prove too heavy a burden for one so conscientious, so devoted to the interests of the university and so anxious to prove that such an important position was not too ambitious for a mere woman.'[23]

Appointing Jean at that point to 'act as registrar with the official status of Assistant Registrar'[24] must have been routine: there simply wasn't anyone else on the ground to take over, and as the Principal's Report noted, 'the present work of the office can be efficiently carried on.' Jean received a salary increase at this point – an additional $600 a year[25] – although it was still insufficient for her needs. At the Ontario Ladies College, room and board had been included; her small salary could be put to other uses.

At Queen's she had to moonlight: in exchange for her room, she took on the wardenship of Gordon House, a residence annex. 'I don't think I could have managed,' she allowed, 'because my salary was relatively low as an assistant registrar and then as registrar. I wanted to send my mother money every month, and I liked to buy books and I liked to travel.' But she didn't take on the additional responsibilities simply to make ends meet. The days when a young woman had her own apartment as a matter of course were still in the future. As Jean put it: 'I didn't actually know the city people and I thought that I would enjoy living in residence.' Moreover, she had 'great fun setting up' in Principal Gordon's home after his retirement 'at the same time [as] working in the university proper.'[26] Jean had worked for Gordon's daughter, Minnie, Queen's first female instructor,[27] liked her very much, and had some good stories about her. On one occasion, when Jean was an undergraduate, 'the men stormed Grant Hall' in the middle of

Levana's Candelighting Ceremony welcoming first-year women. 'Minnie stomped down the hall' – she was rather lame and carried a stick – and the men 'turned and fled.'[28] It was a thrill to live in Minnie's house.

Jean's happy recollections of settling back into Queen's make no mention of the important moment when, after the death of Alice King, she was appointed registrar. Her version suggests entitlement – and why not? She had been doing the job; she had prevented the university from falling into chaos; and more to the point, there was no one else capable in the office.

Yet it is more likely that her appointment was not routine, and that others better placed wanted the position. The Depression, then at its height, made all jobs attractive.[29] Jean, young and female in a world and a university that valued neither youth nor women,[30] might easily have been passed over once Alice King was safely dead, after a proper search had been undertaken. The university's record for hiring senior women does nothing to counter this argument. In 1933 there were only three women on permanent faculty at Queen's: Hilda Laird, Dean of Women,[31] Minnie Gordon (first hired while her father was principal), and Queen's alumna May Macdonnell. May was hired in 1917, 'when all the best men were at the front.' Former Queen's professor and Principal Gordon's recruiting agent in Britain, W.B. Anderson, had advised that Queen's 'would have to be satisfied with a disabled veteran or with a man over forty, and forty, in his opinion, was too advanced an age for adequate adjustment to Canadian conditions' – a point few survivors of Canadian winters would dispute. Anderson urged Gordon to make a temporary appointment or even – God forbid – consider 'female labour.' If the principal was inclined to follow what Hilda Neatby described as this 'last counsel of desperation,'[32] he had someone in mind. This is how May Macdonnell was appointed to the Department of Classics.[33]

The history of administrative positions provides a similar story. During the Fyfe regime, Gibson notes, 'two women were appointed to senior administrative offices – Miss Royce as registrar, and Winnifred Kydd succeeding Hilda Laird as Dean of Women.'[34] Although Gibson's account covers the following thirty years, he is never obliged to repeat the line, 'two women were appointed to senior ... offices.' There is also photographic evidence or, more precisely, dearth of same: in all of Gibson's book there are only two pictures of women. One is 'our Jean Royce'[35] and the other is Dr A. Vibert Douglas, the astrophysicist and first woman president of the Royal Astronomical Society of Canada,[36] who could only procure a full-time university position as Dean of Women.[37] Given the history of the university, it is astonishing that Jean Royce was ever appointed registrar, and there must have been controversy. I didn't expect to be able to confirm this hunch, but I was reckoning without the unembarrassed sexism of the day.

One month and eleven days after Alice King died, Jean received a letter from the secretary of the Board of Trustees 'thanking [her] very warmly indeed for [her] most efficient and unwearying work during the past weeks [and] appointing [her] as Assistant registrar from April 1st at salary of $1800.' The trustees had a further message. 'I am asked to make it clear to you,' the letter continued, 'that it is the policy of the trustees to appoint to the Office of Registrar a male, a conclusion which I ask you to note but not to approve.'[38] Whether they expected her to be grateful that they weren't asking her to approve this policy, who can say? But the wording reveals that the man who wrote the letter imagined dissent.

Six months later, however, the Board of Trustees approved a joint recommendation from Principal Fyfe and Vice-Principal McNeill recommending that she be appointed as 'Registrar at a salary of $2500.00.'[39] Clearly, there had been a protracted behind-the-scenes controversy: what follows is a small piece of the puzzle, which hangs upon a childhood memory.

During the period when a successor to Alice King was being contemplated, ten-year-old Eleanor Smith was in a Kingston bicycle shop with her parents. She was excited; it was her birthday and a purchase was imminent. Despite the joy of the occasion, her father, Gordon, was out of sorts, and Eleanor asked her mother why. It seems that he was looking for a way to escape the family jewellery business: 'He didn't like to work there. Every time a chance came up to not be there father took it.'[40] Gordon Smith had found a foot in the door at Queen's, as part-time secretary of the newly formed Alumni Association,[41] but he wanted more.

'Father had his finger in the pie and I guess Jean did too,' Eleanor recalled. 'Father was so upset about the job. He was one of the candidates, put it that way. My mother told me he wanted the job and she didn't know what would happen if he didn't get it. Well, she found out.'[42] Nor, it seems, did he lose the job fair and square, for as Cecil Smith told her daughter: 'The women had a lobby and got [her] into the job – Charlotte Whitton, Mrs. Douglas Chown.'[43]

Charlotte Whitton had made her mark at Queen's; she was the first female editor of the *Queen's Journal* and an excellent student, receiving an MA in 1918 in recognition of her high undergraduate standing.[44] A decade later she became the second woman appointed to the Queen's Board of Trustees. She was a member of the search committees that secured Principals Hamilton Fyfe and Robert Wallace.[45] It was she who made the notorious comment, 'Whatever women do they must do it twice as well as men to be thought half as good. Luckily it's not difficult.' She was not known for keeping her opinions to herself, for suffering fools gladly, or for accepting defeat. She would have been a formidable advocate had she chosen to go to bat for the acting registrar.[46]

But did she? I have found no direct evidence. But Charlotte did record her views on the treatment of Jean's predecessor. In 1920, after thirteen years as *de facto* registrar, Alice King – 'hurt and bleak ... in her treatment from an institution she loved too much to leave' – watched as William MacNeill succeeded G.Y. Chown as registrar. Seeking commiseration, Alice looked up Charlotte in Toronto, and the two women had dinner together. Ten years later, as a board member, on MacNeill's suggestion, Charlotte nominated Alice King as registrar. 'You did not know,' she wrote to him years later, 'what real joy it gave me [to bring] fortune's wheel a little closer to the full turn for her.'[47]

G.Y. Chown – no fan of public recognition for women – had insisted that McNeill succeed him. In 1960, Clara Brook recalled, 'there was a move to name a new residence after his daughter, May, one of those who had worked valiantly for women's residences. But May insisted that "if my father knew one of the buildings was being named after a woman he would turn over in his grave." We finally persuaded her, but it was never May Chown, as we wanted – just Chown Hall.'[48]

Alice King had been passed over in 1920, and a real possibility existed that Jean Royce would suffer the same fate. Given Charlotte's belief that Alice King had been unjustly treated, Cecil Smith was probably on to something. Jean thought highly of Charlotte, unlike her sister Marion, who was vocal on the subject. In a glowing tribute after Whitton's death in 1975, Jean lauded her as a 'writer, critic, editor, administrator, [and] warm personal friend of people in all walks of life.' Jean acknowledged 'the very great part she played in establishing women's residences at Queen's [as] one of the little coterie of women who worked unremittingly on this project,' and traced her career as Director of the Canadian Welfare Council and, later, 'practis[ing] the art of the possible ... as Mayor ... of Ottawa.'[49] A few months before she died, Jean declared that Charlotte was 'a brilliant person' and that one should not 'be put off by her brusque manner; she had great capacity; she was astute.' Although 'the men all hated Charlotte,'[50] Jean had many reasons to admire her. The handful of women circulating in Queen's corridors needed one another and often supported one another.[51]

The language that the principal, and later the board, used to rationalize their change of heart on Jean Royce's appointment provides a head-shaking illustration of what it was like to be a woman in a man's world in 1933. 'The work of the Registrar's Office is being admirably conducted by Miss Royce. To appoint a man to learn the work under her and then to succeed her' – (as had happened with Alice King) – 'would involve two disadvantages: increased expenditure and the loss of Miss Royce.' (She would have left or – more likely – she would have been dismissed after training her successor.) 'For many years,' the report continued, 'the offices of registrar and Treasurer were held together and gave to the holder a predominant position such as the registrar does not hold in any other university. Now that these offices are separate the efficiency of the registrar is still essential [but] the position is no longer one of predominant importance.' As evidence, it pointed out that 'the work can be done and is indeed at present being very well done by a woman.'[52]

The sophistry involved here is obvious. The registrar's functions had been hived off from those of the treasurer in 1930, and this had made way for Alice King's appointment. Nothing had changed since the board's letter enunciating its unequivocal men-only policy. But this was how Fyfe and McNeill, either together with or pushed by board member Charlotte Whitton and other university women, made possible the appointment of Jean Royce. Fyfe's declaration that Jean's appointment did not constitute an 'omen of matriarchy' was, it seems, more than a routine sexist joke. There were men who wanted the position, and in all likelihood they had their supporters. Perhaps the spectre of matriarchy arose as much from trepidation about lobbying women as from female presumption. In these circumstances, Jean's appointment had to be justified. As Principal Fyfe asserted bravely, 'Miss Royce's imperturbable efficiency made the appointment inevitable [and] would go far to justify any system of government.'[53] Presumably, even a matriarchy, though that threat seemed unimposing then, just as it does now.

It was a coup for Jean to land this job in the midst of Canada's worst depression when she was still in her twenties. She was already known as a hard and efficient worker whose head would not be turned by some cheeky young man. Now she had secured her future and found satisfying work to last a lifetime. 'Jean dear,' her friend Mary White wrote, 'if ever anyone earned and deserved appointment you have. However, men are rather chary and grudging of giving women their desserts, which makes it doubly a triumph.'

Mary's 'pride' and 'joy'[54] notwithstanding, we mustn't exaggerate the importance of the position of registrar at Queen's in 1933. There are two aspects of the position that, when considered together, will keep us earth-bound: the first involves its history, the second its place in the scheme of things.

Alice King was, formally speaking, the university's first full-time registrar, although she had done the job as deputy registrar under McNeill and as chief of staff under his predecessor, Kingston businessman G.Y. Chown. Chown, 'widely viewed as "the real manager" during the Gordon principalship,'[55] held both jobs along with the secretaryship of the (still nominally independent) School of Mining. He did not give up his business interests until he acquired the other posts.[56] We have to go back to his predecessor, George Bell, to find another registrar with a strong following among students. Bell was the university's first graduate,[57] having arrived in March 1842 as an ordained minister.[58] In 1881 he returned to Queen's as teacher of theology – and as registrar, taking the latter post off the hands of fellow graduand and theology professor J.B. Mowat.[59] In 1889 Bell was invited by the students to address the special convocation, held to mark the fiftieth anniversary of the first endowment campaign.[60]

The second aspect of the registrar's position concerns power and prestige. Neither Jean Royce nor William McNeill shared Gibson's view that this was 'a senior administrative post.' McNeill's story reveals the meaner side of university politics, and his trials parallel those of Jago in C.P. Snow's *The Masters*. In 1919 the first head of English, James Cappon,[61] resigned, and O.D. Skelton, the new Dean of Arts, recommended to Principal Taylor that McNeill be his replacement. The university's treasurer-registrar, G.Y. Chown, had contrary notions. He was anxious to leave his own post in competent hands and recommended that McNeill 'be promoted to full professor and then moved over to succeed him as registrar.' McNeill strenuously declined the second part of the deal. Taylor, 'reverting to Dean Skelton's advice,' persuaded the finance and estate committee of the Board of Trustees to recommend to the full board that McNeill be made Head of Department.

But the Board of Trustees refused to play. In McNeill's own words, written some fifteen years later to Charlotte Whitton, 'a former Principal [Gordon] objected to my appointment, saying that I was dull and uninteresting and could not inspire the students.' For good measure, another board member, in words closer in spirit to the end of the twentieth century than to its first quarter, said that 'the university must have a man who could go out and make speeches.' McNeill called the rejection the most painful injury of his life: 'For ten years I could hardly enter the Arts Building without tears.' Adding insult to injury, 'the Trustees ... thought I was good enough to be a clerk. *I was made Registrar* [my italics]. I could hardly hold up my head in Faculty meetings thereafter.' Being registrar left him no vote and 'no voice except to give information.'[62]

One savours the irony: Alice King was heartbroken because the university refused to name her registrar, McNeill because he was virtually forced to take the position. Charlotte Whitton wrote to McNeill: 'I asked [Alice] whether she [feared] that the situation would be more difficult because you would also be suffering from a great hurt of an unjust wounding. I always remember what she said: that it was the understanding that you shared from a similar treatment that made the whole thing endurable ... and, in the end, perhaps a happy undertaking together.'[63]

Educated at Prince of Wales College (Prince Edward Island) and Harvard, McNeill had been lured to Queen's ten years earlier to teach English and – ironically – public speaking.[64] Until 'his most painful injury' it never occurred to him that he should be an administrator. Nor did he ever change his mind. By the terms of his will, he endowed the James Cappon Chair in the Department of English and provided an explanatory preamble: 'My best contribution would have been as a teacher of English, for which my earlier formal education prepared me. [By this bequest] I wish to help provide through others that service as a teacher of English which I was not long permitted to render.'

McNeill's attitude toward the position of registrar must, of course, be understood in the context of his aspirations and his disappointment. That being said, Jean Royce's perspective was not so different. When asked in 1977–8 whether McNeill would have had any 'hesitation supporting a woman in a senior executive job,' she replied unambiguously: 'That would have been heresy to him – [not as] vice-principal or anything like that.'[65] For Jean, the job of registrar, at least in retrospect, was 'a basic position in a university which has its rewards from that standpoint.' But she added, '*I had nothing to do with the funds or anything like that* ... I didn't have anything to do [with] the treasury or finding money.'[66]

Her unsolicited interjection about finances, juxtaposed with her comment about the rewards of the job, demonstrates her insight even during her last years, when she was so physically constrained. When McNeill shed part of his job in 1930, it was no accident that he handed the registrarial functions over to his former assistant and kept control of the purse. (Indeed, the finances at the university have never been in female hands.) Jean was right to emphasize her absolute lack of fiduciary power. Jean's appointment as registrar was less a break from patriarchal practice than an indication of the registrar's low prestige; certainly, the world had not been turned upside down.

But of course that is not the whole story. If we have learned nothing else from Michel Foucault, it is that power circulates. During the Royce years a lot of power circulated through the Registrar's Office, or so I shall try to demonstrate. Also, William McNeill and Jean Royce do not have the last word on the place of the Registrar's Office at Queen's University. For example, university historian Hilda Neatby judges the registrar in the 'growing university' of the 1880s to have been 'an even more important officer' than the secretary-treasurer.[67] From the tenure of George Bell to that of Jean Royce, no two registrars had the same background, experience, or duties. The record of the office during the Royce years underscores how easily institutional terrain can shift. People 'make their own history,' but not in circumstances of their own choosing.[68] Jean Royce picked up the reins in the Registrar's Office in 1933 and shaped something very new – something larger, more complex, more influential, and more rule-bound. Yet she constantly bent her own rules, and practised a form of charismatic leadership that would inform the entire institution.

All of this suggests yet another point about the position of registrar. Not until May 1906 did the board appoint deans in the Faculties of Arts and Theology and, even then, Principal Gordon 'admitted to considerable uncertainty' about their powers and functions.[69] Two more deans entered the scene after the relationship between the Presbyterian Church of Canada and the university was legally severed in 1912,[70] which opened the way for the reintegration of the Faculty of Medicine with the university and the formalization, in 1916, of the relationship between Queen's and the School of Mining (thereafter called the Faculty of Applied Science).[71] Just before the First World War, faculty boards in Arts, Medicine, and Mining were created,[72] both as rational steps to accommodate university growth and as compensation for faculty who had lost their seats when the Senate became a representative body.[73] The Senate also organized itself into standing committees to make academic decisions that 'in default of any other authority' (and this is the key point) 'had been hitherto left to the registrar.'[74] As Hilda Neatby disclosed, 'in the beginning was the registrar,' whose decision-making powers were gradually taken over by principals, deans, and faculty.

This is a rough sketch of the university structure at the dawn of Jean Royce's registrarial odyssey. At the time of her appointment, the registrar shared administrative billing with the vice-principal and treasurer, William McNeill, and the principal, Hamilton Fyfe. Fyfe's appointment three years earlier had been an attempt to cast a principal-as-scholar after the dismal thirteen-year term of Robert Bruce Taylor. Board members and faculty alike agreed that Taylor had left the university sinking deeper into provincialism and financial ruin. Gibson's account of those years presents a litany of failure at every level: poor finances, abysmally low faculty salaries, and students who weren't very good and whose parties led to local disgrace, disciplinary measures, and student strikes.[75]

Finding a replacement for Taylor was excruciatingly difficult.[76] Roaming England in search of a leader, the Queen's committee finally turned up Hamilton Fyfe, English-born, educated at Fettes College and Oxford, and a classical scholar.[77] Though 'everyone liked' him, his insistence on a salary of $15,000 – three times the salary of the most senior professor – left him 'half defeated' before he started.[78]

Fyfe would enhance Queen's scholarly reputation, but he had no experience as a university administrator. Since no one expected him to be adept, the board appointed William McNeill as vice-principal and – to all intents and purposes, since he was to remain treasurer – the chief administrative officer. Together, Fyfe and McNeill, scholar and administrator respectively, would lift Queen's out of the doldrums. Who would have thought that the young woman appointed registrar three years later would outlast and outshine these two worthies, and several of their successors as well?

As Jean remembered it decades later (24 November 1977), the pressures of the Registrar's Office 'were the constant flow of students in and out, the tremendous number of students, the secretarial work – it wasn't typing – minute work for the Faculty of Arts and Senate, the Committee of Departments and the Board of Studies. [Even when Alice King was still there] I was secretary to various committees and [occasionally] to the Board of Trustees.' This involved 'taking down the minutes, and writing up the material, letters to people. Perhaps the work was not so difficult – but there was so much of it. And our staffs were small then.'[79]

Several months later, in early 1978, she elaborated: 'There were some insuperable problems, some very difficult things that had to be discussed and [Dr McNeill] was very helpful.'[80] Perhaps she had in mind some of the same problems that Hamilton Fyfe catalogued when he resigned from Queen's in favour of the principalship at the University of Aberdeen in Scotland. His final report was so incendiary an indictment of Queen's – and the Canadian educational system generally – that the trustees dared not sanction its release, fearing the political and financial consequences to the university. Times were hard enough. The board commissioned McNeill to produce a substitute report that could be taken out in polite – that is to say, Canadian – company.[81]

Fyfe acknowledged that during his tenure the Depression had blighted enterprise of every kind. But he also decried 'deep-seated flaws in the fabric of Queen's, and ... found the worst of them in the students --their abilities, attitudes, and amusements – and in the governing bodies of the university.'[82] After blasting the lack of university-initiated entrance standards and students with 'neither the will nor the ability to learn,' he set down his mission statement for a university: 'Our concern is with minds capable and desirous of increasing intellectual power, and our job is to provide an environment in which such minds will eventually go after knowledge and use it when acquired.'[83]

Fyfe's new registrar would never have engaged in such a diatribe. Such intemperate language was much more likely to have incensed Jean. Certainly, it infuriated McNeill, her sponsor and the ghost writer of the principal's 1935 report.[84] Unlike Fyfe, she did not disparage new forms of popular culture, nor was she critical of students who revelled in the games, the dances, the newly relaxed social and sexual mores, and the 'golden age era of radio and movies.'[85] Yet she undoubtedly agreed with much that the outgoing principal had written. In her 1970 CFRC Radio address on the history of Queen's, Jean praised Hamilton Fyfe more than any other principal. Fyfe, she told her audience, 'encouraged scholarship ... supported the establishment of national scholarships [and] devoted much time to the strengthening of the Honours BA Program.'[86] Armed with 'strong scholarship' and possessed of 'a rare and subtle wit, he brought to Queen's a strong influence for high standards.'[87]

Jean would become notorious for her own high standards. Dr Gordon Dunn recalls: 'Jean Royce as I encountered her at Queen's from 1948 to 1954 was renowned for her rigid application of the rules. I remember Robertson Davies referring – without naming her – to how academically exacting the rules were to get into and to stay at Queen's – so he migrated to a place with more relaxed standards – Oxford.'[88] Jean was still new in her job when Principal Fyfe left for Aberdeen, but clearly, his views on scholarship and standards made a strong impact on her.

Others at the university who took the trouble to record their feelings were glad to see Fyfe's backside, though it is worth noting that neither were his two predecessors – Gordon or Taylor – hailed as worthy stewards of the place.[89] Principal was a difficult job, and the glory days of Principal Grant, who served from 1877 until his death in 1902, cast a long shadow over them all. Although Grant died two years before Jean was born, she had no difficulty in describing his successor, Principal Gordon, the father of her close friend, Minnie, as 'a man of great dignity [but] by no means the quality of Dr. Grant.'[90] Against the eternal myth of Grant's perfection, Hamilton Fyfe comes off very well in Jean's recollections.

While principal, Fyfe provided for the new president of the University of Western Ontario what he deemed 'an inadequate catalogue of the multifarious trivialities on which the head of a university fritters away his time.' Topping the list was responsibility 'for all advice concerning the appointments to the staff, salaries, dismissals and all other academic matters.' Though the deans, treasurer, and registrar had 'each their own department of work,' the principal had to act 'between them all ... as a telephone exchange and an oil-can.'[91] Interestingly, Jean gave no indication that her relationships with her colleagues were oiled by Hamilton Fyfe – or any other principal. She referred much more often to deans, heads of department, and members of faculty. But certainly she met the principal often in those days, before so many of his tasks had devolved onto vice-principals, deans and their associates, department heads, and chairs of undergraduate and graduate studies.

If the first rule of politics is to be there, Jean was consolidating her position at the university, serving on as many committees as the principal including special and ad hoc committees. 'God, I was on the library board, I was secretary to the senate, I was secretary to the faculty of arts, I was secretary to all the committees,' she recalled with some amazement and a retrospective sigh of exhaustion.[92]

The registrar had not always been secretary for all these committees. Until November 1936, Jean attended Arts Faculty Board meetings whenever she had business to conduct relating to student grades and scholarships. The minutes of those meetings, however, heralded a new regime, with Jean Royce signing as secretary. This developed into standard practice for her on most of the boards and committees, except for the Board of Library Curators, where the chief librarian doubled as secretary.

Serving as secretary is an onerous task. Agendas must be set and prepared, and then minutes have to be taken and prepared. All of this involves countless microdecisions about tone and style, about what to include and exclude. There is, in short, a politics to agenda setting and minute taking. Sometime in 1936 the members of Faculty Board decided that the secretary would no longer be one of their own. Finding a secretary from among the faculty often resembles the childhood game of 'hot potato'; they must have been only too pleased when Miss Royce assumed responsibility. Even so, some professors perused her minutes carefully, taking exception to any omissions and commissions and to any infelicitous wording.

For nearly thirty years Jean prepared the minutes while faculty walked to and fro. Once appointed secretary, she introduced a 'detailed agenda.' As she explained:

> I thought an agenda was essential if they were going to do some thinking about what was to come up.
> *They didn't know until they got there what was going to be discussed?*
> Well, the Committee of Departments might enlighten them, I suppose.

Faculty members were vigilant about any poaching on their terrain, and the usual suspect was the Committee of Departments, a settled group made up of department heads, the principal, the dean, and the registrar, who in her *ex officio* capacity knew that it was 'a *very* strong body' indeed. McNeill's exclusion from this charmed circle when the English headship was denied him made him very unhappy, and with good reason: headships were fiefdoms, held at the pleasure of those above, and Jean's memory that a man never 'gave up his headship' rings true.[93] Heads wielded considerable discretionary power over their colleagues and students, and over curricula, standards, and scholarships. To their younger colleagues they were a gerontocracy. Providing an agenda to Faculty Board, so that members did not have to depend on uncertain enlightenment from department heads, may have been a quietly subversive act. But more important, preparing an agenda ensured that *her* issues would be discussed, and in the order *she* determined. She was also trying to shorten the board meetings and raise their tone: meetings animated solely by whatever spontaneous thoughts seized the members must have been hard to bear.

The Committee of Departments proved also to be a thorn in the side of the long-time dean, John Matheson, obstructing any divide-and-rule tactics and alienating his younger colleagues. A year before Jean became permanent secretary, he unsuccessfully moved its abolition.[94]

For nearly three decades Jean was everywhere. The registrar's job expanded every time a new committee was struck. Who could bring information better through time and space than Miss Royce? Principals came and went, as did the occasional vice-principal and dean. As for faculty, while some were there for the duration, many weren't – and their enthusiasms for things administrative waxed and waned. Finally, all administrations know that they can outwait the demands of any particular cohort of students, for whom university is a *rite de passage*, not a life sentence.[95]

Jean was even there when she seemed not to be. She was clearly the secretary (and chief administrative officer) for graduate studies, first in its location within the Faculty of Arts and, after 1943, when it had its own board supervising programs for all faculties. But when the Graduate Survey Committee made a preliminary report on 16 February 1961, she was not named as a member. Only the introduction to the final report, nearly a year later, bore witness to her presence. 'I am grateful,' the chairman wrote, 'to Miss Jean Royce for serving as secretary and for contributing so much to our discussions.'[96] The tribute notwithstanding, biology professor Harold Good's suspicions that 'her influence was felt very clearly but recorded very inadequately' are borne out.[97] In the official records she is sometimes hard to spot and often difficult to hear.

Though she was not considered an interventionist secretary[98] she participated actively, clarifying issues, providing information, and, importantly, deciding what to bring to members' attention. She later explained that when she took something to a committee, 'my strength lay that I knew the case from stem to stern because I had prepared the material.' Though the case would have to be judged by those regulations already in place, 'I [had] drafted lots of [the] rules.' Once drafted, the new rules were discussed in committee, and 'we'd change the phrases and words; it was a pretty democratic set-up.' After the new rules were approved, they joined their predecessors to constitute a (revised) usable past: Jean noted: 'It was very helpful to say that the faculty has agreed that this must be so.' When those very rules needed bending, 'I usually went to the man [faculty member, department head, or dean] and we'd talk it over.' In most cases 'the man' must have relied heavily on her knowledge of the situation, for as she recalled, 'I knew the regulations in a way nobody else knew them [because] I [prepared] the calendar, you see, in my office.'

Someone who knows the rules – especially when he or she has also developed them – is endowed with sweeping powers to exercise discretion. As Jean put it, 'in a sense the rules and regulations laid down in the calendar were flexible enough to give a different interpretation. But you didn't do that too much because you weren't [just] dealing with one student.' Having one person largely in charge provided for consistency.[99] Clearly the process that developed at Queen's provided not only for consistency, but also for the registrar's growing authority. As Jean saw things – and most faculty members would have cheerfully agreed – she had her mandate and they had theirs.

Indeed, Jean firmly reined in a former student who wanted to complain that the faculty paid too little attention to students: 'A man who is teaching has his lectures, his plans for a year away from time to time, his book that is coming out.'[100] Jean realized that faculty interests and hers did not necessarily coincide, any more than those of faculty and students. 'People of course would go off in the spring,' she explained. 'They would take boats just as soon as examinations were over. It was really a racket to go away on the last day of classes and to leave everything to a clerk in their office to see that the stuff got in. [At one point] I put forward the suggestion that until their marks were in they should stay. So that was improved a bit.' But she seemed generally unexercised about these rapid getaways: 'I never remember people coming to me and complaining about not getting results – they may have gone to Frances Gibbs, the person responsible for marks. It was an *easy-going* system and it didn't always work but usually it did.'[101] She took great pride in the accomplishments of Queen's faculty; as alumnus David Slater recalled, 'she took it to be an almost sacred mission to perpetuate, indeed strengthen the accomplishments of Queen's students, graduates, and faculty.'[102]

Hans Eichner, professor of German, remembered how 'wonderfully effective' she was on committees:

> She used her presence [to root] for the very bright students – and of course she had an eye for it. Though no one would have said so, she was a feminist. She had a way of seeing to it that the really bright women got their fair share of prizes and recognition. [The Prince of Wales Prize was] very prestigious, and in the early days there was only one. [The committee would] end up with two or three students from physics and so on – men of course and maybe one or two women whom Jean would know. She would sit quietly, maybe fairly early on talk about the student she had in mind. She picked people who were brilliant.
>
> At precisely the right time she would – 'I move that so and so ...' Precise timing, right to split second. You couldn't do it too soon, before people were ready to vote, or too late ... I am not saying she was manipulating. She had a knack for picking the best person. She was knowledgeable, accessible, helpful.[103]

Jean well realized that principals, deans, and faculty were often busy elsewhere and so not available for students – or her – to consult. For example, she remembered never being able to find Dean A.R.C. (Sandy) Duncan. In these situations, the place had to be run: that was her job, and she had little choice but to press on undeterred, though this wasn't always understood. Another 'phantom' was W.A. Mackintosh, the eminent economist, and principal of Queen's during the 1950s, a man for whom Jean had the greatest respect. One day she stopped him on the street to tell him his daughter had again won major scholarships. He 'groan[ed] about having to put out so much money because he was determined that he wouldn't take any money from the university coffers.'[104] She admired his integrity; moreover, he 'succeeded in creating a happy place to which staff liked to come and from which they were reluctant to leave.'[105] But she took it as matter of course that he could be hard to track down, and no wonder: 'At one time, Mackintosh was the Dean of Arts, the Head of the School of Commerce, the Head of the Department of Economics and on leave most of the time – a great deal of the time – in Ottawa.'[106] The consequences were clear: at times 'it was necessary to take a decision' – sometimes more than one – in his absence.

Faculty members also posed dilemmas in their varying attitudes toward student counselling. 'I knew whom I could pick within the [faculty] who could do this sort of thing too' (that is, as well as she herself could) 'and some of them were very glad to do it.'[107] In the early 1960s some faculty members began aspiring to a counselling role, but, as she recalled, 'they'd never be there at the time they were supposed to meet the students, so the students would come running along to the Registrar's Office ... If it was in my power, I got as much within my hands from the student as he could give me, and if he didn't understand what it was all about I called [the faculty member] myself to see what he was getting at.' Judith [Plumptre] Wedderspoon remembered that the registrar was not necessarily deterred if *he* did not see what *she* was getting at. In her third year, she wanted to drop a course in French – one of her major subjects – in order to continue with an Elizabethan drama course 'which was a complete optional extra.' As she expected, Jean's response was that 'no arts student should leave without some knowledge of the Elizabethan dramatists.' The French Department 'was not pleased.'[108] The displeasure could be reciprocal. Jean remembered that she was constantly battling with P.G.C. Campbell, one of her best friends. She added carefully that the 'French people here seem to think that it is their job to discourage students [from taking French].'[109]

Jean was aware that her methods did not please everyone, and viewed this as a minor occupational hazard. 'I remember Mackintosh asking me once if I had sent [a student] to someone in French.' She hadn't, and replied that she had 'handled it the best way' she could. Besides, she asked rhetorically, what would have been the point of such a referral? 'That person [wasn't in] town,' and moreover, 'he knew nothing about scholarship opportunities in the European universities.' What mattered was that 'the boy won the scholarship.'

On another occasion, after interviewing a student, she did call the dean, who sent letters to all faculty members concerned. But this strategy failed to yield a satisfactory resolution. This story began with a specific incident that she would 'never forget,' but, in her retelling, twenty or thirty years on, the specific story became generic: the problem 'would come back to me and I'd have to pick up the pieces.' Some people thought she had too much power, but Jean herself never saw what she was doing in terms of power: 'I usually consulted people – if I could get hold of them.'

One sometimes senses that Jean ran the place *in spite of* the professors and deans. Each year, she remembered, course materials submitted for the calendar by department heads and deans 'had to be looked at with an eagle eye because they didn't really seem to know what they wanted to [offer].' 'We had bright people,' she remembered with a laugh. 'Some very active and intelligent people – and we had half-bright people and you always knew the man you had to do the most work with because he was the one who didn't ever seem to do anything.'[110]

Professor H.L. Tracy, on the other hand, knew what he wanted. He was appointed head of the new Department of Classics – a merger of Latin and Greek – during the same period that Jean became registrar,[111] and he shared many of her values, in particular a profound distaste for racial and religious intolerance.[112] But he wanted her to change some of her ways. 'I don't think he had anything against me,' Jean recalled, 'but he displayed once in a meeting how he would register a student' by telling them about every subject. Tracy had a practical concern: 'Latin and Greek were very small departments [with] very small classes.' If only the registrar would do her job properly, surely more students would enlist.[113] But Jean reasoned that there wasn't time for such a litany, and more important, 'no student is going to be bothered. It's too tedious.'

Making university materials more accessible – and less tedious – involved some splendidly co-operative ventures with faculty. 'There were certain staff members very interested in running the university – not for very long! George Whalley [head of English] was one of them, and he taught me an enormous amount about good printing and design.' Sitting on Jean's living room floor on a Sunday morning, Whalley, his brother Peter, a well-known cartoonist, and Jean 'worked out what [she deemed] a delightful cover for the calendar. We decided the colours related to each faculty, and Peter drew these little figures.'[114]

The registrar had several irons in the fire. When her former assistant expressed amazement at her ability to keep track of everything, Jean explained that she 'probably initiated it in the first instance and developed it and changed it as time went on.' Some faculty were against her playing such a key role, asking, basically, how she could know '*this* about *that*.' For example, Martyn Estall told Jean that she 'didn't know anything about philosophy.'[115] She knew there were people who 'thought that I thought I was important.'

It isn't clear whether she knew this at the time, or whether this insight grew from her cold-blooded dismissal. But her claim that 'it never dawned on me that *that* was a matter of importance – it was all [about] getting things done,' strikes me as being as close to the truth as our post-Enlightenment sensibilities will allow. This was her refrain: 'I had this enormous amount of work.' She remembered arriving at a meeting 'in the Old Arts Building [and receiving a] cold shoulder' from some people because 'an administrator [i.e., she herself] had just come in. [But since] I [always] had the facts in my hand, you see, I was never worried about that.' Of course, 'there was the occasional [academic] snob, [but] nothing like the attitude now – at least I never felt it; perhaps I wasn't very perceptive or perhaps I just didn't think about it.'[116] If she minded, she didn't let on, not then, and not to historians – and not to herself, I suspect. At some level she probably knew that most faculty, if they thought about it at all, were happy enough to let her get on with things.

For most faculty she was a peer and sometimes a confidante. 'I got an extra-ordinary raise last month,' a friend dashed off on a postcard, adding that he was 'sworn to secrecy lest [his] colleagues turn green.'[117] 'Your address was a prose poem,' Rollo Earl, Dean of Arts, wrote on 11 April 1953. 'The concept beautiful and execution perfect. Every word was apposite and selected for the right effect. Your audience was spell-bound. No one else could do that.'[118] 'You alone,' wrote Gerald Graham shortly before her death, 'had the stature to follow Dr. McNeill, and in the opinion of the Alumni, join the select ranks of the Queen's immortals.'[119]

Her archival papers include scholarly publications inscribed and sent to her by the authors. According to Harold Good, Jean Royce was 'essentially equivalent to full professor.' Given that Jean wrote and delivered papers on the philosophy of education and educational policy, and that it was then still respectable for faculty *not* to publish, this assessment had a solid basis. Hilda Laird, head of German, was 'not a productive scholar,' as Hans Eichner noted – there was 'no pretense.'[120] In the 1960s, Queen's named the new biology building after Rollo Earl, who was described by his colleague Harold Good as 'no hell as a scientist – [he] produced essentially nothing in the research line.'[121]

Good recalled telling Jean that he was perhaps 'a generalist by nature, interested in a lot of things,' but that the university wasn't headed in this direction. Her response was a spirited 'defence of the generalist: Why don't you spit in the eye of the university? (She didn't put it that way.) And so I did.' Jean, he thought, 'was opposed to narrowness.' That's true, in a sense. But, on other occasions she argued for a healthy tension between specialization and generalism: 'I think that we need both in this society. You have to have really good research done, you have to put your mind pretty closely to developing your ideas about your subject. But I don't think that precludes general interests.'

She rejected pigeon-holing. 'I've never classified myself [a generalist or a specialist],' she mused, 'but I knew that I wasn't a specialist.'[122] Her support of Harold Good was partly rooted in her belief that he should not pummel himself into a category unsuited to temperament, talent, or interest. But she also believed that generalists like Good and Earl who taught well – and who acted as university ambassadors to the high schools – were as important to Queen's as dedicated researchers.

The Faculty at Queen's, Jean recalled, 'were mostly my friends – people whom I knew and went about with and this kind of thing.' Elsie Curtis wrote: 'I often think of the times you would phone here and ask to speak to "my favourite dean."'[123] Clifford Curtis 'got below the stern side of Jean,' Elsie told me, 'not that many knew her as we did.'[124] Engineering professor Joe Brooks thought she liked him because he was 'the only one she [could] get along with.'[125] But Jean bestowed favour more widely than people thought. Though there was a gap between her professional, sometimes brusque, public demeanour and the warmth and fun of her private demeanour, she actually permitted many to see both sides. My interest lies in how her willingness to let people in – at least occasionally – helped create the cooperative environment in which she did so much of her work. The stern, brusque lady registrar could turn it on or off when she wished. This accounted for the ease with which she enlisted faculty support for students, and for the high regard that surrounded her. There was 'a kind of *trust*,' Jean recalled, with particular reference to her relationship with deans Matheson and Clark,[126] but this trust was widespread.

Faculty members across decades spoke glowingly about the key role Jean played. Mathematician John Coleman remembered that to an 'innocent new faculty member' in the 1940s, 'it seemed that Queen's was governed – and that *was* the operative word – by principal Wallace, Dr McNeill and Jean Royce. It was clear that [she] was by far the most important for ensuring the internal well-being and smooth functioning of the university.' When W.B. Rice arrived in the early 1950s as an associate professor in the Department of Mechanical Engineering, he found 'a community, its acknowledged leaders principal W.A. Mackintosh and the registrar Jean I. Royce. While the principal provided exemplary scholastic leadership, Miss Royce managed the affairs of the community, efficiently, elegantly, and humanely.' By the

1960s the school had grown too big for such easy encapsulation, but young physics professor David McLay found Jean Royce 'not only the Secretary of the Faculty Board' but also the Faculty's 'chief administrative officer.'[127] Vernon Ready, the first Dean of the Faculty of Education, 'marvelled at all the responsibilities she had at Queen's. It seemed in fact that she practically ran the university.'[128]

According to Harold Good, if opposition existed it was easily explained. 'If you get somebody as strong willed and who has very strict standards, they can easily get a reputation for being autocratic [when] at least half of the problem is that the people on the other side were not preparing their cases properly and they might feel that they were being bulldozed partly because they were inherently weak themselves. You decide something is arbitrary when you are not sufficiently in the picture yourself to mount a coherent discussion.' He recalled no confrontations and 'warm memories of our association.'[129] On fundamental issues, he and his colleague Walter Smith were on the registrar's wavelength. '[We were] somewhat academic snobs – prepared to say if you can't hack it you don't belong here.' Jean was not 'unsympathetic to people who had trouble with university work, but [not] to the point of altering her standards.'[130]

Jean's 'imperturbable efficiency,' which had made her hiring almost a *fait accompli* (according to principal Fyfe), was confirmed a decade later by the Chairman of the Board of Trustees, principal Fyfe's successor, Robert Wallace,[131] and by the Dean of Applied Science, Arthur Lewis Clark. Clark's tribute warrants closer examination. First, his prejudices reveal the rocky terrain that Jean negotiated in her early years in office, as well as the daunting task faced by 'the women's lobby' that sought her appointment. '[I always opposed] the appointment of a woman to this office believing that the science students would not talk as freely to a woman as a man,' Clark admitted. But he added that in this case at least, he was wrong. 'It is extremely unlikely that the work of her office could have been done any better by a man, good as he might be.'[132] To Jean he wrote: 'You have filled the position magnificently. We have only rarely disagreed and when we have I fancy that you were right.'[133] It is not surprising that Jean remembered Arthur Clark 'as having a very happy approach to students.'[134] Their mutual admiration society sprang from their desire to serve students well. But it was Jean, not Arthur, who had to jump the gender hurdle to prove herself.

The second part of Clark's tribute provides an excellent opportunity for looking more closely at how the Registrar's Office actually ran.

'Possessed of an accurate memory, a quick mind, unfailing good nature and unlimited patience,' the dean concluded, 'she has organized the work of her office so well that it goes on quietly and without apparent effort.' Not true. In fact, it could be hard to work for Jean Royce: her office did not at all lack for noise, emotion, fuss, and effort. She had developed her own approach to working with faculty and deans; in the same way, she had a style of office management to facilitate her expanding work load. Not surprisingly, some of her employees didn't like her methods.

All concur that Jean ran a tight ship, one that penurious undergraduate student Priscilla Galloway remembered appreciatively. As a second-year student in 1948, she was delighted to give up waitressing in Ban Righ Hall for work in the Registrar's Office, and not only for financial reasons. 'Jean's confidence boosted my self-esteem. She did not hire anyone lightly.' But, she continued, 'neither a medical association office, nor the typing pool at a canning factory, prepared me for the Registrar's Office, [where Jean Royce] was the principal of the "if a thing's worth doing, it's worth doing well"' school of thought. Luckily for Priscilla, her mother had been one of the school's disciples.[135]

In the age of typewriters and carbon paper, well before whiteout and correction ribbons,[136] strikeovers and erasures were forbidden and abbreviations were banned. 'She had the eagle eye of all eagle eyes, and if she did not read every word that went out from that office herself, lowly minions like me were well convinced that she did.'[137] Yet working in this 'gloomy' and 'austere' office in the Douglas Library, with 'dark wood, high ceiling ... worn hardwood floor, certainly no carpet,'[138] Priscilla 'quickly learned to take pride in "our" standards; we were her support system, not her competition.'[139]

Priscilla, of course, was not in the Registrar's Office, nor in a secretarial and clerking position, as her life's work. Eleanor Smith – whose father had hoped to be registrar – recalled Jean Royce in rather more caustic terms, though with considerable amusement. Every morning she would 'nab Marion Darbyshire ... as soon as she got to work and say smartly, "Miss Darbyshire, I'll take you on now."'

'What on earth did she mean?' I inquired, wondering if Miss Royce was in training for the women's lightweight title. 'That she should come in to her office and take the letters down in shorthand,' Eleanor explained. 'Marion was a good-natured soul, though – she didn't seem to mind. I'd have been up the pole.' Eleanor took a dim view of Jean's famous reputation for personal and prompt correspondence: 'Most of the time in the letters she wrote she said the same thing: "I did this." "I did that." "I transcribed your entrance card." And I'd think: "Like heck you did. *We* always did it."' Of course this is the convention in hierarchical organizations: those above take credit for the work done by those below and upon whom they depend. This is the quiet, seemingly effortless, work lauded by Arthur Clark.

'If you ever lost anything, she'd skin you alive,' Eleanor remembered. 'I was rooting around looking for something I couldn't find, and I went back in her office and told her, and she said, "Things don't just disappear" and I thought, "I have news for you."'[140] Years later, Rona Wilkie discovered that if Jean 'was looking for something that couldn't be found temporarily, woe betide ... The whole place would be in a furor, everybody running about, no taking no for an answer. Nothing casual about it!'[141]

Her staff tended to believe that the lost items were most likely on the great lady's own desk – a familiar story to office workers in the pre-computer age. 'She'd have this pile on her desk, and there'd be a record card someone would need very badly at the bottom of the pile, and we always waited until she went home to lunch, and then we'd root through all her stuff. We'd have a spy, and she'd say, "Here's Miss Royce coming up the street."' At that time, home for Jean was the second floor of a small house on Queen's Crescent. From her promontory in Douglas Library, the 'spy' could follow Jean's progress back to the office from the time she turned onto University Avenue, about four brisk minutes away. When people are willing to go to these lengths to ensure the smooth running of an office, it may be that they fear potential wrath if tasks are botched; or they may be taking the initiative out of concern for students awaiting news; or they may be taking personal pride in the work of 'their' office, as Priscilla Galloway suggested.

But the assumption that cards 'got lost' on Miss Royce's desk was well established: 'One day she wanted a [student] card and called in Margaret Brown – who probably stood there and shivered – and ordered her to go find James Jones's card. Of course, the kid rooted around in all the files and couldn't find it. On advice, Margaret then went upstairs to the Department of Extension because "they were always coming in and taking the cards." Someone there cheekily suggested that she "go back and tell her it's on her desk."' Ever obedient, Margaret returned and told Jean she'd been upstairs looking for the card.

'So where is it?' Jean asked.

'Well, someone told me to tell you it's on your desk,' replied the honest but foolhardy Margaret.

'The nerve,' replied the registrar.

I asked Eleanor Smith if the registrar was like the general. She replied swiftly: 'No, the sergeant major.'[142]

Kingston is an army town, and even civilians know that sergeant majors bark orders: generals presumably have other ways to impose their will. 'She had a very commanding voice,' said Rona Wilkie, looking back on her stint in the Registrar's Office in the summer of 1956.

> The tone of her voice gave you a sense of what she expected. I was the furthest [from her office]. She would come to [her] door – this not very large person, but very prepossessing – and standing in the door she'd call out [my name].
>
> *Did she call you Rona?*
>
> Noooo. *Missus Wil-kie* ... She was a very hard taskmaster. I personally never worked so hard. I'd come out [of her office] with my [shorthand] notebook half-filled, which was a day's work right there, and then in half an hour ... she'd be at the door saying, 'When you have finished, please come in.' *When I finish!* There's masses of work here.

Magda Davey joined the office in 1960. She remembered clearly her first glimpse of the office. 'She had her desk sitting at the back and she had a long table at right angles to it, both of which were piled high with papers, files, coloured cards ... it looked very disorganized to say the least ... She also had a gorgeous painting of Picasso that I've wanted all my life.' Magda believes she was the first to dictate letters, at least routine ones. Jean would sign them all, but 'once in a while, something would catch her eye and she wouldn't be very pleased and she'd just sit at her table and screech – Mag-da ...' 'Nowadays it's all done very quietly through the intercom, but then there might be a whole lineup of students. You realize now how funny and undignified it was. But it worked – another little quirk of hers.'[143]

Nor was Jean always tactful in monitoring office behaviour. 'In 1945, some of the boys ... back from the war [came] into the Registrar's Office,' Eleanor Smith recalled. 'I went over one day to one guy because I knew him and she walked by and said [in a brusque, annoyed tone], "We don't have time for that in this office." Imagine her saying that. Poor guy. I felt sorry for him.' Though Jean went out of her way to encourage the returning veterans who wished to become students, her warmth did not extend to permitting their fraternizing with her staff on company time. Nor did she extend her kindness to those in her office who had family overseas: 'Jean McBratney got pretty mad at her. Her brother was coming back from the war. Jean wanted to go meet him at the station. Miss Royce wouldn't let her go.' There was plenty of work for Jean McBratney, 'who usually did the minutes of meetings like Faculty Board, Arts and Science, and Applied Science.'[144] But was there really no time for a sister to go meet a brother returning from war?

Maybe not. A *Queen's Journal* headline from 10 October 1945 announced: 'Registrar Reports Record Enrolment; Emergency Accommodation Established.' Reporter Garth Gunter explained that 'the record enrolment is attributed to approximately 840 ex-service men and women.' Even this late in term, recently discharged soldiers were seeking admission. Hoping to curb the flow, 'Miss Jean I. Royce, university registrar,' had announced that 'under absolutely no circumstances are additional applications for registration being accepted now.'

Four years later, Principal Wallace reported that 'the heavy strains of the war years and postwar influx of students have taken their toll in the health of our staff ... Too many breakdowns have taken place, and several others are at the breaking point.'[145] Between 1945 and 1948 the faculty offered two full academic sessions a year in order that the newly returned veterans – at university at the (partial) expense of a grateful government and a country woefully depleted of [man]power – be degreed as soon as possible.[146] Some of the distressing consequences, historian Brian McKillop concluded – contrasting Queen's unfavourably with other Ontario universities – stemmed from the lack of postwar planning in a university 'hampered by an ineffectual Senate, two decades of straightened circumstances in its faculty of arts, and ... a generally demoralized professoriate.' Indeed, in September 1945, when the 'university's registrar reported [that] nearly half' of the intramural students 'were returned veterans ... its senate appeared startled.'[147]

Whether or not the registrar tried to galvanize her colleagues earlier, the demands on her office – 'the inrush of veterans, acceleration of courses, problems of adjustment, housing accommodation and classroom space'[148] – were mind-boggling.[149] The registrar was stoked during this period, self-cast to serve those men who had fought valiantly, lived to return, and were now as ready as she to build an educated postwar society that might find alternatives to war. 'The end of the war,' Jean wrote decades later, 'was a time of great intellectual excitement and development [and] the whole tone of the university was pitched to a high level.' In those 'happy days'[150] she was a woman with a mission. In the aftermath of the Great War she had been all dressed up (in ideological terms) with nowhere to go; this time she – and her staff – had to get with the program. From all reports, they did, but the sharp memories of Eleanor Smith and her co-workers, harboured so carefully over the years, suggest the informal response of some of those (wo)manning the mission.

Perhaps Jean knew that without strict supervision, 'girls' just out of school, working long hours five-and-a-half days a week, most of them with their eye on boyfriends and marriage – and poorly paid to boot – could not be counted on to demonstrate proper diligence. William McNeill, the university's treasurer, was a hard man with a dollar. After Alice King died, Jean did not inherit her salary of $3,500. Even at a reduced rate, however, Jean was doing well relative to those women who worked for her.

Many of them failed to make a living wage, although Gibson put a warm cast on the situation. Single women at home, he opined, 'found in a salary of $624 a year a welcome supplement.'[151] Certainly this was still the dominant view of the day – that parents support daughters until marriage. Even so, Gibson's remark, offered some fifty years later not as ideology but as fact, displays the staying power of this particular variation on patriarchal rationalization. Jean never embraced this ideology: 'I was very concerned about the salaries the girls were making and I pushed that for them as far as I could, without much success.'[152] Perhaps she realized that young women, receiving such inglorious compensation, were unlikely to offer body and soul to their work. Jean herself had a strong sense of duty and an unassailable work ethic, and was herself from an impoverished background, so she tried to counter any fall from grace that she detected in her employees.

Clearly, Jean had little in common with the young women who worked with her. Several of them recalled that 'we had a little thing going that [she] didn't make enough to buy herself a new dress. Aggie had a chart and marked off all the days that she wore the same dress.'[153] Aggie and her friends would not have been caught dead wearing the same dress day after day. Perhaps, as Frederick Gibson assumed, the young women who lived at home – and worked for one-fifth of Jean's salary – did have more discretionary income than she did. Jean's account books show every penny accounted for and few savings during the first two decades of her tenure. Far from receiving help from family, she sent regular monthly sums to her mother until Katherine died in 1946. But even after that, as she accumulated substantial savings, she spent little on clothes. During her last decade as registrar she always wore – wore out, in fact – 'very nice but tailored-like dresses and suits.' Dawn Kiell remembered 'one outfit in particular, an iron grey coloured suit which she wore ... regularly day after day until ... the elbows wore through. We were happy to see it replaced.'[154] There would be little argument with Jean Richardson's observation that though 'formally dressed ... she didn't give two hoots about her clothes.'[155] Her discretionary income was marked for travel and books.

There was the usual speculation about why the registrar was as she was. Perhaps she'd been 'thwarted romantically,' was one suggestion – albeit one that flies in the face of Miss Rayson's earlier assurances that Jean wasn't interested in men.[156] (Perhaps, on the other hand, her job in the library had permanently ruined her chances. Did Robertson Davies know something? His heroine's romantic possibilities weren't 'first-rate ... working in the Waverley Library [that] graveyard of matrimonial hopes [alongside] Miss Ritson, "her great enemy."' Did art imitate life?)[157] Jean's staff naturally speculated about Miss Royce. She was said not to sleep well, 'that she'd get herself all excited about [whatever was going on].' Jean Richardson, her assistant, knew she suffered from bad headaches that made her irritable, though she never complained. But Jean's larger problem, she thought, was that she 'lived in her head rather than her heart.'[158]

Jean Richardson had a long time to observe Jean Royce. Hired first in 1936, soon after finishing her BA and business training, she became the registrar's assistant in 1939, thus assuming the post that had remained unoccupied since the death of Alice King. Jean Royce recalled suggesting her promotion to Dr McNeill, who 'thought that it was a good idea.'[159] The arrangement lasted twenty-three years, to the registrar's great satisfaction: 'Jean Richardson [is] a very remarkable person – you'd like her very much – she had *all* the [necessary] qualifications and qualities. [Accurate, pleasant, very able, and a good person,] she took a lot of the burden off me.' Then she added, as if to give authority to her words, 'she shared the registrar's duties as her first assistant.'[160]

Jean 1 depended heavily on Jean 2 not only on a day-to-day basis, but also for taking charge when she took holidays and conference trips.

According to Eleanor Smith, Jean Royce had a curious way of dealing with this reliance. 'She'd plan a holiday, and she'd march into Jean Richardson's office the day before and say "I'm off tomorrow," and Jean would say, "Where are you going?" Then she'd have to take over the office.'[161]

Jean's style reflected her workaholic nature. The prospect of leaving produced anxiety. By informing her assistant at the last moment, she kept the knowledge of her departure from others and, more importantly, from herself. She was 'The Office,' and she was there until she wasn't there. After that, out of sight out of mind.

Jean Richardson remembered those disappearing acts and how her boss 'just sailed into the sunset.' She must have been the perfect assistant. She had no aspirations for promotion and no ambition to shape policy, yet she also knew almost everything about the office's daily operations. As gentle as her employer was brusque, she was often the first recipient of bad news, because of her manner and because she was willing to be the messenger. She knew, if others didn't, that 'behind the brusqueness was a kind of pussycat [who couldn't show herself] in the man's world.' Though 'it wasn't all peaches and cream' working for her, 'if a member of her staff made a mistake' she always supported them.[162]

Clearly, Jean Royce did not hesitate to leave the office in Jean Richardson's hands, even pending major changes. For example, during Jean Royce's trip to the Netherlands in July 1955, the entire administration moved from the Douglas Library to Richardson Hall. In the new building, strongly decried for its opulence by Vice-Principal Emeritus McNeill,[163] the Registrar's Office ceded pride of place and circumstance only to that of the principal. 'It was a magnificent office,' Shirley Brooks remembered, 'and she really looked the grande dame of the university.'[164]

The point here is that Jean Royce could have cared less. By the time she returned from the Netherlands, Jean Richardson had arranged the office. 'She didn't change much around when she got home,' she recalled, 'so it must have been all right.' Just as she assumed that her office could run without her – and without direction – so she took the arrangement of her physical space as a given.[165] Perhaps she agreed with McNeill that the new building was unnecessarily opulent, but it is more likely that she was oblivious.[166] Nor would she have picked up on the impression of her importance that her new office promoted. Her more spacious surroundings simply meant that she had to talk louder so that the Miss Wilkies could hear her.

She was oblivious to office and university politics because her mind was uncluttered by noise. What mattered was the work to be done, and that her staff do it with dedication and without fanfare. Surely her practice of signing memos 'R' was a time saver for one whose desk was buried in memoranda every day. One observer took a different view: 'Who does she think she is? The Queen?' She gave another example: 'The post office [which was under Jean's jurisdiction] was just down the hall and [she] was always coming out and saying, "Hold up the postmistress!" So the person would have to wait.'[167]

Had anyone dared to ask, the registrar might have explained her management style in terms similar to those used by Jean Richardson in discussing whether Jean was nicer with students than with her staff. 'Well, yes,' she replied in a tone meant to banish any negative implications of my question. 'The students were in a sense her employers, weren't they? She was very interested in the students. She was interested in her staff but not in the same way – you're there to help the students.'[168]

The word 'perfectionist' figures in nearly every staff member's recollections of the registrar. 'Jean Royce was a perfectionist and so demanded perfection from her staff.'[169] 'She demanded near perfection from her employees ... I can affirm and attest that she was VERY VERY demanding; I can't think of another word.'[170] 'Jean Royce was a perfectionist ... and expected the same from her office staff. Some were not able to work under this pressure and changed jobs. [But those] who could enjoyed working for Jean Royce and admired her never changing energy.'[171] 'As a boss she could be formidable and demanding, and second best was never good enough.'[172]

Like other new employees, Magda Davey was thrown into the deep end, with three hours of dictation the first morning and not a word of instruction about what to do next. 'If she decided you were a worthwhile person and were capable of doing it, she just ... expected you quietly to do it ... which is a very good way of doing things, but mind you, I didn't even know what a transcript was! [But] once Jean Royce put her trust in you it was there wholly. You'd have to do something terrible to lose that.' Magda emphasized how much she learned from Jean: 'Admissions, standards, quality grades, universities, you name it – [all of] which I took to my [next] job at York ... Jean wrote very good references for me.'[173]

Magda Davey's most enduring memory is of Jean's kindness. In 1963, quite ill, she required an operation. When she returned to her hospital room 'there was a vase with one rose in it and that was from Jean Royce, and every single day for the whole time I was in, one rose arrived. It taught me that one big bouquet is not the same as remembering [someone] on a regular basis.' Jean and the staff visited every day 'even during office hours.' Magda remembered: 'You had to earn [Jean's compassion] or there had to be a real bad problem ... She had no patience or time for people who fussed through their lives [but] she did have this wonderful caring for everybody.'[174]

Connie Martens, Jean's secretary after 1965, remembered well her second day on the job. 'While taking dictation, I asked her to repeat a professor's name, and she brought her fist down on the desk with an admonition to "read the Calendar and know your staff." That night I took the Calendar home and studied it well and I never again had to ask her to repeat a name.'[175]

Through the years, Jean's drive for perfection remained constant. Yet however exacting she was 'about small things,' Jean Richardson recalled, '[she] had great patience [for] things that mattered.' Especially memorable – nearly legendary – was the 1940s equivalent of a computer crash, when half the registration records were thrown out by mistake. Only after the Christmas examination lists had been submitted were all the registrants finally known. As Jean Richardson tells the story, there was 'not a word of reproach from Miss Royce, although this created unimagined difficulties for the first term.'[176]

Rona Wilkie quaked in her shoes when she had to give notice of her resignation only months after starting her job. 'I thought, she'll be so cross because it takes a little while to get into a new job and you have to train someone else. I simply dreaded it and I had to summon up my courage.' But when she did, Jean Royce 'was very gracious and offered all kinds of concessions to me if I wished to resume when I came back to the city.'[177] Ruth Bialek wrote that if Jean 'spoke a hasty, unkind word to someone [because of] high pressure with too much work and problems, she was never too proud to apologize after.' Every Christmas 'she took the time in choosing and wrapping a gift for each of her office staff along with a note of good wishes' – a practice that her successor didn't continue. 'The personal touch was gone.'[178]

For Connie Martens, Jean became 'a very true and loyal friend.' Even so, her experiences in the Registrar's Office were mind-boggling. 'I learned not to be surprised if the phone rang around six a.m. on a weekend and I was greeted with the brief injunction to come to the office as there was some work to be done.' One night, before Convocation, they worked until one a.m.: 'I was all but dead on my feet [but Miss Royce] appeared as fresh and full of energy as when we started. She told me to sleep in the next morning and that she didn't want to see me before nine o'clock – little realizing that this was only half an hour after normal starting time!'[179] Once, after a long week with many extra hours, Jean said to Connie, 'Try and get away early on Friday.' 'Ha!', retorted Ralfe Clench, 'What she really means is: *try* and get away early on Friday.'[180]

Ralfe Clench is another story (unto himself). His presence alone ensured that the Registrar's Office was unique. Jean will introduce him: 'I think you must know Ralfe Clench. He was a very able person, always a character. One year the front door of the Arts Building refused to open at May convocation.' Ralfe used the kit of tools that he carried permanently on his belt to take 'off the door – and the students emerged! He is very good with his hands, very quick-witted, very prejudiced, and has a low view of mankind generally, and he had a marvellous set of keys.' The question is: Are you any further ahead in understanding the role of Ralfe Clench?

After graduating from Queen's, Ralfe went to McMaster, but he did not get along with his PhD supervisor. 'So he wrote to me in the middle of the year,' Jean explained, 'and asked if there would be a place for him in my office. And he was prepared to do everything. He did come, and he was invaluable.' He was a mathematician, a timetabler, a locksmith, a man of all trades, and Queen's leading candidate for eccentric of the twentieth century. 'He picked up a great range of responsibilities – in particular, all the examination scheduling. Taking *that* off my shoulders was the best thing that could have been done.'[181] Magda Davey remembered: 'He wouldn't change his clock so he was on a different hour to us. When the clocks went forward, his stayed the same – it got very very awkward!' But after 'Ralfe joined, we had no problems getting things fixed. All we had to do was literally yell and he'd come trotting in. Both my boys had him for maths and ... thought he was [the best]. Once [we] got used to him he was [a] breath of fresh air.'[182] According to mathematics professor Jim Whitley, Jean defended Ralfe against all comers 'because he was the hardest-working person around.' Jim offered proof of her spirited advocacy: 'One day in 1966 I was in her office and George Whalley and Martyn Estall charged in, speaking very elegantly but complaining about Ralfe Clench.' Whitley enjoyed the memory of their short-lived intervention: 'She tore strips off them, and they retreated with their tails between their legs. She was delighted, charged up, and invited me home for sherry. [She kept] expensive sherry.' They had several glasses and a wonderful talk.[183] Ralfe Clench returned the support, writing just before he died: 'I owe a great deal to Jean Royce, her ability, her kind personality, everything she did. [She was] more than a thousand times the Registrar than the combination of those two who followed her.'[184]

In 1962, after a national job search, Jean hired Margaret Hooey – a graduate of the University of Toronto and Bryn Mawr, then doing an apprenticeship with the federal civil service.[185] In acquiring Margaret Hooey, Jean Royce had found herself more than a registrar's assistant. As she reflected later, 'I suppose it's a matter of choosing people; it's always a gamble in the beginning, don't you think? You have to have good relations in an office. I think that I was pretty fortunate in some of the people I had, particularly Miss Hooey.' Jean listed her qualities: 'She's easy to approach; she came from a personal tradition and handled people well, and she isn't short-tempered, which I am sure I am accused of lots of times.'[186] All of which goes uncontested. Jean abandoned her detached description at one point, halfway through an interview: 'Margaret just gave new life to me at that time.'[187]

Margaret Hooey was twenty-eight, a year younger than Jean had been when first appointed registrar. In her tribute to Jean in August 1968, she provided a sweet version of her first day in the office, which coincided with the first day of registration.

> At the end of the long and gruelling day, Jean and I made our way back to the office. I had just slumped exhausted into my chair when Miss Royce bounced in:
>
> 'Well, how did it go?'
>
> 'Well, it was very interesting – but I'm exhausted.'
>
> 'Don't worry – you'll get used to *that*.'[188]

Over the next weeks, Margaret began to wonder. Daily life in the Registrar's Office was turning out to be quite distressing. The staff worked non-stop – though of course, no one harder than the registrar herself. From early morning until long after her last employee had left for the night, Jean went flat out, appearing periodically, jacqueline-in-the-box style, to summon the name of the next petitioner, usually a student. Margaret was thrown into the deep end with no life jacket, no special instructions, and no time to familiarize herself with the complicated sets of rules and regulations that animated the whole operation. Worse, she never had the opportunity to consult the boss-lady.

One day, in desperation, she placed her own name on Jean's appointment calendar. When the moment came, Jean emerged from her office, looked at the schedule, and shouted out 'Hooey!' When Margaret dashed out of her office, Jean looked up, spotted her, and snapped: 'Oh, it's just you – I can see you later.' Looking for some explanation for this behaviour, I told Margaret's story to her predecessor. 'That's the way it was,' said Jean Richardson. 'It's a little hard to describe. She herself could see all around a situation, and she didn't think others needed direction.' Yet 'after the first few months Jean came to depend on Margaret – more than she had on me. When Margaret came, she was getting older and probably needed a friend.'[189] The story of this remarkable friendship, recounted in chapter 4, is linked to Margaret's growing realization that the problems of the Registrar's Office were rooted outside that office, in the corridors of power.

The Registrar's Office was the heart of Jean Royce's domain. An enormous amount of work went on here, and without that work, her regime would not have endured. She extracted prodigious amounts of labour from her staff, and many felt that her 'innate knowledge' of their capabilities brought out their best. Connie Martens found herself 'tackling tasks of which I thought I was quite incapable, and because she ... never entertained the thought that I might fail, I somehow came through, much to my own surprise.'[190] Jean herself deemed her office a 'very happy [place]. They enjoyed their work – [perhaps] I pushed them too hard, I don't know.'[191] Also, 'they were all personal friends [and] did lots of things together. Sometimes I joined them.'[192]

In many ways, however, her office was only the necessary backdrop to her operations. She had a broader mission: to attract a large and diverse band of good students to Queen's, to make sure they received an excellent education, and then to turn them out to fulfil their promise. How she carried out that mission on a day-to-day basis requires a close look at her approach to interacting with students. Success at this level demanded innovative policies and practices that would put a university education on every good high school student's agenda and then – most important – delivery on the promise of a good education.

Students flooded Canadian universities after the Second World War, thanks in large part to subsidized education for veterans. However, until the 1960s postsecondary education in Canada remained the prerogative of the very few.[193] Jean Royce set out to change that, and she engaged herself on several fronts with all her force of character. Although her role as secretary at university meetings often masked her specific contributions, she formulated her own educational philosophy and her own ideas on educational practice and policy and expounded them in written speeches and papers. The interviews she gave later in life are full of references to her extensive outreach program.

Soon after the war, in the middle of a long statement on the purpose of a university degree, she wrote: 'Education cannot be satisfied with imparting knowledge ... It must send the student out with a definite spiritual attitude to life and the material and basis for a definite philosophy of living.'[194] Two decades later, in a paper on the population explosion, she argued that 'the student is a privileged person but educational opportunity cannot be restricted to a privileged few. Society must make the fullest use of its resources, [and] its members must be prepared to share the burden of responsibility.'[195]

These statements illuminate her project. So do the recollections of a brother and sister who met her shortly after their family immigrated to Canada from Germany in 1950.[196] Jean lavished attention on them, hiring Mary-Louise despite her admission that 'my English was dreadful, my commitment to work lukewarm, and I had absolutely no intention of studying. [Jean Royce] pushed me from knowledge-known into knowledge-unknown, and she demanded excellence in the process.' It seems incredible, but Jean hired her even though she was unsuitable, and even though *she had not even applied for the job.* Jean had asked her brother whether he had any siblings. On learning he had a sister, Jean hired her 'conditional on [her] taking a first-year university course in English.'[197] Ed Funke concluded that Jean saw 'her job as a mission to develop the human resources of an emerging country.'[198] That is the correct explanation, I think. How better to demonstrate this conviction than by making sure the children of a recent enemy had the opportunity to contribute to their new country? Her high school language of Huns and Allies was long gone. Jean now embraced education, tolerance, and peace.

As the registrar of Queen's University, she rode the rails around Ontario, bringing the good word. 'It was strongly felt,'[199] she explained, 'that certain people should be encouraged, and I caught a lot of good people in the schools who [wouldn't otherwise have thought] of the possibility of a university education.' These jaunts also promoted Queen's. 'We were very much afraid of just being limited to eastern Ontario [in the way that] Western had become a university serving one section.'[200] On these trips – to as far away as Kapuskasing, and even Moose Factory[201] – she tried to kindle the interest of good high school students, wherever in the province they lived.

Ever since the days of principal Grant, Queen's had harboured wider ambitions, and means had to be found to attract students from places farther afield than a registrar might travel in a week's work. That was why, Jean explained, 'we introduced provincial scholarships. Queen's was obsessed with the fact that it was a national university.'[202] By carefully developing and distributing these scholarships, she ensured that good students from all regions of the country came to Queen's. 'We offered tuition, a cash award, and railway fare – third class! Can you think of third class? We used [the term] day coach, and some [students] sat up during the night.'[203]

Her use of the prized General Motors Scholarships also reflected her interest in ensuring that people from afar came to Queen's. Douglas McCalla remembered that his offer of a GM scholarship from Queen's followed 'a frosty letter [from the University of Toronto] that I could hardly expect to be considered for a scholarship on the basis of a mere Alberta high school diploma.'[204] McCalla's encouragement to apply to Queen's came from an Edmonton neighbour. Many others who applied from the West, as Jean recalled, were the children of graduates who 'wanted to send their sons and daughters back to their home university.' This custom continues. The Canadian predilection for internal migration meant that Queen's is now known paradoxically as a 'national' university and a 'family' one simultaneously. Her knowledge of so many of the applicants came to be seen as remarkable. She explained: 'If I didn't know that particular person, I knew his uncle or his cousin or his aunt. Queen's has been a closely knit place.' A transparent understatement.[205]

Although Jean took some interest in subsequent generations of students, by no means was this a plank in her admissions policy. From the beginning she cast her gaze widely, focusing on quality rather than simply depending on legacies. Thus she encouraged Ed and Mary-Louise Funke, the German emigrés; Bernard Champagne, the Quebec College Classique graduate, with his rudimentary knowledge of English; Benjamin Scott, whose Jewishness precluded admission to McGill; and Bob McLarty, admitted because 'Queen's wanted to encourage workers to upgrade their qualifications.' In this way she was stretching the university's national, Presbyterian, and Anglo-

Canadian ethos.[206] As the following chapter will attest, her policies and personal practices altered the profile of the student body and enriched its social, national, and ethnic composition.

In her quest to demystify university education, Jean welcomed high school students to Queen's 'on Saturdays for weeks and weeks and weeks during the winters ... On those occasions the students questioned [me] and there was give and take. I had a very exciting job, really.'[207] Although these visits were helpful, 'much more' could be gained, she thought, 'from working weekends with teachers and other university officers.'[208] For several years she organized 'teachers weekends,'[209] and her lively reprise of the 1955 weekend reveals that there was no stinting on the intellectual content. George Whalley held forth on how to undertake critical readings of poetry, assuring his audience that 'analysis does not destroy a poem but may increase its value.' Eric Smethurst argued that the Roman Revolution was 'purely a struggle for power by the demagogue.' Frederick Gibson addressed the question, 'Who makes Canada's foreign policy?'

Nor was the life of the mind neglected at the dinner that followed: Henry Alexander 'told wittily of his researches in Linguistic Geography [in the] Maritime Provinces'; John Meisel discussed 'the voting habits of Kingston people'; and 'with the careful accuracy of the scientist and something of the skill of a C.P. Snow in building up a situation, B.W. Sargent told the story of the construction of the National Research Experimental Reactor at Chalk River.' The development of the NRC, continued the registrar, 'was a magnificent enterprise with all the elements of the drama provided by a project that involved the expenditure of vast sums of money, the technical skills and creative genius of scientists working under the oath of secrecy, the possible hideous dangers of tampering with forces of nature, political intrigue, a new principle of international collaboration approved by President Roosevelt, Prime Minister Churchill, and Prime Minister Mackenzie King at the Quebec Conference of 1943.'[210]

Little wonder that in 1968, in her last days as registrar, at a registrar's conference, Jean insisted that these weekends become a staple of university outreach. She was certain they paid more dividends than the increasingly obligatory student romps across the campus.[211] Jean saw high school teachers as privileged mediators in her efforts to attract students to Queen's, yet only a cynic would argue that this was her main reason for inviting them to the campus. She opened her discussion on the weekends by quoting Dr J. Robert Oppenheimer's view that 'the influence of one good teacher is incalculable [in instilling the] courage and faith that the creative man must have since he cannot know what the final results of his work will be.'[212] More than once, she summarized in writing the closing 'wise lecture' by A.R.C. Duncan, who presented 'a cogent argument for a study of Philosophy as a force in determining one's objectives.'[213]

If Jean's objectives were lofty, her methods were pragmatic. Within the space of fifteen minutes she could take her listeners from peaks of abstraction to the nitty gritty of how to find students, prepare and present accessible materials, process their applications, and admit them. For example, at her last registrar's conference in 1968, after a generous swoop through Duncan's philosophical exegesis, she advised her colleagues to write their requirements in unambiguous prose, simplify their entrance requirements, modify their common application form, and work toward an earlier application deadline. She provided a detailed list of thirteen kinds of information that universities should include in materials prepared for high schools. To her it was vital that such statements 'challenge the students' minds.'

She then addressed the question, 'What do universities want from the schools?' Her answer was formidable. They wanted students who wanted to learn and who had the potential to do so. They wanted students who were ready to devote several years to finding out things not previously known, and who were ready to clarify ideas only dimly apprehended, to look at accepted views critically, to distinguish fact from opinion, and to develop ideas through investigation and questions that could be tested against the criticisms of their teachers and contemporaries. They wanted students who were prepared to argue and to reason, and who would not take anything for granted.

In her office – first in Douglas Library and later in Richardson Hall – she worked like a human dynamo six days a week for all but six weeks of the year. On 'vacation' she disengaged from daily tasks only to immerse herself more fully in the cultural pursuits that were, for her, the *raison d'être* of the examined life and a key part of the historic mission of universities. Though she knew the world was changing, her parting words to her colleagues were clear: universities 'may seem to be emulating big business [but] the fact remains that they are a community of teachers and students who believe that learning is still a positive good.'[214]

These were more than pious words. Few students doubted Jean Royce's expectations. We turn to their stories in the next chapter.

Chapter Three

Keeping a 'Watching Brief'

Soon after she was appointed registrar in January 1996, Jo-Anne Bechthold received an unusual letter of congratulations from Dr Benjamin Scott: 'I hope,' he wrote, 'that one day someone will write about your tenure with as much gratitude and appreciation as I write of Dr. Royce and Queen's.'[1] On the surface, Jean Royce had done little to earn such a tribute. In the summer of 1934 she had simply accepted Scott's application to study at Queen's, along with those of hundreds of others with the requisite grades and courses. Sixty-two years later, however, he still could not 'express the intense joy and profound relief' at the news of his admission. 'In those days in Montreal and elsewhere there existed a very strict quota for Jewish students trying to get a university education and so it was that *my* Quebec universities were closed to me. The possibilities that they would never be open would have made my later life intolerable – I *had* to graduate in Medicine.' Dr Scott's memoires, written in his eightieth year, just two years past his retirement from medical practice, convey his youthful vulnerability and his hopes. 'You cannot possibly imagine,' he wrote, 'with what heartache and desperation I applied to the Faculty of Arts and my utter disbelief when I was granted an interview with "The Registrar" ... Jean Royce.'

Dr Scott provides a crystalline picture of the registrar at the beginning of her second year in office: 'I vividly recall her quiet demeanor, her efficient but kindly questioning, her reassuring answers and, above all, the feeling that she could "see thru me" – that she understood my yearning, my fears ... and I sensed her decision to help. [The registrar was] a MENSCH, a person of grace, empathy, kindness, and understanding.'[2]

As a descendent myself of Montreal's Jewish community, I was moved by this story. Though born and bred in a small and strict Christian congregation in small-town Ontario, she had apparently resisted the 'normal' anti-Semitism of the 1930s. The story beckoned me to admire her and to share Ben Scott's gratitude.

Yet the contemporary postmodern voice invites contrary thoughts, opinions, experiences – and narratives – to be embraced and mined for colour or overlap, or to parade in parallel formation. Current perspectives permit the fragmented and the destabilized. They permit a reading of the self as the outcome of shifting and even competing discourses, in defiance of traditional biographical imperatives to create linearity, coherence, solidity – a convincing core. This new way allows space for all the stories. Yet if there is to be a biography, the writer must still orchestrate their arrangement.

Writerly bias is not the biggest obstacle to including all the stories about someone so recently departed as to be in many ways still among us. Grandmothers are reputed to say, 'If you don't have anything nice to say, then don't say anything at all.' Perhaps this explains why almost all alumni stories are grateful and/or amusing and why so few stories suggest that Jean Royce ever acted unkindly or maliciously. Can it really be that in thirty-five years almost no one felt her ill will or left her office discouraged by the tone or substance of her remarks? Or left believing that others were more favoured? Is there no one to suggest that her advice was ill-considered?

If so, that would be a remarkable record. It is worth remembering here that people may gossip happily over the back fence or in locker rooms, but balk when reaching for a pen. The most spirited negative reaction to her name I ever heard came during a casual, front yard introduction. 'She had her favourites,'[3] my new acquaintance told me, bristling. If you weren't among them, 'it wasn't just that she wouldn't single you out; she would do things that negatively affected you.' She and her husband and daughter had been among those harmed by Jean Royce's decisions, she told me.[4] The stories about Jean Royce that speak of anger, pain, or hurt are important. Somehow within these covers I will try to include all the ones I have heard – an impossibility when it comes to the myriad tales from grateful and often amused graduates.

It took a long time for me to realize that Jean Royce's response to Ben Scott and to those who followed him – whether from Africa, the Caribbean, Eastern Europe, or postwar Germany – was not strictly a matter of her being untouched by anti-Semitism or racism in its endless varieties. Her response stemmed also from her boundless curiosity about place and culture – a curiosity stimulated by admiration for certain applicants. Through their admission, she stood to learn and the university stood to be enriched. She had a talent for landing on the good, the interesting, the learned, and the fascinating. More than forty years later she recalled: 'McGill wouldn't accept Jewish people – they had to have extremely high averages.[5] But think of the contribution Jewish people have made to education.' When asked whether quotas existed at Queen's, she replied simply, 'Not when I was registrar.'[6]

The year after Ben Scott arrived at Queen's, a fellow Quebecker, Bernard Champagne, landed in Jean's office without an appointment. A Catholic and graduate of a classics college, his English was 'quite rudimentary,' so the interview took time. 'I took in about 20 per cent of what she said [but upon my return the next day] she went through it all patiently again, stopping often to ask if I was understanding.' After taking her suggestion that he should audit courses for a year to improve his English, Bernard registered in 1936. For him this was an act of rebellion. During a visit to the Champagne family home later that year, the parish priest charged him with going to a 'communist university, a Protestant university.' Queen's was non-denominational, Bernard replied, and he refused to kneel for the priest's blessing. He contrasted the priest with Jean Royce, who 'was ecumenical with no prejudice. She leaned over backwards to accept people from Quebec.'[7]

Jean was against the move to charge higher fees to students from other countries: 'I think that's a very limiting thing for a university to do. Queen's has always welcomed anybody who seemed able.'[8] The evidence is overwhelming that she did just that for thirty-five years. Yet her simple statement about ability belies the effort she expended trying to spot this elusive quality. For example, those who seemed able in the 1930s could be quite different from those who seemed able in the 1960s – a time when entrance requirements were rising.

In September 1936, John Matheson presented 'documentary proof' that he had passed a supplemental examination in high school Latin, a prerequisite for admission, but not to be taken as evidence that he was 'one of the great thinkers registering at the time.' In Matheson's words, 'one did not need to be a near genius to come to Queen's in the good old days.' Nonetheless, Jean had high hopes for him, as he discovered in his third year, when she summoned him to her office and suggested he apply for a Rhodes Scholarship. No doubt she was impressed by this attractive young man, who 'liked to flirt with her just a little bit' and who had sampled 'all the lesser endeavours of campus life.' Matheson, however, was closer to the ground than the registrar, and quickly spotted an obstacle. Have you, he asked, consulted my marks lately? She hadn't, but she did: '"O dear, John," she said, rather primly, "applying for a Rhodes with these marks would be entirely inappropriate."' As well he knew, for 'the sole award [he had] ever merited was a Quebec City Morin College bursary requiring only that the recipient be a Protestant.'[9] While this must have been the last time Jean neglected to consult grades before offering postgraduate encouragement, there is perhaps more to the story. As Matheson concluded his reminiscence, 'Jean Royce saw in the students potentialities that we dared not recognize in ourselves.' Perhaps she took his later accomplishments in the war and in the peace that followed as indications that she had been right in her earlier assessment. It just took time for her to be right.[10]

Matheson presents an attractive portrait of 'this shy little lady with the artificial smile and twinkling eyes behind big black Nana Mouscouri glasses.' But to some dress-conscious young women, at thirty Jean Royce was already 'rather daunting in appearance ... very plain, big glasses, no makeup and very old-maidish clothes.' In her role as warden of Gordon House, she 'tended to be stiff and rather managing.' When invited to her room for social occasions, Phyllis Nunn and her housemates were 'on our best behaviour.' Never renowned for small talk, Jean would fix one of them with her eye and 'ask some serious question' about studies or the political situation. But the behaviour that created awkwardness in social situations disappeared when they went to see her as registrar. 'Such a welcoming smile you would get as you timidly approached her. And such interest in your plans, petitions and hopes.'

'Perhaps,' Phyllis suggested, 'she felt more comfortable behind a desk [and found it] easier to interact with students within the context of her position.'[11] When Evangeline Phillips arrived for registration in 1936, her mother in tow, she advised the registrar that she wanted to take Greek. 'This shocked my mother [who considered Greek too intellectual for her daughter]. However, Jean was talking to me and listening to me. She put down "Greek."'[12] Doris Burns retains 'very warm thoughts of that lady! [Although certainly efficient], she would take a few minutes to give words of encouragement which certainly helped me to get through my first year in particular.'[13] For Mariam Fletcher,

'Miss Royce was my unfailing friend. No matter what my problems concerning courses [as a summer student in the 1930s], I could always count on her sound friendly advice.'[14] Like Mariam, Lester Anthes remembered, some fifty years later, 'the kindness and special consideration given a *struggling* young extramural student. She seemed to understand some of the difficulties of following that route toward a degree.'[15] When Douglas Smith sent a contribution to the Jean Royce Fellowship, he noted that she had been appointed to the staff of the Registrar's Office while he was still an undergraduate. 'I have always remembered her as efficient and knowledgeable, and very pleasant in her dealings with bewildered students. Not all the members of the staff were as easy to approach.'[16]

'I had no idea of what she was or was supposed to do,' Alan Gold recalled, 'but she [was] a kind of faculty advisor to me. I indicated my future plans, and before I knew it we were talking.' Jean gave Alan a lot of advice. 'I told her that I was going to go to the law so she pointed me in the direction of political science, [making] sure I took a course from Alec Corry [then in his first year at Queen's]. Jean knew he was a lawyer. He became a friend, very dear to me.' Jean also steered him to 'economics and, above all, English literature.' For the dreaded science, 'she told me to take geology – "it's easy and you're out in the fresh air." We used to go on field trips with hammers, pair up – if you were lucky, you got a good-looking girl – and we looked for rocks. The professor realized most of us were never going to make geologists.' Alan's 'dismal' math and science grades prevented him from making the Jewish quota at McGill. 'My father suggested that we go see the registrar at McGill because I was so close and that he'd talk to some of his friends. But I said no, no begging.' Going away to school was difficult, because his father had lost his money in the Depression, but 'my dad was a wonderful man and [told me], "I can spare thirty dollars a month even if I have to stop smoking." [So] I sold magazine subscriptions and I was good at it. My Queen's tam gave me entry into homes that I probably wouldn't have [without it].'

Alan continued: 'Much to my family's despair, because I was thought to be bright, I was a very indifferent student. [But still] Jean pushed me to join the Drama Guild, where we did left-wing plays. I was second banana [to Lorne Greene and] became a good actor.'[17] After the plays, Jean would come backstage to congratulate them. Undoubtedly, she saw Alan's drama career – along with his participation in the Debating Union – as excellent preparations for Law. She once asked him about his politics and 'wasn't shocked' when he said he was a 'socialist.'

'She made sure I took Minnie Gordon's Shakespeare course,' Alan remembered. 'She was a real character – she didn't walk, she ran, gown trailed in the wind all the time.' When Alan's extracurricular life took precedence over essays 'I went to apologize [and] ask if I could do them over Christmas.' 'I can see you have been busy,' she told him, 'we'll just tick them off.'

Alan wondered whether Jean 'felt I would be a stranger [at Queen's]. She thought it desirable that I meet members of the Jewish community. They were exceedingly warm. When they found out my mother's father was a rabbi and that I was well educated in Yiddish culture, they asked me to give three talks on three great Yiddish writers, including Sholom Aleichem.' Alan recalled that 'some of the best years of my life [were at Queen's and] not just because I managed to get a degree without too much work. We all smoked, drank, took girls out, went to the Splendid Restaurant. And suddenly I liked learning.' At the university, 'in my time Jean Royce – I want to use a legal term – kept a "watching brief."' As he explained it, when a client wants a lawyer to follow a case – not his own – to monitor any repercussions for him, this is called a watching brief.[18]

In 1938 John Hanna received a call from Jean just before his final examinations. Two years earlier, he had transferred from the University of Toronto. In his graduating year he had more exams than his classmates, and the registrar called to see whether she could do anything 'to make [the schedule] more palatable.' John declined 'with thanks – and a renewed determination to do well.' She had remembered that the special program in honours chemistry that had been mapped out 'might give me trouble at exam time.'[19]

During the 1930s, Jean perfected the peppery response that became her stock in trade whenever she wanted a student to shape up, quickly. When she asked freshman Jake Warren what courses he had chosen, he replied that he wanted to become an officer in the new Canadian Foreign Service. 'Miss Royce informed me that I was no longer in high school and was expected to do my own course selection! I retired in some disarray with my Queen's calendar.' He returned with an appropriate list.'[20] Kathleen Butcher vividly remembers 'the dressing down' she received during her first year after failing 'miserably' the Christmas exam in English. 'We don't expect a scholarship student in Mathematics to get great marks in English,' Jean railed, 'but we expect them to pass!'[21] In thinking back, Kathleen wondered whether Jean paid particular attention to girls. She learned later that her brother got 'bawled out for failing a physics course. So she had her eye on the men too.'

But when women did well, Jean's interventions made all the difference. Kathleen recalled: 'In my senior year she sent for me [again, to see] if I was intending to go to graduate school. Frankly the idea had never occurred to me. I had no money [and] it was not as common as it became later. She said they (whomever that was) had been watching my work since I was a sophomore.' Though Kathleen's first response was no, she reconsidered and returned.[22] Kathleen's friend, Mary Jeffery, a psychology student, on being summoned to Jean's office, was advised to apply for graduate school and a scholarship to Radcliffe. 'Kay's experience was the same as mine,' wrote Mary. 'It was Miss Royce, not our major profs, who suggested we apply to grad school, although the profs [Israel Halperin and George Humphrey respectively] enthusiastically agreed and helped.'[23]

By the end of the 1930s, Jean Royce had established her reputation as staunch upholder of rules and standards. James Courtright recalls that 'core curriculum subjects [and] limited failure in specific courses were *de rigueur* for yearly advancement. And the rules were hard and fast [regarding] the number of supplementals allowed without penalty of repeating an entire year.'[24] But for the determined student, the registrar could usually see a way. For instance, in the spring of 1936, fourteen-year-old Raymond Phillips travelled from Ottawa to meet her. Raymond had a problem: he was too young. Neither McGill nor Toronto nor RMC accepted students before their fifteenth birthday. Perhaps he might persuade Jean Royce. Scanning his transcript, she spotted another impediment: 'Jeannie Royce looked up and said, "We can't let you in. You don't have Latin."' Raymond pointed out that the school in British Columbia where he had received his grade twelve diploma hadn't offered Latin. His father had just retired from the Navy, the family had moved to Ottawa, and young Raymond didn't relish attending Lisgar Collegiate. Now there was a bigger problem – no Latin. 'So then Jeannie Royce – bless her, super person – told me what to do: go to Lisgar for grade thirteen and do four years of Latin on the side.' Extraordinarily enough, he did this, and registered at Queen's the following year. Raymond laughed at his memory of the university in those days: 'It was all pretty simple. Jeannie was a great girl. She had one helper. The student/faculty ratio was twenty to one. There was one woman running Ban Righ (residence) and someone to fill the swimming pool.'[25]

Things were indeed simpler then. But as war approached, Jean Royce found herself at the helm as 'the university's "queen bee,"' in John Matheson's words, 'the important arbiter not only for the intellectually endowed but for marginal scholars as well.'[26] Shirley Brooks, who later became Jean's friend, remembered that in those days she 'ruled the roost, and [her word] was God's word. We always admired her.'[27] Even this early in her career, among many students Jean was provoking disquiet, awe, and a sense of expectation.

During the 1930s she learned to make and enforce rules. After that – stimulated by the war and its aftermath – she perfected the art of bending them. 'You may already know,' wrote Arthur Ross, that once she admitted students she was 'not prepared to see them fall by the wayside if it could possibly be prevented.' In 1943 his classmates in chemistry included the candidates for the newly inaugurated Bachelor of Nursing Science, and most students from Kingston did poorly at Christmas. After interviewing them all, the registrar decided 'that their preparation [was] under par [and] persuaded Professor Clarke to allow them to continue.' Ultimately, with the help of some extra classes, 'the group did well.'[28] The nursing program developed at Queen's as a result of the war.[29] So those students were destined to pass chemistry come hell *and* high water.

But students didn't require a special wartime mission to engage the registrar. Anne Ginn recalled that she wasn't 'a very good student [and would have] fallen through the cracks without [the registrar's] special help.' Mid-year in 1939, 'my father was posted to Halifax [and] I was forced to follow. So Miss Royce (as we all referred to her) carefully wove all my subjects into similar courses at Dalhousie.' A year later, when the needs of the nation brought the family back to Kingston, 'Miss Royce and Dalhousie [once again] arranged my education, and I graduated with a BA from Queen's in 1941.'[30]

But the exceptions Jean Royce made came packaged with her customary sharpness, as Jake Warren discovered during his second encounter with her, during the winter term of 1941. 'I was doing naval reserve officer training and [by the end of the previous October] had pretty well given up attending classes.' After explaining that he expected to be on active service by the fall, he asked her whether the university would give him 'an ordinary BA the coming spring. Miss Royce's reply was typical: "What, Mr. Warren, makes you believe that you are entitled to a BA? Where are your languages and sciences?" I was able to satisfy her on my French (summer courses at Trois Pistoles in '37 and at Tours in France in '39) but sciences I didn't have!' Perhaps, Jake suggested, she might check his first-year geology marks. Good bet: 'The card I think showed 99 – it was a course I immensely enjoyed. Miss Royce smiled and said, "If you pass your Spring examinations you may have your degree."'

That seemed fair enough, but as Jake noted, he always 'wondered whether she knew at the time that I had skipped all my classes. The next five weeks were borrowed notes and endless cramming which in due course allowed me to skim through and earn a degree. There is no way of knowing what course my life and career might have taken had Jean Royce not given a 'second' chance to this wartime negotiated degree holder.'[31] After the war his cram-till-you-burst degree positioned him 'as a serving naval officer to write the first post-war exams for External Affairs.' In later years, Jean expressed admiration for Jake Warren's work as Canada's Ambassador to the United States. Perhaps unlikely outcomes like this one confirmed, in her own mind, the wisdom of her ways.

Some students didn't need the Royce jump start. Kenneth Binks had left school at sixteen, worked on senior matriculation at night and during the summer, and eventually passed nine papers. At that point he came to see the registrar, requesting admission as an extramural student. 'Miss Royce did not say anything while listening to my story and when I finished she said, "Is that all you have to say, Mr Binks?" and I said yes and she said "Queen's would be proud to have you." I will never forget that day. What she said and the way she said it.'[32] Her response, he elaborated later, 'is neatly catalogued in my brain because it gave me confidence when I needed it most.'[33]

When Mike Lafratta finished high school he wrote to three universities. From the other two 'I got a perfunctory acknowledgment, a calendar and other sheets produced from worn-out stencils. I remained grossly uninformed with little inkling of what to do next.' But Jean Royce sent a 'personal two-page letter [and] using my grade 13 results, suggested several programs and related them to possible careers. For a callow 18-year-old with immigrant parents, this letter was an incredible welcome to higher education. Guess where I now wanted to go? [Once at Queen's], she always saw me immediately when I showed up in her office listening to my concerns and offering advice. Small wonder that I saw Miss Royce as the essence of Queen's.'[34]

In January 1939, first-year student Frank Ritchie arrived back at Queen's from his home in Windsor with no money for tuition. He went to see the registrar. 'She said, "You've got a record. We'll loan you tuition if you can manage the rest." I said I'd try.' That summer he got a job with the Ford Motor Company at 16 cents an hour. His mother waived room and board so that he could send 'the first eighty dollars to Jean Royce. I worked hard, scraping and scheming, and I [have] prospered. One of my regrets is that I never went back to express thanks.'[35]

For Margaret Cutten, Jean Royce was 'a terrifying person, because she looked so much more austere than the teachers I had known.' Margaret registered in 1939 as 'the greenest 17-year-old from a small town that it's possible to imagine. Family dynamics [meant] that I had never been allowed to make a decision on my own, even on the smallest matters of hair style and dress.' Her good academic record was not a result of study habits: 'I had none [but] school was where I got all my personal affirmation and affection.' Later, Margaret realized that 'Miss Royce was keeping a kindly eye on me. My allowance of $2 a month for everything except room and board didn't go far even in those days and the "little prize" worth $5 that she declared I won sometime during the winter can only be explained as a camouflaged gift.'

Jean also gave Margaret advice on non-academic matters, insisting, when she was ill, that she stay in bed except for lectures. When Margaret stayed in Kingston to work during the summer after first year, Jean kept track of her, 'entertaining the one black woman student (from Bermuda) and myself for tea.'[36] Jean enjoyed gathering people in her apartment 'for tea and conversation and to meet distinguished visitors to the campus,' and students were often included.[37] 'The conversation,' Shirley Brooks told me, 'would be just marvellous. Absolutely. Jean was up on everything. She read the latest on everything – politics, everything. It wasn't small talk.'[38]

Jean didn't dwell on the personal, but she still made time for students' troubles. Kay Mein remembered how caring and helpful she was when her father died suddenly during her final exams.[39] Mary Collier was surprised when Jean referred in some correspondence to the 'death of a very close friend. I had not realized that she knew about the friendship.'[40] In a letter enclosing a contribution to the Jean Royce Fellowship, Joyce Hemlow wrote: 'The wonderful thing about the registrar was that she seemed to know us one and all. Someone knew and cared.'[41]

Jean extended Donald Gormley's routine visit to her office by asking him 'how I was getting along in Kingston, the condition of my rooming house, and whether I had any problems in or out of school. I was to see her any time I needed help of any description.'[42] For Donald, the simple offer of help was enough to make him 'an instant fan.' David Moyer did need assistance when his 'standing became abysmal following a nervous breakdown.' 'There is no way,' he wrote, 'to describe how highly I thought of Jean I. Royce. She was like St. Peter at the gate of Heaven. She still found a way to let me struggle through.'[43]

A vague rumour circulates that Jean went out of her way for 'Queen's family.' Certainly she seems to have kept track. According to Elizabeth Marsh, Jean advised her younger sister to 'emulate my older brother rather than my older sister.'[44] But the reminiscences of two alumni with long pedigrees do little to suggest that Jean played favourites in this way. David Sweezey was the grandson of John Watson, who figured in the last chapter and for whom Watson Hall is named. He also knew May Macdonnell and Jean Royce as his mother's frequent bridge partners. Jean and May shared more than a bridge table, as David recalled; intentionally or not, they resorted to terror in their struggles against the forces of darkness. '"My God," Robertson Davies told me,' upon hearing the name of the woman who had been his classics professor some thirty years earlier, "Is May Macdonnell still alive? I used to be terrified of her!" [May] was demanding, insisting on excellence. For somewhat the same reason I, David Sweezey, was terrified of Jean Royce.' When he applied in 1943, Jean provided 'serious formal guidance [stressing] the need to be dedicated and hard-working. Her consistent demeanour at that time was *stern* and *authoritative*.'[45]

May's niece Kate (Macdonnell) Lawson – whose father was long-time chairman of the Board of Trustees – thought Jean Royce 'wanted to be helpful if she could. She knew my father well. In those days, she was young for the job and inclined to be a bit of a martinette and had overly firm views about what courses she thought one *ought to take*.'[46] But Kate knew 'from the time I was five' that she would be coming to Queen's. She knew her way around, and even when she was seconded to the air force for three years, she found little occasion to meet with the registrar.[47]

Neither David Sweezey nor Kate Macdonnell required any bending of the rules to get on with their lives, though Miss Royce might well have obliged. But Alfred Bader did. Once he was released from internment camp – on 5 November 1941, into the care of the Wolff family of Westmount, Quebec – he required some registrar somewhere to take a leap of faith to allow him to move along. Both the University of Toronto and McGill declined the opportunity. Alfred had a Queen's connection, however, and perhaps that made the difference. Rosetta Wolff was an extramural student, and her father was an engineering friend of Queen's professor Richard Low. 'When Daddy called Dickie Low,' Rosetta's sister Annette told me, 'he said, "Well, if he's your responsibility, of course we'll take him."'[48] This rings true, though no one got 'taken' without the permission of the registrar.

As Alfred made his way to meet Jean Royce on that 'rainy Thursday,' he was 'scared for so many reasons.' Given the instructions 'never to tell anyone' where he had been, and 'to report weekly to the RCMP,' what on earth would he say if she asked where he had been to school? But 'in her kind and firm manner,' which he learned later was 'her trademark,' she discussed the results of his junior and senior matriculation exams – taken in the internment camp – asked about his academic plans, introduced him to the professorial secretary of applied science, and sent him on his way.

Admitting a student two-thirds of the way through term was a bold act, or so thought the stockroom manager in the Department of Chemistry when Alfred turned up later that day. Had Alfred already paid his fees? To Al Heiland's astonishment, the deed was done. 'Why, that is highway robbery,' Heiland told Bader. 'This is November 15th and you don't have the chance of a snowball in hell passing at year end. Go get your money back and return next September.' Alfred stayed put. 'I was no judge of people,' he confessed, 'certainly not of Canadians, but Jean Royce and [the secretary of applied science] were no highway robbers.'

During the war, the federal government had interned many Jewish refugees as enemy aliens. Alfred Bader was the first of these to gain admittance to Queen's. Among those following him were Carl Amberg, [later] Dean of Science at Carleton, Arno Cahn, Director of Research at Lever Brothers, Kurt Rothschild, the founder of a successful electrical engineering company, and Willy Low, the founder of the Jerusalem Institute of Technology. 'Most of us,' Bader wrote, 'justified Jean Royce's trust in us.' He passed that first year, 'eventually getting the medal in chemistry.'[49]

Alfred and his fellow refugees weren't aware that Jean was well informed about their situation – and undoubtedly supported the efforts by various pacifist, religious, and Jewish groups to have their internship ended.[50] To ameliorate their situation in the camps, Queen's had offered 'correspondence courses to the refugees at reduced fees,' and the Student Christian Movement (of which she was a member) had 'subsidized' the remaining fees and textbooks.[51]

The war brought this group of refugees to Queen's; it also created challenges for those students whose arrival had been less dramatic – and for the registrar. 'In my second year as a full time student,' wrote Vernon Ready, 'a crisis developed at [Kingston Collegiate] which resulted in a sudden vacancy on staff. As so often happened, the [school] principal appealed to Jean.' The registrar cast her net and came up with Vernon and another student, Martha Jamieson, who agreed to fill the vacancy. The plan worked, although its execution 'involved a complete rescheduling of [our] Queen's classes as well as considerable juggling of the [school's] timetable.' Whether Jean had the longer view in mind or not, Vernon believed that this emergency plan led directly to his career as a teacher (later principal) at Kingston Collegiate.[52]

James Martin's stories indicate that both during and after the war, Jean Royce did as she thought best. For going out on a limb for him not once, not twice, but three times, he gives her – what else – three stars, concluding that 'there is nothing adverse to report.' Indeed.

Star 1. After he displayed 'total ignorance' in mathematics, Martin's professor instructed him to go over and see if the registrar could change his course. Without jeopardizing his desired degree in commerce, Jean obliged by enrolling him in French – not realizing, perhaps, that his high school French was almost as bad as his maths. He passed the year by 'being in KGH with pneumonia' during final exams and received 'standing of 65% in all courses and permission to continue.' Who could have produced this result but Jean Royce?

Star 2. James's first term back didn't go well, and he withdrew, married, and joined the army. By war's end, Warrant Officer Martin had three children and 'was desperate to return to Queen's on reestablishment credit.' But his captain 'also wanted out [of the services] to return to university,' and one of them had to stay to finalize 'end-of-war details.' James telephoned Jean Royce. Could she help? 'She wired my CO stating my presence was necessary at Queen's to enter 3rd year Commerce: "Please discharge James E. Martin."' The now discharged NCO brought her 'a bouquet of roses.'

Star 3. Twenty years later, James was a Category 1 teacher (the bottom rung of the pay scale) in Ottawa. On the advice of a Queen's alumnus, he wrote to Jean, who in turn informed the Ottawa school board that his 1947 pass degree was actually equivalent to honours level, as he had achieved an average of 75.1 per cent in *Commerce* subjects. With five children now, he was pleased to move up to Category III, gaining 'a substantial increase in salary.'[53]

It was widely known that Jean Royce watched out 'for the vets on campus and did what she could' for them. 'One can only write one's own story,' noted Sylvia Mercer, who also came to Queen's in 1945, but the veterans 'worked so hard and sometimes hit roadblocks in degree "regulations." [Jean Royce] was an enabler. I think it was this combined with high standards that made her special.'[54]

She was also a 'magnificent advisor,' noted Kathleen Bowley, the only female war veteran from whom I heard. After 'a hectic fortnight' in late October 1945 getting from England to Halifax, then by train to Ottawa for a day with her parents, Kathleen arrived by bus in Kingston. Jean Royce perused her high school record and 'announced that I should enter Honours English and History and that [I had to] take first-year French, Latin and Philosophy ... to qualify for my degree.' Without missing a beat the registrar added: '*And*, Miss Barclay, you have time to get to Dr. Tracy's Latin class *right now*!' Miss Barclay 'nearly fainted dead away – *Latin*!!' Glancing out her door, the indomitable registrar 'spotted a passing second-year student, *called her by name* and instructed her to take me' to Dr Tracy's class and perform introductions. 'The student was just as overpowered as I was, so we numbly took our leave [and Tracy] installed me in [his] Saturday morning Latin class.'

The gown Kathleen received that day covered her uniform and 'the sad collection of clothes [she] was able to acquire over the next four years.' In time, the registrar learned of Kathleen's 'straitened circumstances' and secured her a tutoring position with her friend, Minnie Gordon – 'Dr. Wilhelmina Gordon' to Kathleen – as well as bursary money sufficient to ensure that she could complete her last year.[55]

Jean's 'rare combination of intelligence, efficiency and sensitivity' greatly impressed George Jewett. While still in Halifax in August 1945, he wrote to Queen's and to the University of Toronto seeking admission to secure his 'early release from the Navy.' Four days later, to his great surprise, he received Jean's 'unqualified acceptance! On receiving my letter [she] had picked up the phone and called my high school for transcripts.'[56] The same month, Fred Moote stopped off in Kingston, 'still in uniform,' to apply for admission to Queen's. 'Standing on opposite sides of the counter, an indication of her energy and the lack of time and space for leisurely office interviews, [Miss Royce] told me that she first needed my high school records.' Fred told her he had sent in copies in the 1930s. On hearing this, 'she just wheeled around to her files, found the records, and told me my admission was assured.'[57]

However, when David Slater applied to do an honours degree on the strength of a pass commerce degree from Manitoba, Jean asked him by return mail to come see her. 'I managed to travel [at army expense] from Winnipeg to Kingston and she welcomed me in a friendly, business-like and helpful way. She must have seen something in my record that was encouraging.' So did Frank Knox, senior professor in the Department of Economics and Political Science, to whom he was subsequently dispatched. 'Within hours [of arriving],' Slater recalled, 'I was enrolled in Honours Economics with credit for a minor for mathematics from Manitoba.' His Manitoba transcript showed good marks in the first two years, mediocre ones in the third and 'horrid but passable ones in fourth year, reflecting many distractions.' Perhaps Jean was sympathetic to someone who had been distracted in 1941–42, just prior to his next assignment – with the Canadian army in Europe. And after all, he had travelled a long way to let her see the whites of his eyes. David did well at Queen's. 'Before long she was encouraging me to apply for scholarships at the best graduate school in the world.'[58]

John Collins hadn't been a very good student, either. 'Like many of my class-mates [at Humberside Collegiate], I was more interested in "joining up" and doing my bit for the war effort.' Four RCAF years later, he was accepted into the January '46 engineering class at the University of Toronto. In preparation, he attended evening refresher classes at the Rehabilitation School.[59] He found this so useful that he stayed the next term to sit the exams. Because Queen's had a class entering in May '46, he wrote to Jean Royce. Her reply came quickly, and essentially said that Queen's would be pleased to accept him 'if and when, [he] upgraded [his] marks to an acceptable level.' In short, Jean would not 'lower Queen's entrance standards' because Collins was a veteran. This response acted as a 'powerful motivator,' and he arrived that May with 'excellent marks' to join the class of Science '49½.[60] Though John never met the registrar, he 'saw her many times on the campus: [she was] the "omnipotent presence" that represented and maintained the high standards that made Queen's an excellent university.'[61]

In those days, James Scanlon recalled, 'Queen's was known as the poor man's university, and that was true for many of us who came from different parts of the country.' Fresh from a veteran's school in Fort William, James recognized his grade ten teacher from Geraldton in the long registration line down University Avenue. He had left teaching to enlist and go overseas. 'For some of us,' James remembered, 'the business of registering and selecting courses was a bit confusing [but] Jean Royce came to the rescue,' giving him and many others personal interviews.[62]

When Hartwell Illsey registered in 1945 – one of the first of the veterans – he had been out of school more than twelve years. His high school marks were not stellar, averaging between 50 and 60, and Jean Royce noted that he 'certainly [was] consistent!' Responding to his 'particular deficiency in math [she] applied a condition on entrance – geometry.' This became a real hurdle: 'I needed every precious minute to conquer the necessary subjects. I was eleven years older than the other students; I had been out in the business world; and overseas as an RCAF pilot in the horrendous war.' Pressed for time, he opted 'to let the geometry go.' After three years in the scholarly trenches, 'the results of the Arts Degree were posted.' He and his wife 'rushed to see the results; and there was [his] name, included.' Still, for confirmation he phoned Jean. 'She realized this had passed through, but in order to save face said there was a review that afternoon, and she would bring it before the powers that be.' The powers-that-be, in their collective wisdom, decided that Hartwell should graduate and proceed with his theological studies.[63]

Jeffrey Kelly did not *want* to graduate. In 1946, after a year at Queen's, he re-joined the Army to get back to parachuting. In '48 he was sent back to Queen's for a degree, which would lead to a commission.' Two years later he was horrified to receive a notice of graduation.

> 'Miss Royce! I only have fifteen subjects and I need sixteen!'
>
> 'I'm quite aware of that, Mr. Kelly, but you are a veteran and I spoke to the Senate and they agreed to graduate you.'
>
> 'But Miss Royce!! I'm scheduled and planned for three years here and I want to continue!'
>
> I can still see her impish grin: 'This is most unusual, Mr. Kelly, but if you insist.' And I had another glorious year at Queen's, taking care to get a C in at least one subject.[64]

It was not only veterans who felt the helpful touch of Jean's common sense when, at the end of the road, some course was missing. When Vernon Ready was planning his final year, 'Jean discovered that I had not taken a "required" science course.' But she pieced together extra math credits and the Dean of Women's astronomy course and 'used her authority to grant the equivalent of the missing course.'[65] Bill Craig *had* taken the required French course – often – but the numbers wouldn't add up to 50. 'When I was in the fourth year of my honours course, Jeannie Royce called me in and said, "You've taken French four or five times; you did get up to 48 one year. I've consulted with the French department and we've decided [to] give you a few extra marks." [So saying] she took a pencil and ticked it off my record.'[66]

When John Carmichael arrived from Saskatchewan in 1946, Jean Royce 'was at her zenith, a household word with the students. I came out to do arts but I was really hoping to get into medicine. [But] I got in with a bunch of ex-service people from Regina and we did a lot of partying. [Also] I was trying out for the hockey team.' Just before term's end, John became 'desperately ill.' He was hospitalized, and probably given the wrong drugs, and was released the day of the exams. He went home immediately, expecting to return in January. But his father had contracted lung cancer and asked John to remain at the local college.

Unfortunately, the college wanted a record of John's Queen's marks – and he assumed that he was out of the game. But he had figured without she-of-the-watching-brief. In her letter, she noted his problematic standing but added the following unsolicited testimonial: 'Mr. Carmichael was ill during the Christmas examinations and we do not feel that his marks indicate the real quality of his work. We feel that Mr. Carmichael is a man of promise.' So John took courses at the college, and that fall – after his father died – he gained admittance to medicine at Queen's. The letter from Jean Royce still exists. At the time he received it, it seemed like divine intercession. 'She was just the greatest and she affected everybody.'[67]

To preserve standards, Jean spot-checked new registrants as they 'wound up the stair case' for the first time. In 1946 she found time to refuse to accept for credit two courses that Glenn Wilms had completed in psychology at Regina College. 'Hmm,' wrote the otherwise admiring Reverend Wilms, adding that 'because she kept the eagle eye on the frosh she was present to supply info to the Deans when midterm exams were in the grey. Though not an academic, [and] resented by some students, she knew what smacked of excellence.'[68]

David Slater went without interruption from student to sessional lecturer in 1947, and saw Jean 'cope with the explosive expansion of the student body, with the inflow of veterans.'[69] Yet despite the numbers she faced, she offered inspiration and leadership 'to countless students, as she had [to] me.'[70] As the war ended, perhaps no one felt her shepherding more than Ian Vorres, whose letter of acceptance 'arrived by special messenger on a drab morning in the spring of 1944 in war-torn Athens while stray bullets were still buzzing in the air. Jean Royce, larger than life, had thus entered my world as a beacon of hope in a dark tunnel of despair.' His account of his arrival at Queen's is well worth quoting: 'Crammed for 28 days in a stuffy, mice-infested cubicle that served as my cabin in a war battered freighter, and up to the very day I was disgorged along with a shipment of olives on a dock in Mobile Alabama, the main question churning in my restless mind during that tortuous crossing was about Jean Royce: Was she pretty, young, old, thin, blond, brunette, tall, short? Arriving in Kingston late for registration, I rushed to her office looking haggard, exhausted and confused and with a deep feeling of awe.'

As he observed Jean Royce 'counselling a timid freshman,' Ian felt in the presence of 'an Olympian divinity capable of striking earth with lightning and thunder.' From 'behind her spectacles' her eyes looked 'hard and rather cold, like a pair of lasers penetrating one's inner being.' But when he introduced himself, 'the image of cold reserve dissolved into smiling warmth and compassion.' Fifty years later, he still remembered her greeting: 'How nice to have you here finally, Mr. Vorres. I can well imagine what you have been through these past years. Relax, you will find much understanding here.' She told him that as the first European student since the war, he was 'in a way a celebrity in town.' The local paper wanted an interview, and she would, if he wished, make the arrangements. So began 'the start of an inspiring life-long association.'[71]

It is not surprising that she made special time for Ian Vorres. But the Canadian boys and girls also felt her interest and concern – and sometimes more – in those years. 'During my undergraduate years,' Vernon Ready recalled, 'our relationship blossomed into real friendship.'[72] 'Her capacity for keeping track of students and [their courses] was astounding,' wrote Stewart Fyfe. '[As students we accepted that] Jeannie occasionally made mistakes, but this was acceptable because she was so good so often.'[73]

Priscilla Galloway found Jean 'a little less [miraculous] than the angels, but not much!' At the end of her first year, Priscilla discovered that her 'parents had suffered financial catastrophe' and could no longer help her. 'I don't know that I've ever had a greater shock. I loved Queen's, and was determined to complete my degree.' Jean told her 'that it was possible to do a four-year honours degree in three years.' She also offered her a job in the Registrar's Office.[74]

Although Jean had less to do with Applied Science, she was the registrar of all Queen's students, and as she had with Alfred Bader, she involved herself as much as necessary. One rumour has it that she tried to talk good students out of engineering.[75] The evidence runs to the contrary. In 1937, MacKinnon Lynch presented himself in her office, wanting to pursue a (quick) three-year Commerce degree. He was already in the air force and was seeking the degree route to a commission. Unfortunately, he had 'outstanding math and science marks,' and Jean reportedly told him, 'Young man, you're going into engineering.' The Queen's Alumni Office records that Capt. John Andrew MacKinnon (MacK) Lynch graduated in 1941 with a BSc (Eng.).[76]

The demand for engineers during and after the war produced some innovative schemes. While still in Grade 11 in Chipman, Alberta, Anton Chiperzak was advised by his principal to take an eight-week senior matriculation course at Queen's.[77] If successful, he could enter first-year engineering in the fall. 'You will appreciate,' he wrote, 'that being away from home under very demanding and trying circumstances was stressful, to say the least.' The registrar and her staff arranged accommodation, and 'Miss Royce personally met many of us and stayed in contact through the summer. Her interest help[ed] immeasurably. I'm not claiming that I was a personal friend or anything like that. My point is that she was a kind and understanding individual and the memoirs should reflect this.'[78]

On entering first year, in fall 1943, Anton's class was joined 'by an equal number of military cadets who were billeted in various buildings on the campus – notably the gymnasium and Fleming Hall.' Once the war ended, the 'engineering faculty was put on a year round basis to process men coming out of the services. Many of these had special needs – some were blind, some had families' – and Queen's still had no accommodation at all for men. 'Miss Royce,' Anton noted, 'must have had a jolly time.'[79] Despite all the confusion in those days, this 'pretty naive boy from Western Canada' earned the BSc in 1947.[80]

In 1949, Neil Black arrived at Queen's with nine others from Fort William and Port Arthur to enter second-year engineering, having completed first-year courses at the Lakehead Technical Institute. The young men were looking forward to Queen's, 'but with some trepidation. We had heard rather disquieting stories about Miss Royce and registration, and thought we might be in for a rough time.' But it wasn't like that – at least not for them. 'She treated us with kindness and respect and gave us all the help she could. She was a very fine lady and I will never forget her.'[81]

Despite all this, there was tension between Jean and the engineers. Al Hyland told me that when he was at Queen's, '[his fellow] engineers didn't like Jean. I don't know why because they didn't have anything to do with her.' Al came from Trinidad, and 'not from an affluent family. She told me to go see her whenever I had a [financial] problem. Jean was my friend. When I came back for [Convocation in 1961], she called me by my first name, and I got quite a ribbing from the others.'[82]

Jean's help to engineering student Michael Humphries ran in a different direction. At the end of first year he failed three subjects – a performance he repeated in all three supplemental exams. Soon afterwords, Jean summoned him and quickly came to the point.

> 'Mr Humphries, Dean Ellis and I have come to the conclusion that the field of engineering in Canada would be better without you.'
>
> 'Oh, I couldn't agree more, Miss Royce.'
>
> 'What are we going to do with you?'
>
> 'I would like to go into Arts.'

And so he did. Miss Royce was 'a big supporter of the Drama Guild,' Michael added, 'and I was in the Drama Guild.'[83]

Pauline Jewett, the politician, academic, and university president, was mainly a jock in her first years at Queen's. 'I was [on the] tennis [team], I was centre forward on the basketball team, I was catcher on the baseball team, and I was goalie on the hockey team – and I figure skated too.' If you're wondering how Pauline managed, she 'hardly ever read a book.' She was a B-C student set on a pass degree and then law school.

Suddenly, in her third year, 'the world of ideas just came clattering down.' At Christmas she landed four top A's.[84] Her professor told her she 'just might be able to do an honours degree,' but she'd have to see Jean Royce. As Pauline told those assembled at Jean's memorial service, 'I went with fear and trembling because I heard she was a dragon.'[85] Jean began by stating the obvious – that Pauline had 'apparently decided to do some work, or ... what had happened?' 'Oh, it's just so exciting, it's just so exciting!' burbled the recent convert to academia. 'And everything [is] beginning to tie in, you know.' 'Well then,' asked the registrar of all the people, 'Why are you leaving at the end of your third year?'[86]

'Well,' Pauline admitted, 'I would really like to do an honours degree.' Then the gauntlet fell: 'You'll have to take seven courses next year and write a thesis.' Pauline wasn't stupid: 'That does seem a lot.' 'Nonsense, you want to do it, you can do it. But you've got to really want to. You've got to love to do it.'[87]

For students in the 1940s, Jean Royce was a 'somewhat remote but all-seeing person,' according to Elspeth Baugh, daughter of Principal Robert Wallace. 'She appeared to keep track of the academic records of each student and legendary [were] the tales of those [summoned] to receive admonishments about their lack of [progress]. Yet her interest was often immensely helpful, and many students benefitted from her wise advice.'[88] One day, Sylvia Mackenzie was haunting the Registrar's Office, 'the intelligence centre [for those] seeking to do post-grad work and [apply] for scholarships, [when] out popped Miss Royce.' Did Sylvia know about the Queen's/St Andrew's exchange? St Andrews had a very strong faculty in her area, and the opportunity to study abroad would be worthwhile, even though 'the exchange year could not be used toward a further degree.'

Sylvia had excellent reasons to remember that next year at St Andrews: 'the fine scholarship, life in a large women's residence, and the opportunity to join the throng of European students wending its way through countries so long isolated by the war.' In time, she married a young St Andrew's lecturer. Forty years later, their family included six grandchildren. 'Those of us who studied away from Queen's,' concluded Sylvia, 'became more aware of the unique quality of our Registrar's Office.'[89] (Sylvia isn't claiming that Jean had the slightest interest in matchmaking. Neither am I.)

Sometimes Jean's suggestions for the future seemed impractical. 'When I was applying to graduate schools,' Elspeth Baugh remembered, 'Jean called me in to suggest that I should study in Vienna, and not set my sights as low as the United States.' Her endorsement was appreciated, but 'my linguistic abilities would not [permit] graduate work in another language.' On an earlier occasion, however, Jean gave her 'wise' advice, based – at least in part – on Jean's knowledge of Elspeth's father, the principal. She had been granted an (unearned) grade of 50 in a statistics course. In distress, she sought Jean's advice. 'Without hesitation, she said firmly that I was to remain silent about this, as my father's rage against the hapless professor would know no bounds if he discovered I had been favored.' Not only did Elspeth heed her words, but she left Jean's office feeling she had been 'to a confessional and had been granted absolution – such was the power we perceived [Jean Royce] to have!'[90]

In the same year that Elspeth Wallace graduated, her father notified the chairman of the Board of Trustees that he intended to retire two years later. When that time came, in 1951, the war was six years over, the challenge of double cohorts had mercifully ended, and the 'golden years,' as Jean later characterized them,[91] were just ahead. With Robert Wallace's departure, Jean had seen the backs of two principals, and most students, with their short memory spans, must have thought she had been there forever. After so much practice dealing with students, there wasn't much that threw her for a loop. But if the letters from the next decades are credible, she wasn't bored – not with them, not with their successes, and not with their occasionally astonishing failures. On the contrary, she was on guard for thee, for them, for Queen's.

In 1950, Ed Funke met Jean Royce to discuss registering in Applied Science. He had emigrated from Germany with his family two years earlier, and was now working in a small factory in Morrisburg. He had just started high school evening classes and had no grades to confirm his eligibility: 'All that I brought with me was some evidence of real determination.' Jean responded well to those, like Ed, whose reach exceeded their grasp. To Pauline Jewett she had proposed an absurdity – seven courses and a thesis. If Pauline rose to the challenge, the registrar's risk was rendered void; if not, she had no obligation. Win–win. 'So she questioned me,' as Ed remembered, 'in great detail about the courses I was taking,' and suggested some changes. 'Fortunately, there was still enough time to make a few changes and additions in midstream. Although this was difficult,' he added.[92] Indeed, that was Jean's point.

Some months later, twenty-two-year-old Douglas Ross decided he wanted to become a minister – a daunting prospect. With three years of vocational training at high school, he had been advised to start at

Grade 11. 'This would have meant 3 years of high school, 3 years of university, and 3 years of seminary,' wrote Douglas. 'I didn't think I had ... the money or the stamina to last 9 years.' Jean proposed a short-cut: 'Ross, here are five Grade 13 subjects I want you to take this year. If you pass those subjects, come and see me one year from now and I will let you into Queen's.' He passed, and she acceded.

These encounters – one notes with interest – took place long before the days of mature admissions. Jean cared enough to offer the challenge, and she likely – in the Reverend Ross's words – possessed the 'unique ability to size up a person and to have confidence in their ability, determination, and perseverance.'[93] How many of her seedlings fell by the wayside, we will never know. But at her memorial service, Ann Saddlemyer described Jean as a modern-day 'Ceres, goddess of seed-time, nurture and harvest.' In rhetoric suitable to such commemorative occasions, Ann told her own 'Jean challenge story':

> Sitting late one winter afternoon poring over rare books and dusty records of the past in the depths of Douglas Library, careless of and – I naively assumed – unobserved by the outside world, [I was] breathlessly sought out by an anxious member of the library staff. "Miss Royce is on the phone, and she wants to speak with you!" Panic-stricken, I followed my guide, searching my brain for errors of omission, commission, or – God help me – *both*.
>
> 'You haven't entered the McCulloch thesis presentation competition. The deadline is today.'
>
> 'But Miss Royce, I haven't got a thesis to present.'
>
> 'Nonsense. I'm setting your name down. You have three weeks. Besides, you could use the money.'[94]

Ann did as she was bid. But Jean's challenges weren't always taken up – especially those winging in from left field. When Michael Humpheries went to say good-bye, he happily reported that he was about to accept a job offer. 'She didn't look pleased. "If you were my son," she opined, "I'd send you on a tramp steamer. You'll be married in two years and you won't have seen the world."' Michael understood her comment to be less about marriage and more about the value of broadening one's horizons. 'She was right,' Michael added. Two years later, he was married.[95]

Perhaps Jean felt grumpy with young men that year. Some weeks later she produced another unsolicited (and disregarded) gem. At the time, she already knew John Ashley, whose father was a Queen's graduate. John was perfectly bilingual, which perhaps is why he confidently addressed his application to 'Mr. Jean Royce.' And why not? Jean Royce would have fit right in with his townsmen: 'Louis MacDonald, Jean-Paul Alexander, Francois Smith and Sean Sequin.' Jean must have shared a chuckle with Archibald Ashley, who put his son right. Once at Queen's, John apologized. Backstage, his peers laughed up their sleeves at his naïve bravery in facing 'Jeannie.'

A year later, John again visited her office, registering 'during pre-season to save hours later. Miss Royce smiled: "Hello, Mr Ashley. How is your father?" Then the smile faded. I was wearing my new football jacket. In a cold, assertive voice [she] stated that I was wasting my time. If I wished to play football, then I need not register in an honours course. She was also disappointed in my father [for] allowing it and, when I reminded her that he had been a member of a Queen's Dominion Championship Team in 1931, she merely grunted and noted that I was not my father (whatever that meant).'[96]

Was she simply out of sorts? Or did she share the views of her first principal regarding the 'baneful influence' of football? In his infamous final report, Hamilton Fyfe railed against the annual fever created by 'press propaganda' and fed by 'the infantile enthusiasm of the middle-aged' that kept from their work 'all but the most sensible of students.'[97] Yet John Matheson remembered rather warmly the registrar's support for football players. 'Jean was one of the first of the academic community to recognize character!' he wrote. 'Football stars like Johnny Munro, Reg Barker and Eddie Barnabe relied heavily upon Miss Royce's goodwill, and Coach Ted Reeve could never have produced his winning teams without her imaginative help and cooperation.'[98]

But those were prewar victories. Glenn Wilms remembered ruefully that just after the war 'we lost the pride of the Golden Gaels to Western when he was not accepted for second year because of failure in first year Meds!'[99] Perhaps this was the occasion for the 'campus skit' that Elizabeth Kennedy remembered, 'featuring a football player in full regalia coming to the registrar, bragging of the great things he could do for Queen's reputation. The skit ended with "Miss Royce" reaching for the phone and referring the athlete to Johnny Metras, Western's renowned football coach.'[100] Jenny Weir, Director of Nursing, illuminated Jean's stance toward 'the gladiatorial games' that Fyfe had so deeply lamented.[101] 'I don't know if Jean ever attended a football game,' she wrote, 'but she understood the fall enthusiasm which helped to meld the students together (and the faculty like myself who came to enjoy the "Queen's spirit"). But Jean was adamant that although the football players might get assistance such as tutoring, [no] academic concessions [could] be considered.'[102]

Years later, John Ashley began 'to suspect she was baiting a sophomore and challenging him to succeed in both academic and extracurricular endeavours.' Whether she was baiting him or simply in bad temper, she would have appreciated the effect her words had on him. 'I believe,' he wrote, that 'my perseverance and success was in no small part due to Miss Royce's comments. There was simply *no way* I'd ever let her say, "I told you."'[103]

When her unsolicited advice arrived unbarbed its impact could be just as surprising. In the spring of 1963, Douglas Slack met the registrar to select his next year's courses. 'In the course of our discussion,' he noted, 'she took a legal account from her desk top and quoted from part of it "... To reading and understanding – $15.00." "That," said Miss Royce, "is what lawyers do, Mr. Slack – they read and understand. You should consider being a lawyer."' The result was no Road to Damascus epiphany; however, he did attend the University of Toronto Law School. Ten years later he returned to practise in Kingston.[104]

Kristian Palda wasn't looking for long-term academic or career advice; his needs were more strategic and financial. Kristian, 'a penniless refugee from Czechoslovakia who had 3 semesters of university before being expelled,' was anxious to resume his studies. From his new home in Niagara Falls, he wrote to several universities, but 'the only pertinent and welcoming reply, with practical suggestions,' was signed by Jean Royce. After two extramural courses and further correspondence, Kristian called on the registrar in the spring of 1953. 'I was very impressed by the authoritative, but very helpful, lady who was willing to back me up provided I showed myself worthy in my studies.' Did Jean enjoy setting the challenge, observing the course, the vicarious success?

Or was it the roses and peaches she liked? Kristian remembered: 'On the way from Niagara Falls [that fall] I stopped in Beamsville and picked up from my grower friends a basket of specially selected peaches. On delivery Miss Royce was pleased and seemed less stern as she thanked me.' The next summer's recession and the dearth of jobs brought Kristian back to Queen's without enough money. 'I had won all the prizes and scholarships it was possible to win [but] this time, the registrar seemed metamorphosed. Her sternness vanished and I was warmly welcomed.' Bursaries and loans were forthcoming. 'I had the strong sense of having a friendly supporter in a key position at Queen's. It was a reassuring feeling for somebody without family and fortune.'[105]

In 1956, the year after Kristian graduated, the Hungarian Uprising resulted in a new group of refugees arriving at Queen's, among them Tom Fahidy. Tom learned quickly that 'compassionate understanding' lurked behind Jean Royce's 'somewhat stern exterior.' By stern he meant nothing derogatory: 'I think it was Miss Royce's duty to be firm, and when she thought that some students were trying to pull a fast one, she did not fall for that.' To Tom and his compatriots, she was 'very helpful in many ways,' some financial, some bureaucratic.[106]

People with a passion for their subject – whatever it was – also found support from the registrar. When this passion joined special strengths forged in adversity, she was especially captivated. 'Unlike many who came to Queen's in September 1949,' Eugene Cherniak was the first in his family to attend university. His father, a cabinet maker, had brought with him from Slovakia some quarter-century earlier 'a Central European respect for learning and scholarship, [and an attitude of] obedience to authority figures.' When Eugene's high school principal, a staunch United Empire Loyalist, insisted on Queen's, 'scoffing at his plans to attend a university in Detroit and live at home,' Eugene did as he was told.

Eugene remembered many meetings in Jean Royce's office. Little by little, Jean Royce dispelled his anxiety and fear, which stemmed from his leaving home for the first time and from 'the inferiority complex ... expected in one born to Slovak parents.'[107] What bound Eugene and Jean, however, was her delight in his passion for chemistry which 'increased in intensity after every session.' It is hardly uncommon that love for a subject blossoms in a cathected relationship between a student and a professor;[108] however, this was the early 1950s, and the teacher was female and not a chemist by trade. Remarkably, their relationship developed, apparently oblivious to gender, ethnic, or disciplinary differences.

Almost always her first encounter with a student was by letter. 'The quality of her letters,' wrote Stewart Fyfe, 'made a day's impression and I suspect they were a deciding factor in my coming to Queen's.' Perhaps, as he later imagined, 'she had a set of very good form letters which were personalized.'[109] Whatever the case, many students remembered their first letter from her, for good reason. Margaret McKenzie's family assumed that if she went to university, it would be to Victoria College. But Margaret 'desperately wanted to get away from Toronto,' so in April 1951 she quietly wrote to the registrars at McGill, McMaster, and Queen's. 'Presently form letters, calendars and applications' arrived from the first two, and 'then a wonderful letter from Jean Royce [outlining at length] an entire 4-year honours program in English and history' and offering a room in residence. Her father's response was immediate, and highly pleasing to Margaret: 'Any institution and registrar which will go to this much trouble gets my daughter.'[110]

Jean's letter to Diane Polson, whose great-great-great-grandfather, the Rev. Robert McDowell, helped found Queen's, 'made reference to a recent sporting achievement of mine.'[111] When grade ten student Catherine Eddy wondered if she could 'take Greek and drop science and still get into honours English and history,' her mother, a Queen's graduate, as her mother before, suggested she write to Jean Royce. The reply was 'thorough and sympathetic,' sanctioning her plan provided she take a science course once at Queen's. 'No doubt,' Catherine wrote, 'someone else wrote the letter, but I was impressed.' Actually, there is little doubt that Jean had dictated it, as well as the 'prompt friendly' reply to a second letter Catherine wrote, in grade thirteen.[112] The same year – 1965 – Miss Royce wrote a personal note at the bottom of a Macdonnell letter of acceptance: 'It's nice to see another member of your family at Queen's!' Frances was impressed with Jean's memory.[113]

But it was the student differently placed, like Bob McLarty from Algoma, who really gained from her personal attention. 'I finished high school in 1951,' he wrote by e-mail, 'and thought I knew all I needed to take on the world. My parents did not agree. So, when I attempted to become a bricklayer's apprentice, my father, perpetual Secretary of the Carpenter's Union and of the local Trades and Labour Council (TLC) announced that he would kill anyone who accepted me as an apprentice.' Bob found a loophole: Algoma Steel organized by the Congress of Industrial Organizations (CIO) hired him as a sampler in the quick test lab. One night, Bob had 'just sampled 25,000 tons of pig iron being loaded into the *Sir James Dunn*' when the lab rang to report that the iron was too brittle. Bob's suggestion that the sample be retested was refused. So 'I crawled in and out of the *Sir James*' – for nothing, as it turned out, since the first sample was retested and found healthy. 'The next morning [when] I ran into Neil McIntyre, my school guidance counsellor ... I was in a bad mood.' Never off the job, the counsellor noted that Bob was the one 'who had to crawl through the *Sir James'* because *he hadn't gone to university.*

At home, Bob found the Queen's engineering calendar and application that his cousin, a Queen's '37 graduate, 'had just happened to drop off,' and discovered that the money saved for a new MG would pay for two years of engineering. 'Before I cooled down I mailed in the application. [Jean Royce replied] that my scholastic record [was] not quite good enough, but *Queen's* wanted to encourage workers to upgrade their qualifications and, with letters of recommendation from my employers, *they* would consider me' [my italics]. Although the letter from the chief metallurgist was no problem, the general yard only had letters of recommendation for citizenship applications. But Bob was told, 'If you'll write a letter, Len says he'll sign it, provided you don't say you're good looking.' Bob wrote it, Len signed it, and Bob was admitted to Science '56.[114]

Jean believed that people would rise to the tasks she set them; she also trusted her own judgment. Catherine Harland graduated from an American high school in 1965, but her Canadian parents wanted her to consider a university in Canada. She loved the Queen's campus, and friends urged them to 'just talk to Jean Royce.' Jean questioned Catherine about her academic background, her hopes, and her intentions. Then she said, 'In my experience, American-educated students with your sort of background either finish at the top or the bottom of the pile. If you want to come to Queen's, I'll take a chance on you.'[115] A chance, Catherine recalled, that 'neither the University of Toronto nor McGill would even consider.' Although Elizabeth Hamilton, also an American high school graduate, was just seventeen, Jean accepted her the same summer she admitted Catherine, noting to the 'amazement' of Elizabeth's father that his daughter's high school was 'one of the better academic institutions in the State of Pennsylvania.'[116]

Jean knew even better the standards at Kingston Collegiate and Vocational Institute. By 1965, Vernon Ready was principal there. That year Jo-Anne Hawley, the school's high-flying English student, failed the province's senior matriculation exam in that subject. She and her parents were thunderstruck. Her plans to cross the street to Queen's for honours English, Ontario Scholarship in hand, had crash-landed. A visit to Ready's office elicited sympathetic astonishment, along with advice 'to live with' the results. At the board office in Toronto, an official held up her paper – no touching allowed – so that she could identify her handwriting. In the left margin she glimpsed a vertical row of 'zeroes.'[117]

From the vantage point of the litigious years of the beginning of this millennium, it is scarcely credible that thirty years ago there were absolutely no official appeal routes – and that without passing grades in English, a student would be barred from all Canadian universities. Still, Jo-Anne did attend Queen's that fall because Jean Royce 'was more practical and sensible than the bureaucracy. She not only let me in to Queen's, but into English, into honours English.'[118]

Less dramatically, the registrar admitted Steven Leikin in the fall of 1959 despite the late discovery that he lacked a high school credit. With his 'dream of going to Queen's in big time jeopardy,' the universal gatekeeper lifted the barrier, provided he take the missing course concurrently. Steven admitted that 'Jean Royce was frightening (for such a little lady she was terrifying, actually) but understanding.' That June, Steven crammed for a week 'and got a dazzling 55.'[119]

Most students, of course, gained admittance routinely, without the need of the registrar's discretion, and subsequently appeared on campus with their eye on initiation, friends, and, yes, studies. But in an interview, scholarship winner Jerry Simon remembered arriving in 1956 'at the old railway station on North Montreal Street ... I thought, oh my God what have I gotten myself into? I had just turned 17 years old. I had left home; got on the train; gone 2000 miles. A kid from the prairies, never away from home, frightened. I didn't know what to do.' He continued:

> So I went to the Registrar's Office – because she had been in correspondence with me – and she greeted me with open arms. She was warm. She welcomed me to Queen's, found out I had no place to live, and right away called Padre Laverty, who came over, took me under his wing, and got me a place to live. They were both extraordinarily kind. I was just some kid who had gotten off the train.

I reminded him that he won a major scholarship. 'Yes, but I think she would have done the same thing for anyone. She was that kind of a person who paid a lot of attention to students and who cared for them.'[120]

Probably the same week that Jerry Simon stepped off the train, the registrar herself greeted a party of three on the same platform, and accompanied them to their new accommodation. 'Miss Royce was very protective of those students whom she considered worthy of entrance to Queen's,' Rona Wilkie told me. 'There weren't as many foreign students as now – [some] from Europe. But [these three] were Africans; I think from the Ivory Coast. I was most impressed. They came to her office the next day for the formalities.'[121]

However, by the mid-'50s, fewer students were having more than cursory dealings with the registrar. Her earlier admonition that students should select their own courses seems to have given way to something less time-consuming for her and less challenging for students. Mabel Corlett wrote: 'Grumbling in the coffee shop, at the time, [often took the form that Jean] had "told" students what courses they "had" to take ... With a student's entrance record in her hand, and the graduation requirements in her head, she certainly could – and would – rattle off a list of five first-year courses suitable for undecided students.'[122]

This is not the stuff of which living legends are made, and this wasn't Mabel's own experience. But Jim Shute provided the following description of an unnegotiated first-year itinerary. 'When I turned up in Miss Royce's office for registration and related guidance, she opened my file, looked up at me and said, "So you're Jim Shute. You'll be taking English, history, French, psychology, and your science course will be geology." Thus ended the interview, the guidance, and most, as I recall, of the registration process. I don't recall saying a single word; and I did indeed do those very courses.' He graduated in 1957.[123]

Would Jim have liked more discussion? 'In retrospect,' he noted, 'I'd have appreciated some conversation and at least a flicker of personal interest from Jean Royce. It was all slightly intimidating at the time (and a matter of no consequence at all in the long run).'[124] However, Zander Dunn felt quite differently about Jean Royce's direction: 'It was the good old days when we all went to Grant Hall to get registered and I happened to fall into Jean Royce's lap. I had read the syllabus and knew that I didn't need a science because I had done zoology and botany in grade 13. But she said I did.' After rechecking the regulations, he went to her office, and she said: 'Mr Dunn, it's too late to change and you'll be glad you took this course.' He wasn't glad. 'The course took a lot of my time; I didn't need it and I have these ungodly memories of looking at dead cats. Miss Royce caused me no end of grief and I managed to avoid her from then on.'[125]

Other students retained more pleasant memories.[126] 'I had two occasions to converse with her on a *one-to-one* basis in her office,' Brian

Mosgrove wrote. 'She was very helpful, and "user friendly" in that she was a human being who acted like one. I personally liked her, and this is the nicest thing that one human being can say about another.'[127]

'During my years at Queen's,' Neil McNeill wrote, Jean Royce was 'professional, compassionate and understanding. When the situation called for it she could be "tough" – no one walked over or around Jean, but if you needed her help you got it. My needs were routine and without incident, yet she knew me by name.'[128] Lionel Lawrence applied to Queen's from Chibougamau, Quebec, where he worked as a prospector's apprentice. 'Although at registration I was one in a long line Miss Royce referred right away to our short correspondence, and my distinct background, without any reference to documents. For me, it was her actual presence, greying (permed?) hair, conservative dress, sensible shoes, thickish glasses in steel rims that I connected with official sanction to attend Queen's.'[129] 'Jean Royce,' Cornelis Keyzers wrote exuberantly, 'was an Administrator with a human face: God bless her soul!'[130]

Six weeks after registering, John Olsen knew despair. 'I was told to go into civil engineering out of some romantic notion my parents had, having met expatriate engineers in Cuba.'[131] Not only did he find socialization into the 'engineering world view ridiculous [and] abusive,' but his Alberta boarding school's regime in mathematics and science proved entirely inadequate. 'I was really out of it. And I could tell this wasn't going to work. And you're really on your own. I was really quite vulnerable because I had [no] resources, [no] advocate,' and parents in Cuba who in any case lacked knowledge of universities. 'I had no idea what the rules were. I had been admitted to engineering, not to any other faculty.' He went to see Jean Royce and 'threw myself on her mercy.'

On the spot, there was 'a complete faculty switch. Everything, the works, at six weeks. Maybe geology was her idea. She made it all work and the year wasn't lost and there were no sparks or recriminations. She really got to the point of the matter very quickly. What's going on here? What's the problem? She could figure things out. She was quite sympathetic to the plight of the stranded and I [was] stranded. Her intercession had the quality of magic.'[132]

A year after John made his big switch, Esther Jamieson met Jean Royce in similar circumstances. Her description of the registrar rings similar to John's. Esther hoped to transfer from architecture at the University of Toronto and had written to University College and Queen's.

The College took months to answer and would only allow credit for two courses 'from the two and a half years of architecture's demanding curriculum.' In contrast, Jean Royce's reply was prompt, 'decisive and encouraging. [She] recognized five credit equivalents and helped me identify an interesting course of study.'

In her subsequent contact with Jean, Esther found

> a very straightforward, businesslike person who radiated enthusiasm. She [had] an open smile – accentuated by bright red lipstick – and just slightly lopsided which made it particularly disarming. Her eyes were always bright and engaging, and although she wore thick glasses, she tended periodically to tilt her head forward so that you could see her eyes directly. Her gaze was direct and open and one felt she had the capability to sense dark secrets, but would not seek them out, and would not judge them if she found them. Rather, she seemed interested only in the best you had to offer.
>
> One felt the need to come straight to the point, for there was a sense that she had other things to do. She could be abrupt, for she listened carefully, quickly arrived at a conclusion, and was impatient to move on to the next topic. But she sat perfectly still when she engaged you in conversation, totally focused on the matter at hand, without fidgeting nor gazing off in other directions. When you had her attention, you had it one hundred percent![133]

Sandra French came to the registrar's attention when she burst into tears – an event that so transfixed Jean Royce that she produced an ingenious, against-the-grain reading of the rules. 'During my first year at Queen's,' Sandra wrote, 'Miss Royce had been described to me as cold and unapproachable. My only experience with her, however, was memorable: she was sympathetic and helpful.'

> I had been a very good student all through high school, and had a satisfactory first year at Queen's. I was in honours math with a minor in chemistry. I struggled so badly with the chemistry courses that I had to drop a math reading course. I plugged away at my courses, seeking help wherever I could, studying intensely. But alas, after writing my final exams, I knew I had failed *both* of my chemistries, and badly. I went straight from my last exam to Miss Royce's office. She saw me immediately. I tried to control myself as I asked about the rule that you had to have three credits

> out of five in order to write supplementals. I explained that I would only have two math credits.
>
> 'Well what can I do about that?' she asked, in a very brusque tone.
>
> I dissolved into a bucket of tears. I was the first person in my family, on either side, to make it to university. I'd let everyone down.
>
> She jumped out of her chair, grabbed some kleenex and melted into a soft pile of mush.[134] 'There, there, dear. Let's take another look at this.' She informed me that I would have the opportunity to write supplementals since the rule could be understood to say that I must have no more than two failures out of five credits. They would not hold the fact that I had dropped my reading course against me.

'It probably had not taken her long,' Sandra concluded, 'to understand that I had not failed because of too much partying and/or too little studying.'[135]

Sandra Sinclair benefitted from Jean's innovative reading of the rules. Another student, in her office some years earlier as emissary of his family, had a very different encounter, related to me by his sister. 'When Miss Royce's name comes up – oh, wasn't she wonderful or whatever – my brother says don't talk to me about her. Our sister was ill – she died at twenty-two – and had never been able to do what the others did. Our mother had the idea that it would be good if she could take a course at Queen's. Audit it, and we'd pay. It would give her something to interest her. My brother came to talk to Miss Royce and made the case for our family and sister.' Jean replied, and the words remained with him, 'Mr S ... We are not a charity.'[136] I try to hear those words in a tone that does not grate, that does not bespeak insensitivity, that does not place a narrow understanding of institutional interest ahead of compassion, but without success.

On a lighter note, Jerry Simon's scheme was also shot down in a flash, Lone Ranger style. By then the frightened kid from the prairies was class president,[137] and he had had 'a brainwave.' He had added up all the arts and science courses mandatory for medicine and discovered, as he reported to his classmates, 'enough ... for a bachelor's degree.' Their response was predictable: 'Hey, that's great – we can all get bachelor's degrees and we don't have to do any extra work.' Happily, Jerry went off to see the registrar, whose welcome, as earlier, was warm. He explained the purpose of his call. 'And she looked me in the eye, and she said, "Simon, that's just degree collecting and we wouldn't want that, would we?" And I said, "no ma'am." And that was the end of that. I went back and reported that my mission had been a complete failure.'

In this encounter, Dr Simon told me, he saw Miss Royce's 'feisty self.' In contrast, on first arriving from Saskatchewan he had met her 'kind and charming self.'[138] Neither ever seemed far away, with other 'selves' stage centre as the occasion warranted. On Barbara Excell, Jean had a 'calming influence' that helped create space for a change of mind. In 1956, Barbara began a PhD with Dr Bob Semple in the Department of Physiology 'on the bleeding disorder reported following the use of dextran, a plasma expander used extensively in the Korean War.' As Barbara explained, 'The problem was fascinating but the standard approaches then available proved negative.'

> To ease my anxiety (high to all PhD students who think that their work is getting nowhere), Bob put me in touch with Dr. Monkhouse of the University of Toronto. I became convinced that I needed a Supervisor actually working in the field and I should move to Toronto. At my insistence, Bob and Dr. Monkhouse agreed and I arranged an appointment with Jean Royce to get permission from Queen's.
>
> I can still visualize her sitting behind her desk – not the face, but bright sunlight on fair hair and a splash of orange on her blouse, and a projection of vitality and authority, of a person completely attentive to what I had to say. She quietly questioned if my work was really going as badly as I thought and if a move was necessary. However I was in a highly emotional state insisting that it was so and realizing that argument would only wind me up further, she agreed that the necessary transfer could be arranged.
>
> Having got what I wanted, from people who were so genuinely interested in me, the emotion subsided to be replaced by a more accurate perspective of the situation.

In her next interview with Jean, Barbara reported that she woud be staying at Queen's. 'She smiled and quietly said that she was pleased. Though the contact was fleeting, the impression was indelible.[139]

A letter Jean wrote on 13 May 1953 to Denzil Doyle, after his first year of engineering, reveals her as earnest and encouraging. 'I am sorry to learn,' she wrote, 'that you are so distressed about finances. You have done so well that I think it is important for you to continue.' She provided suggestions but no concrete solution, and concluded, 'I feel strongly that a student of your quality should be supported to the hilt.' Where Denzil turned, he doesn't remember. But he did return to Queen's, and graduated with his class. 'I was so encouraged by her letter that I have kept it to this day. That was the kind of impact that Jean Royce had on many of us at Queen's.'[140]

For able and committed students, Jean seemed unable to imagine either failure or the abandonment of dreams. In the spring of 1959, while reviewing with Esther Jamieson 'some rather mundane administrative requirement,' she suddenly asked: 'Esther, what do you *really* want to do?'

'The question came out like one from a genie who would grant me any wish. I felt suddenly empowered – the world was sitting in my lap and I had only to define my wish. An Honours BSc in geology was the fantasy, but one with little hope due to parental [disapproval] and minimal financial support. As I reviewed the dismal why-nots, she countered with how-to's – for scholarships, teaching assistantships, and room and board as resident warden. So I left her office that day on Cloud Nine.'[141]

Mabel Corlett also 'loved geology.' At the end of second year, when she decided to make the switch from chemistry, she made an appointment with Jean 'with much trepidation, [perceiving] her to have little patience with people who drifted aimlessly through their university careers. But I still remember her delighted and enthusiastic response.' Yet despite Mabel's subsequent success, none of her professors suggested graduate work. That encouragement came from Jean Royce. 'Mostly,' she recalled, 'I was insulated from the ingrained discriminatory attitudes in the profession, by the staunch friendships of my (all-male) classmates, and simply studied for joy. But one memory rankled still: [When] my thesis supervisor finally looked at the material I had assembled,[142] he said it would make a grand master's project for somebody – by implication not me.'

This sort of sexism is startling, and Jean was neither oblivious to it nor uninformed. But how much of it did she confront – and how? She left few comments to suggest that she was aware of the pervasive nature of a discrimination for which – in its singular incarnations – she had no sympathy. Her words, collected together over the decades, do not add up to a satisfying feminist tract. Yet her impact on clever women with educational ambitions but no patrons was astonishing. She took the high road, providing encouragement where no one else did.

In 1952, Lin Good reluctantly accepted the fact that her husband's career would keep her in Canada. The move from England had been 'harmful,' especially, she explained, 'because my academic specialty was European diplomatic history, as a background to Foreign Office work. I decided to try to pick up my PhD programme and so met Jean Royce the Registrar.' Jean sent her to the History Department. When Lin discovered that no one there could supervise her field, she declared willingness to change. She was referred to Professor Arthur Lower, 'the famous "name"' at the time. She wrote him a note, and the departmental secretary called to set a time. When she entered the room, Professor Lower was clearly taken aback.

'You're a woman!'

'Yes,' Lin replied. 'I assumed you knew from my note.'

'No, I thought your name was Jim. Well, I don't like English people and I specially don't like women.'

Lin left. 'But raised as I had been, it did not occur to me to accept the comment. Instead I went to Jean Royce. She listened carefully and sympathetically, making no hasty judgement, which I respected, but saying she would look into it. A few days later I received a call from Professor Lower. With a little trepidation, I went. He did not explain or apologize. But he did offer me some tutorial work and a small stipend, and suggested I register in some of his graduate courses. All of which I accepted and enjoyed.'

When Lin went to thank Jean, she expressed the hope that she could work with Lower 'without fear of retribution. Jean smiled: "Queen's is a community of scholars and students. Retribution has no place in such a setting." To her, it had not. And there wasn't for me, thanks to Jean Royce. [She] was unique. Her personal dignity enabled her to survive unpleasant situations with grace, however she may have been hurt inside.'[143]

Esther Magathan echoed this sentiment: 'Unfairly, I think she was the butt of many campus jokes generated by male students and professors who perceived her as imperious and insinuated that she was trying to run the whole university. She certainly had the administrative capability of doing so, but if she was aware that students disliked her, she never conveyed it, so I admired her for grace under pressure. I never saw her as imperious, but merely more competent and decisive than any woman most students had previously met!'[144]

From early days, Jean 'gave enormous encouragement to women that she thought would likely go on.' Pauline Jewett well knew this.[145] So did Lin Good, to whom Jean became 'friend, mentor, counsellor and confidante.' Esther Magathan noted that Jean 'seemed to take a special interest in female students – a fact that was particularly appreciated [during the late 1950s] because women were not taken very seriously in courses such as engineering and geology.' But Jean's attitude toward women students crossed disciplines and spanned the decades. Cheryl Creatore, an arts student between 1962 and 1966, remembered that 'sometimes the male professors would just play with us. Again you just accepted it. One professor called me cherub in class – and they didn't give us the help and support that they would give a male student because I guess they thought we would just get married and have children.'

Jean Royce found marriage a rather difficult concept to get her head around, and she didn't try: she simply encouraged Queen's women to pursue their interests and talents. In Cheryl's words, she was 'always trying to push us on to do things.' On one occasion, Jean put her in touch with her old friend, Charlotte Whitton, 'because we were doing something on women in the *Queen's Journal*. We interviewed her. It was eye-opening for me, [realizing] that these women had really had to fight. That was why Levana was formed – it was there to protect the women. It was the first time I was aware. For us Levana was just, you know – you'll marry an engineer, and the candles.'[146]

In those prefeminist days, few educators or parents sent their progeny to interview the likes of Charlotte Whitton. But as Esther Magathan remembered, Jean did not 'seem to be on a special mission for women's rights, and the concept of "feminism" never entered our discussions.'[147] Several respondents took pains to tell me that Jean's support for women did not mean that she supported men any less. This is interesting, because for so long men comprised the only academic game in town. Once the monopoly was broken, and men had to share the fine words, mentoring, scholarships and jobs, some felt aggrieved.[148] And the fear lurked that the tables would be turned. Poetic justice?

But there is no evidence that Jean ever parcelled out her encouragement, bursaries, or conversation on the basis of gender. Throughout her decades as registrar, men who were 'serious and gifted,'[149] or gifted but not yet serious, were treated the same as women who were.

Here are five boy stories from the 1950s and 1960s. The first comes from Robin Jackson:

I entered the university with a rather low average mark but with As in the two English papers. Few registrars would have had time to waste on me, but Miss Royce added me to her list of waifs and strays and used to have me in for [biannual talks]. She would begin by asking me what course I was finding most interesting and what was the best book I had read recently. Then she would ask me to remind her of my plans for the future. (None.) Then the painful moment:

'I've been looking at your marks.'

And she would ask about the lowest:

'How are you going to improve it?'

Then energetically:

'I see that you are doing very well in x!'

Then she would ask if I knew some senior student (I never seemed to) and would tell me about the interesting things that he (I think it was always he although I did learn that there were many distinguished women in the years above mine) was doing, and she would suggest that I should start thinking about doing the same kind of thing.

She always took my breath away. She seemed to have faith in you that was entirely unjustified, but when you came away you felt exhilarated by the possibilities that she had revealed and you had the beginnings of a plan, even if it was only a reflection of someone else's. I used to go to my appointments with her in a state of considerable anxiety (I knew that she was over-rating me), but I always came away from them full of enthusiasm, determination and hope. No teacher (and I was lucky to have some very good ones) ever had that effect on me.[150]

Douglas McCalla was a better student, earlier, and he benefitted more tangibly from Jean Royce's enthusiasms. 'She was probably my main academic adviser and more of a mentor than any of my professors (with whom I got on well enough). Despite my meagre Alberta high school French, she sent me to the course for Ontario senior matriculation graduates, who had vastly more formal training than I had; and in second year she pushed me to take J.A. Corry's course in Canadian politics and constitutional law while it was still available. In short she kept an eye on the progress of her scholarship students.'[151]

Doug's General Motors Scholarship was

large and flexible ... based on a budget you submitted; it would pay the difference between what you had and what you needed. Jean was very helpful to us in organizing our budgets, so much so that GM scholars at

Queen's had the highest average awards in Canada. GM officials visited every year to meet with university officials and with us, and were under no illusions about such things as my European grand (youth hostel) tour. They seemed to accept Jean Royce's judgement in interpreting their mandate; or at least that was my impression from one of the GM executives I got to know quite well.

After third year, Jean suggested I attend a six-week summer school on international affairs, held in Connecticut, and then helped with funds from Queen's for the tuition fees. I thought of her then (and still do, I realize) as having the best kind of understanding of education, which extended far beyond formal classroom credits. She had high standards and pushed you to be ambitious. These she tempered with realism, for example in her tolerance for extensive extracurricular activity that could lead to academic difficulty. I never knew where the bottom line was [for keeping my scholarship] although in my first two years I know I tested it.[152]

During the same period, David Wilson skated on much thinner ice, putting scholarship and standing in jeopardy. Jean Royce was in good form the day she took him on, as he well remembered.

Boy was it ugly. The wind came off Lake Ontario and chilled you right through your flimsy satin red Arts jacket. But it didn't matter, it was January 1961. I was in my second term as a freshman and it was Friday at noon. Saturday's class with Ralfe Clench had been canceled. I was the epitome of cool. All that was required of me for the next twenty-four hours was to figure out a way to tell my parents that my performance in the fall term had given me a real opportunity to demonstrate improvement in economic history and geography and politics. In truth, I left ample room for improvement in all five courses. I had, however, managed to fail Pol 2 and Eco 4 with a panache rarely witnessed.

And then came the call. 'Would you be in the Registrar's Office at 3 this afternoon?' The invitation would, in no way, be construed as an invitation to tea. I didn't know who the Registrar was or what a Registrar did. [But upon being] ushered into the spacious corner office I met a diminutive grey haired lady who resembled any number of aunts. So this is what a Registrar is. And this is Jean Royce.

Jean Royce was not pleased with my academic performance. It was tragic [she said] that I should come to Queen's and squander the opportunity so cavalierly. 'You have the potential, Wilson, to do well. You apparently have chosen to waste it. I hope I never have to see you in this office again. If I do, it will be the last time.'

Jean could not have spoken to him like this nowadays. She would have been tempted, certainly, but in the current therapeutic and litigious climate, visions of bridges and lawsuits dance in the head. What's equally astonishing is that her words had precisely the effect she intended: 'Jean Royce knew that what I really needed was a good swift kick. Many members of the Queen's faculty took the time to advise me. But none would have been able, had it not been for the strong firm hand of Jean Royce who saw an immature but not dumb freshman and cared enough to read him the riot act.'[153]

When things were much better – but still not as she wished – the registrar could be a trifle more subtle, as she was with Peter Taylor, scholarship winner and mathematics student:

> In the fall of my second year (1962) I was called into the registrar's office. 'Yes Taylor,' she said. 'How are you?' I was fine.
>
> 'You got a B in English.'
>
> 'Yes I know.'
>
> There was an embarrassed silence. It was a course I had enjoyed a great deal. That year for the first time, some 20% of the exam was multiple-choice, and I knew I had got every such question but one wrong. In a sense that was good news in that my mark indicated that I had done well on the essay writing part. So during that interminably brief silence I struggled with the question of whether to try to explain all this. But she did not let me struggle for long.
>
> 'Is everything else all right?'
>
> 'Yes ma'am.'
>
> 'Good, I'm glad to see you again.'
>
> And she stood up and extended her hand.[154]

In his third year – and Jean's penultimate year – Douglas Patriquin nearly lost his Alumni National Scholarship. 'I was uninspired academically, but I was very concerned about losing that scholarship. I had to go to see Miss Royce. I [had met her] after arriving at Queen's – a short, rather steely eyed person who carried herself with a good deal of authority, but not stuffy. If there was anyone at Queen's who had moral authority over me (and there were some formidable characters there at the time, including Dr. Corry, Padre Laverty, Dean Duncan and

David Smith), it was Miss Royce. [On this occasion] she looked at me with an expression that let me know I had disappointed her and said, "Patriquin, I had thought of you for the Rhodes."' (Visions of John Matheson, 1936.) 'While this was not the track I was on, Miss Royce's combined admonishment and reminder of future potentials encouraged me to pick up my socks the next year. She understood the ups and downs of an undergraduate's life and continued my stipend.'[155]

Even at Queen's – 'that bastion of content'[156] – the sixties contributed to the 'ups and downs'; that is to say, they produced options for the undergraduate life. In 1965, her last year, Cheryl Elliott lost her GM scholarship. 'By that time,' she recounts, 'I was so involved in political things that I didn't care.' Knowing the registrar's reputation for following 'her' scholarship students, I asked Cheryl if Jean Royce knew she was politically involved on campus. 'I think she did. I remember once she asked me who I was living with, and when I answered I think she said something like, "Ah ... the campus Marxist." She was very aware of what was going on. It was a small place. I wasn't one of the leaders.'

Did she cast any negative judgments?

'Oh no, no. There was always a twinkle in her eye. I remember her with these great curls, this fiery energetic woman, bright blue eyes. Over the years we met a few times. She would do things. She invited me to tea to meet some people, and I remember her looking at my marks and saying, "Humph – French isn't good; well, you're from Saskatchewan you probably don't have a good background."'

For this problem Jean had a solution: '"I hope you're reading every night. You should have a French book open by your bed." The fact that she cared enough to say that. When I was leaving she was concerned about what I was going to do. And she was ready to help me get a scholarship somewhere or contacts for jobs. And of course that was all lost on me because we were all more interested in running off to Toronto and Yorkville than getting jobs. Being young, I didn't really appreciate how she concerned herself and cared for the students, but I would like to be able to say so now.'[157]

Those closest to Jean insist, like Cheryl, that she was non-judgmental. Cheryl's memories hint that Jean derived pleasure and interest from observing the full gambit of students, as well as – to quote Jean on the sixties – 'the revolutionary character of the present.'[158]

But there were those who found her out of step. Gordon Dowsley was a student during the same years as Cheryl Elliott. He recalled that earlier generations of students – especially veterans like his friend

George de Hueck – 'could not speak too highly of Jean Royce. It is not a stretch to say she was loved and respected by his group.[159] [But] by the time I got [to Queen's] she certainly was not loved, more feared. A meeting with her was filled with trepidation.' In particular, he remembered that she sent back a bursary he had been awarded on the grounds that, having won another, he was ineligible. 'The resident don had her meet with me and I showed her how the eligibility was not what she thought. I lost that money and all she said was, "Oh, well don't go around saying Queen's cost you that money." That was the end of it. No one was to question her and her decisions.'

Robin Jackson, much more of a fan, told a similar story. 'I had received a graduate fellowship from Princeton and a travelling one from Queen's that was more valuable. It was decided that I should have the honour of the travelling one and funds up to the amount of the difference. When I received the funds they were $400 short (at that time a significant sum). It turned out that she had misread my handwriting. "Well Robin," she said, "you will just have to learn to write more clearly," and that was that!'

Perhaps Robin came to see this incident – or the registrar herself – as amusing because of another piece of advice that she (perhaps) winged his way. 'She suggested that I should "improve" (i.e. initiate!) my ability to speak French by spending the summer in a monastery in Quebec; only later did I learn that it was a Trappist institution with vows of silence. Did I invent this occasion? I don't think so but it all took place a long time ago.'[160]

The registrar held stronger ground in her ongoing campaign to enlist graduate scholarship applicants. Here she went into full chief-of-staff mode. 'In the fall of 1960,' Judith Rice Lave wrote, 'I got a call from her asking me to come to her office. Not having the slightest idea about why she wanted to see me, I went with a considerable degree of curiosity. She told me (as I remember it) that I *should* go on for graduate work in economics and that I *should* apply for a Woodrow Wilson Fellowship. At which point, she handed me the forms and told me to talk to my professors. To say that Miss Royce changed the direction of my life is an understatement.'[161] Two years later, Judith Plumptre was summoned in the same way and handed 'a huge sheaf of forms' for graduate scholarships, among them a Woodrow Wilson. But, Judith informed Jean, she didn't want to go south for postgraduate work. At which point, '*Dear* Jean fixed me firmly with her most compelling gaze and said: "This university has done a lot for you. If you win any of these, it will be good for the university's reputation, whether or not you decide to take them up."'[162]

The two Judiths both won, thus contributing to Queen's remarkable success rate in these years. But although the students emphasized that Jean orchestrated these achievements,[163] her name is absent from Frederick Gibson's account, which is drawn from official documents only. 'Mackintosh's principalship,' Gibson wrote, 'ended in 1960–61 with a particularly fine flourish of scholarly awards.' The principal himself was pleased, writing to his successor, J.A. Corry, that 'having had one Woodrow Wilson last year, we have eight this year, and seven honourable mentions.'[164]

But whether Corry knew or not about Jean's role on the scholarship front, he never joined her fan club. The student grapevine of the day provides intriguing evidence. Sometime in the mid-1960s, Gordon Dowsley heard a story from a friend, George Murray, who was at Queen's from British Columbia. At a meeting with Jean Royce petitioning for something, George became upset when the registrar turned down his request. He was especially unimpressed with her accompanying words: 'You have to realize that BC has an inferior education system.' 'George went to the Principal, Alec Corry,' who was similarly unimpressed and told George 'just to go ahead with whatever it was.' The principal is reported to have added, '[Jean Royce] thinks she is in charge of everything; pay no attention to her.'[165]

In the last year of his principalship, Alec Corry acted on this belief. In the next chapter I revisit the politics of the last years that led to the retirement of Jean Royce. Or was it a dismissal? A gentle push or a determined shove? Was she out of it? Was it past time? Did those who wanted to rid the place of her have any idea what they wanted to do once she was gone? Was her way with students – and faculty – no longer appropriate? Was she blocking progress? the computer age? democracy? ambition? Was it an exercise in good old-fashioned, time-tested misogyny? Or was it the reasonable action of a fair-minded and long-suffering administrator?

But this chapter concludes on its own terms, with a student story from Jean Royce's last year as registrar. In 1968, Catherine Harland pondered graduation and her future. Jean sat across the desk from her and asked: 'So your father wants you to be a scholar and your mother wants you to be happy. What do *you* want?'

'I confess,' Catherine wrote, 'I found her penetrating intellect and straightforward attitude a little intimidating. I realize now, many years later, that she was one of the first people I ever met who tried to show me I might see my life in relation to my own self, my own needs and desires. I can still visualize her trying to suggest possibilities for a woman's life that were new and different at the time. She was really an extraordinary woman.'[166]

Chapter Four

The Prime of Miss Jean Royce

In late March 1960, David Sweezey arrived at Kingston's CNR station on Montreal Street after attending his mother's funeral. 'Walking along [the platform] at a vigorous, snappy pace, close to jogging, all the time pleasantly cheerful, carrying what looked a very heavy suitcase,' was Jean Royce. 'Her vibrant youth and utter charm stand out in my memory most vividly,' he wrote. Her taxi driver had just asked her what help she needed. She made it clear that she needed none. But David, seventeen years past his own graduation and properly raised, equally cheerfully told her she was getting old and feeble, and carried her suitcase to her seat in the parlour car. Jean did not know his mother had died. When he told her, she 'simply and directly' extended her sympathy.[1]

At fifty-seven, Jean was in her prime. She had a great job; she was interested, by turns, in hundreds of students, all of them bursting with potential; and her work took her to interesting conferences and meetings, where she often played key roles. Furthermore, nearly every summer after the war she travelled to Europe.

No woman at Queen's ever exerted anything like her influence, though she would never have suggested as much. 'The Registrar's Office,' she explained to the Commission on University Government in Canada, 'has no place in the "power" structure of the organization.[2] Probably, the most useful descriptive term would be ... the centre of "academic housekeeping." Its basic function has been to provide a consistent, unified and coherent record of decisions made and action taken in relation to academic matters.' No wonder Jean never saw herself or her position as a threat to anyone. No wonder she never grasped the growing opposition to her in the last years of her regime.[3]

But there is another reason why she didn't see the future – and that was the past. For over thirty years she had enjoyed the apparent support of principals, vice-principals, deans and most faculty. Each year, with little fanfare, her office produced an incoming class of students, and each June there was an elegant convocation to congratulate those who had completed the course. Agendas, minutes, awards, calendars, class and exam timetables, and student transcripts: all appeared in synchrony with the seasons.

Jean's professional life had started easily enough, back in 1931, when William McNeill first offered her a position. Jean Royce and William McNeill were natural allies; their affinity for each other consolidated her position at Queen's while leaving him free to manage the university's finances during the Depression, the war, and the first years of peace. Judging from Jean's personal account books – which record each coin spent on a newspaper – she lacked sympathy for those who believed that McNeill was nickelling and diming the university to death. A decade after her retirement she invoked McNeill's 'proud statement that [during the Depression] nobody lost in salary.' When Dean Rollo Earl defended McNeill's policies, on one occasion 'noting Queen's as the only university in the province' to manage to hold the line on salary and positions, he drew wrath from a faculty member who said that 'he didn't want to hear' anyone praising 'administrative officers.' Jean's description of McNeill's detractor left no doubt as to her own view.[4]

Jean and William McNeill also delighted in the properly placed comma, expressed enmity for careless typos; more seriously, they took pleasure in language well crafted. McNeill's will, which funded the Cappon chair in English Language and Literature, included a clause trumping that bequest in favour of the McNeill Professor of English Composition, should the university ever establish a professorship with the main purpose 'of extending instruction in the effective writing of English and of giving students pride in their language, a desire to maintain its beauty, and the ability to use it with clearness and accuracy and with distinction of style.' His will included three references to Jean. Along with the will's executor (the university treasurer) and John Orr, she was to take any books and records she desired, and to distribute books to deserving students.[5]

Until McNeill retired in 1947, they had adjoining offices. Eleanor Smith claimed:

He used to drive her nuts because there was a connecting door, and he'd come [into her office] unexpectedly.

I understood they were friends.

Well I don't think they were enemies. They got along all right as far as I know.[6]

More than that, according to May Macdonnell, that redoubtable professor of classics so feared by all. On one occasion May told a young Margaret Hooey 'in no uncertain terms that [the two] were more than friends.' One night, just months before her death, Jean cried as she recalled their close collaboration over so many years: 'He had such a good sense of fun. He was a *very* special man.'[7] The two shared an Old World enjoyment in good conversation, and they understood each other. Both were respected, from a distance. During the Fyfe years, while Jean was creating and consolidating her own role, she and McNeill ran their respective domains quite independently, but cooperatively.[8] Although Principal Fyfe lamented McNeill's financial policies, he left these two stalwart Canadians plenty of space to stamp the institution with their own values of civility, frugality, hard work, ever higher standards, and no nonsense.

For the most part, so did his successor, Robert Wallace, who held the post during the turbulent years 1936 to 1951. 'These dates,' Jean informed a radio audience in 1970, 'tell their own story. He came towards the end of the Depression at a time when the clouds of World War II were gathering.' With the war, the university became 'in the fullest sense a service institution. The university's centenary observation, in 1941, had little of spontaneous joy; everyone was saddened by the destruction of war and the untimely deaths of friends and acquaintances.' War's end brought 'seasoned men from overseas service [who] knew what they wanted at the university and were determined to get it.'[9] Despite all the schemes to process more students, lay on double cohorts, and speed the production of engineers, the registrar and her office remained virtually invisible to Robert Wallace. He was concentrating on attracting and keeping good scholars – a daunting task, given the frugal financial policies of William McNeill and the Board of Trustees. Their 'overzealous' reserves policy yielded uncompetitive faculty salaries, Wallace argued, with devastating consequences for the university's stature. Even after his 1947 retirement, McNeill thwarted Wallace's ambitions for Queen's, for he was elected to the Board of

Trustees where he continued to orchestrate the university's financial strategy.[10]

Indeed, McNeill influenced the selection of Wallace's successor, W.A. Mackintosh, whom he welcomed in 1951 as 'one of the ablest men we have ever had.'[11] No principal, he assured Mackintosh, had 'come to the position fortified by the loyalty and admiration of the whole staff' – which knew him well. The first graduate and member of faculty to become principal, Mackintosh had already clocked in four decades as a 'Queen's man.' Sydney Smith (his counterpart at the University of Toronto) wrote in his letter of congratulation: 'You have the very ethos of the place in your marrow.'[12] Yet ironically, during his decade in office it was Jean Royce who came to personify the university – and not just for her admirers. 'Jean Royce *was* Queen's,'[13] a detractor charged, the indignation no less fresh with the passing years. For this, one must credit William McNeill, who provided her with the opportunity to create the cultural space to become just that.

For Jean herself, looking back 'from the turbulent days of the late sixties and early seventies, the ten years of Principal Mackintosh's service seemed to have an atmosphere of calmness that allowed for reflection and an appreciation of fundamental values. Of problems there were many,' she told her radio listeners, 'but for a time there seemed to be respite from stress.' Though money was still short, 'there was not the constant pinch of earlier days. Salaries were brought into line with those paid at levels in effect elsewhere [and] building went on apace. [This] was in a sense a golden age.'[14] Certainly the registrar and her domain thrived during these years.

Yet by the late 1950s the university treasurer, Morley Tillotson, would not have had such a sanguine view. William McNeill had conducted the fiduciary symphony since 1920, first as vice-principal and then, between 1947 and 1956, from his action on the Board of Trustees. His departure left a huge vacuum. Tillotson continued as treasurer as he had been – in name only – since 1951. But without his predecessor's authority and prestige – and vice-principalship[15] – he carried little weight.[16]

Not surprisingly, McNeill's final exit, coinciding as it did with the pressures of expansion, 'subjected the principal and treasurer to heavy strain.' Symptomatic of the new tensions was a 'stinging memorandum' that Mackintosh sent Tillotson on 17 January 1957: 'There is no reason why this list [of current staff salaries] should not be available by October first each year, and if your staff does not know how to prepare it, I am willing to take an hour to show them how.'[17] Many would have thought this style out of character for Mackintosh. But Gibson suggested that the principal's 'customary demeanour of unruffled detachment' actually represented 'a triumph of self control over temperament. Duplicity enraged him [as did] incompetence and stupidity and pretension.'[18]

Mackintosh's memo predated by two years his invitation to Price Waterhouse for a review. The consultants found 'the university's central financial and administrative services thin and overloaded.' In the resulting shuffle, Tillotson retained secretaryship of the Board of Trustees under the broader mandate of secretary of the university; however, he was relieved of the position of treasurer. This position disappeared, and re-emerged cloaked as a second vice-principalship – for administration. Mackintosh expressed delight when his former student and head of economics at UBC, John Deutsch, accepted his offer to be the first incumbent,[19] thus ending a three-year period during which the university had no chief financial officer who carried authority. The new arrangement, which united the roles of treasurer and vice-principal, simply reinvented the practice abandoned during the period when the 'retired' William McNeill managed the financial life of the institution from the Board of Trustees – except that now the university had two vice-principals.

On becoming principal, Mackintosh had appointed a man with 'neither financial training nor inclination' as vice-principal. Perhaps he felt free to choose such a person because McNeill remained *de facto* financial administrator. J.A. Corry, Hardy Chair of Political Science, was Mackintosh's 'closest and most trusted colleague.' While a department head, Macintosh had brought Corry to Queen's, and fifteen years later he still had 'the highest opinion of [his] quality and good judgement.' When Mackintosh retired in 1961, Corry was such an obvious successor that no search of any kind was undertaken. Indeed, Mackintosh proposed splitting the positions of principal and vice-chancellor – and retaining only the latter – in order to ensure that Corry did not accept the presidency of the University of Saskatchewan.[20]

Corry's appointment as principal heralded the demise of Jean Royce as registrar. Piecing together this story – the context, actors, motivations, and strategies – requires a close look at the documentary record. Yet this will not tell the whole story: some pieces are still missing. Retiring Miss Royce was clearly a drawn-out affair that percolated on Corry's back burner from the beginning of his tenure through to the moment during his last year in office when – in a short, infelicitous conversation – he terminated her career.

Early in 1962 the new principal travelled the country, waving the Queen's flag to the alumni. These trips could be arduous, but Corry must have been pleased to visit Saskatoon. He was a graduate of the University of Saskatchewan Law School, and only five years earlier he had been offered the presidency of the university. His visits meant unsolicited work for the Queen's local alumni associations, especially in Saskatoon, where the president had recently left town and 'dumped' the job on Bill Craig. He knew that Corry had been a law professor at the university and that he had practised law with a small group of downtown lawyers. 'So I decided that this wasn't just the usual alumni meeting [and I] fixed up this schedule [including a newspaper column] about the returning Dr Corry, now principal of Queen's.'

'When he came,' Bill continued, 'he wanted to see his lawyer friends downtown as well. He wanted to go down there for tea – tea, I think, being a euphemism for something a little stronger before he met the alumni – and he decided to have dinner down there too. So I took him and of course we talked about Queen's. I inquired about our registrar, Jeannie I. Royce, who was known to everybody. How was she getting on?' Corry didn't respond, but after the alumni meeting, intrigued by his silence, Bill returned to the question: How was the registrar's office managing with the growing numbers of students?

Perhaps 'he was fed up with my questions but he just suddenly opened up [and] revealed that he wanted Jeannie I. Royce out.' In a nutshell, Jean had too much power. She was 'secretary to so many committees, she knew everything, and could influence' things before Corry ever heard about them. 'She had no business in any of the university affairs where she dipped. He wanted her position reduced to running the registrar's office.'

'I was quite surprised,' Bill continued. 'I realized that Jeannie I. Royce – as we all called her – was not so respected as we students supposed.' And then he recalled 'all sorts of undercurrents and behind-the-scenes goings on.' But Bill had 'always found Jean Royce to be a very kind and concerned person.' So he suggested that Corry 'make use of her and keep close liaison with her so that he could influence policies through her without actually doing the work himself.' But the principal was candid: Jean Royce had to go.

Not surprisingly, Bill Craig never forgot the episode. Things were not as they seemed, and not as students had assumed.[21] His story, moreover, is unusual as Corry did not make a practice of sharing his views on Jean Royce. Indeed, those with whom he worked (including Jean) respected him, and most of them were unable or unwilling to comment on Corry's innermost thoughts.

Queen's Principal Emeritus Ronald Watts (and his wife, Donna, who knew Corry from childhood as a friend of her father's) gave Bill Craig's story no credence. Ron recalled that he had 'got to know Alec very well' when he first arrived at Queen's in 1955. As first head of the men's residences, he reported to Corry, who was then vice-principal. 'Alec was a very even-keeled, charming, sensible person, not what you would call a sort of power-hungry sort of person, and very highly respected by everyone. And I always had the impression that he and Jean got along well together. I never sensed any animosity between them, and I never heard Alec say anything derogatory or negative about Jean.'[22]

But Bernard Trotter, who had been Corry's executive assistant, found Bill Craig's story 'quite credible.' Bernard and his brother Hale were students at Queen's, and their father was head of the History Department. 'Jean Royce was a friend of my parents,' Hale wrote, 'and I knew and liked her ever since I can remember. My father felt that she was a great asset to Queen's, and I came to admire her too as I grew up and came to understand her contribution.'[23] Bernard recalled that their father 'had good relations with Jean Royce. I never heard of any difference of opinion; but he was always very punctilious about getting things in.'[24]

Twelve years after his father's death, after establishing a successful career elsewhere, Bernard returned to Queen's to work for Alec Corry. He speculated that Corry's attitude toward Jean Royce went back to his time as vice-principal: 'I think probably Jean Royce would have initially resisted strong suggestions from Corry about what to do. He may have crossed swords with her in a very gentle way. He didn't ever want to do anything in a spectacular way. Corry obviously wasn't a brute.'

Corry, however, did not act alone. Like Corry, his vice-principal Hugh Conn received his administrative jump start from Mackintosh, who in 1955 appointed him to replace D.S. Ellis as Dean of Applied Science. Until that succession, as far as records and memory serve, Jean's relations with that faculty had been harmonious. But Hugh Conn, as Jean remembered, was 'always very difficult'[25] – a sentiment that Conn more than reciprocated. 'He would have strangled her if he could,' one of his close colleagues from Applied Science stated bluntly.[26] Ominously for Jean, the new dean's 'organizing abilities [had] soon marked him out for still larger tasks.'[27] With the departure of John Deutsch, Corry appointed Hugh Conn vice-principal. With Conn's promotion, Jean had two adversaries at the highest level at the university, both determined to banish her.

Conn's animosity, the same colleague explained, derived from Jean's predilection for steering the most able students interested in engineering toward arts and science. 'Because of her position as registrar there was nothing he could do about it.'[28] There is no corroborating evidence that Jean proselytized, or even held the view that the best students should go into arts and science. One emeritus professor in the Department of Mechanical Engineering wrote: 'We, who were members of the Community, did not fully appreciate the quality of [her] leadership until after she retired.'[29] Every engineering student interviewed spoke warmly of her support, whether they were successful, or needed money, or had to be bailed out because of failure.

As the saying goes, however, there's nothing like being there, and we weren't. We could speculate, however, on how Jean acquired the reputation that she steered good students away from engineering. First, given parental and social pressures in the late 1950s and early 1960s, many boys felt that there was only one game in town, and that was engineering. My fellow don at Carleton delighted in relating his dubious academic history. His father insisted he follow engineering at Queen's. He failed. His father then chose science. Peter failed again. His father threw up his hands and let him do what he wanted. So Peter got a PhD in political science. There is every reason to believe that if he had been in Jean Royce's office, torn between the vicarious desires of a father and his own inchoate ambitions, he would have been encouraged to discover his own talents and interests.

Second, the decline in engineering enrolments may have complicated the relationship between the registrar and the Dean of Engineering. The terrific wartime and postwar expansion in engineering students peaked in 1957–8 at 998, and then, in response to 'a business recession and the opening of new engineering schools,' tapered off, down to 785 by 1963–4.[30] If Conn blamed the registrar, it wouldn't be the first time that a messenger has been shot.

When I mentioned to Bernard Trotter that Conn was reported to have more or less hated Jean, he noted: 'I think that's probably right. I think that there were quite a few of the male faculty who found her intimidating or couldn't relate to her, as we say.' So we sense something that passes as motivation for Hugh Conn and Alec Corry. Perhaps Conn would have knocked her out of the box sooner, but Corry had a whole university that needed transforming. As a faculty member, vice-principal, and political scientist, he possessed ample time to observe the university and gauge the broader social and educational climate. 'He knew universities were in for a big expansion,' his former assistant recalled. Even though Queen's was determined to hold fast to current enrolments, 'Corry could see some radical changes coming.'[31] Each time he turned his attention from one sector to another, he drew on the advice of an outside consultant – or in Bernard Trotter's more telling phrase, 'the *deus ex machina.*' First up on Corry's agenda was the Faculty of Medicine. In 1962 he brought the outsider – E.H. Botterell – inside, and made him dean.

'Until Corry recognized the need for change, department heads [at Queen's] were there for life,' Bernard Trotter explained. '[And] the medical faculty [was] far behind the other faculties. Botterell came in and said these old guys have got to go. He was an amazing character, very strong and powerful, and he upset a lot of people. Tact was not his major quality [so Corry] did a lot of very delicate work. He just had quiet little chats with all these people.' During the five years Bernard worked for him, Corry 'spent close to half of his total effort on the Faculty of Medicine, trouble-shooting' for Botterell.[32]

None of those 'whose existence was changed' by all this went public. 'The closest we came was with D.L.C. Bingham [who] was brought here, as head of surgery, from North Africa where he had been a colonel in the British army. He cut a very wide swath in Kingston.'[33] When Bingham threatened to sue, Corry arranged for him to see the board's most powerful member, Donald Gordon, then president of CNR, and 'it died down soon after.' Given this account, it is not surprising that Jenny Weir, then Director of Nursing, found Corry 'of little help when Dr Botterell, Dean of Medicine was driving me out of Queen's.'[34]

'So how does all this relate to Jean Royce?' I asked. Bernard continued: 'Well, I gave you the example of the Faculty of Medicine but Corry realized that there had to be change throughout the university and a lot of decentralization. The library was one of the first things. Pete Gundy was still here, and he was close to retirement.' For the '*deus ex machina* in the library, he got Dick Logsdon, who was the librarian at Columbia University.' Bernard drove Corry to pick Logsdon up in Watertown, and 'Corry gave him his briefing while I was driving.' He explained that 'our library was pretty old-fashioned' and needed to be 'beefed up' under a 'forward looking' leadership in order to accommodate future expansion.

'Logsdon wrote his report, which foreshadowed a lot of changes in the library. So, the look for a new librarian. We scoured the continent pretty well before we found Don Redmond. So that was his way. It was a pretty good way, even if he knew what he wanted' before the consultant was ever selected.

Robin Ross – registrar and Director of Student Services at the University of Toronto – was the *deus ex machina* for the Registrar's Office.

> I know Robin Ross very well. I am still in touch with him. I know Robin had tremendous respect for Jean Royce. She was such a prodigious worker, so many balls in the air. Not everyone liked her but I think there were very few who didn't respect her. And in several cases I think she put the fear of the Lord in them, if they were tardy about doing something.
>
> She had a very strong presence. But in a social situation she was great fun and relaxed and a good sense of humour. But she was living in a man's world. And I have to admit that, in retrospect, all those people of that earlier generation – and I imagine McNeill too – I can't imagine that he didn't share the general chauvinist attitude of the time. And Corry and Mackintosh did too. But nevertheless, she earned respect and she got respect.
>
> I think that students could well get the idea that she was running the place – bright students especially, of both sexes. She wasn't pushing the women's envelope particularly, but she liked to promote talent. And I think that she was just as interested in the men.

Would Corry have wanted to reimagine the Registrar's Office? And would part of that have involved bringing in a new registrar? Bernard replied in the affirmative. And that would have been very early in his tenure?

> Yes, I think so ... What Corry said to Robin Ross, I have no idea. [Nor was I] privy to any talks Corry had with Jean, but my impression was that he felt he couldn't wait. I think he felt he had to move. And I think quite understandably she didn't want to be pushed. But I think she was pushed.
>
> There had to be a whole restructuring of the registrar's office to cope with the [expanding] university [and how could one] expect anybody

who had been doing the job for thirty-five years to suddenly turn around and do it differently? Maybe it was a very unfair judgment. Maybe if he'd told her we have to revolutionize this and you go and do it, maybe she would have done it. But there wasn't that confidence there.'[35]

Instead, a series of events commenced in 1964, part of a concerted effort to make Jean leave of her own volition. Some years after these events, the concept 'constructive dismissal' emerged within the field of labour relations as the basis for legal redress when working conditions become so problematic that a person 'chooses' to resign. In assessing the following events, we need to remember the notion of constructive dismissal, all the time remembering that the woman who left virtually all her money to Queen's would never have sued the university, no matter what the provocation.

Not only would she never have sued, but she never believed that her increasingly difficult working conditions were aimed to make her quit. No, she just soldiered on, until Corry was 'forced' to fire her. Some of Corry's friends insist that he neither could – nor would – have taken such a draconian measure. For them, terminating Jean Royce would have been so out of character for him as to be impossible.[36] But whether or not Corry gave Jean her walking papers – and he most assuredly did – he already had proved himself more than capable of giving notice to those who had provided long-standing service to the university. This was an aspect of providing leadership that he displayed no sign of shirking, not in medicine, not in nursing, and not in the library.

Let us turn, then, to the evidence for constructive dismissal before proceeding to the larger issue of Jean's competence to do the registrar's job during the changing conditions of the 1960s. Shortly after Corry talked to Bill Craig about his plans to dismiss Jean Royce, her new assistant, Margaret Hooey, was offered a senior administrative position at the University of Waterloo. It was an attractive offer – to run her own show – and she discussed the possibility with her boss. Margaret recalled that Jean 'was pleased [and] saw it as an opportunity' for her, and suggested that she seek advice from Corry. When Margaret saw Corry, she allowed that she found it difficult to work with Jean. Jean had little time for her staff, and it was stressful to deal with so many complex situations without advice. Even 'her formal manner, "Old World,"' wasn't what this girl from Sudbury – albeit from a professional family, and with two prestigious degrees under her belt – found comfortable. Jean also had 'a short fuse,' though she displayed it in the form of short, cutting remarks rather than harangues. Her staff knew intuitively when she wasn't pleased. Corry heard Margaret out and advised her to stay at Queen's. Jean Royce, he explained, wouldn't be there much longer and she, Margaret, stood to succeed her.

Margaret stayed, and over the following months her attitude toward the registrar and her office shifted dramatically. 'I matured in the job quite quickly, and I [got] a much better perception of Jean's range of responsibilities – and the pressures that she was working under. But also I remember that I simply had to persist to get through to her, that it was well worth [the effort]. I began to realize that if I stayed in the office until seven p.m. when Jean had done what she had to do at that time, then I could get some time with her.'[37] '[Jean] started talking about how much fun it was to work together on projects.'[38] 'She began to see the advantages of talking things over with others.'[39]

But it is also fair to say that Jean wanted the new assistant registrar to shoulder some of the burdens of the office. In the university's submission to the Commission on University Government, Jean wrote that until Margaret's appointment 'the assistant registrar served as the recorder,' but now 'the position is being developed [and] the work includes advising the Registrar on matters affecting the successful working of the office.'[40] The rest of Jean's report to the commission is similarly clear, upbeat, and businesslike.

Though this report was clearly not the forum to air troubles, the registrar had in fact already been kneecapped. Fifteen months later, when worse things were afoot, she took pains to remind the vice-principal. 'In January 1964,' she wrote, '[despite increasing correspondence], service given in the past by the post office was withdrawn and as a result mailing work takes the major part of the time of one clerk.' Jean's prompt attention to all letters of inquiry was legendary. No university in the country could boast a faster turn-around, and prospective students perceived this courtesy as a sign of genuine interest in them. Now that service had been withdrawn, the registrar could no longer 'hold up the post mistress'[41] if the daily batch of letters was not quite done. Nor did she receive replacement staff. That she reminded Conn of this over a year later indicates that it wasn't only latter-day historians who read something symbolic in the severing of her direct connection with the communication system of the day.

The cut in the registrar's postal service was an omen. For reasons impossible to explain in financial or organizational terms, during the winter term of 1965, Vice-Principal Conn made an even deeper cut to her budget. The lady who had never peeped during the cash-starved days of the Depression did her best to oblige, providing Conn, on 30 April 1965, a 'sheet outlining budget reductions to a total of $28,080. I have wiped out 016-519-04 and reduced 08, 31, 32 to the maximum degree possible.' But she added a warning: 'I am not at all sure that the office can function with so drastic a cut. The work load is already so heavy that practically every member of the staff is putting in constant overtime, the present equipment is being used to the fullest degree, and present indications are that there will be a substantial increase in registration next year. Unlike many offices, the Registrar's section is affected by every extra student both extramural and intramural.'

She listed specifically all the greater and additional tasks: examinations, fees, records, counselling, mailing, postal service, correspondence, the more complicated bursary system (including the principal's new plan for assistance to incoming students), elections to the Board of Trustees and University Council, financial aid. 'As you know,' she continued, 'the work of the Registrar's office is closely intertwined with all academic work of the University and includes many non-academic functions. In view of this it would seem only equitable for other offices to bear in their budgets part of the costs of work associated with their programs. The figure (some $6 per student) as you gave it to me the other day is artificial.'[42]

At the end of her memo she provided an alternative 'solution to all this: to set up entirely separate offices – Records, Fees, Financial Aid, Admissions, and so on. This would undoubtedly greatly increase the overall expense but it would give a fairer picture of the distribution of costs.' This last suggestion must have been ironic, intended only to make a point about the invisible reliance of the entire university on the Registrar's Office.

Clearly, the registrar and her staff were hard-pressed. Her secretary, Connie Martens, recalled that although Jean 'thrived on work as few people do, the strain inevitably took its toll.'[43] Late in January 1966, 'during the biggest snowstorm in years,' Jean gave a cocktail party. She loved entertaining and saw to all the details herself, including that highly regarded Canadian ritual, shovelling the walk. During the party, Jean sidled up to Margaret and asked her to see to the drinks as she was 'a bit breathless.' Then she disappeared into her bedroom, followed by two of her guests: her own doctor, and Margaret's father, also a doctor, who rushed her to hospital. That night the cardiologist reported that as a result of high blood pressure her lungs had filled with fluid and she had suffered heart failure. Margaret sent for Jean's sister, Marion. 'Of course, by the next morning,' Margaret recalled, 'she was asking for files to be brought down from the office.'[44] On 1 February the student newspaper reported in a tiny front-page story that delighted her: 'Jean Royce OK.'

She was OK, but perhaps the experience motivated her, two months later, to provide the principal with plans for a revamped Registrar's Office – one that would enjoy the senior administrative support that other Canadian universities provided. 'With the present complement of help,' she wrote, 'the office is overloaded and understaffed. The registrar does not have adequate support in that there is in no branch of the office a secondary group capable of assuming major responsibilities.' She noted that Guelph had three assistant registrars, Manitoba five, and Waterloo six. Her plan included a lengthy brief asking the principal to appoint an assistant registrar for admissions. 'The handling of admissions has become a craft in itself,' she explained. 'The complicated educational structure of the provinces of Canada, the changing admission requirements, the adoption of new techniques, the constant demand for statistical information, the dependence on universities for information and direction on the part of School Principals, Guidance Officers and students, the complexities of certification, all contribute to the necessity of building up specialized personnel with adequate secretarial help. Queen's is the only university of like size in [in Canada] that has not adopted this practice.'[45] Of course, Jean herself was an expert in this whole area, and it was only when the university expanded and the external environment became more complicated that she needed to cede the responsibility. But now, when she knew she had to delegate, her words went unheeded.

Some months after Jean's death, Margaret provided Robert Legget with an account of these years. 'When I first came to work with Jean in 1962,' she wrote, 'she was super vigorous, productive, incredibly efficient but severely over-loaded. She was anxious to delegate tasks, but was extremely short of staff. The place was growing rapidly. She was coping splendidly but at great personal cost. She knew this. She asked for middle management staff [but] was repeatedly refused help. I think this was the first time she was not supported by the principal with whom she worked.'[46]

Margaret knew even at the time that Jean Royce didn't have the support she needed. In 1966, in the same week that Jean dated her request for more staff, Hugh Conn tried to draw her into the plot against Jean. This was three years after Margaret had confided to Corry her misgivings about her job – misgivings she shed soon after. So it wasn't until years later that she realized, with great regret, that that conversation must have been what led to Conn trying to enlist her as an ally in getting rid of Jean. She was summoned to a meeting with Conn and Bill Wright, the Director of Personnel, ostensibly to discuss the work flow in the registrar's office. But when she got there she was 'grilled on the workings of the Registrar's Office.'[47]

At that time, Margaret was barely thirty and politically unseasoned, so several days passed before the penny dropped. Even after it did, she still didn't realize that the group had the support of the principal. Unaware of that, she took an exceptional step for a young assistant: she wrote to Corry to express her dismay. Though 'I was quite pleased to have the opportunity of discussing work-flow methods, and organization of the Registrar's Office with Vice-Principal Conn,' she told him, 'my enthusiasm for the meeting was somewhat dampened when I realized that the purpose of the meeting was to discuss a "situation" in the registrar's office about which judgments apparently had already been made.' Those judgments, she stated, 'were subjective' and in some cases bore 'no resemblance to the real situation.'

'I was handicapped throughout the discussion,' she continued, '[because the others had] little awareness of even the broad structure of the present office organization (which in fact is fairly sophisticated) and while I circulated a number of figures, I soon saw that they were not particularly meaningful without a knowledge of the framework from which they had come.' For example, she pointed out, 'Vice-Principal Conn erroneously assumed that money for scholarships and bursaries was administered by the Secretary of the University.'

Margaret ended her memo in a conciliatory tone: 'We have perhaps failed to communicate properly. I would be glad to spend some time and effort in outlining only in a general way the present organizational structure. Surely this information is an essential prerequisite in any effort to assess present needs and in planning for the future. I would be pleased to have an opportunity to discuss this with you if you should have a moment.'[48] But the principal was a busy man, and as it turned out, he didn't have that moment. There would be no response to Margaret's memo.

Immediately after her meeting with Conn and his colleagues, Margaret wrote to Bill Wright explaining that 'if a work-flow study is to be worthwhile' it would have to be delayed until November and December, when 'the personnel in the office may participate freely. An extra effort of this kind is not possible during peak periods such as Convocation, end-of-term clean-up, admissions and registration, all of which are immediately ahead of us.'[49] Margaret was whistling in a strong wind. Once Corry and Conn realized that Margaret wouldn't agree to an immediate work flow study – the real purpose of which was to demonstrate that the registrar was out of her depth and needed replacing – they hired Robin Ross from the University of Toronto as their *deus ex machina*. Ross submitted his report in July.[50]

Ross wrote that he had spent three days at Queen's, 'discussed the work of the office at considerable length with Miss Royce and Miss Hooey,' and spoken also to deans, the vice-principal, the principal, and Bernard Trotter. He noted that he had been asked to examine and report on the 'present functions and structure of the Office and to suggest either functional or structural changes should either or both of these seem to be required.'[51]

Ross found that the registrar's functions were consonant with those of most other Canadian universities: Jean held less administrative power than registrars in the United Kingdom but more than her American counterparts. He confirmed the situation that Jean had outlined in her earlier memos. Both the registrar and the assistant registrar were 'very heavily burdened,' making it 'physically impossible for them to spend the time that they both consider desirable and essential on the training and supervision of the general office staff.' The problem lay in the 'very small numbers of supervisory personnel ... [as a result] the registrar herself finds it impossible to be as free as she would wish, to exercise the general policy control of the office which she believes (correctly, in my view) to be her primary role.'

In his recommendations, Ross reiterated that the registrar and her assistant were 'greatly overburdened.' Nor was it an exaggeration 'to describe the shortage of key staff as dangerous. Without wishing to sound alarmist, if the present shortage of supervisory personnel is permitted to continue, there is a lively possibility that the office may simply be unable to deal with the mounting complexities that face it immediately and in the future.' Following Miss Royce's earlier brief, Ross called for the admissions services of Applied Science and Medicine to (re)merge with the rest of the university under an assistant registrar and sufficient staff. Historically, Medicine had processed its own admissions; Applied Science had only set up its own service in 1965.

Yet Ross noted that the Registrar's Office should provide service to all parts of the university.

At the same time, he argued that some of the academic services 'might better be done by members of the academic staff in the faculties concerned.' Jean Royce might well have been expected to resist this measure. For over thirty years she had provided academic counselling, often consulting faculty on behalf of students. However, by the time of Ross's report she had delegated much of this responsibility to her assistant, who had come herself to believe that the service belonged in the faculty office.[52] In fact, it was not the registrar who might balk, Ross noted, but rather the Dean of the Faculty, 'who quite properly wants the central office to provide teaching divisions of the university with as much general service as possible.'

That objection was overcome in February 1967 when an English professor, W.C. (Clint) Lougheed, was appointed assistant dean in the Faculty of Arts and Science to 'to undertake student counselling ... and generally relieve the Registrar's Office of these and other long-standing and burdensome responsibilities.'[53] Lougheed's memories of Jean Royce went back to his postwar student days, when students generally considered her 'more omnipotent than God and certainly more than all professors combined.' But, as he recalled, from the time of his appointment he had 'closer contact' with her. 'I warmly remember,' he wrote, nearly thirty years later, 'the wise advice and generous counsel that Miss Royce and Miss Hooey gave me.'[54]

In his briefing by Corry and Conn, Robin Ross perhaps learned as well that Jean Royce did not favour modernizing her office – specifically, she hated computers.[55] If so, he took pains to note: 'The Registrar made it clear that she was fully aware of the assistance that the use of the computer' could give in registration and recording procedures. Ross suggested securing a 'consultant for this purpose.' Clearly, he did not perceive Jean Royce as an obstacle to computerization of the office.

Not surprisingly, Ross's report followed Jean's own recommendations. During his three days on campus, he spent more time with her than with anyone else, and he found her views sound. How, then, did his report come to be used as a weapon against her? There is one convincing explanation: the response to his report had been formulated long before he was invited to the university.

However, one of Ross's recommendations *was* implemented by the Queen's administrators, and used to help pry Jean out of her office. 'I suggest,' he wrote, 'that it would be wise to appoint an Associate to the

Registrar, both on the grounds that the Registrar requires such help in the present difficult circumstances, and also because I think it important that there be an obvious "heir apparent" for the present registrar when she retires after her long and distinguished service to the university.'

Ross's homage to the registrar was no mere formality. Later, he noted privately that he would never have agreed to come to Queen's had he realized that his report was going to be used to oust her. On 18 August 1997, I wrote to Ross asking him some questions about his time at Queen's and the aftermath. Sadly, he died following a tragic accident shortly after receiving my letter. Nor could his wife, Elspeth, add anything to the report except that 'Robin would have been very much interested in your research. Remembering back to the year when he worked on his study of the Registrar's position at Queens, I do recall that he developed a great respect for Jean's work there, and for herself personally. Indeed, they remained great friends for years afterwards.'[56]

This point is corroborated in Jean's correspondence with her sister, Marion. In a letter some six years after the report, she wrote: 'I had a long chat with Robin Ross on the telephone tonight. I think he is growing weary of the changes at Toronto and the constant shifting of places. I wish we had something for him here.'[57] Then she wrote several more lines, with the word 'confidential' up the side: 'We are losing my successor as Registrar and a search is now on but the job has no meaning for Robin. He is much over qualified. Like all Army men the present incumbent has whittled down the job so that there is not much left.'[58]

From the outset, Ross's arrival at Queen's must have been humiliating for Jean. Without any consultation with her, one of her peers, younger and less experienced,[59] had been hired to evaluate her office. There he had discovered the same problems that she herself had flagged earlier to no avail. In keeping with her stalwart Protestant soul, however, she scarcely mentioned the event or any feelings that she might have harboured. Margaret Hooey was not as restrained. She sensed that Jean's greatest liability was her political naïvete, that is, her trust in those around and above her. At work, Margaret was increasingly protective of her boss, and there is little doubt that this infuriated Jean's adversaries.[60] Indeed, during Jean's hospitalization in January 1966, Margaret felt suspicious when offers of help began emanating from the Principal's Office. She had responded cagily: they were all doing fine, thank you.

Immediately after it was announced that Robin Ross had been hired as a consultant, Margaret decided to inform Jean's family about the plot against her. She was certain that Jean would tell Marion some version of current events, but she did not have great confidence either in the gist of that account or in Marion's ability to call up the suitable response spontaneously, so she sent her own version to Marion, asking her to respect her confidentiality. Six months earlier, her first foray into promoting sororal communication – when she had called Marion after Jean suffered heart failure – had turned out well. Jean had asked brusquely, 'Why did you call her?' But she had cried when Marion arrived, obviously moved that her sister cared enough to travel through the still raging snowstorm.

Marion appreciated Margaret's second intervention; Jean might not have been grateful for it had she known. Certainly she had no intention of revealing her work situation – or anything else – during those unhappy days. 'I have been a bit stunned by Jean's silence,' Marion replied to Margaret. 'The last time I called her she was not very communicative. Jean is so reticent that I am thankful that she can talk to you. That is therapeutic but also difficult for you, as in such a situation one can scarcely know what to do.'

Marion provided some solace to Margaret by sharing what she knew about Robin Ross from 'a U of T Round Table several years ago.' He seemed, she wrote, 'a sensible and rather perceptive person. That may help. It is difficult to understand the attitude of "the Administration" – as impersonal and inconsiderate as the word itself!'[61] In a second letter, written after Ross's report had been submitted, Marion expressed thanks 'for the forewarning about the job situation Jean is facing.' Having some 'mental preparation was ever so much of a help when she finally told me about it herself.'[62] What Jean said when she finally got round to it, we don't know. According to Margaret, Jean never interpreted any of these events – not the budget cut, not the failure to respond to her requests, not the Ross consultancy – as attempts to drive her into retirement. Rather, they were difficult circumstances to be tolerated with good grace.

Jean seemed to take all in her stride. Sometime in late 1966 she was shown a résumé for Brigadier-General George Leech, Corry's choice for associate registrar. Little in Leech's distinguished record of military service indicated preparation for his new appointment, though some observed that he had been a note taker in Vietnam. But this was a time when the relationship between two of the largest three state-run enterprises in Kingston – the university and the military – was especially close. The military's habit of retiring men who would have been in mid-career elsewhere released many army officers onto the job market. Those hired at Queen's were known as 'Conn's Commandos.'[63] Whether Brigadier Leech was qualified remains moot at best. Neither the paper record nor his time in office suggests that he was well suited to the Registrar's Office.

Still, he was a charming man, and Jean showed him the ropes as best she could. Together they wrote to Corry on 27 January 1967 proposing a reorganization of the Registrar's Office based on Ross's recommendations – a note, incidentally, that bore a close similarity to Jean's earlier submission. Corry took another year to puff up his chest sufficiently to tell the lady what she had failed to discern. When he finally did, in February 1968, she told him she hadn't reached retirement age. He expressed surprise. He had been mistaken, but now 'surely she could see that it would be embarrassing for Mr Leech to have to tell his friends that it would be another year before he would be registrar.'[64] Perhaps Corry made a genuine mistake. His executive assistant – and Margaret's close friend – Donald Gow, believed that to be the case.[65] And of course there are some mistakes that people *want* to make. Most likely, as Bernard Trotter put it, Corry 'felt he couldn't wait – he couldn't wait till after the end of his term. I think he felt he had to move.'[66]

Whether or not Jean Royce was up to meeting the challenges of the brave new world (filled with Conn's commandos), there is nothing edifying in the way she was treated during Corry's tenure. Given Bill Craig's contention that Corry's underlying attitude toward her had nothing to do with her competence and everything to do with her influence, this does not surprise. But a biographer must take note of the mumbles, of the half-spoken lines. Yes, she had been there so long; she must have been set in her ways; she would/was resist(ing) change; and after all, she was nearly halfway through her sixties – the age that makes all women old and some men wise. With cautions about hindsight notwithstanding, these questions remain: Was Principal Corry justified in adding concerns about her competence to resentment about her influence? Was it only his methods that were faulty? Would it have been irresponsible to bequeath this registrar to his successor?

It was only during an interview, in 1997, that Ronald Watts discovered that Jean had not retired voluntarily, and he speculated on why Corry fired his registrar. During Corry's tenure, Ron pointed out, 'the university was undergoing a total transformation – from 2,500 to 7,000 students. I would suspect that – but I have no first-hand reason here – that some of that change may have been very hard for Jean. She'd been here from the thirties [and] things would have gone on much the same during that period. If that happened to me in the last five years of my career, I would have found that upsetting.'

Given the 'enormous pressure to change in a 101 different directions,' Corry might have found it 'hard to find just the right sort of niche for Jean. I may be putting the best construction on it.' Later in the conversation, Ron reiterated that 'it was terribly tough for Jean in the last three or four years.' Until then, 'things had been pretty stable. Her style had been enormously effective. It's not a time when you're ready to change everything upside down.' Donna Watts agreed: 'Remember she's overworked [and] she's in her sixties. You get all that change.'

Ron continued: 'Something may have happened that I am totally unaware of that led Alec to the conclusion that change had to be made before Jean retired. It's an easier thing to do, to say, well, let's wait until she retired. I could see Corry saying we've just got to have change and Jean was resisting. And I would find that natural on the part of both individuals.'[67]

This is certainly a reasonable hypothesis. It takes account of a widely held view that Corry was a sensible and confident person who would have acted only for sound administrative reasons. But at the same time, such an interpretation depends on the notion that the registrar was failing. Several avenues exist for exploring this speculation, three of which already have appeared in other contexts: the briefs she presented on internal organization to Principal Corry, the recollections of students and faculty, and the policy papers she presented during and after the last years of her regime.

By the mid-1960s, as noted, Jean realized that she needed more managerial staff to help with her work. After 1962 she delegated major tasks to her assistant, Margaret Hooey, and she based additional requests on this model. Her brief to Principal Corry in April 1966 explaining why the university needed an admissions officer makes a cogent argument based on her grasp of the interconnections between the changing internal and external environments. She informed Corry that there was 'a state of chaos in the Province of Ontario. All sixteen universities have announced new entrance requirements, and there is a great deal of variation. Since prerequisites for different fields of study do not vary (for example mathematics is obviously essential for the student interested in the sciences, and desirable for some branches of the social sciences), there is surely a strong case for common entrance requirements. The Registrar with the help of an Assistant Registrar (Admissions) could play a very helpful part in a move in this direction.'[68]

Jean revealed her usual sensitivity toward the task faced by high schools seeking to help students negotiate the university landscape. In the previous month alone, she informed Corry, Queen's had been invited to take part in career nights at twenty high schools. It was not enough, she assured the principal, lest he think it might be, 'to send someone who will give a pleasant and amusing talk. The person must have exact knowledge of requirements for all Faculties, costs, financial aid, living conditions at the university, and answers to a host of incidental questions. Parents [also] want expert information.' Jean's quintessential admission officer would 'speak well, make a good impression and most important of all, give the information that is requested.'

In the matter of what universities were (and weren't) up to in the mid-1960s, and what they would come around to in the next decade or two, she led the pack: lots of contact with high schools; get out there and strut your stuff. Since the 1930s, in fact, she had pioneered such liaison in her quest to encourage those students who never would have considered university, let alone Queen's, to imagine the improbable. But the problem was different now. The Ontario government's commitment to provide higher education for all qualified postwar baby boomers had spawned new universities and vast changes and variations in admission criteria, programs, and standards. There were new reasons for her time-honoured practice of going out on the academic hustings.

Jean's response to the Commission on University Government in Canada – better known as the Duff-Berdahl Commission – provides another opportunity for assessing her reactions to change. On the recommendation of the Canadian Association of University Teachers, the commission was established in response to the desire of faculty to wrest control of the universities from administrators and boards of trustees. In the words of the commissioners, 'the hope was specifically expressed that the study would examine the charges that one so often hears today, that universities are becoming so large, so complex and so dependent upon public funds that scholars *no longer form or even influence their own policy* [italics mine], that a new and rapidly growing class of administrators is assuming control, and that a gulf of misunderstanding and misapprehension is widening between the academic staff and the administrative personnel, with grave damage to the functioning of both.'[69]

Though the commissioners succinctly captured the complaint of the day, they had no mandate to interrogate the assumption that a golden age of faculty leadership once existed. This was taken as a given, and the claim to be restoring old rights is of course a precious legitimation tactic. But as the two official volumes on the history of Queen's make clear, this never had been a town hall–style democracy. The board, the principal, and sometimes a vice-principal, with varying shuffles, made the major policy decisions and appointments. The occasional faculty member aspired to a policy or leadership role, and some involved themselves temporarily when they felt aggrieved. Perhaps the size of Queen's facilitated many informal conversations and gentlemen's agreements, depending on the personal proclivities of the principal. At the same time, the department heads, who held lifetime appointments (at the pleasure of their institutional masters), often wielded considerable power over the lives of their colleagues.

In the face of this traditional paternalism, the faculty began demanding a larger, formal, collective role in the running of the place. The commission made many recommendations regarding how this should happen and just how much of this heady stuff was appropriate. But paradoxically, just as the faculty were beginning to define administrators as usurpers of power, some faculty also began aspiring to places in the expanding administration. Contrast these new ambitions with William McNeill's jeremiad chronicling his forced march out of teaching into more mundane administrative pastures. Now, for the first time, enough 'ships' existed – vice-principalships, deanships, associate deanships – to create the possibility of an alternative career path or at least a secondment detour for many ambitious, bored, or idealistic faculty members. After 1951, even the principalship – once the object of prolonged external searches – was grown at home.[70]

The move to restore democracy and academic prerogatives also found voice in the growing conviction that the faculty should manage their own administrative affairs. Hence Arts and Science decided that the secretary of Faculty Board should be drawn from among the academic staff. And so we come, by this seemingly circuitous route, back to Jean Royce. I have been told that 'Faculty Board decided to elect a secretary from among their numbers,'[71] yet there is no mention in the minutes of the board of any decision or election. Instead, the minutes of 19 March 1964 record that 'Principal Corry marked

Miss Royce's retirement [as secretary of the faculty] with the following words.'

> I am glad to come on this occasion when Miss Royce takes leave of her duties as Secretary of the Faculty of Arts and Science, because I know more than most members ... about the length of that service. For more years than she or I will talk about, she has given her best to this office. She has given unstinted thought and energy to the needs of the Faculty. She has made a full knowledge of its rules and practices, and its lack of rules and practices, her peculiar province. She has shown as much insight into the idiosyncrasies of its members as observation and reason will reveal.
>
> She has given all this with full loyalty to the ends and purposes of the Faculty. I am glad to have been reminded recently of how another Royce [Josiah Royce, the philosopher],[72] defined loyalty: 'the willing and practical and thorough-going devotion of a person to a cause.' The fitness of the definition here is complete.
>
> For this service and loyalty, the Faculty of Arts and Science expressed its gratitude, tinged with the sadness that comes when we realize that something has happened for the last time. It wished Miss Royce to accept this gift to mark the completion of her duties as Secretary. It is only a little thing, a token, but the spirit in which it is given make it much more than it is in itself.

At this juncture, Corry presented 'orchids to Miss Royce who received a standing ovation from the Faculty Board.' Clearly, this was a big deal: the principal himself had come to the meeting and made a gracious speech. Perhaps 'the completion of her duties' had been his decision alone. But henceforth some willing or unwilling faculty member would have to do the job, and every assistant professor knows that minutes of meetings don't count as scholarly publications. Whoever made the call to end the Royce-as-secretary show, which had been on the road since 1936, it is quite staggering that a gift without value – 'only a little thing' – was perceived as preferable to, for example, a return ticket to Paris. But this gift was in line with her pension, and seems to suggest that women – elderly women? Miss Royce in particular? – have no needs, let alone desires.[73]

In the commission's report there is no mention of this sort of transfer of tasks from administrative to academic staff. However, I have been told that the faculty's decision to run its own show was in the spirit of the report. As chair of the faculty association's response to Duff-

Berdahl, Ronald Watts recalled the Faculty Board's decision to have an elected chairman 'and about that time we also decided to elect a secretary. And this didn't arise out of any dissatisfaction with ... I don't recall anyone ever complaining about Jean's role. It was just part of a change as things got bigger, more structured.'[74]

Did Jean mind that she had been deposed as secretary of Faculty Board? Not so you would notice. Yet there is a sense that Jean lost in the changing order, and that this made her not only passé, but also better gone – lest she stay on nursing resentments that others sense they would hold in her place.

Yet the written record reveals Jean's active role in making the spirit of the commission live at Queen's. As secretary to Senate, she worked closely with Frederick Gibson, then vice-principal responsible for creating – constitutionally at least – the world according to Duff and Berdahl. Delegating expansively, as was his custom, Gibson relied on Jean for most thinking and writing on Senate reform. She had recorded Senate deliberations for more than three decades, and although criticism was never her weapon of choice, she had pretty firm ideas about what was needed to transform the body into the 'central educational forum' proposed by Duff-Berdahl. In a memorandum to Corry[75] she grappled with the commissioner's warning that with all Senate's new powers, 'care must be taken [lest] it be drowned in trivialities.'[76] Duff and Berdahl were both academics and knew of what they spoke. But Jean had endured a few hundred Senate meetings herself – and she knew too.

'As I am sure you agree,' she wrote to Corry, 'there is reason for concern at the multiplicity of business now being transacted over the table at formal meetings. The Senate has wide responsibilities and must be informed of many activities, but routine matters should not be occupying so *much attention* that insufficient time is left for debate on fundamental issues.' One can imagine Corry cringing when she went on to remind him that 'if there was ever a period when first principles needed to be grappled with, it is the present. The meetings should not be cluttered with discussion of *minutiae* that could have been handled in Committee and action should be taken forthwith to avoid this.'

Jean provided four recommendations. The first was explicitly Gibson's, the other three her own. Gibson's suggestion 'that a subcommittee of the Senate be set up to serve as a clearing house for the *Agenda* [has] distinct merit,' she told the principal. 'Such a body would sort out and group the various items [and ensure] that all preliminary research [is] carried out. This would allow immediate consideration of vital questions. [This material] would be circulated with the agenda as at present but could be presented at meetings as a separate entity.' As a result, she added, 'the members of the senate *having been informed of the detail should be fully aware of its content.*' Jean's italics indicate that this process would only work if senators did their homework. Having watched them come and go for over thirty years, she wasn't making guarantees.

'As a second desirable measure,' she continued, 'I would suggest that a series of standing committees be set up with carefully defined terms of reference.' This mundane and sensible suggestion heralded a broader purpose: 'It would probably [not] be sound,' she told Corry – and she touted few qualities above soundness – 'to select the membership ... exclusively from the elected members of the Senate [or] as representatives of Faculties but from the university as a whole and to include staff in all ranks who have special interest in the subjects concerned.' Committees constituted in this way would 'be able to report with authority because they would be working on problems of which they have special knowledge.'

Through this proposal, Jean also sought to circumvent the problem that the Senate, 'by the very nature of its structure, is a diverse body with strong vested interests and a feeling of responsibility and obligation to the individual Departments and Faculties rather than the university as a whole.' As registrar, she felt certain that she had a bird's-eye view of the whole place, and she looked to bring others similarly minded into the decision-making process. These colleagues might be less interested in jockeying for position than in making recommendations that would help students.[77] Her third recommendation – to provide an adequate secretariat for the Senate – would also be implemented in the fullness of time.[78]

Jean's fourth suggestion countered the recommendations of the Duff-Berdahl Report. She reminded Corry that the commissioners regarded presiding over Senate as 'virtually [the principal's] most important task. Faculties should realize,' they warned, that 'if the President does not preside over the Senate, he will feel less obligation to be the Senate's effective spokesman to the Board.' Though Jean allowed that the Duff-Berdahl statement had 'merit in theory,' she urged 'a strictly neutral Speaker in accordance with Bourinot's Rules of Procedure [who] would free the Principal from the distraction of procedural matters and allow him opportunity to give the most effective leadership.'[79]

In making this proposal she was aligning herself, in the words of Duff-Berdahl, with those university professors who unjustifiably 'fear their outspokenness may jeopardize their own prospects. [For] under our proposed reforms, the professorial future of a faculty member could not be subject solely to arbitrary judgments by the President or his Deans.' Besides, they added, with the assurance of those who have had power and security for too long, 'if professors are too timid to say what they think, they should not be on the Senate.'

Jean's argument seemed to skirt this problem entirely, raising neither the possibility of autocratic principals nor that of faculty who shouldn't be in the kitchen if they could not stand the heat. 'I realize,' she wrote to Corry, 'that there is a delicate balance between leadership as defined by the Duff-Berdahl Report' (i.e., controlling things from the chair) 'and the leadership [through] free range of expression on the part of the principal that can come only if he is unfettered by the chairmanship.' Her argument that Corry cede his chair of Senate was tactful – and unequivocal. This outspoken memorandum was dated the same month she and George Leech presented to the principal 'their' recommendations for restructuring the Registrar's Office.[80] Was Jean being courageous? Or oblivious? Or was she just doing her job as she saw it? Certainly, she did not exhibit in this memorandum any of the political naïvete that underlay her lack of awareness regarding her own treatment. But Jean would not be the first person who failed to bring her analytical skills home.

Judging from this reading of her response to the Duff-Berdahl Commission, she was attuned to – and even prescient about – the shifting university environment. Only her recommendation that the principal not chair the Senate failed, and here she seemed more in touch with the need to create a more democratic and participatory Senate – and a university that displayed a more collective purpose – than the commissioners or those at Queen's who accepted their recommendation.

Yet this conclusion contradicts important evidence. Donald Macintosh arrived as a professor in the School of Physical and Health Education in 1965, and he never knew the registrar personally. But he recalled that faculty members – including Ron Watts – believed that Jean Royce was an obstacle to their goal of 'democratizing the university.'[81]

'That's interesting,' Ron replied on learning this:

> I think that [Don] got what I was trying to do correct. I was chair of the

> committee that made recommendations [to Duff-Berdahl] on behalf of the faculty at Queen's. Fortunately, at that time Queen's was already pretty collegial so it wasn't revolutionary. Queen's was one of the few universities ... where the faculty really did run the place. Or more or less, and became more so subsequent to that. I don't recall thinking that Jean Royce was the one I had to overcome.
>
> [But] thinking back on Jean Royce, I can see that this was not something that she would have been particularly sympathetic to, if you see what I mean. I don't recall struggling with [her] but I can see how Don Macintosh might have arrived at that conclusion because Jean Royce was used to the time when everything was run from the principal's office and the registrar's office and that was it. [So] that's probably perceptive on Don's part: she represented the old style in terms of running the university. [But] oddly enough, I don't ever recall thinking of Jean as the barrier that had to be overcome.

Nor did Donna, who added, 'I always thought she cooperated.'[82]

Yet the perception endures that Jean Royce resisted, and we have to wonder why. As Ron Watts intimated, the obstacle to faculty democracy at Queen's came not from the registrar but rather from the usual suspects – principals, trustees, and contrary-minded faculty members. Clearly, the obstacle wasn't Jean Royce. But perhaps ousting her brought other satisfactions. Some men feel an urgent need to throw off the maternal yoke – especially when dad is urging them on. For others, Jean's packaging would have said it all: she was an older woman, a self-styled icon representing an unlamented past.

The knock against Jean from the administrative ether was that she wouldn't accommodate change. Yet most of the chat from below – as related in the two previous chapters – suggests otherwise. I am thinking here in particular of two faculty members who wrote about their experiences working with her during her last years. When her old friend, Vernon Ready, returned to Queen's in 1969 as the first Dean of the Faculty of Education, he established an advisory committee. 'Even though I knew how overworked she was I dearly wanted her wisdom on the Committee. When I asked her she accepted immediately, another indication that she was never too busy to take on a new task which she believed in.'[83]

Physics professor David McLay chaired the Board of Studies in the Faculty of Arts and Science in 1967–8. It was then, he wrote, 'that I discovered the caring nature of Jean Royce as we wrestled with the problems of students afflicted by bereavement, [parental] divorce, illness and poverty. She was not only open to helpful consideration of individual cases but often made the proposals that were approved by the Board.' McLay identified two of the accomplishments during that period. The first made it 'easier for students to increase or reduce their academic load by 20% [thus reducing] substantially the number of appeals to the Board. [The second] established the important principle, which endured for the next two decades, that very bright students could take enriched programs without extra payment.' McLay found Jean 'a compassionate, sensible and wise officer of the university with a delightful sense of humour.'[84]

Like many former students, Judith Plumptre continued to drop in to see Jean.

> After my first year of graduate study I came in to see her (*of course* there was time; that busy woman was great at finding time). She asked about graduate study, and I said something to the effect of 'a great life – interesting work, interesting professors, wonderful living abroad.' After another year or two I came back again and she asked the same question. This time my reply was 'it's dreadful. It is so lonely, and such a grind, endless minutiae. And all the other graduate students are absorbed in *their* thing, so communication falls to nil.' Jean looked at me and said quite quietly, and not without compassion, 'that isn't what you said two years ago.' I had forgotten but she had listened and remembered. Those later years were very difficult but the talk I had then with Jean helped a lot.[85]

Even so, in a later interview – in response to a direct question – Judith suggested that 'it had passed the time when her approach to being university registrar was appropriate. It was [no longer] appropriate to handle students as she had, and I don't know this but it probably wasn't appropriate to handle faculty that way either. I can see that it was time for her to go, time she retired.'[86]

Quite possibly, Jean's formal, often clipped style was increasingly at odds with the challenges and casual mores of the revolutionary 1960s. Yet she seemed singularly *not* flummoxed by the 'student of the sixties [who] has wanted to be involved in every phase of the structure and pattern of the University.'[87] On one memorable occasion, she met in the revered Collins Room with student politicians, who were exercised about one thing or another. At that time the Collins Room was for formal business only and, as Margaret Hooey recalled, 'the conference table was considered sacrosanct, guarded by Kaye Roushorn in the Secretary's Office. When Jean came into the room and sat down she looked up to see a rectangle of feet atop the table. She surveyed the [scene] and remarked, "My, what fine large feet you have." The feet came down and the discussion went on.'[88]

Her clever response must have deflated the revolutionaries. But whether she was amused or disapproving, her interpretation of the student body's changing character was quite sympathetic and sophisticated. A year after her retirement, she wrote to Ronald Watts:

> As late as the early sixties, although a coming change was apparent, most policies of the university progressed along established lines. Students came to the university ready to follow established patterns: indeed, they were attuned to them. I think they were as socially conscious as their present counterparts but those who looked forward to public life had a sense of urgency to get ahead in their background studies in preparation for later professional work. They were concerned about poverty and human rights and misgovernment, but the university represented a respected and all important source of knowledge and they were eager to imbibe as much as possible. [Both the serious intellectual and the playboy] would have looked askance at the student who aspired to a place in university government at the higher levels. [But postwar students were also] angry about many things – paternalism, poor teaching, inadequate housing, rising costs, and the inadequacy of student aid.
>
> Ironically, it is the children of these groups who, having been reared in comfortable circumstances, now want to take over the reins, to do away with what they label as social injustice and to found a new order. Parents having had to cope with almost overwhelming difficulties themselves, have indulgently eased the progress of their progeny. The carefully-guarded child provided with every facility and yet subservient to parental dictate is impelled to express disdain for all his advantages, to claim special insight into the weaknesses of society, and to give his activities a righteous tone by espousing anti-war movements, the cause of the underprivileged and other social problems such as pollution. [Although] every progressive adult is concerned about the same problems, many students, some of them very able indeed can find no relation to reality in their first year at the university.

Her response to this problem was so distinctly unlike Queen's as to take one's breath away: 'I suggest that study followed by practical work or such work done concurrently, has value. I advance the idea because students have withdrawn from the university in order that they might remedy their own situation. The beginning of wisdom gained in a year or two of practical work has proved invaluable to them.' Nor was society, she added 'likely to support Institutions restricted to a small, highly selective academic group working on esoteric research.'[89]

In her letter to Ronald Watts her voice resonated as strongly as ever, and her views seemed 'sound.' However, in the three years since she had written the memorandum on Senate reform to Principal Corry she had navigated her way through occupational and personal oblivion, and that story also needs telling.

In retrospect, it seems clear that Corry had expected George Leech to take control of the Registrar's Office whether Jean retired or not. He was to be the *de facto* registrar. But Leech lacked both the ambition and the stomach for this.[90] The registrar's job, as presented to him by Corry, seemed to suit him well. Corry's working assumption, as expressed in his conversation with Bill Craig, was that the Registrar's Office could run itself – it was more or less routine office work, after all. Certainly Corry wasn't looking for a Jean Royce clone who would insist on playing in the big league, laying out the implications of policy decisions and exposing bottlenecks that needed unjamming. Leech was perfect: he was charming, and nice, and had no interest in running the Registrar's Office, let alone the university. As a result, after he was hired Jean continued to run the show as she always had.

Corry now moved into high gear, at a time when Jean was becoming absorbed with the issue of Senate reform. Situated as she was in the nexus of discussions, meetings, and briefs about the nature of a reformed university governance, she was, not surprisingly, blown away by his words of dismissal. But she never admitted to others that she had been sacked. It was a secret. Corry had no reason to tell, and every reason not to, and to his credit he kept quiet. Jean had every reason to shout it from the roof tops, but that, as you know, would have been out of character. She did tell Margaret Hooey, who kept the faith until after Jean's death. Only then, did she write to Jean's friend, Robert Legget, in response to his many questions: 'I went to Jean's for lunch the day of her conversation with Mr. Corry. She was stunned, deeply hurt, and sobbing asked, "What have I done wrong?" It was a terrible day.'[91] No one else saw the tears. To Eleanor Smith, who met her downtown and asked how things were going, she was her usual feisty self: 'I am going to retire. I'll be replaced by ten brigadiers and fifteen lieutenant colonels.'[92]

The budget sheet for administrative salaries for July 1968 to June 1969 reveals more than the fiscal story:

016-519-22	Administrative Salaries	Annual Salary
Registrar	Royce, Miss Jean I.*	$10,334
Associate Registrar	Leech, George C.	$17,000

Beside the asterisk was the following explanatory note:

> *Miss Royce retires as Registrar Aug. 31, 1968–
> continues as consultant until Dec. 31, 1968–
> On leave of absence with pay Jan. 1, 1969–
> Feb. 28, 1969– 8/12 of $15,500 (July–Feb.) = $10,334

Also listed on this budget sheet were four assistant registrars – Margaret Hooey ($11,800), D.N. Ellis (Student Awards, $10,800), H.W. Sterne (Admissions, $13,000), and Rudolf Ziola (Statistics and Records, $11,000) – and two admissions officers. As Margaret told Robert Legget, 'Mr Leech was [immediately] flooded with middle management types – six [is] a very modest estimate.' Yet what is most staggering about this budget was George Leech's salary. Even as associate registrar, he was being paid 11 per cent more than Jean Royce ($17,000 vs $15,500), who had been registrar for thirty-five years.

Jean's name was not the only one that did not appear again on the budget sheet of the Registrar's Office. In her memorandum on Senate reform, Jean had called for a secretariat located within that office, and in her 'joint' presentation with Leech she had noted that Margaret Hooey, continuing as assistant registrar, would be 'an excellent person to head up this work.'[93] Once in office, Leech repeated the recommendation, and Corry offered Margaret the position of associate registrar and Secretary of Senate.

By then, Margaret had more than one reason for wanting to bolt from the Registrar's Office. 'Leech was a very delightful man,' she recounted, 'but he didn't do much except throw out files.' On one occasion, he had had to take notes for a meeting. 'Jean laughed about it because the one thing everyone kept saying about him was that he had been a note taker in Vietnam and this was something he could do. Well, when she came back from her holidays he told her that he didn't know how to write up notes. [So] she had to write the minutes for a meeting that she hadn't attended.'[94]

The brigadier general clearly needed Margaret Hooey. When he offered her the associateship he provided a list of everything she would do:[95] 'all the things that he was appointed to do, really, all the work that he didn't know how to do.' Working for Leech, Margaret insisted, would have meant 'a lofty title and all the joe jobs. [So] I held out for a separate unit for the newly reorganized Senate.'[96]

In her last months as registrar, Jean never missed a beat, continuing to run the place and to represent the university in the outside world. A month after Corry dropped his bombshell, she delivered a 'think piece' on the new intelligence/achievement tests, which some thought would take the guesswork out of university admission policies. She warned her audience:

> Aside from techniques, the important thing to keep in mind here is that we must not make the system our Master, that in all our operations we remember that we are dealing with human beings whose futures are in the making. How often must a Registrar have wished that some magic wand would open up a vista ahead and reveal the true quality of a candidate for admission, particularly the border-line candidate. How often would the wisdom of a seer be a help as one ponders over a school record of limited achievement but with evidences of untapped ability.
>
> [How easy it is with the] able student well adjusted and oriented to consistent application [who] is almost certain to succeed if given normal opportunity. [But with] the less well adjusted student of ability we have no certitude. Given the right atmosphere, the benefit of stimulating teaching and contact with mature and well stored minds, he may develop to a degree far beyond expectation. Without these stimuli, without motivation, he may join the dull throng of the unfulfilled. This points up at once that the teacher is really at the core of this situation.

But teachers weren't the only factor. The vagaries of history, 'inspiration from peers [and] an atmosphere that infects him with the excitement of learning' also mattered. 'All this means that we cannot foretell with true accuracy; we are subject to the winds.' Having reminded her audience that they were not gods – 'that it would be depressing if we were to reach a state of complacency that would cause us to think that we have selected in any one year, the perfect group' – she allowed that the tests would 'prove useful as an extra source of information.' A more important indicator, though, was the 'complete high school record [despite] the loss of the external subjective examination which provided a common standard and tested the analytical capacity of the student.'[97]

To her colleagues she threw a challenge, and it was not to come up with a better test. Research into 'factors that seemed to hinder or improve student progress, problems of interpretation of university work to secondary school teachers and students, problems of financing university education, studies of scholarships patterns are long overdue.'[98]

Only days before the end of her registrarship she addressed the National Association of Registrars in a mode similarly philosophical and practical. 'We want [university] to be a rich experience allowing for the fullest development of the capacities of the student and at the same time we want to avoid waste of time and energy through wrong choices. I suppose we might digress here and think for a moment about whether a choice can ever be wrong. Certainly every learning experience bears within it seeds of development.' There was, she told her audience, 'new strength' in the educational system in that teachers were increasingly 'concerned with having a part in educational development and the students have become self-conscious about the quality of their education and want to have a voice.'[99]

Two months later, registrar in name only, Jean received an honorary degree from Queen's University. In the photographs of the ceremony, she is smiling; she appreciated the warm display of affection. Perhaps she alone, having attended every Convocation for three-and-a-half decades, would have known whether hers was the first standing ovation. Jean's family attended, and afterwards she wrote to Marion describing the dinner that evening. 'It was a very pleasant affair, indeed. They had set up the Great Hall with the dining tables at the south end and at the north arranged big comfortable chairs around the hearth which had a glorious blaze. Waitresses served a variety of drinks from trays and for a long time we sat or moved about at will before sitting down to eat. It was all completely informal with no toasts and no prepared speeches but several of the guests were moved to "ad lib."' One of her fellow graduands, René Dubos, 'made an interesting comment. He said – "I find that Queen's has a sense of proportion. Today it gave Miss Royce a standing ovation but did not do so for [honorary graduand, Pierre Elliott] Trudeau. It was honouring one of its own members in a very special way."'[100]

'With all of you gone,' Jean confessed, 'my house felt like a tomb when I got back from the Dinner. It was a happy day for me and having all of you there was its peak. I only wish it hadn't been so hurried.'[101]

Nor did she wish her exit from the university to be so hurried. This ceremony, which brought together colleagues and family, friends and adversaries, students and alumni, marked the end of an era at the university and in her life. As registrar at Queen's, Jean occupied centre stage for thirty-five years. Her work, her self, her energy, her inquisitiveness, her views – all had been there to see and hear. They had been public performances, open for scrutiny, subject to approval, dismay, respect, resentment, anger, and amusement. But if her work sustained her, so also did her rich intellectual commitments, her immersion in literature and art, her unbounded enthusiasms for travel, people, and places, and her engagement with family and friends. All of these shaped and gave meaning to her life wherever she happened to be. The students, faculty, and staff at Queen's – and beyond – were the beneficiaries of all her enthusiasms. Hers was a life lived in the fluid intersections between private and public, a very public life fuelled by interests nurtured while travelling and meeting people, and during quiet hours reading alone, curiosity and wonder never far away.

Working at a small university in a small Ontario town, Jean Royce was an internationalist, a cosmopolitan, a sceptical student of the Enlightenment. Perhaps this is the Jean whom Robert Legget deemed the 'other' Jean. But my reading is that there was enough traffic between the two to blur the distinction. Of course, she displayed different styles for different people. But the person who was out there, in the academic trenches, alternately admonishing and praising the troops, was driven by her own unquenchable curiosities and by the desire to see others take off, each in her own way.

As a single woman with a demanding job, she permitted the impression that her life began and ended with Queen's. Outwardly, a dutiful and parochial life. But the categories – work, leisure, single – occlude and distort the range of interests, the varieties of people, the ideas and questions that made life the grand affair that she took it to be. In the next chapter, Jean the registrar cedes pride of place to Jean the book lover, traveller, gardener, sister, and aunt, the friend, the woman who loved and was loved.

Chapter Five

More Than a Registrar

Appearances often deceive. Many people believed – then and now – that Queen's was Jean's whole life, and the previous three chapters do little to modify that impression. As she steered students, faculty, and administrators through the bureaucratic architecture of her own design, Jean seemed married to her job. As Queen's alumna Priscilla Galloway wrote, '[Jean] was extraordinary in her devotion to Queen's [and] became established as an administrator in an era when a woman was not expected to have a personal life if she had chosen to have a professional one. What was Jean's personal life? I know so little.'[1] There was, Robert Legget would have assured her, the 'other Jean, a perfectly delightful and very human person, so completely unknown to all but a few.'[2]

There are perils to writing about the 'other' Jean(s), occasioned both by her character and the nature of available sources. How puzzling it is to be in the presence of a person who seems to exclude her own self from her wide-ranging interests. In her letters, interviews, and papers, and in the recollections of others, there are no excursions, no detours, on self. This would seem less surprising in a conformist. But those whose lives run against the grain of expectations tend to produce rationalizations for their behaviours and convictions. Yet Jean left no traces of this sort of commentary. Was her nonconformism conscious? Did she experience constraint? How did she feel about her choices? Did she desire, seek, or have a shared intimate life?

In *The Last Gift of Time*, Carolyn Heilbrun expresses regret for the years she spent writing the biography of Gloria Steinem: 'How confounding it was that I, who had urged women to delve deeply beneath the surface, found myself with a subject who had little interest in delving.' Steinem was an activist who had 'not known herself, not in the sense of acting from hidden, unadmitted motives – this she never did – but in the sense of not having needed, for her own survival, to penetrate her own psyche.'[3]

Heilbrun's declaration brought me up short. My own history intertwined with feminism's first consciousness-raising and therapeutic generation. We turned to psychoanalytic thought to illuminate women's subordination, and to each other and to a range of psychotherapeutic practices for help in personal navigation. This fuelled scepticism of Foucault's take on psychoanalysis – that it is simply another regulatory discourse that inscribes itself on bodies, shaping rather than explaining the maladies of mind and spirit.

Certainly Jean was not of the therapeutic era. The Royces, men and women alike, appear to be dead ringers for David Riesman's 'inner directed' person.[4] Marion once lamented that Jean would not talk about herself, and Jean that 'Don [did] not ever reveal himself at all.' Don's wife, Celia, insisted that they were all alike in this, and that she never understood how Jean and Marion – let alone her husband – got by with so little talk about themselves, their relationships, their emotions, or their hopes and fears.[5] 'Why are the Royces so emotionally stunted?'[6] her son, Ian, wondered aloud. For all their differences, did Jean Royce resemble Gloria Steinem, who had 'required a personality ill at ease with introspection, or indeed any deep sense of a self in conflict with her mission'[7] If so, what did that mean to me?

While turning all this over, I chanced on John Bayley's comment about his wife, the British philosopher and novelist Iris Murdoch, that she was 'extremely sociable and liked to hear about other people's lives, [yet was] very incurious about her own.'[8] Jean reported a similar sentiment in Nathaniel Micklem's memoir, *The Box and the Puppets*, nearly fifty years after she met him at Queen's.[9] 'He claims,' Jean wrote, that this book is 'not an autobiography [for] he has not found the contemplation of himself edifying or even an interesting exercise.'[10] There is gentle irony conveyed in Jean's choice of the word 'claims' – for why would someone write such a book if it were so tedious a project? Nor did she share Micklem's aversion to what he described as the 'curiously popular' trend toward 'psychological nudism.'[11] When she was twenty-five, she had reviewed the letters of Charles Lamb, declaring that 'there is an indefinable charm in the letters written by a man to his friends. For the letter is as a mirror reflecting one's inmost thoughts and desires. The reader is given an inner glimpse. He sees beyond the portals of another self.' All her reading life she retained this interest in the 'personal quality' that distinguished Lamb's letters, letters that were 'so intimate that I feel I have acquaintance with all the Lambs.'[12]

Yet in her personal practice, Jean hewed the Micklem line. She listened to others if they cared to speak of personal dilemmas, but there is no written or oral record that she ever reciprocated. Her preferred conversations were of the sort that animated the Micklem's Sunday night parties – covering, among other topics, history, philosophy, religion, politics, music, and the arts. As her friends Marie-Jeanne and John Coleman wrote, she tried 'to exchange views about as wide a range of topics as came to mind (none superficial!)'[13] and was 'a wise human being of universal culture and extraordinary vitality.'[14] Parting from Heilbrun, I decided that I could learn something from a woman who had no discernible desire to 'penetrate her own psyche' and whose attention always seemed to be 'out there' – albeit an out there that she carted inside to develop and sustain that most precious of resources, a 'well-stored mind.'

In writing any biography there is a lot of surmising to be done – or to be left undone. Jean's imbrication within the dense network of institutional and social relationships at Queen's permitted me to render her work life with some confidence. Not so with the rest. I had plenty of glimpses, enough to say that other lineaments of her life, criss-crossing the university as they did, neither began nor ended in that small place. I knew enough to destabilize easy truths about her, assumptions spun from observations and appearances, from the condescension of married to single, old to young, young to old, men to women, academics to administrators, the stylish – whether in matters of dress, sexuality or language – to those paying less attention. But there is an unnegotiable distance between this postmodern project and the writing of coherent parallel narratives about a woman who spoke little of herself, who lived most of her life alone, and who left few personal records. My motley array of sources left many spaces and untranscribed years: experiences without words, companions without names, tears without witnesses, untraceable pleasures.

Yet there is enough here to make a general claim. Jean's extracurricular life was primarily neither diversion nor escape. Her major institutional involvements, first in the Student Christian Movement (SCM) and later with the International Federation of University Women (IFUW), helped forge her identity as an internationalist and cosmopolitan. Her participation in these communities shaped and legitimated her world view and bolstered her commitment to challenge parochialism at Queen's. She came to Queen's, she recalled, for extramural studies, because it was the best available program. 'You know how hide-bound Queen's people are,' she added. 'I don't think that particularly interested me.'[15] That she confidently charted her own course for so long attests to her identification with those values she found in the SCM and the IFUW, and to the strength she garnered from working closely with people whose broad vision and sense of purpose she shared.

Jean's advice to students to remain untrammelled, to read broadly, to spend time away, to cultivate a spirit of adventure and open-mindedness, reflected major themes in her own life. From early childhood on, she mind travelled through the auspices of the public library and her love of books. She was never unkind about the narrow confines of her youth, nor later about the limitations and parochialism of Kingston and Queen's. She didn't have to be: much of the time her head was elsewhere. All her life, Jean's voracious reading took her on long nightly excursions.

Her modest bequest to the Kingston Public Library acknowledged the hundreds of books she had borrowed over the years. 'Today we were surprised to receive the cheque for one thousand dollars,' wrote the chief librarian, Moira C. Cartwright. 'It was always a joy to listen to her opinions of the many books she read and to accept her suggestions for purchase.' She was, Cartwright added, 'the sort of person who attracted high quality in library service.'[16] Some might have called her demanding, but those who also loved books responded generously to her informed enthusiasms.

During the 1930s and 1940s, book clubs and study groups provided a forum for an intellectual life, especially for women. On one occasion Jean contributed a paean to 'Books' – makers of revolutions, lonely archives of the past, the only promises for immortality – or so she posited. 'The pomp of ancient kings is no more. The glory of their cities is gone. What are these now? Names in a book, nothing more. Mighty men and great cities have perished, but the humble book has survived. No doubt Time will lay the same mortifying hand on our own civilization. In future when men shall puzzle over our crudities, and, let us hope be charitable for our ignorance, only in our books shall we make our defense.' She is up and away: 'history, biography, poetry, drama, all these and more, for with what Mr. Henry Sidgwick calls the altruism of literature the reader is led into the fields of the sister arts, painting, sculpture, architecture, music. A many-sided mistress is Literature, and the book is her medium.' This is the voice of Jean Royce – herself mistress of the book – in a 1940s living room, reading aloud, somewhat flushed by the end, her concluding metaphor resonating with her listeners, who would have been offended at the presence of a mistress. Her story of literature's influence is autobiographical: since childhood, books had been her licit and illicit companions. By the time she spoke these words, they had enticed her to art galleries and concert halls at home and abroad.

Not surprisingly, a person who read as greedily as she did, and whose interests and curiosities were so lively, yearned to travel. Even so, it is astounding that as early as the spring of 1933 – at the height of the Depression – she applied for a passport. Although others were worse off in those lean years, Jean was poor, too – even if her prospects were improving. In 1934 – after a considerable raise – her account book recorded her net assets as (minus) $13.81. At the time of her passport application, she hoped to be named Alice King's successor. By the time her passport reached her, however, the Board of Trustees had simply raised Jean from 'assistant to' status to assistant registrar. (Just so there was no misunderstanding, the board's letter of 10 May clearly identified her disqualifying distaff status.) Her new salary of $1,800 was retroactive to 1 April. This provided a modest windfall that financed her first trip abroad.

Jean's passport application reveals that over the same months she was establishing her indispensability at Queen's, she was also making getaway plans. Given her straitened circumstances, modest beginnings, and lack of connections, her desire for a passport reveals her to be exceptional. Young, single women of her background lacked cultural capital[17] and were unlikely to travel abroad, especially alone.[18] Jean's salary had a similar function to that of one of my more worldly colleagues, who explained that he made his money in Kingston but spent it elsewhere. Modest though it was, Jean's income provided her with the means to cultivate her love of art, indulge her endless curiosity about people and places, and develop an internationalist and cosmopolitan persona presaged neither by birth nor by circumstance.

Her passports and account books reveal her destinations and her expenses. The only other glimpses of her first two decades of travel are retrospective, found mainly in letters to Marion, in the travel advice she dispensed, and in her reminiscences. On a visit to Philadelphia in

1973, she succeeded in a project she 'failed to do about thirty years ago' and spent three 'rewarding hours at the Barnes in Merion.'[19] At a conference in Washington in 1961, she managed to 'slip away one morning [to visit] again the National Gallery' as well as the Phillips, 'one of the most delightful galleries' she knew. 'The new wing makes it more spacious and the paintings and the sculpture are displayed superbly. There is an intimacy and restfulness about the rooms that have a special charm.' Her last visit to Washington had been years earlier, and she had 'forgotten what a beautiful city.'[20] The travails of a small innkeeper near Kingston in 1974 reminded her 'of the Grand Hotel in Bruges where [she] stayed for a short while in 1948. There too they had all the difficulties apparent at Pine Lodge' – finding adequate help, a 'balky' furnace, high costs, and purchasing 'on a scanty scale.' She wasn't kidding: the Pine Lodge had been 'out of eggs last Sunday although the luncheon menu offered omelettes and egg salad sandwiches.' But the hotel in Bruges had 'one great advantage – an overall manager, an impressive Belgian woman, elegant in black satin and a long history of family experience in the business.'[21]

On her maiden voyage, in the summer of 1933, before she had secured her future as registrar, she went to England. What she did, whether she had companions, and how she managed to scrape together the money, can only be conjectured. She did go to Oxford, but we know this only because Marion asked her over four decades later whether she had read Cushing's life of Sir William Osler.[22] She had, and the book had made a big impression. 'At the time I was reading it,' she wrote, 'I happened to be in Oxford and I was taken out to the centre for older citizens for which he was responsible. This was forty-three years ago and Osler's idea of such a community was new.' She recalled the 'neat little square surrounded by small houses for singles and married couples [many] having tea on their doorsteps.' But the book remained the important thing: 'I still cherish my memories [reading] it [and] keeping it out of the Library a very long time to savour its contents.'[23] Her 'best friend' from Queen's days, Mary White, graduated from Oxford that summer. Perhaps they explored together, with Mary providing a bed or a piece of floor. Perhaps she visited Nathaniel and Agatha Micklem.

Another Queen's friend, Sarah Common, certainly awaited her. 'Your last letter was superb,' Sarah wrote. 'I am so glad that you're coming to England. Do let me be your guide sometimes in London. I know the place in its many moods and phases but I don't know it completely – no one ever does.' She raised many possibilities: 'I'd love to pilot you through Picadilly, then drop you a dozen yards or more away in Shepherd's Market and have you think you're in a quiet country village.' Jean proposed a trip to Germany, but Sarah couldn't 'say definitely yet. My thesis must be in by June 5th and my viva comes off a month later.' Sarah had 'a perfectly grand idea' for her thesis that involved Virginia Woolf's *Orlando*. 'I'm getting madder and madder ideas,' she enthused, 'ideas they're everywhere.'[24]

Sarah's plans for Jean invoke the same language that Jean employed in a short literary travelogue – presumably written for her study group on her return – titled 'Some London Byways.' The first person singular is absent; the piece could be derived entirely from the experience of others.

> 'Fine night. All's well.' This is not the call of a mediaeval night watchman as he makes his rounds, but the voice of the gold-braided porter of Ely Place, just off Holborn circus. Ely Place is a private thoroughfare in the heart of London, free from the jurisdiction of the City. If, at nightfall, we were to ask the porter for admission, he would produce a gigantic key to open the gate.
>
> But morning is the time to visit Ely Place. Then we may see the glory of the great east window of St. Ethelreda Church. St. Ethelreda is said to date from Saxon times. But regardless of its antiquity, the oak roof, the fig trees flourishing in the quiet cloisters, and the beauty of the windows make it one of the most interesting spots in London.

One of the most interesting to her? To those whose books she has devoured? She takes her sedentary travellers from Holborn 'through an archway into the aloofness of Staples Inn ... an old court set about with plane trees [behind] the noisy Strand [to] another oasis – the Temple [where] we may vision up Knights Templars walking in the garden in the evening, the plucking of the red and white rose, the crowds gathering to see Twelfth Night.' She conjures up Samuel Johnson, 'his solid figure coming and going from Fleet Street,' Charles Lamb, 'child of the Temple,' and, in Lincoln's Inn Fields, 'Sir John Soane, architect by profession, collector by hobby,' whose wife, someone 'suggested ... must have been a woman of infinite patience.' Did Jean follow this route? 'We have turned but a scant few of the pages of the book of London,' she concludes. 'Endless delights await our further searching.' Was 'the book' the source of her adventure or a metaphor for being there? What

ine? 'When a man is tired of London he is
on all that life can afford.' Is her voice com-
of Charles Lamb throughout? Or has she
n to evoke her own experiences?
cipher the sources for a paper she wrote on
. Echoing in these pages is the theme of her
dmother awaiting news of the military call-
th of her grandson. But now Jean is a cool,
sentimentality is absent as she draws from
of French history to illuminate the contem-
For nine years the Great War was awaited;
t: and its aftermath has been regarded as a
is a compelling read even now, more than
with a long book review and a similar trea-
reveals her extensive historical knowledge
world events, as well as the rigour of her
thought and the breadth of her vision.

The biggest 'problems dividing France today,' Jean informed her group, 'are largely legacies of the great revolution for the path of constitutional advance by revolution is difficult. Having run the gamut of political experiment through republic, empire and constitutional monarchy, she finally adopted the republican form after 1870 not so much because of any positive enthusiasm but because of the absence of any agreed alternative.' Also persisting as divisive forces from the revolutionary period, she continued, were both the 'great cleavage between the Republic and the Roman Catholic Church' and the open faultline over property. 'By making the mass of Frenchmen property holders, the Great Revolution ensured that the 'mass of public opinion' would be 'politically democratic but socially illiberal' and therefore in continuing conflict with the 'town industrial class.'

Jean's talk was dense with descriptions of the French Constitution and explanations for France's instability. However, when she discussed contemporary politics and news of the day, she made few concessions to her listeners. Her account of contemporary French politics – including mention of all thirteen political groups from left to right – must have been drawn from her experience travelling the country during the summer of 1934, but once again she never recruited a personal pronoun. 'It may be a cynical view,' she continued, 'to maintain that the only fascination left for the civilized Frenchman is the overthrow of government and yet may it not be the natural reaction of the disillusioned citizen who looks on hopeless division in political, social and religious issues, who sees treaties disregarded, financial panic in the air, increasing antipathy between liberal and conservative policies, disputes between capital and labour, profiteering, greed and unemployment, in short universal unrest?'

Aggravating this incendiary situation, she reminded her listeners, was 'the prospect of war, [for] every step that Germany has taken toward recovering her military power has increased the feeling of insecurity. Taxes to meet the growing military situation grow along with resentment against a government which has permitted the German menace to appear.' Yet, on that winter night in 1935,[25] the question she left in the air for her listeners to ponder did not concern Germany's ambitions, but rather internal French politics: 'Is the French stage being set,' she asked, 'for the entrance of a Fascist dictator?' Widening her lens, she observed that 'mass democracy ... is not educated, and is not noticeably in love with freedom. [A] vulgar, rough-shod dictatorship may express the unpleasant side of democracy's personality rather more truly than do the polite parliamentary politics of the educated middle class' – of which she also expressed few illusions. 'At certain times,' she suggested, 'a dictatorship may be the only means by which something of civilization can be saved from democracy.'[26] Nor could '[we] look at the present condition of Europe and North America without being struck by the docility of modern democracies to dictators.'

With these problems in mind, she returned to contemplate the future of France: 'In a country in which the Caesarian idea has already been twice embodied by Napoleonic action,' she wrote, 'it would be foolish to ignore its strength. The appearance of a popular leader or the recurrence of financial scandal may well bring to a head the distaste which is felt for the parliamentary machine.' Perhaps such a popular leader was already in sight, and she assumed that her audience knew the man: 'It is impossible to prophesy whether or not [François de] La Rocque will provide this leadership. His organization, originally nothing more than a small body of veterans, has grown to an army numbering over 300,000, and it is said that he has 600 recruits a day.'[27] La Rocque led the Croix de Feu, the largest of the right-wing leagues. Though all of them aimed to decimate the socialists and communists through popular action – including violence – most were also committed to ending Republicanism.[28]

The foreword to the English translation of La Rocque's book, *The*

Fiery Cross: The Call to Public Service in France, commended La Rocque for attempting 'to form a party which would appeal to all men of good will regardless of their political creed.' Yet 'he [has] been attacked [by the right] for remaining hitherto within the bounds of legality, [and] his personality has been described as lacking in those dynamic qualities which have made adored leaders of Mussolini, Hitler and, in the calmer atmosphere of English politics, Oswald Mosley.'[29]

French historiography generally insists that La Rocque and the Croix de Feu were not fascist, and Canadian historian William Irvine asks 'why so many French historians have so much invested in denying its fascism.'[30] For decades after the Second World War, accounts of French collaborationism took a back seat to those of French resistance, the history in which everyone wanted to believe. Seen in this light, Jean's focus on the emergence of (homegrown) French fascism and her invocation of La Rocque is striking. On his future, she wisely hedged her bets: 'La Rocque's slogan is "Take France away from the politicians and give it back to France." He has excited the anger of the communists, the socialists and some of the radicals. But up to the present his attitude has been fairly passive; he seems to be holding his forces in reserve for some unknown emergency. I will not venture an opinion as to how it will come out. Make of it what you will.'

Four years later, in an evocative review for her book club of *Fallen Bastions* by G.E.R. Gedye, 'one of the few Anglo-American journalists who stayed to see the curtain fall on the play,' Jean revealed her profound dismay about the step-by-step capitulation to Nazism. She lamented that 'the urgency of the situation' compelled Mr Gedye 'to compress the Austrian and Czech tragedies into one book. I feel sure that he must have had enough material on Austria, even though the Nazi arrival forced him to burn his archives, to write many further chapters ... If he had space and time he could have made his breathless and horrifying description of the last months of Czechoslovakia even more valuable by giving it a solid background of the Republic's evolution during the preceding decade, as he himself witnessed it.'[31]

Gedye's publisher, Victor Gollancz, had rushed *Fallen Bastions* into print. It appeared less than a month after Munich, with a foreword by the author warning that 'there is still time, but, I think, only just time. That is why, at whatever cost, I had to write this book – while there is still time.'[32] Jean described *Fallen Bastions* as 'tragic reading, and no one of his chapters have a more terrible quality than those in which he pictures the unleashing of Anti-Semitic and Anti-Marxist violence upon the helpless populations of Vienna and the Sudeten.' Jean must have completed her review just after the invasion of Poland, for at the end of the typewritten copy the following words appear in longhand: 'In the last few days, the world has learned of how Hitler has repaid Britain's services to him ... what is to come we know not – but ...'

After Pearl Harbor, Jean offered a paper exploring the economic, political, and cultural background for Japanese militarism.[33] 'Western powers had long since begun to divide China into spheres of influence for themselves. The New Japan began to want some of the cake too – therefore she made war on China in 1894 and set up an independent kingdom in Korea.' Subsequently, 'the War of 1904 made Japan an Eastern Power [and] the World War made her a World Power.' But, Jean assured her audience, 'the foundation of a prosperous national economy cannot be laid on war, [and when] war orders ceased to come in Japanese statesmen found themselves faced by a terrible problem.' By then 'every inch of land that could bear a crop was under cultivation [while] the population of the cultivated areas was nearly four times as dense as in England.'

Although both political parties that emerged after the Great War were 'opposed in principle to the militarists, they were not without interest in military expansion – the one stood to gain by expenditure on the army, the other by expenditure on the navy. As elsewhere, the politicians of Japan ... were corrupt, [representing] not the interests of the community but the interests of the two rival clans [and despite] the illusion of democracy ... the majority of the people remained very far from the control of their own destinies. The economic inequality became rapidly worse through the deepening of the abyss between the classes, wrought by the capitalist system of making labour a commodity, bound to a machine owned by the rich.'

She painted a devastating picture of life for most Japanese people in the decades after the Great War: 'the survival of certain remnants of the old feudal system, with its paternalism and unceremonious exploitation of employees; the earthquake of 1923 – a catastrophe from which she has not yet recovered'; the unrecognized struggle for trade unions, and the depression of 1930 which 'hit Japan with full force.' For food the people were left with the 'unsaleable residue of the rice crop [as] the World Crisis robbed their ships of cargoes and knocked down the price of silk and cotton goods.' And if this were not enough, she continued, 'the Chinese had set a boycott on Japanese goods and the British Dominions were building new tariff walls which Japanese exporters could not penetrate.' There was something of a moral to her tale: perhaps it was 'not surprising that Japan turned to war as the way out of the crisis.' Not a radical thought, in retrospect, but Canada was at war, and anti-Japanese sentiment had been mobilized by an appalling racialist discourse, light years from Jean's reasoned historical interpretation.

A paper titled 'Mexico,' dated January 1941, provides a dense history of the country from before the Spanish Conquest, couched in her own social and political views. 'In New England the Pilgrim Fathers busily shot the Indians and wrested their patrimony from them and then sent ships back for their wives [while] in Mexico the sons of the land survived and with tough temerity ... maintained their identity.' But, as she took pain to note, it wasn't easy. Spain 'introduced' not only the usual litany of diseases, but also the hacienda – 'a giant farm under the absolute domination of an individual.' The hacienda had to 'produce a crop large enough to keep the local Indians from starving, thus conserving the labour supply, and to keep the señor in velvet, wine and other extravagances.' When 'the Indians rose in rebellion the white Mexicans captured the revolutionary movement and forced the third estate back into their places. Matters went from bad to worse until 1857, when a Zapotec Indian appeared [named] Benito Juarez and his is probably the greatest name in Mexican history.' Though his reforms, '[which] separated church and state, wresting from the former the vast feudal possessions which had been amassed through native offerings and tithes,' were short-lived, she applauded his 'cold Indian cunning that cut straight at the heart of the evil.' But Juarez was succeeded by Porfirio Diaz, 'who made himself a Dictator and the country safe for foreign bankers and for tourists.'

Jean's prewar and wartime papers reveal that she was a woman of the world, internationalist in perspective, open-minded, and a harsher judge of political leaders than of those whose lives they affected. Her study of Japan displays especially her critique of the prevalent racialist discourse. Her engagement with the historical record provided complex explanations – though certainly not an apologia – for the wars raging in Europe and in the Pacific. Some of her economic critique is in the language of Marxism, but her commentaries on power and corruption, on the one hand, and her observations on the fragility of democracy and the dangers of putting stock in 'the people,' on the other, suggest that she wore no political labels. Clearly, she believed in education as humanity's best hope, though not as panacea for the ills, injustices, and inequalities of the world, which were complex and thoroughly informed by greed and ambition.

Jean's involvement with the Student Christian Movement provided the social and cultural context for much of her analysis. Founded in 1921, a critical spin-off from the YM/YWCA and Christian student groups,[34] and in tune with the Social Gospel movement,[35] the SCM sought to make a new world on this earth, a world in which people would settle their differences without war and treat one another with the love and respect embodied in their understanding of the life of Jesus. The SCMers were not at all fair-weather friends. 'We believe,' read a 1942 declaration, 'that the apparent tendency among Canadian students ... to discriminate against racial minorities, especially at this time against those of Japanese origin ... is contrary to the mind of Christ and is a challenge to the SCM to witness on the basis of its Christian convictions against all forms of race discrimination.'[36] The issues that captivated the SCM throughout its existence were 'peace; international relations: minorities – the Japanese Canadian, French-Canadian, Indian, Eskimo; and workers and industrial life.'[37] Within the SCM, Marxist ideas were taken seriously, and attempts to reconcile these ideas with a humanist Christianity informed discussion, created dissension, and led to strategic alliances with other peace and socialist groups.[38] The SCM was attacked in the 1920s for being 'modernistic' and for 'de-emphasizing doctrine,' and in the 1930s for being 'radical' and even a cover for 'potential communists.'[39]

Within the SCM, the social gospel phase predominated until the Depression, when radical Christianity began to gain influence. Throughout these years, SCMers gathered at conferences and workshops and at retreats such as Elgin House in Muskoka.[40] Elgin House was one of Jean's haunts in the late 1920s and 1930s, as she mentioned nearly half a century later, in a letter to her sister which she wrote after learning about the sudden death of an old friend, Marjorie Bier. Although Jean had not seen Marjorie for years, she kept 'a precious recollection of companionship at Elgin House. I am overwhelmed at the feeling that something good has gone out of the world.'[41]

In conference papers and oral histories, the idealism, enthusiasm, and dedication of the young people gathering at Elgin House stand out clearly. An SCM-sponsored petition to Prime Minister R.B. Bennett, aimed at influencing the 1932 Geneva Conference on Disarmament, garnered 10,000 signatures.[42] The SCM's principal project before the Second World War was pacifism, but it was a strategic pacifism that would later be abandoned in the face of 'German Fascism's' denial that men were 'brothers in the fatherhood of God.' Just after the Nazi invasion of Czechoslovakia in 1938, the SCM declared 'that the threat to the freedom of the Czechoslovakian people is a threat to the freedom of all peoples, including the people of Canada.'[43]

In the 1930s, Jean served a year as honorary president of Queen's SCM. In that decade and later in the 1950s she made occasional small donations to it. Then, from 1963 through 1966, she provided an 'annual gift' of $100.[44] By then the SCM had protested against nuclear weapons and the war in Vietnam, and against 'racial injustice,' especially in South Africa.[45] 'In the mood of the sixties,' historian Doug Owram noted, 'the SCM translated the idea of Christian stewardship into a radical critique of contemporary society.'[46]

Though Jean's views on the key issues of the day in the 1930s, 1940s, and 1950s found a congenial home within the SCM, her financial support in the 1960s reveals that she never lost her affinity for this 'theologically liberal and politically left-wing'[47] student movement. It isn't clear how much it was the Jesus side of SCM that compelled Jean's attention. She never wrote about this. After she left home she went only irregularly to church, and later not at all. But SCMers were religious folk, and Jean's religious knowledge was extensive. Over the decades, debates within the movement swung the pendulum between religious thought and social action.

Although Jean's papers and SCM involvement indicate her engagement with economic, political, and social history, only snippets survive detailing her early interest in theatre and the arts. When she visited Ottawa in August 1934, most likely driving with a friend, her only expenses were a nickel for an *Ottawa Gazette* and 50 cents for a picture from the National Gallery. At Christmas the same year she visited New York, the entire adventure setting her back $60. If her later New York itineraries are any guide, she was there to go to the theatre, visit art galleries, and imbibe the atmosphere.[48] After spending Christmas 1959 in New York, she wrote of 'rediscovering a city' noting that she had forgotten how stimulating it was. 'I liked the Beekman Towers very much and enjoyed the neighbourhood. There is a quiet elegance about the little streets on the River side of the Hotel and the Drug Store on the corner of First Avenue – where we had coffee several times at midnight – brings together an amazing collection of types.' Who 'we' were remains unclear, although her notebook includes the names of New York friends from the International Federation of

Women, as well as the plays they saw: *Heartbreak House*, 'with a galaxy of stars including Maurice Frays and Diana Wynyard,' *Five Finger Exercise*, 'a rather slick British production directed by John Gielgud,' and *At the Drop of a Hat*.

Jean praised *A Raisin in the Sun* as the best play she had seen for some time. She was not alone in her assessment: the play subsequently won the New York Drama Critics' Circle Award, making Lorraine Hansberry, 'at 29, the youngest American, the first woman and only black [playwright]' to win the coveted award.[49] Jean wrote: 'To me, [the play] represents the problem of poverty rather than colour. Indeed the problem of the latter begins at the play's end.' As the play ends, a Black family stretching economically into the middle class discovers the entrenched *de facto* residential segregation of northern cities.

Jean also visited New York's galleries. 'On the second try we got into the Guggenheim (the first time we went, there was a queue as far as Madison Avenue and growing). It is monstrous and wonderful. The first adjective applies to the exterior. I found the interior very satisfying indeed. I have never before been able to see paintings from so many angles.' This was a pleasure trip: she informed Marion tersely, 'I did not make any contacts at the United Nations.' In effect, she was telling her sister that she hadn't taken her advice on how to spend time in this Mecca. Marion worked for years in the international arena, and her political commitments to peace and women rated high on her agenda. She expected her younger sister not only to share these commitments, but also to respond in similar ways. Jean's accounting for how she spent – and didn't spend – her time confirms that childhood practices die hard.

On the other hand, in the same letter Jean shared a different sort of thought with Marion, one of well-disguised intimacy. 'I was amused,' Jean wrote, 'at a call from the Leggets the other night. Robert checked carefully on all my activities in New York and expressed surprise that anyone would want to spend a holiday there.'[50] Robert was not, of course, in a position to say aloud: But why are you in New York without me? But his lack of comprehension seems a discreet lament, and neither sister would have been deceived. Marion must have endured many visits with Robert in which Jean was the spoken or unspoken object around which conversation swirled.

On one occasion, in the spring of 1946, Robert moved heaven and earth for a few hours with Marion, who was on the staff of the International YWCA in Geneva:

> I had to make a special 'Top Secret' mission to Switzerland, to see a new snow and ice laboratory. Decked out as a temporary Lt. Colonel and, in uniform, [I] traveled to London, Frankfurt and on to Berne and Zurich. My schedule was, naturally, so tight that there was no possibility of seeing Marion in daytime and I felt that I must see her being so close. So, with her full agreement, I got a train from Zurich to Geneva [arriving] at about two a.m. Marion met me; we spent a delightful hour or two, walking the lovely streets and parks of Geneva (by moonlight) before having a meal around four a.m. at an all-night restaurant. Marion did, naturally, unbend a little during this escapade which we naturally kept to ourselves but Jean knew of it and, I think, approved of the efforts I had to made to see her sister.[51]

Robert provided the story to emphasize that Marion and Jean were 'so very different, it was hard to believe they were sisters. Jean, small in stature, full of fun (i.e., the "other Jean") and so lovable (for want of a better word); Marion ... much taller, always reserved, or almost always and always serious!' Perhaps serious, but Marion was also observing Robert. As she once confided to Celia, 'Robert had been in love with Jean all those years.'[52]

We also have Robert's account of how he came to know Jean. He and his wife, Mary, came to Queen's in the fall of 1936, the first hire, he wrote, since the crash of 1929. The Kingston welcome in those days was – shall we say – restrained. 'We were "observed" by proper Kingstonians to see if we were socially acceptable [while] only one of the four full Professors who made up the staff of the Department of Civil Engineering ever called on us.'

Robert's walk across the 'pleasant park to his University duties' brings us (slowly) closer to our story:

> Gradually I got to know the regular walkers along this route. Quite the most unusual was a middle-aged man ... After seeing him a number of times, I made an attempt in greeting but got no response at all. Nor did I succeed in doing so throughout the two years I used that walk. If he saw me approaching, he would make the most hilarious efforts to avoid looking me in the eye and so not once did I ever get even the suspicion of a smile out of him.

The man who wasn't looking for a friend was Professor George Humphrey, who gave his name to the Psychology Building at Queen's.

> But there was also a young lady who was also a 'regular' on that walk, always plainly but nicely dressed, always walking with a firm lady-like stride. It was not too long before we exchanged smiles, shy youth as I most certainly was. And that [was] how I first met Jean!

He recalled, however, that it was Mary who first invited Jean 'to drop in for a cup of tea one Sunday.' With her young son in tow, she also clocked in time in the park. One day 'Jean stopped to pat David on the head. Soon Mary and she were exchanging greetings, shyly since my dear one was not an extrovert.'

> All this was in the spring of 1937. By the start of the 1937–38 session, we had happily slipped into a regular pattern for Jean's visits – every Sunday afternoon! For she, too, was 'lonely' in a sense, away from her office. She would come along late in the afternoon for an initial cup of tea and some happy talk. After 'high tea' (the only hang-over, I think, from our British upbringing!), and more good talk our evenings together always finished with me getting out my portable 78-rpm gramophone. At Jean's request, we finished our evening with the music of Bach, and with these wonderful sounds in our ears, I would walk with her along the deserted Wellington Street to see her safely home, Mary joining us occasionally.
>
> In our late evening walks, she would confide in me (and Mary, too if she was with us) some of the problems of the week, the difficulties she faced, initially, as a woman in such a position and naturally I did what I could to help. I must add that those lovely walks were of help to me, too ... as I would tell her of my struggles to be a good lecturer under the watchful eye of the great, and unique, Sandy MacPhail.

Robert's travails, in this respect, were rather unusual, and Jean was not amused by his account of them:

> After my interview with Dr. Wallace, 'Sandy' said, as we walked away together, 'I'm sure that Dr. Wallace will be a good Principal but the dear man knows nothing about teaching. Now this is the way we'll work together. When I come in on Tuesdays and Thursdays, if I feel up to it, I'll take the three lectures; if I don't, then you can take them.' And so I never knew until a few minutes before the first lecture if I was to take [the others]! Jean was so cross when she heard this, as she was when she found out that I was doing all the (sub) editorial work for the Q.Q. [*Queen's Quarterly*].

In the spring of 1938, Robert received a 'third request from Dean C.R. Young of the University of Toronto, to join his staff.' It was a difficult decision, and 'giving up those wonderful evenings with Jean was one of the very real factors we had to weigh.' Jean helped them reach the decision to accept, as did Sandy MacPhail, who told him:

> 'You don't know how good one University is, Legget, until you've seen another. Go, and see what the place is like but *come back*.' And so I accepted, with the full intention of coming back to Queen's, so had Jean inspired me with her own devotion to her Alma Mater.
>
> The memory of those late evening walks are still vivid and it was in this way, I feel sure, that Jean and I became such close friends – in a strictly platonic way! I can not now recall ever kissing her in the happy social way that men may kiss their closest women friends, until her last sad days when holding her tight and kissing her were the only means left of real communication. I was often amused when Jean would go out of her way at any social gathering, to keep me at my distance (so to speak) so that others would not know what close friends we were, so jealous was she of her independence as The Registrar!

What did Jean think of all this? Only a small fragment remains. One evening, in the last years of her life, she slipped lucidly into the past and had a conversation with Robert. 'Will you be alright if I send you away?' she asked. Margaret was certain, then and now, that Jean was remembering the spring of 1938 when Robert moved to Toronto.[53]

Robert recorded an encounter from 'just before the end of the war [when] Jean and I both managed to attend one of the rather exclusive Hazen conferences held to develop some clear thinking for what lay ahead.' Though Jean was 'her usual serious self,' keeping her customary public distance from Robert, she did suggest – much to his surprise and delight – that they 'spend one of the free afternoons in a boat!'

Although Robert 'was far too shy to suggest' such a madcap idea himself, he made her wish his command. 'I rowed us up into Sand Lake on a simply perfect day, and there we spent a truly magical afternoon together, recapturing the strange intimacy of our late Sunday evening walks, talking about "everything under the sun" as we drifted around the lake, enchanted by the lovely scenery and the serenity of the day.'

Strangely enough, despite 'the happiest general recollections,' Robert remembered but one detail from their adventure – that 'Jean brought with her a most elegant [and unneeded] rain coat.'

Robert was of the old school (the age of chivalry was not dead), and his great regret was that 'in her hour of need,' when Alex Corry axed her, Jean did not call on him, 'her closest male friend. This baffling question,' he wrote, 'dominates all my thoughts about Jean.' Essentially, he believed he could have saved her. His simple but air-tight plan involved his long friendship with Queen's Chancellor John B. Stirling, whom he first met in 1935. 'In spite of the difference in our ages (almost twenty years) a special sort of friendship grew up between us [growing] stronger and (for me) more valuable as the years went on.' And, as with conversations between Robert and Marion, there were few visits or phone calls in which 'we [didn't] get round to Jean, for whom he had the greatest respect and admiration.'

'If only Jean had called me,' Robert anguished, 'if only she had just let me know when the blow fell, I would have called J.B. instantly and I can, in imagination, hear him say so clearly, "Get your hat on, Robert, and we'll go and beard Alex Corry in his office. As Chancellor, I will just order him to rescind that disgraceful order."' And the good boys would have triumphed over the good old boys, saving the damsel in distress. 'I am as certain as I am sitting here that between J.B. Stirling and me, we could have had that terrible action of the Principal reversed so that Jean could have finished her great service to Queen's as she had hoped, expected and (probably) planned. If only ...'[54] Perhaps it is not that surprising that Jean did not tell Robert.

We don't know whether or not there were other men in Jean's life. If so, they were not so obliging as to provide memoires. That said, Jean had many intimate encounters over the years. Once, in her later years at Tanglewood, after she had seen – for the umpteenth time – Leonard Bernstein conducting, a young friend asked her: 'Would you like to go to bed with him?'

'No, I don't like to go to bed with people I don't know.'

'But you do know him.'

'Not in that way.'

A woman who knew nothing of such pleasures would not have replied in this way. For women of Jean's generation, whose flirtations were with men and who did not intend to marry, little room existed for love affairs. Single women took risks if they turned would-be lovers into lovers: pregnancy, reputation, and livelihood, to note three. Would

Queen's have stood for a libertine registrar?[55] Jean knew the score. Women of her era who entered the work world found limited scripts, and the one that Jean Royce opened was normative for the time. She played her part well, cultivating that manner of dress and tone that invited respect, conveyed authority, and permitted assumptions of asexuality. But as Robert Legget's memoir reveals, not everyone was meant to be persuaded that the packaging told the whole story.

But packaging never tells the whole story, especially when it comes to the complicated terrain of sexuality. Above I used the term 'flirtation' rather than desire, because for many people sexual orientation is not signed, sealed, and delivered early in life. In the past few decades there has been more social acceptance of homosexuality and a good deal more drifting across boundaries. Jean enjoyed the company of women; in another era, who is to say how she might have lived? My intention here is to resist labelling, to resist treating sexuality – her sexuality, in this case – as an 'essence.' Sexual practices, desires, and fantasies have histories, and arise from complex psychic negotiations that bear more than the casual markings of cultural context.

I have puzzled also over the place that Jean's family had in her spatial and emotional map during the years she was at Queen's. Outwardly, Jean seemed a dutiful, even perfunctory daughter, sister, and aunt, but little more: she helped support her mother; she visited Toronto regularly, but not often; her letters to Marion include references to her brothers' various children, but until after her retirement none of them got main billing. Her nieces and nephews – with the exception of Gail – retain few childhood memories of Jean; their other aunts register higher on the Richter scale.

Yet from small things, I concluded that her attachment to her mother was profound and that this informed her affections and attitudes toward her siblings and their children. 'You get more than anyone I know out of the ten-cent stamp,' Jean wrote Marion when they were both well retired, 'and as always the letters are delightful. I find myself thinking often of the pleasure with which we received them when you first went to Toronto. They were a weekly refreshment for the whole family. They took us into a new world which we all enjoyed and mother was literally captivated. They seemed a kind of recompense to her. I am sure she read each one of them over and over again.'[56]

Katherine Royce was clearly an exceptional woman. She raised five children in conditions of respectable working-class poverty, and all of them achieved middle-class status. Her two older daughters, departing from her example but probably not her advice, remained single and childless, and each made a considerable public mark, mainly through paid employment.

Their brother Donald was convinced that Marion was the more extraordinary.[57] First in her church, then with the International YWCA in Geneva, later – in her prime – as first director of the Women's Bureau of the Federal Department of Labour, and finally in her 'retirement' years at OISE, she lived an uncharted life, pressing pragmatic pacifist and feminist agendas all the while.[58] When both were in their seventies, Jean urged her to consider 'writing [her] autobiography [for] there cannot be many Canadian women who have had so varied a life as you.'[59] This was not just a random thought. A few months later, while writing the citation for an honorary degree for Sylva Gelber, Marion's successor at the Department of Labour, Jean realized 'all over again that she is following in your footsteps.'[60] But Jean was 'rather shake[n] by the differences' between their budgets, and appreciated 'more than ever how much you did on so pitifully small a sum. I feel very proud of you and of what you accomplished. You are a distinguished woman.'[61] What a formal way to describe a sister! – but no less true for that. Marion led the way in negotiating a life of professional commitment and social and political engagement. She cut a wide swath, providing both space and foil for Jean.

But there was no easy comfort in Jean's relationship with Marion, no maternal substitution. When Katherine Royce died, in Kingston on 26 March 1946, Jean was bereft, and not just in the short term.[62] So she suggested in a letter to Margaret on the death of her mother. 'I know that we have talked of this more than once,' she wrote, 'but I shall speak of it again. Life is never the same after one's mother death. There is no one to whom one can talk to in the same way, no one who can give the same reassurance and comfort. And yet there are warm memories of courage, endurance, warm companionship and understanding that remain always. They are rooted deeply within the consciousness and give strength to life.'[63] No Hallmark sentimentalist, Jean revealed that with her mother's death came a new loneliness that she sought to accept rather than counter. New confidantes were not there for the asking, and besides, one never asked.

We might wonder why Katherine was with Jean when she died, given that her apartment was in Toronto and that most of her children lived there most of the time. But in the aftermath of the war, Marion was in Geneva and Donald in Washington working for munitions procurement for the Australian government.[64] Catherine, married for ten years, was thought fragile by her family, and perhaps her marital status provided immunity, as Jean once suggested when a friend, 'as the single one [took] the heavier toll ... I expect that is always the way.'[65] Stewart was immersed in his own family tragedy. In 1945 his wife, Nina, was diagnosed with multiple sclerosis, and their eight-year old daughter, Gail, was sent to board at Moulton College, where she stayed – through her mother's death in 1947 – until she was a teenager. Alone among her siblings and cousins, Gail declared Jean her favourite. After Nina's death, her father purchased a car, and she remembered weekend visits to Kingston. She enjoyed them, as did Jean.[66]

From her comments, it seems that at least when it came to Gail, Jean displayed a maternal side that her other nieces and nephews with their more straightforward lives didn't see. 'She looked adorable,' Jean wrote, just after Gail had arrived for summer school at Queen's. 'She had just washed her hair and after a day or two at camp had some tan.'[67] The adorable-looking girl was twenty-four, and Jean wasn't in the habit of 'adorable-ing' adults, nor remarking on their last hair wash.

Ian, the oldest of Donald's children, recalled that neither Marion nor Jean had any 'ability to have an emotional connection with a kid. Kids were foreign things. [But] I am sure they cared about me a lot.'[68] Gail was born when Jean was thirty-three. All of her six other nieces and nephews were born after she was forty-six. So except for Gail, the children had an older aunt, perhaps more remote than she had been to Gail.

Through rose-coloured glasses, Robert Legget certainly remembered another Jean, from the halcyon days of their early friendship. 'When our son's bedtime approached, she would don one of Mary's large aprons and lead him off to undress him, and then bath him [and tuck] him into bed. She loved doing this, displaying so clearly her "motherly" instincts, later to be submerged.'[69] This last remark was not such a long-shot, though there are only bits of supporting evidence. On 7 December 1941,[70] Gleb and Valentina Krotkov had friends for tea, their eleven-year-old daughter Mary helping serve. 'But why,' Mary wondered, 'was everyone clustered around the radio, great tension in the air?? Jean Royce took me on her knee and held me. I remember [her] well and [this is] my fondest memory of her.'[71] Young Harold Harkness, whose father, R.D., had joined the Physics Department in

1938, was also one of Jean's 'great favourites.' Every afternoon after school, he would cross Union Street over to Queen's, where one person or another kept an eye on him. Jean used to say, 'not by way of criticism,' 'Maud was never home, so we all looked after Harold.' Harold's mother, Maud, was 'a bigwig in the alumni association,' her daughter-in-law, Elizabeth, told me, and she preferred being out and about. 'Jean was like a babysitter, but not a mother hen,' Elizabeth related, 'she had great dignity – and she just loved Harold.'[72]

But Lord help the child who turned up uninvited. 'On Saturday mornings,' Duncan Sinclair remembered, 'my brother and I took piano lessons from Miss Phyllis Knight,' Jean's landlady and downstairs neighbour. 'On more than one morning, I fear, [Miss Royce] appeared at the head of the stairs, distinctly not amused, when my brother and I, arriving before 9 a.m., chanced to ring the wrong doorbell. Stern of visage and very firm of voice, I still recall being enjoined *never* to mistake the bell again!'[73]

Jean's comments about her nieces and nephews are fond,[74] sometimes anxious, and in later years even admonishing. When Ian was nine, visiting Marion in Ottawa, Jean wrote from England: 'Do tell him how much I envy you having him for a bit.'[75] Two weeks later she repeated the sentiment: 'Your letter about Ian filled me with envy. I had a note from him addressed with meticulous care telling me that he had seen the Changing of the Guard, and had been to Hull with the Leggets. He mentioned that you had given him some coins but that he did not have any Belgian, Swedish or Finnish money and would like to add to his collection.'[76]

After a visit with Donald's children, when Shelagh was four, she sounded every inch a fond, observant aunt. 'Celia and the children plus the dog were just back from the Island,' she wrote. 'They had had a wonderful time. Shelagh's face lighted up with enthusiasm as she talked. She was particularly excited about some pigs they had seen; [their] size impressed her tremendously. Brenda chimed in from time to time and Ian with the wisdom of his advanced state made suitable explanations ... Both girls were intrigued that I was going to Mexico that night. They asked me to bring them diamonds, but later, after they were in bed, called Ian and asked him to tell me not to bother with diamonds.' On reflection, they decided 'that they would like dolls.'

Jean was especially taken with Shelagh's question to her Aunt Catherine: 'Do you know her,' she asked, pointing at Jean, 'as well as I know Brenda?'[77]

Royce family picture, 1909. Left to right: Jean, Katherine, Catherine, David, Stewart, Marion

Marion Royce, high school graduation, 1918

Jean, Queen's University graduation, 1929

Levana Executive, *Tricolour* 1929. Back row: Margaret Clarke, Geraldine Boyce, Maude Whattam, Edna Baird, Mary White, Fern Johnston. Middle row: Ruth Walker, Jean Royce, Helen Grange, Korleen Ball, Mary Van Dusen. Front row: Janet Allan (president), Mrs R. Bruce Taylor (honorary president), Agnes Pretty (vice-president)

Katherine Royce's Birthday, 7 May 1937. Left to right: (Unknown), Gordon Alderson (Catherine's husband), Celia, Katherine, Marion, Catherine, Donald

Jean with her niece Gail, 1937

Jean with friends, 1940s. Eleanor Tett is on Jean's right.

Jean at her desk, early 1940s

Students registering in Douglas Library. Jean is visible, seated at the third desk on the right.

Jean at Palazzo Pitts, Florence, June 1948

Jean in St Cergue, Switzerland, 11 July 1948

International Federation of University Women, Helsinki, July 1959. Jean is second from right, in the front row; A. Vibert (Allie) Douglas is second from left in the front row.

Robert Legget, after receiving an honorary degree from Queen's, 14 May 1966. Front row: Principal J.A. Corry, Robert Legget, Chancellor J.B. Stirling, A.B. Kinzel (honorary degree recipient), J.H. Brown (Dean of Applied Science). Back row, third from right, Vice-Principal Hugh Conn

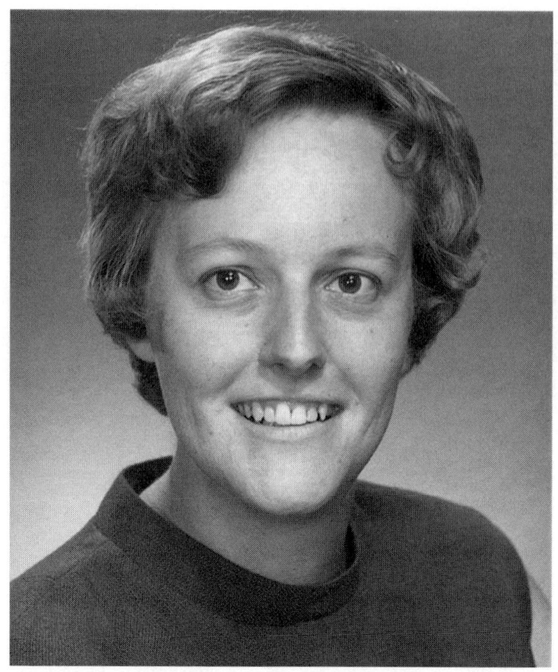

Margaret Hooey, 1968

Jean with Phyllis Knight, spring 1968, in front of their home, with the Queen's campus in background

Jean on the eve of her retirement, 1968

Jean receiving her honorary degree, 8 November 1968. Front row, left to right: Chancellor Stirling, Rector Gratton O'Leary, Vice-Principal George Harrower. Behind Harrower are Principal Emeritus W.A. Mackintosh and the Ontario minister of education, William Davis.

Jean and Margaret, October 1968, embarking on the *Leonardo da Vinci* from New York to Lisbon

Jean, Bill Cannon, Margaret Hooey, Dawn Cannon, Bill Clarke, Jessie Jean Cannon in Margaret's garden, summer 1980

Jean in front of Margaret's house, fall 1981

But Jean's interest in and fondness for her brothers' children didn't keep her Kingston-bound. Lyn doesn't remember her much at holiday times, and imagines that Catherine's vivacity monopolized all the space reserved for aunts.[78] For most of Lyn's childhood, in fact, Jean passed on family Christmas, following up her 1959 trip to New York – Robert's incomprehension notwithstanding – with four more Christmases in that cultural haven. In 1962 she actually travelled to New York on Christmas Day. Since most of the continent's travelling aunts reached their destinations in time to watch small nieces and nephews open presents, she bagged a very low train fare. Her Christmas holiday included a 'morning at the public library, an interesting afternoon at the exhibition of sculpture (Henry Moore, Daumier, David Smith) at the Guggenheim, [and] much walking through the byways of this area and up and downtown.' Though she found herself sighing for London theatre prices she 'saw one good play (The Affair), a talking academic situation with some delightful caricatures of university types' and a 'so-so' play with Joseph Cotton, 'the story of a family's struggle to maintain control of a woollen mill and succeeding in doing so by rather skillful manipulation of a manipulator.'[79] She also 'sandwiched in three excellent movies – an enchanting French film "Sundays and Cybile," and "Electra," a new Greek production with magnificent photography,' though, as she pointed out, the title was misleading: '[The play] was based directly on Euripides.' But it was the third film, *The Loneliness of the Long Distance Runner*, 'a harsh comment on the problems of adolescent delinquency with all the roots, but no suggestion of a solution,' that she recommended to her sister.

Jean's many travels suggest that after her mother's death, she felt unencumbered. Without financial or emotional dependents, she planned her discretionary time in ways that satisfied her desire to see interesting places and kept her abreast of generations of students. 'I had occasional letters from her during the years I spent in Chicago and Zurich,' Mabel Corlett recalled, 'and from these gained some inkling of her diversity. There was no place that I ever mentioned visiting that didn't evoke some anecdote from her – even the Lido beach in Venice.'[80] Ann Saddlemyer's 'first excited trip to Italy called forth rhapsodies of Florence and Rome, monuments and libraries. Had Jean Royce been everywhere? Deciding whether to go to the University of London or Trinity provoked a lyrical description of Georgian architecture and the quiet Irish countryside.'[81] Jean's own one-liners, casually dropped years later, reveal yet another small thing. In 1976, Billy Daniels was entertaining on a cruise. 'He is an old man now,' she wrote, 'but he still sings magnificently.' Inadvertently, however, he elicited 'one regret: the other night he sang "Ole Man River"; a long time ago I heard Paul Robeson sing the same song and to my mind nothing can touch his interpretation.'[82]

Jean could only leave town for pleasure – for longer than a weekend – twice a year. We have spied on her Christmas holidays – often in New York City – and this leaves her month-plus summer vacation. Even in the barely captured glimpses that remain, her love for travel and for variety (of people and place) shines through. By the time war broke out, she had made three round trips across the Atlantic, and after 1948 it was only the occasional summer that left her passport unstamped. In 1948 she launched herself in Naples and travelled in Belgium, Switzerland, and England. All we have, in her own words, from that trip is the black-satin lady of Bruges, although she did hold the members of the University Women's Club 'spellbound with a colorful and sensitive description of her travels and of the many interesting personalities she encountered.'[83]

Not until 1954 do we have any first-person reportage, and this on flimsy air mail paper that must have torn even as Marion removed it from the envelope – confirmation, if any were necessary, that she didn't expect someone to be swotting over it nearly half a century later. Despite the missing words and the fading ink, this fascinating letter helps compensate for the dearth of earlier material. For three weeks that year, and two summers thereafter, she attended sessions sponsored by the Netherlands Universities Foundation for International Cooperation. 'The summer course is an interesting project,' she wrote, 'and obviously very dear to the hearts of the educational authorities. There is strong competition for it among the universities; they vie with each other.' That first summer she was at the University of Utrecht, on return engagements at the University of Groningen and the Technological University of Delft. 'Authorities co-operate by helping to find accommodation,' she explained, 'in providing free transportation and in giving free admission to all Museums and Exhibitions.'[84]

During these 1950s summers she studied 'Trends in Modern Civilization' with various subtitles: 'Vital Forces in Western Europe,' 'Civilization and Technics,' and 'Communications in Our Shrinking Modern World.' At the end of the first week of the first summer, she waxed enthusiastic: 'I think the lectures must include Holland's best; certainly I have never heard better presentations.' She didn't spend all her time in the lecture hall. The day before, the whole cohort were 'guests of the city of Amsterdam with a reception, a luncheon, [and] a conducted tour of the Rijksmuseum.'[85] The next week they were off 'to Drenthe and North East Polder to visit the Zuderzie land reclamation project'; in the final week it was Rotterdam and the Hague and the Van Gogh Centre at Hage Veleuwe.' Jean was 'particularly pleased' about the last: 'I have wanted to go there for a long time.'

'For the most part,' she reported, 'there is no nonsense with the Dutch; they do things with great seriousness and thoroughness; there is a sound background of reading and factual knowledge that is impressive if a little lacking in humour.' Her fellow students ranged from a college president and a justice of the court of Idaho (both retired), through teachers, and people from Ireland and England, 'to a large group from Nigeria and the Gold Coast, most of whom were at London, Oxford and Cambridge.'

However, Jean told her sister – newly appointed as first director of the Women's Bureau of the Department of Labour[86] – that she feared 'we shall not be giving much time to women. Mrs Verney Jonker who was asked to deal with women's social position is unable to do it and they have not succeeded in finding a substitute. "We are not interested in women," said Mrs Brandt, the ambassador's wife whom I met in London last summer and I think she is fairly representative. Indeed, several women with whom I have talked appear to be somewhat consciously superior about filling their place in the home. They have all mentioned the irresponsibility of American women towards home and children.'

One of these women was her hostess's neighbour, 'a charming girl with a very modest but attractive house and two darling children, one of four and one of two. She told me that she had graduated in Law and had worked for two years but had given it up gladly to marry. She added that, "unlike American women I do not work out. I stay at home and look after my husband and children."' Jean added some corroborating evidence for the prevalence of her life choice: 'The characteristic early morning sound of Holland is the beating of the rugs – I noticed it in Amsterdam and I hear it in Utrecht.' But she didn't lose hope of finding contrary-minded Dutch opinion: 'I am going to dinner tomorrow night,' she wrote, 'with Dorothy Hefting, an I.F.U.W. person and I shall be interested in her comments. She is unmarried and may have other views.'

Jean sounded a native and had much to say. 'I have become a householder of Utrecht,' she continued. 'My hostess has gone to Nijmegen for the weekend and I have the flat to myself. It is an attractive place in a new section of the city; the living room windows look out on the Utrecht-Amsterdam canal and farm meadows lie beyond. All day long barges slide by on their way to Amsterdam, carrying every kind of freight.' Her letter ended with a weather report: 'quite the worst I have ever experienced and the houses are not very comfortable. Hot water is the chief lack. [W]e have to admit that the people on the American continent have a genius for making life physically comfortable. I wish we carried with it the Dutch love of books. All these modest little houses have full book shelves and the book shops are wonderful.' She squeezed her name along the side, and then mobilized the little space above the salutation to inform Marion that she had encountered 'great interest in the uses of atomic energy, [which] is approached as a moral issue.' She also told her to 'take C.P. Snow's *New Men*' along on vacation. 'Britnells will know of it,' she added confidently.[87]

Many of her travels, before and after her studies in the Netherlands, focused on the IFUW. From 1947 through 1962 she attended the federation's triennial meetings – in Toronto, London, Paris, Helsinki, and Mexico City. In the postwar atmosphere of determination and hope, the IFUW offered her a generous mixture of friendship, shared interests, and political and social engagement.

The IFUW was founded in 1919 and was organized at international, national, and local levels. In 1943 the Canadian federation began promoting local groups as well. Within three years the number of clubs had risen from thirty-eight to fifty-four.[88] One of the first off the ground, in November 1943, was Kingston's. At the twenty-fifth anniversary of the club, on 9 October 1968, Jean delivered a short history lesson, a modest founding myth. At the time 'there were experienced and sophisticated advisers living in the city,' among them 'Dr. A. Vibert Douglas [who] awakened them to the value of the [international federation] and the world scene [and] Dr. Ursula Macdonnell [the president of the CFUW] who had come to live in Kingston' following her retirement from the University of Manitoba.

That night Jean 'pinch-hit' for Betty Phillips, 'who sparked the enthusiasm' for the club's establishment. Jean herself had been but 'a cog in the wheel, [albeit] the only current member of the club who served on the [first] Executive.'[89] Jean invited her audience 'to think back a quarter of a century and try to recapitulate the scene in November and December 1943. We were at the height of the Second World

War; plans were in embryo for the launching of the D-Day Invasion.' It was a time, she reminded them, of scarcity, uncertainty and confusion, when bad news from overseas seemed always to diminish the good. 'It was a time when people wanted to establish roots, to have the companionship of friends. They wanted to have a part in the building of a better and wiser world and they wanted opportunity for constructive talk.'

She tactfully explained the club's inauguration: this 'pleasantly residential city was growing apace. The war brought a large influx of military personnel,' and the new aluminum plant attracted staff 'whose wives were university graduates [as well as] female personnel with degree status.' For this new crowd, which had 'lived for the most part in large urban areas and had enjoyed the intellectual benefits of metropolitan society,' Kingston no doubt felt – though Jean didn't say so – like the end of the world. She noted that the new residents 'were up and coming women with ideas about the development of society, [interested] in public affairs, the international scene, in music and art and ballet, in education, in recreation in the various disciplines, in the place of women in the community, in satisfactory opportunities for their children.'

Within two or three years, she continued, the club had established itself as a force in the life of the community. It was approaching the government with resolutions, participating in regional and national meetings, contributing to overseas relief funds, forming study groups, and establishing local scholarships. Notwithstanding her self-description as a mere 'cog in the wheel,' Jean had played a noteworthy role at the local level in the early years. The year her mother died she was the club's president, and before and after that she was program chair. Her own interests are evident in the speakers she selected: her friend André Biéler addressed the question 'What about Modern Art?' and Hilda Hays described her experiences in a Japanese internment camp. Executive meetings often took place in her apartment, which was also used as drop-off centre during a clothing drive for refugees.[90]

A stenographer's notebook that Jean used during the 1940s corroborates her empathy with the club's internationalism and points to her later involvement with the IFUW. In it she drafted her paper on Japan as well as notes for a paper on India. She devoted many pages to a select German vocabulary, which suggests she was planning a post-war trip by sea. How else to explain the preponderance of seagoing terms? Departure, ocean, home port, railing, homeland, leaving, steamer, fellow passenger, concert tour, vacation, acquaintance, reclining chair, steamer band, 'the rest of Germany,' mountain air, health resort. She was already proficient enough in French to lead the club's French conversation group.[91] Although she sailed to France in 1937, for a second time, and flew abroad in 1948, 1950, and 1952, she didn't have the opportunity to practise her German until 1953.

That year she also attended the IFUW conference in London. In 1956 she checked out early from the modern civilization course at Delft to attend the conference in Paris, where she spent 'a delightful period' at Reid Hall, the IFUW clubhouse.[92] Although no letters from Paris survive,[93] she provided the University Women's Club 'with an interesting description' of the conference, which was attended by 110 women from forty-eight member associations and included discussions to promote 'international understanding and relief work.'[94]

By then she was an officer of the federation. At the meetings in Zureik, in absentia, she had been elected Convenor of the Standards Committee. She was re-elected in 1953, and earned special mention the same year for work 'on admissions and organizing.'[95] After the 1956 Paris conference the outgoing president, Dorothy F. Leet, paid tribute to her 'excellent work' on the Standards Committee, which had made possible 'the prompt admission' of seventeen national associations, thus raising the number to forty-eight.[96] Leet was succeeded as president by a distinguished French scholar, Jeanne Chaton, a woman whom Jean came to admire immensely, and whom she first met in 1947, in Toronto, at the first postwar triennial.[97]

In 1959 Jean travelled to the conference in Helsinki by way of London. By then – though we have seen precious little of her there – she was an old hand in the city. 'Today,' she wrote, 'has been a bit like old home week. I went over to the Senate House to find Muriel and met Dick Preston from R.M.C. and some people on our staff. Later on Oxford and Regent Streets I ran into acquaintances of all vintages and from a variety of places.' As in the past, she stayed at Crosby Hall, the IFUW clubhouse in London, which twice had been the beneficiary of fundraising campaigns by the Canadian federation – first in the 1920s and then in 1949.[98]

Whenever she was in New York or London, Jean saw as many plays as she could afford. Later she dispensed advice. On one occasion, when she knew that brother Don was going to see a production of Pirandello's *Henri IV* in Toronto, she provided quite a rap. She asked Marion:

> Do you have a copy of Pirandello's Henri IV or does Gordon? If so I suggest that you lend it to Don. I think he would get much more out of the play if he has read and understood it. I understand that the original English company is playing, and Rex Harrison should be a thoroughly good interpretation of the mad savagery of Henri; the mask of insanity and the insanity of the masquerade need preparation by the spectator as do indeed the contrasts between history and reality and/or art and life. (*Six Characters in Search of an Author*). I still recall the middle of the six characters – in a superb production that I saw in London in the middle fifties. Pirandello can be a deep philosophical experience.[99]

In 1959 Jean took a five-day motor trip with friends that had some 'unforgettable moments: a gray evening in Dartmoor, a morning in the market and potteries at Barnstaple, a choir practice in Wells Cathedral, a group of tiny girls of Brenda's age in white frocks and straw boaters playing ring-a-round-a-rosy in the outer green at Salisbury, and within the Cathedral rows of absorbed faces listening to a wise sermon on the use of leisure. It was the end of term service for a girls' school.' But though the motor trip was 'sheer delight,' she regretted not seeing the Victoria and Albert or the Impressionists at the Courtauld Institute. Next time she would stay 'the whole time in London.'

But sailing for Stockholm in 'a small and quite unpretentious boat' elicited such joy that regret must have been easily shelved. 'I bought Dr. Zhivago in London, thinking that I would spend most of the time reading; however, the company and country side were so beguiling that I scarcely opened it.' Her sailing companions included 'a charming family from Florence, an engaging young couple from the American Embassy in Warsaw and a Swedish commodore and his wife who interpreted Sweden for us.'

'At times the channel was so narrow,' she continued, 'that the branches of trees brushed the deck. It was like travelling through a tunnel of green. This was offset by the open waters of the lakes which are really great lakes. I had not realized that the interior of Sweden was so generously watered. The latter part of the journey was in the open Baltic from which we moved into the Malaren waters and up to Stockholm. The approach to the city was quite magnificent. I came in by train at night the last time and thought it a brilliant scene but this was really a wonderful experience. [But] in spite of this, Stockholm does not have for me anything like the richness of London or the charm of Paris. It seems a kind of soulless city.' She spent three days there, visited the

National Museum, and finished work on her 'report and the agenda' for the conference. In London she had been told that 'there were to be 700 women at the Conference, a rather big project for the Finnish Federation.'[100]

That is the last word we have from Jean on this trip. She did write to Marion from Helsinki, and Marion kept all her sister's letters – except this one, which she forwarded to Catherine and Gordon, who in turn did what most people do with letters, once read.[101] Had Jean not been invited a few months later to speak to the Belleville District University Women's Club, Helsinki would have lined up with IFUW conferences in London and Paris: JR there, but no comment. The *Belleville Intelligencer* covered the event under the gripping headline, 'University Women's Club Enjoys Talk on Life in Helsinki, Finland.'[102]

The unheralded reporter wrote that 'Miss Royce found the old town with the new look to be more provincial than cosmopolitan, [with] the women attending the conference from many parts of the world [making] an exotic contrast. She admitted that the Western women who had drip-dried their way across Europe were easily outshone by the Eastern women in their colorful saris.' Through 'amusing sketches of many of the delegates,' Jean provided something of an exegesis on national character: 'the woman from Ceylon who looked so deceptively feminine but was actually a lawyer with a mind like a steel trap; the Brazilian women who have entered men's professions and occupations to a degree unknown in most other countries; the watchful, legal-minded Dutch, the solid, steady British.' Though she only 'touched briefly on the conference program, [she] spoke feelingly of the refugees' helped by the IFUW and assured members that their contribution, approved earlier in the meeting, 'would be greatly appreciated.'

Jean in this talk focused mainly on the resettlement of the hundreds of Karelians who 'became refugees when the Russians seized their lands during the war,' and on general postwar reconstruction. She dwelt especially 'on the children's hospital, as remarkable in its financing as in its layout.' After the war a paediatrician visited the United States and 'canvassed the Finnish settlements, [but] instead of bringing the money back' he sought government 'permission to buy coffee which was selling in Finland for high prices on the black market. [T]his proved such a good investment,' Jean reported happily, 'that a magnificent hospital was built' from the profit.

Some years later, when Marion was in Helsinki, Jean mentioned the hospital and catalogued other highlights of the Finnish capital: 'I am wondering whether you have discovered the great church and the market below it on the waterfront and if [there is] an abundance of fish, and ducks, vegetables and flowers presided over by women in smocks of varied colours and great butchers with clean white aprons. There should be a little booth there with onion soup fully as good as that sold in Les Halles. Have you walked in The Memorial Cemetery [and] enjoyed morning coffee and a newspaper in one of the tiny street-side coffee houses and have you listened to Finlandia.'[103] In a later letter she hopes that Marion 'bought [herself] some winter underwear in Scandinavia.' Did Marion chafe at this advice, as Jean did when she was on the receiving end? Or does advice from a younger sister sound more like fondness than the desire for control (hopeless in any event)?

The next IFUW Congress after Helsinki was scheduled for Mexico City in 1962. But the summer before, Jean had overdosed on conferences: Washington, D.C., Alpbach, Austria, and London, Ontario. She left a record of each of these events that provides a more critical view of her hopes for the federations. 'The Washington Conference [of the American Association of University Women] was quite an experience,' she reported, 'There were 2000 women [and mostly] I saw those with I.F.U.W. connections and they are very pleasant people.' One evening, 'Dr. [Althea] Hottel had a delightful little dinner for visitors [including] Juanita Hefting from Holland [and] a visiting scholar from New Zealand.' Their hostess was 'very keen' on pursuing some research ideas presented by Cora du Bois, an anthropology professor at Harvard, who had 'really talked about women and the contribution they can make – the special aptitudes they may have, the kind of education that meets their needs, the institutional adjustments that may be necessary to allow for a contribution* to the economic, political and cultural life of our times, the need for constant questioning of what is known and what is taken for granted. She deplored the wastage of women's skills. She suggested research** that deals with the bio-physiological and socio-cultural functions of women' (asterisks in original). The asterisks allowed Jean to elaborate points at the end of her letter.[104]

This missive provides convincing evidence that Jean shared Marion's abiding interest in changing the position of women in society. It also indicates clearly that these questions were on the intellectual and political agenda of women's organizations during feminism's supposedly quiescent decades. Though Jean appreciated several of the lectures at the Washington conference, Cora du Bois clearly gave 'the finest address.'[105]

At the time of the Washington conference, Jean was chair of the CFUW's Committee of International Relations. So three weeks later she left for the meeting of the IFUW Council in Alpbach, Austria. Not surprisingly, she went by way of London, where she spent a week in the new wing of Crosby Hall. She enjoyed a 'rather lazy week mouching about Chelsea, chatting with people in the Hall, sitting in the garden in the sun.' George and Berta Humphrey came for tea (the same George who had walked so resolutely past Robert Legget when they were both young men on the make), and they enjoyed 'a wonderful gossip about old times.' Prompted by the chilly weather, she purchased a suit at Harrod's,[106] 'a grey tweed that [would] be useful in the fall.'[107]

In a note two weeks later, she reported having an 'interesting time in Munich.' However, she added (quite uncharacteristically) that she found 'the crowds very tiring and the Germans rather unpleasantly aggressive.' She expressed surprise 'at the extent of war damage, they were rebuilding very slowly, and in somewhat shoddy fashion.' On this trip the Austrians received the kudos: 'They have so much grace and innate courtesy.' She was enchanted with Alpbach:

> It is a lovely place – a tiny village in the heart of the mountains built around a little church. The church is 12th century, restored in 1953, the exterior beautiful in its simplicity, the interior rather a bad copy of baroque. You must have stayed in places like this in the Swiss Alps, but Alpbach is really quite special. The villagers treat us like personal guests – they entertained us the other evening with their band and young people's chorus. At the blessing of new fire equipment on Sunday they likened us to the fire engine as instruments of help to other people. The storekeeper, the postman, the priest always begin a conversation with 'Do you like Alpbach?' And on the roads they use the old greeting 'Gruss Got.'

In this lovely place the council members held 'a good meeting, relaxed and without any of the tensions that are sometimes apparent. For once the British delegation has pulled together and no anti-American feeling has evidenced itself.' Jean mentioned some of the 'distinguished' participants from India and Pakistan, and the 'dear Mlle Chaton.'

We know nothing of Jean's post-conference tour – Hailigiulylest, Volckvirnedekt, Graz, Senimbering, Eisdistadt, and Vienna. However, a vignette from a tour through one family's castle shows her talent for evoking time and place. 'The family [of one of our members] still lives there and maintains it largely by renting the lower acres to summer campers. The area along the roadway was filled with tents of every colour and the campers were going hither and yon as they prepared their evening meal. The castle was built in 1576 and is unchanged except for electric lighting and some rather indifferent plumbing. Apricots were espaliered on the south wall of one of the stables and were yellowing in the sun. It was a peaceful glimpse of a century in which the castle must have known many hazardous moments.'[108]

Only one day home from Alpbach, Jean headed for the CFUW triennial at the University of Western Ontario. Perhaps she was just tired, perhaps London, Ontario, was a come-down from the other London, or perhaps her sympathies lay so much more with international issues. For whatever reason, she expressed considerable impatience with the narrow interests of those who attended the Canadian meeting, especially in contrast with the broad vision of the 'dear Mlle [Jeanne] Chaton.' She told Marion:

> Getting to know Jeanne is one of the most rewarding things I have had from my connection with I.F.U.W. She is very occupied these days with Africa and what can be done for African women. She left Alpbach to go to Egypt and from there will go on to Uganda to lay the foundations for the Seminar that is being held there in 1963. She talked one night at Alpbach about the meeting in Ethiopia last winter and made the problems so clear that we came away fired with the idea of doing something. I enlisted Mary Winspear's interest in this but by and large the C.F.U.W. is concentrating on domestic matters and will probably continue to do so during the next triennium.

For Jean, 'the C.F.U.W. conference was a hurried affair [just] Sunday to Wednesday night after the Dinner and that length of time only because I had promised to speak.'[109] Some good things happened: 'a young Scotswoman from Belleville gave a brilliant paper titled the "Biological Aspects of Population Explosion."' Jean took special pleasure in this paper because her committee had sponsored the study. She was also 'very happy [that] Madame Guay came up from Quebec. She was delightful as always. She enjoyed everything and this in spite of her doubts. I had to do a lot of persuading to get her there.' No doubt, with Madame Guay, Jean was up against the perennial problem of Canadian federations – the fracturing along national, that is to say Canadian/Québécois lines.

Jean left the conference early: she was needed on the registrarial front, 'inundated' as she was 'by the importunities' from parents for children 'who do not live up to their expectations.' But she was also clearly out of sympathy with the CFUW, which she now found 'pretty parochial. The chief hope is in the younger women who were there: they are interested in something beyond national offices and sitting on the P.M.'s mat and they are beginning to be articulate.'[110]

Four years later, after a CFUW council meeting in Sudbury, she seemed considerably more upbeat. 'It was a good meeting. Laura Sabia carried it off very well and the usual tensions were not apparent. [There was only one] representative of that group of difficult people who dominated things for so long.' Once again, 'the younger women of whom there were a goodly number, were impressive people.'[111]

What she really liked about that meeting was its location: she was absolutely taken with Laurentian University. 'You have probably seen it,' she wrote to Marion, 'and yet I am surprised that if you have, you have not mentioned it. It is so striking. The architect has used reinforced concrete and local stone and the design suggests an Aztec influence. It all fits in to the rough terrain and with the lakes in the foreground, the city beyond the water, and the tall chimneys of Falconbridge in the distance, the effect is magnificent.' At this meeting she agreed to chair the CFUW Fellowship Committee, the same committee that in 1930 awarded her friend Mary White a fellowship for Oxford. Now Jean was a decision maker. Whether here or with the Queen's Marty Fellowship, she was known to spread her interest beyond the winners, often writing to other applicants to suggest how they might pursue their work. She always had empathy for the able but financially strapped students and for the runner-ups. She knew that position first-hand, first with Marion-the-star, later with Mary who became 'a real Oxfordian, she swallowed it whole.'[112] In perhaps a bittersweet way, she clearly relished the task of helping the strugglers. That year's applicants had been 'an amazing group: some of them appear to have great abilities and they are working in fascinating fields. Perhaps the most striking thing, however, is the narrowness of the specialization. It seems to me that our society is going to be woefully short of generalists who are able to communicate but perhaps I am forgetting that enormous group of Generals BAs who are planning to come up for degrees in May.'[113]

Several months later she provided Marion a snapshot of each of the winners of the newly inaugurated Alice Wilson award, stressing that each – a woman 'approaching middle age [with] two well-grown daughters,' 'a young married woman,' 'a woman who had worked for many years as a sub-professional librarian,' – needed the award to complete long-established programs of study. 'I only wish that there were more Alice Wilsons,' she wrote. 'Laura Sabia and I carried on a constant campaign with clubs during the last triennium and as a result several clubs agreed to give annual donations to the fund.'[114]

In August 1962 Jean attended the IFUW triennial in Mexico. Though the city was 'less festive'[115] than it had been when they were there at Christmas, 'a second visit increases its charm.' One afternoon she spent 'at Tula with Dr. Spitzmuller, the curator of a museum in Vienna' and one of the hostesses the previous summer. 'She is especially interested in Indian cultures,' Jean wrote, 'and it was really a great privilege to recreate with her the city of Quetzaleoatle.' The conference had been 'a happy combination of place, people and activity ... probably not so well organized as Helsinki but the Mexican women were most attractive hostesses, a bit diffident and yet proud of what they had to offer.'[116] She was the congress's parliamentarian.

Although she never used the term, Mexico was the only Third World country she had visited, and the experience brought reflection. 'The Medical Centre [in Mexico City] is a magnificent place built primarily for the use of Conferences. One wonders whether there is justification for so costly a building for this purpose when so many people are housed so poorly. Yet there is an imaginative quality in putting up a well-planned, finely executed, and beautiful structure that all may see. In a way it gives a larger view. (I am not sure what a hungry man would say about this.)'

All her descriptions carry this ambivalence, usually implicit: 'I rediscovered our street.[117] This time I drove down and recaptured that lovely sunny morning at the *audijar* the same beggars were sitting at the door of the monastery, a woman was suckling her child in the garden, Alvarado House had the same untouchable look and the rose facade of the House of the Sun across the way glowed in the light. Chauffeurs were still gossiping at the stone seat and their arrogant-looking cars lined the curb.'[118]

Jean was not a star of the IFUW as was her good friend, Allie Vibert Douglas. Jean took pride in Allie. 'Her spacious mind embraces the earth and reaches to infinity,' she said, a reference to Allie's dual career as an astrophysicist and Dean of Women at Queen's.[119] When *Herstory* – the first Canadian Women's Calendar – appeared in 1974,[120] Jean found, to her dismay, that Allie Douglas was 'not cited as the only Canadian woman elected to the Presidency of the IFUW. [Though] we all regard this as a great honour, perhaps she is excluded because this was an election of a woman' by women. Jean named others included in the calendar, the implication being that they were less worthy than Allie, but did admit to being pleased that Marion had been 'included as the first Director of the Federal Women's Bureau.'[121]

Allie Vibert Douglas became the most important link between Jean's life in Kingston and her role in the IFUW. In 1950, as outgoing president, she named Jean as eminently suited for the role of convenor of standards. The two women shared a broad, internationalist vision, yet both were parked – permanently it seemed – in small-town Kingston. They were friends, perhaps more so after Jean retired, but Allie lived an engaging academic life in tandem with some of her more humdrum responsibilities as Dean of Women. Her opportunities for travel – often with the IFUW – continued until she was well past eighty, her presence being sought at meetings in China, Japan, and elsewhere.[122]

One must eventually come to ground with these women. Travelling, saving the world, redrawing the gender map ... these were all part-time vocations. No matter how internationalist or high-brow, unless one is very rich one must get from Monday to Tuesday, fashioning domestic, career, and social strategies that make life peaceful or chaotic, manageable or hit-and-miss. As long as she was dean, Allie had few of these concerns, though precious little privacy: meals, housekeeping, and laundry were stage managed by others, for better or worse. But Jean had to create her own modalities, and on recreating them – mainly from her account books – the observer notes her quiet ingenuity.

According to one of the many students who visited over the years, Jean's apartment was 'a sharp contrast' to the formal world of her office. 'It was warm, friendly and most conducive to enlightened talk,' Mary-Louise (Funke) Campbell wrote. 'I suspect that she gained strength and deep caring [from this place that enabled her] to pursue her task which cannot always have been easy.'[123] In those years most people with jobs as responsible as Jean's had a car in the driveway and a wife at home to carry the daily domestic routines. Jean had neither. She worked long hours, often at home in the evening as well, and on Saturday mornings. She had to devise strategies to ensure that she didn't devote precious leisure hours to the usual litany of errands and household chores.

During her long tenure as registrar, co-workers, students, and friends ran into her at the library, at the movies, at a concert or play, and occasionally at Steacy's Department Store; but seldom (if ever) did they see her at a grocery store, an LCBO outlet, or a laundromat. Indeed, no one remembers seeing her making a vital decision about which detergent would make her wash whiter than white, or puffing along University Avenue with too many bags of groceries, or wrestling her laundry into the back seat of a taxi. Yet she ate well, kept good sherry, entertained her friends and students, and was always well turned out.

After she gave up being a resident warden in 1936, she lived in her own apartment. The first was at 131 King Street East. Living here involved the famous walk through the park, where she first encountered Robert Legget. On King Street she hosted the executive meetings of the University Women's Club, especially during the year of her presidency. This was also where Katherine Royce spent the last six months of her life. In 1947 Jean moved into the separately entranced second floor of Phyllis Knight's house, some three blocks from her office in Douglas Library. By then she was dining with friends most weekday evenings. The estimable May Macdonnell supplemented her budget – and acquired daily company – by providing dinner for Jean and for Phyllis Knight, and for her boarder, Pauline Jewett, then a junior lecturer at Queen's. 'Five evenings a week,' Pauline recalled, 'May Macdonnell, with whom I lived, Phyllis Knight, Jean Royce and I had dinner together, and Jean would let me slip in and have a glass of sherry at her place first, because dear Miss Macdonnell, whom we all loved, didn't provide sherry in abundance.'[124] Pauline left Queen's in 1949, when her contract failed to be renewed,[125] but Jean continued to dine with May and Phyllis until 1958. Not having to prepare an evening meal after a long day at work was a bonus. Jean was good at finding wifely substitutes. And her arrangement meant that she dined in the company of friends.

Then there was Mrs Saunders, who remained on Jean's payroll until mid-1966.[126] Judging by Mrs S's wage,[127] she did cleaning and laundry and other necessary tasks. In February 1962, when Phyllis and Jean moved house after 52 Queen's Crescent was expropriated to make room for Stirling Hall, Mrs Saunders did yeoperson service and was paid $125.[128]

By January 1951, Jean had arranged for Cooke's, Kingston's famous 'Old World Shoppe,' to deliver groceries and bill her monthly – not so unusual, except that the driver purchased what she needed from other shops as well. No one needs as much coffee and jam from the old country as her account books indicated she paid for – $26.52 in January 1951, and $62.00 in July 1956, for example. This arrangement saved her a whomping amount of time, but at considerable cost. After mid-1966 her bills shrank drastically – January $67.05, February $32.55, March $32.50, April $42.72, May $23.06, June $11.99 – and that's it.[129] Her affair with Cooke's ended after her assistant Margaret Hooey observed that Jean purchased these services 'at great expense.' A deceptively casual offer to take Jean along on her next series of errands quickly became routine when Jean, at sixty-two, discovered the pleasures of the modern supermarket and also of the laundromat, whose doors she had never previously darkened.[130] With a friend in tow, these chores become social occasions. Even so, but imagine how many books she read during time not spent endlessly walking the aisles of the A&P or schlepping clothes from washer to dryer.

Fred Bartlett, the director of the School of Physical and Health Education, was a good friend of Jean's. In September 1954 he offered to buy her 'sherries and soda,' and for the next dozen years, as her account books attest, he was as good as his word: FLB $12.00 ... December 1958 FLB $16.25; ... (the last time) April 1966 FLB $34.60. Fred would march into her office to announce that he had delivered the latest cache to her apartment. She would light a cigarette and, judging from the laughter, a jolly time would ensue.[131]

In her early years as registrar, Jean did not pay much attention to sartorial display. But as her salary increased, she spent more on clothes. Her store of choice, from at least April 1955, was the decidedly up-market Holt Renfrew. But why she donned the same outfit for days on end, once her closet was no longer bare, remains a mystery. Certainly the women who worked for her embraced the strict high school outfit code: change your clothes every day and don't repeat the same outfit for at least a week. Even when that option became available, Jean paid no heed.

Perhaps she was just born too soon. By the late 1960s she could have worn jeans every day and, in some circles, been right at home. When Marion sought advice on the appropriate clothing to wear to accept an honorary degree from Acadia in 1975, Jean informed her that Margaret Atwood had received hers at Queen's a year earlier dressed 'in blue jeans, which she wore to lunch' as well. 'I should add,' Jean continued, undoubtedly enjoying her sister's predicted reaction, 'that they were very well-cut jeans, but some people took exception to them.'[132] Not

Jean, though, who had reported earlier that Atwood – who writes 'exquisitely'[133] – gave a speech without 'any content to speak of. I think she thought the whole affair was a kind of joke.'[134]

At one point, Jean disclosed that she did know something about the politics of clothing. Marion's days at Moulton College resulted in a close relationship with a Bahamian family that continued into the next generation, when four daughters – including her namesake, Marion Victoria – studied in Canada, one at Queen's. 'I thought you would like to hear about your Bahamians,' Jean wrote. 'They are a charming quartette They were all beautifully and rather expensively dressed, [and] Ruby is one of the best dressed women at Queen's. The striking thing about it is that she never lowers her standards. She never appears in tight shorts and sloppy joes; she dresses for dinner and so on. Her Canadian friends might well emulate her, and yet I am sure that, in a way, it is a measure of her insecurity.'[135] As in other matters, Jean knew the rules, and did as she pleased.

One of Jean's friends suggested that a woman alone tended to be left alone in the couple-ridden Limestone City. According to Elsie Curtis, Jean was invited to large parties – especially those of the semiofficial sort – but not to more intimate gatherings.[136] Undoubtedly the woman-only-in-a-couple rule functioned in many quarters. But Jean had a wide circle of Kingston friends, and there was a good deal of reciprocal entertaining. She wrote in 1974: 'I had a wonderful evening at the Biélers on Friday night ... a dinner party of eight, and like all their parties it was sheer delight. André who has been in poor health for some time has recovered and as usual he was the life of the party. We were a group who went back in time to the old days before the excess of the present. Archie Day and his wife were there and he regaled us with stories of his work under Pearson.'[137] Jean noted that Day had been a professor of Greek in the mid-1930s and was a 'witty and fascinating conversationalist.' After war service he returned to Queen's for a year in 1947, and 'then was offered a post in External Affairs. He is a competent and gifted person and his career in diplomacy took him to Ottawa, Paris and London. Latterly [as] Mr Pearson's confidential secretary [he] wrote Pearson's better speeches and handled [his] delicate correspondence. He practically rewrote "Mike" and this of course is *top secret*.'[138] Jean recalled seeing Archie at a formal dinner in Ottawa at which Prime Minister Louis St Laurent announced the establishment of the Canada Council. She told Day that his speeches for Pearson were very good. His reply was succinct: 'They were among my better efforts.'[139]

The party's hosts, André and Jeanette, had come to Queen's in 1936.[140] Jean's friendship with André originated in their shared love of art (and her love of his work), and expanded from there. She was delighted when the Agnes Etherington Art Gallery opened at Queen's in October 1962, two days after President Kennedy's 'frightening' Cuban missile speech. She told Marion that though she feared 'reprisals from Russia' and wondered whether her sister should make her planned trip to 'the Caribbean area,' the crisis wasn't enough to bring her home from the gallery for the eleven o'clock news. 'I could hardly tear myself away. It is quite beautiful, I think. I am eager to have you see it. The Zacks, bless them, have loaned some wonderful bits of sculpture and the exhibition of paintings is an interesting one – British Art of the 18th–20th centuries. I missed the French Impressionists, but there were some good things.'[141] A year later, when the gallery mounted a Biéler retrospective, she pronounced the exhibition 'quite wonderful.'[142]

The opening of a new building for the School of Music, in 1974, 'named in honour of Frank Harrison and Hugh LeCaine,' produced similar rapture and memories of old friends. 'Frank Harrison,' she wrote Marion, 'is acclaimed as one of the foremost musicologists of the western world. Formerly the Musician of Oxford and now at the University of Amsterdam, he was at Queen's in the late thirties and forties. He is a dear person –Irish, a gentle soul, and very gifted: [he and his wife] were close neighbours and friends of mine when I lived on King Street.'

Her comments about Hugh LeCaine reveal much about why she was a favourite among those who liked open, interesting, and generous conversation. 'One of our brilliant young physicists in the thirties, and now with the National Research Council, he is one of the people who developed electronic music.' She admitted not liking this music 'at all,' and reminded Marion that Catherine once bought some records 'to try out on us.' But her aversion to electronic music was no impediment to appreciating the invention, or the person – or his worthiness for the honour. She looked forward to seeing him and his sister Jeanne, 'now a professor of history at Oklahoma [who] was one of our first Marty Fellows.' Like Harrison, LeCaine was 'a gentle, very able person.'[143]

Jean also informed Marion that Frank Harrison had 'divorced his first wife' and that 'his new wife also a musicologist is coming for the laureation.' As always, Jean seemed pragmatic about marriage break-ups, although she expressed satisfaction – and perhaps surprise – when a marriage actually produced a 'meeting of minds.'[144] As a colleague, she was closer to husbands than to wives – certainly among the professoriate – so she could be excused for being unfamiliar with the view from the distaff side of the house. But she was not oblivious. A student she knew 'intimately' at Queen's in the forties married 'an attractive young blade' while she was an undergraduate. She supported him through graduate school, working as a teacher. After his graduation 'her husband got a very good appointment in External Affairs and they were sent on a foreign posting,' where he promptly 'fell in love with the daughter of [a diplomat] and simply told [her] that things between them were at an end.'[145]

One wonders if Jean's friendships with men generated hostility among their wives. After all, this was the source of the 'couples only' convention that continues to animate some circles.[146] But it would have been clear that whatever Jean wanted from their husbands, it wasn't love, sex, or marriage. In 1968, while in Edinburgh, 'Professor Roy came in for sherry and we had a gossipy time. I asked his wife to come along,' she noted, 'but she assured me that Hamish enjoyed his sessions with Queen's people on his own, and that she always felt herself an extra piece of furniture.'[147]

In 1960, after J. Robert Oppenheimer's visit, she wrote that her friend 'Reg Sawyer and I were cherishing some of his phrases: "the sobering recognition of our ignorance;" "we must learn to listen and understand;" "we must hear." [Though] he spoke on every occasion with great simplicity in beautiful English [his] very simplicity was deceptive. Every sentence had something significant behind it.' Jean thought everything about Robert Oppenheimer admirable and worth comment. 'At times he chuckles to himself and then says: that was supposed to be funny but it isn't.'[148] 'We have had 'Greatness' in our midst this week,' she wrote, and she meant it.

The timing of this encounter with 'greatness' antedated by one year the ascension of Principal Corry, and her own apogee as registrar – this we can say retrospectively. A perusal of her account books indicates that as she rounded sixty, there were also changes on the extracurricular front. Strikingly, from 1963 through 1966, she made no major trips. Previously, when she did not go abroad in the summer, she enjoyed theatre at Stratford,[149] but during these years, she didn't even venture that far. Perhaps she just wanted to enjoy a quieter life. Certainly she wasn't as young as she used to be, and as the heart failure of January

1966 dramatically points out, her life as a wind-up toy was coming to an end.

Probably, Jean herself was also at low ebb: her work life was increasingly stressful: the upper echelons were hostile to her; and her office faced more work with fewer resources. At work she was in overdrive, and given her age and health, she must have required more recuperation time. A few months after her heart episode in 1966, the Robin Ross consultancy dealt another major blow. That year she faltered even in her obligation to keep up with Marion: she wrote no letters to her and except for Margaret might have stayed completely out of Marion's way. To put all this succinctly: had Jean died in January 1966 – a distinct possibility at the time – the record would show that she was winding down by then, her passing an early denouement to a rich and active life. It would show her undermined at work; without a partner or children; with two sisters (one increasingly kept at bay) and two brothers, and nieces and nephews for whom she was a fond but distant figure; and with friends who were insisting on dying. But that would be reckoning without her own deep internal resources – and without Margaret.

The independent lady who did so much on her own now had a new friend, but not simply a friend who invited her to dinner parties or tea, exchanged letters, cards, and invitations, or dropped in for good conversation. No, she had a friend with whom she shared meals, spent weekends, and went grocery shopping and to the laundromat – and with whom she travelled to Tanglewood and Niagara-on-the Lake, to Portugal, England, South Carolina, Scotland, and the Caribbean. As she put it later, 'Margaret just gave new life to me at that time.'[150]

'Margaret is coming with me,' she wrote to Marion on 4 October 1967, 'on the goodship Michaelangelo. Why Portugal [you ask] and I can only say that for some irrational reason I have always wanted to sail up the Tagus to Lisbon but my real objective is the Prado.' This was Jean's first (recorded) trip abroad with a friend; it was also the first time she had left Queen's during term. The very idea left me in a state of shock: 'Why did you both bolt in October?' I asked Margaret. 'An act of rebellion,'[151] she replied. In other words, if associate registrar George Leech wanted to be registrar, give him a chance to enjoy the full catastrophe. Three cheers for Jean.

In fact, Jean had bounced back earlier that year. 'I am sorry,' she wrote Marion, 'that I missed you in Toronto. I wanted you to come to the Albee play with me. By chance, I got good seats and enjoyed it enormously. It was a beautiful production, acted with great skill. As always, Albee is overly profane and liquor flows too freely; but he stimulates the mind – one continues to think of his dissection of human personality and his assessment of the human.'[152] She and Margaret had recently returned from an extended spring break – a preview of the coming rebellion. 'I am still catching up after the Carolina trip but it was worth doing. The sheer charm of old Charleston grips one – the old houses are miracles of architecture and they are full of beautiful things. It is a city in which to saunter, to explore little courts and byways and to bird watch, the robins, the cedar waxwings, and the red headed woodpeckers were on their way north and out on a plantation one day we saw a cloud of blue birds.'[153] On 7 September 1968, the first autumn in thirty-eight years that Jean did not welcome students to the university, she sailed with Margaret for Scotland. Things seemed to augur well for her retirement.

Chapter Six

Ranging the Universe

'The other evening,' Jean wrote Marion on 10 March 1969, 'I went to dinner with Allie Douglas. It's always fun because we range the universe. She is reading the Bertrand Russell Autobiography and we relished it together. It is amusing, witty, lucid and detached. He is an over-sexed libertine, arrogant to a degree, brilliant, sceptical of his own and other people's ideas and experiences, and as the present generation would say, "he plays it cool."' Purchase a volume, she suggested, 'as a diversion from the business at hand and as a traveling companion.'

The same letter picks up on a story that Marion had relayed earlier. Jeanne Chaton, Jean's great favourite from the International Federation of University Women (IFWU), had been attacked by 'thugs' on 49th Street in New York. Quite in line with her character, she had resisted: 'She is a doughty knight. One of her French friends told me once that to really know her you have to stay with her on her farm and carry through with her daily activities. Apparently she is master of all she surveys from quantities of milk from the cows and goats to quality of the hay, household management and district problems, surveying every question with calm competence and loving the sun and the outdoor life.'[1]

Jean's withdrawal as registrar left intact her fascination with the 'universe' and with other people. Her own spirit remained 'doughty,' her mind active. Her calendar was peppered with activities. If she didn't 'play it cool,' she didn't appear hot and bothered either. A month after the evening with Allie Douglas and Bertrand Russell, she topped the alumni ballot and joined the Board of Trustees.[2] She was officially back at Queen's, this time only for love.

But if she enjoyed the goodwill of the alumni, she was clearly out of sorts with the student temper of the times – sometimes quite harshly so. Publicly, she refrained from comment. 'Miss Royce answers questions with other questions,' wrote an amused interviewer who asked her what she thought of 'present student radicalism'? 'Well they certainly feel a great deal of urgency, don't you think so, Draayer? Perhaps you can tell me why.'[3]

Privately, she agreed with Marion that 'our student revolts are making this continent look pretty silly by contrast with other parts of the world. The Gray affair at McGill and the eruption at Harvard last month seem to be only exercises in rebellion, to get in on the bandwagon. Playing at revolution seems to me a serious offence.'[4] Informed some weeks later that in the past year 'most college presidents of Canada had their lives threatened,' she was not amused: 'So much for our society!'[5]

Yet when Queen's students 'struck a new note' at a University Council meeting, her tone became measured, even ironic:

> After a long afternoon of somewhat complacent reports, the president of the AMS, an invited guest, rose to say that the true picture of the university had not really been given. Indeed, there were immeasurable problems that had not been discussed – housing deficiencies, lack of communication between students and staff, inadequate teaching, lack of summer employment and so on. He was followed by another student who [charged] that the Council was made up of a lot of 'fat cats' – doctors, lawyers, teachers, professors and so on, who knew nothing of real conditions. He warned the Council that although Queen's had escaped violence during the past year, another session would undoubtedly bring riots and offensive action.

'Chancellor Stirling,' Jean continued, 'was shaken by all this. Another council member questioned whether students today really knew anything about problems.' Jack Hannah relayed his own history as 'the youngest of eighteen children who got educational opportunity only by the Government assistance given after World War I, a meagre amount compared with the D.V.A. plan after the second war.' He augmented 'his grant by menial summer employment, living while at college in a small room and getting his own meals.' But, Jean observed, though Hannah's 'saga pleased the Council members mightily it seemed to have little effect on the students.' Nor did she seem surprised: 'Interestingly, the most vocal of them seem to come from comfortable middle class homes. In many cases their parents are strongly humanitarian and liberal in their views. Indeed, I often wonder whether the students are mouthing views that they have heard expressed around their family dinner tables.'

Nothing in this letter of June – full of interesting thoughts and events – augurs personal distress. Jean had received a letter from Catherine, 'always a special surprise and delight'; her garden 'had masses' of tulips, enough for 'bouquets for every-comer,' and the iris, peonies and lilies' were beginning to bloom. An honorary degree to her friend, André Biéler, had 'provided excuse for celebrations,' and she and Margaret were off 'on a bit of holiday' to Vermont.[6] Yet this is the last letter she wrote to Marion before she attempted to end her life. As with so much else, she was efficient, choosing a quiet weekend alone – at the end of June – when she would swallow sufficient pills to ensure success.

Her plan would have worked had it not been for an uncharacteristic gesture a few days earlier when Margaret dropped in before going to visit family in Sudbury. 'As I was leaving,' she remembered, 'she came over and kissed me on the cheek. That was not Jean.' A few days later, Jean answered a call from Margaret after 'many rings [in] a very groggy voice,' and Margaret alerted Connie Martens.[7] I don't think for a minute that chagrin with student militancy contributed to Jean's decision – despite her 'so much for our society' remark – yet there wasn't much else in the letters leading up to her action that seemed to be exercising her. How, then, to understand her despair and her suicide attempt?

Perhaps reformed smokers might find it relevant that around this time, Jean Royce was weaning herself from cigarettes. The previous summer she had tried to go cold turkey. She resumed smoking in October and November, abstained in December, smoked in January, didn't in February, had a few in March, none in April and May, a few in June, and that was about it. She bought a few the following November and December, and purchased her last cigarettes (that we know of) in January 1970. Cigarettes, we now know, are an addictive weed – they get you when you're using them, they get some people when they lay off, and they get others second-hand. Nor can one absolutely reject the hypothesis that nicotine withdrawal fuels (or creates) despondency.

The timing of Jean's suicide attempt coincided closely with the time that she had presumably expected to retire – had the universe unfolded as it should. Was it possible, then, that she had planned to take herself out for the count once her registrarship was over? The question echoes Carolyn Heilbrun's declaration in *The Last Gift of Time*: 'Having supposed the sixties would be downhill all the way, I had long held a determination to commit suicide at seventy. [Indeed], the fact that my sixties ... offered such satisfactions only confirmed my life-long resolution not to live past [the Biblical] "three score years and ten."'[8] Five years later, on the eve of *her* seventieth birthday, Jean declared, 'I have no sentiment about birthdays. Indeed, I dislike giving them significance at my age. To be seventy is not a matter for celebration.'[9] Perhaps we can imagine her saying, with Heilburn, 'Quit while you're ahead was, and is my motto. It's leaving the party while it's still fun ... I don't like parties ... but it's the best metaphor I can come up with.'[10] Was Jean declaring the party over? If so, the decision was probably not long in the making – for years she had made financial plans to supplement her pension.[11]

More likely, however, her abrupt removal from office was a major factor. One sign that something was amiss is that she let her membership in the University Women's Club lapse between 1967 and 1970. Perhaps she found it too painful to see old friends in a social setting. Ten years after her death, Margaret declared publicly that 'Jean had been devastated by the massive negation of her life's work. For some time she lost her will to live.'[12] Yet today, Jean's only confidante no longer accepts this explanation. After leaving office, she noted, Jean had been feisty most of the time, as interested as ever in all and sundry.

May Hambly, who met Jean in January 1969, also recalled a woman in fine fettle. That month, May arrived as a charter member of the Faculty of Education to teach Latin. Widowed, with a son recently graduated from Queen's, she was thrilled with her new appointment.[13] May knew plenty about the newly retired registrar, who had helped her son while he was in residence. So when she arrived with a friend and a carload of some 2,000 books on a midwinter evening and found the doors to the college locked, she called Jean.

'Throw snowballs against the caretaker's window,' Jean advised, and so she did. It worked, too. Jean and May saw each other a lot after that. From May's account, Jeannie – as she still calls her – took her in hand. Jean knew who had an apartment for rent, which church May should attend (and where she might go instead when that didn't work out), and advised her to join the Public Library and the Art Gallery. They went to the theatre and 'quite often would eat out.' They also protected each other – well, in May's words, 'I felt that I was protecting her and she felt she was protecting me. Someone had been raped or assaulted in the park.' To avoid walking alone, they would meet after class and trudge through the snow together, sometimes arm in arm. But in fact, only May lived on the other side of the park, so accompanying her must have been Jean's motive, whether for protection, company, or in the interests of a good walk. One dark evening, Jean advised, 'Don't be afraid, May.' One snowy night she announced, 'May, I'll go ahead and you can walk in my footsteps.' May thought, 'I am walking in the footsteps of Jean Royce.'[14]

In March, Jean was hospitalized for five days as a result of a 'loss of power and sensation in her left leg.' Her doctor called it an 'episode of transient cerebral ischaemia.' Germane here is recent medical evidence that points to a link between silent strokes and 'significant symptoms of depression.'[15] If Jean's stroke triggered depression, however, it went unnoticed at the time. A subsequent silent stroke in September 1976 was followed, two months later, by a clinical diagnosis of depression accompanied by 'paranoidal delusions.' In March 1977, five electric convulsive treatments finally lifted her spirits and cleared the 'thought disorder.'

The hypothesis that the March stroke triggered Jean's depression cannot be ignored. But one cannot reject Margaret's original conviction that Jean's decision was linked to her being stripped of the position she had held for thirty-five years. Was her brusque removal from office – which Margaret deemed 'the sad and ugly incident'[16] – the sort of blow that destroys perspective, engulfs all emotional space, and negates all pleasures, obligations, and attachments? One recalls her reaction to her dismissal: 'What have I done?' Because she never spoke of these matters, she found no new answers. So, for her, it was the trip on a Ferris wheel – the inevitable return to the same point of departure.

In robust times such questions can be banished, permitted only fragments of time, small corners of the mind. But life's meaning is continually created – often heroically – against the odds. Late one evening, just before she died, and appearing 'heavily burdened,' Jean asked Margaret to help her understand 'what went wrong' during her last years at the university. Though she confirmed 'the great satisfaction her work gave her despite the hostile environment of the last years,' she blamed herself – though for what, she didn't know. 'Damn me!' she proclaimed.[17]

By the time she attempted suicide, she had spent a year in her new life. Things had gone rather well: nice trips, nice friends, a few rebellious students – though a long and observant career counselled that the latter were a mere sign of the times. Congratulatory letters continued to arrive, and one of these, from Roland Nadeau, surely cheered her: 'Something needs to be added' to the citation accompanying her degree: 'Jean Royce, whose courage to gamble on the long-shot, long-odd, almost-certain-to-lose dark horse places her in the doubtful but delightfully exciting company of horseplayers, and brought returns which will pass from this generation to, at least, the next. To you – who gambled and won; from me, who ran, stumbled, ran again and "finished in the money."'[18]

Moreover, the alumni – her constituency, after all – insisted that she stay on board and represent them. Nonetheless, the routines that had kept her focused – decent, perhaps – were gone. The days could be long. A lot of people no longer sought her advice. All this, of course, would have been so had she been retired more gracefully, at whatever passes for the 'right time.' But that scenario would have carried a different meaning – a golden sunset without storm clouds of doubt.

When she recovered, she told her doctor not to worry, that was it (for playing God, I imagine her thinking). She thanked Connie Martens for saving her life.[19] In tears, she confessed to Margaret that had she thought of Catherine, she would have pulled back.[20] But that's it, isn't it? We cobble our decisions from reasons disguised as emotions, emotions tarted up as logic. At a crucial moment, if we should leave something out – if we, say, forget about Catherine – we may make a thin decision. But Jean was graced – if grace it was – with the chance to recall time. For the remainder of the 1969 calendar year her daybook, except for two entries – a board meeting and a farewell dinner for J.A. Corry – remained unmarked. This is clear evidence of her dissociation from her life. Yet, throughout this period she kept her account books meticulously, and these reveal that weeks before the suicide attempt she and Margaret had arranged to rent a cottage in July. They had invited Marion to join them for a weekend, but her sister was preoccupied writing a report that Jean called her 'heavy task-mistress,' and Marion stayed away.[21] Nor did she accept their offer to go visit Catherine and Gordon in Lenox, Massachusetts – home of Tanglewood – later in the month.[22]

One wonders at Jean's continuing invitations to Marion. In later years Marion would be rebuffed, Jean unable to tolerate her presence. Yet now, worried that her sister was working too hard, Jean made several overtures. Did she really want Marion's company? Or did she feel obliged? Several times in the past, Margaret had notified Marion when Jean was in distress, first in 1966 when she suffered heart failure, and again, later that year, when the screws at work grew tighter. But this time, no one would know. Marion surely would have been on the next bus – report or no report – had she been aware of Jean's deep despondency.

During this time, Jean was not only urging Marion to take a break from work, but also fretting over Catherine. Gordon became ill while the couple was at their second home, and Jean wished that 'we had gone at once but we were committed to the cottage.'[23] Jean's motive for a visit was sisterly concern. For Margaret, the trip had a different purpose: to make tangible Jean's attachment to Catherine and, hence, to the world. To further the process, she intended – without revealing the big secret – to tell Catherine that Jean's retirement was proving difficult. Though the visit may well have had the desired effect on Jean, Margaret was left frustrated with Catherine. Her confidences had drawn a brisk response: Gordon had retired with no malingering, and so should her sister.

Marion and Jean shared the view that Catherine had a certain fragility of body, mind, and spirit, a sensitivity reflecting her artistic temperament. Burdened also, as they believed, with a neurotic (albeit devoted) husband, Catherine required protection. As much as Royces could, they fussed over her, at least in their minds and letters. Neither Jean nor Marion would have expected the kind of support from Catherine that Margaret sought to elicit that weekend in July – indeed, they might have looked askance at her attempt. Yet, one wonders how Catherine would have responded had she known that her sister had tried to kill herself, had she realized that Jean had named her as the reason to live out her natural life. The three sisters were very attached, but intimate talk was never their strong suit – certainly not with one another.

In any case, Jean proved as good as her word. By late 1969 she had re-entered the spirit of her former life. Focused on Queen's, friends, family, and travel, always interested in history, politics, and the passing scene, and passionate about music, theatre, and art, she left a record of commentary and accomplishment that defies any reasonable desire to categorize or limit. A single, older woman in retirement: a denouement – surely this would be easy enough to capture in a few pages. But after a year of poring over letters, account books, and day books, and interviewing her friends and reading between the lines, I abandoned this assumption.

In these last years – her 'retirement' – not surprisingly, she continued to produce opinions on everything. Some of these were contradictory, some were harsh. Often they were informed by new reading, old memories, and current experience. They are often evident in her many casual comments and off-hand canny judgments.

Two stories reveal Jean's commitment to improving educational opportunities for women. In these stories – of the Aletta Marty Scholarship and the Ban Righ Centre for Continuing Education – we see her as protofeminist strategist. At the end of the day, she clearly saw both projects as successes. Their realization provided her with considerable satisfaction and pleasure, and they are worth some elaboration.

In Jean's words, the Marty 'makes a wonderful tale of rooted prejudices working hand in hand with a genuine desire to provide opportunity.' Aletta Marty, she wrote, graduated from Queen's in 1894 and 'taught for some twenty-five years in the schools of the province including the St. Thomas Collegiate Institute.' In 1919 she was the first woman in Canada appointed to an Inspectorship of Public Schools, and 'in that year Queen's gave her the LLD Degree' – the first woman, she had been told, 'given an Honorary Degree for merit.' Although Marty was 'a sponsor of higher education for women,' it was not she but Wilhelmina Gordon – the intrepid Minnie – who became 'the moving spirit' behind the creation of a scholarship for graduate study that would be 'in Aletta Marty's honour.'[24]

As Jean noted in her 1976 resignation from the Marty Committee, she had been with the project almost from its beginning, and had continued to serve 'by special invitation' after retirement.[25] During this time she worked to 'bring the history of the award up to date, [though] the chief problem' was persuading the fellows to 'write about their accomplishments.' When they obliged, she happily relayed their stories to Marion. The 1953 winner, a marine biologist, was 'one of the first North American women to work on an oceanographic ship. It took ten years for her to persuade the authorities that women are capable of fitting into the accommodation offered.' Soon she was to publish a book 'on a calceolaria group of marine algae.' The 1959 scholar had a Readership in Physiology at Queen Elizabeth College in London, where she pioneered 'micro-electrode techniques for studies in the mechanism of action of neurotoxic components from snake venoms on neuromuscular functions. Her work provided tools for study of membrane structures and synaptic mechanisms.'[26]

Choosing winners was always difficult. In 1977 the award went to a PhD candidate in clinical psychology interested in the emotional stresses suffered by autistic children and their parents. 'You can imagine,' she wrote, 'that her selection involved the Committee in a good deal of discussion. Some members thought that she did not meet the usual requirements; they had a preference for pure research and we did have an interesting candidate who proposes to work on de Maupassant.'[27] Jean allowed that they needed several scholarships but were 'fortunate that the women graduates of the twenties recognized the need for at least one good award.'[28]

Jean often praised the work of the Marty committee. On one occasion, 'a special meeting of some of our really able Queen's women' was held in a member's apartment:

> Evelyn gave us a sumptuous lunch, but food was unimportant. The sheer delight of seeing the group was nourishing in itself – a doctor in a large country practice already bringing her second generation of babies in to the world; a lawyer in University teaching; Anne Saddlemyer fresh from her teacher post at Victoria and her work at Hart House; Gail Stewart who is to my mind a very constructive citizen; a teacher from the Toronto system who has the true gift of exposition; a psychologist from York whom I last saw years ago in London where she was working on her PhD; a delightful woman trained in science (life) now occupied with family matters (3 children) but finding time for useful community work. People of this quality justify our Institution.[29]

On her resignation, Jean wrote that the committee 'had achieved most of the things that I have wanted for the Marty award.' In particular, she was 'pleased that we have removed the age barrier, that the terms of the award have been broadened to take into account the value of creative work, and that we seem to be in tune with changing patterns of learning.'[30]

This last referred to a dispute that surfaced in 1970 over whether the award should be offered to a candidate who was married with children. 'Two of her greatest friends' on the committee were against the award, insisting that 'she had made her choice when she married' and had children. Jean wrote that both women were 'distinguished academics, undoubtedly good wives and mothers [who] do a lot of useful voluntary work. [Yet they] could both be making useful contributions to their fields.' She urged Marion to keep this bit of intelligence confidential. The applicant, Elspeth (Wallace) Baugh, she was sure, 'would be as shaken as I was by this [extraordinary] opinion.'[31]

This event occurred in the same year as the Royal Commission on the Status of Women published its report. The notion that married women – especially those with children – had made a choice and should live by it was hardly 'extraordinary.' If women needed to work for pay, they should get jobs, not PhDs. The members of the committee were not so out-of-step with majority opinion – Jean was ahead of them – though the tide would soon turn.

Jean's second project, the Ban Righ Foundation for Continuing Education (BRF), aimed to facilitate the re-entry of mature women who wished to return to university. Queen's had lagged behind other universities in this area, but the BRF, now thirty years old, more than closed the gap. Though the BRF, married women, single mothers, and women with few economic resources or little confidence were welcomed and sustained in their university studies. As part of the campaign to garner support, Jean provided the *Alumni Review* with a prehistory of the foundation, including a background on the financial capital – the 'largish sum' that made the foundation possible. In Jean's version, the story went back to the turn of the century and Queen's first female graduates. 'They were forward-looking women who, having gained for themselves the privilege of higher education, wanted for their successors an atmosphere conducive to good work and the advantages of corporate life. These values, they thought, could be attained best in residential life, and the campaign for a residence for women began.' Fundraising was long and arduous, and though the Board of Trustees finally agreed, in 1923, to match their efforts, later the women felt betrayed by the board's financial sophistry[32] – an aspect of the story that Jean chose to omit from this version. Through the years, the women's residences flourished under their own board – the Ban Righ Board, which was constituted in part by the original fundraisers and their supporters. Jean knew them all, of course. As a student she had lived and donned in the residence; as registrar she had ensured that female students knew the stories of their benefactors and would promote their legacy. For the *Alumni Review* she focused on a 'story of constant striving and accomplishment, of friendship kept green through the years, and of social living warmed by the flames of a central hearth.' More prosaically, she informed her sister, here was a story of funds accumulated through 'careful management, indeed, one might say "stern pruning."'[33]

In 1969 the university moved to integrate 'the financial operations of the women's residences ... with those of other ancillary enterprises of the university.' In so doing, it made itself the trustee of the accumulated funds. Because the women's residences turned a profit and the men's residences a deficit, this was a smart, if opportunistic, financial move.[34] Once again, the women felt betrayed. The Ban Righ Board protested, but lost its independent status. As Jean put it in her sanitized version for the *Alumni Review*: 'Time marches on. Emphases change.'[35]

Yet the women succeeded in protecting the surplus funds. Jean wrote to the Board of Trustees that 'the accumulation of monies [had been] built up over the years by the prudent management of the women, through careful buying, conservation of resources and the personal efforts of every member of the residences – both staff and students. Their use for a women's project is a natural measure, and any thought of spending the money on other than a women's project would be unacceptable to the women of Queen's.'[36] Jean based her argument for the funds not on any notion of women's disadvantage within the academy, but rather on a claim to natural justice: this was the women's money.

Jean was well positioned to play a key role in this protracted debate about 'the money.' In January 1970 the board appointed her to the Ban Righ Residence Board, where 'a great deal of discussion [eventually ensued] about the wisest use of the monies and, to bring matters to a head, [a six-member subcommittee was struck] with myself as chairman.' Shortly after, the secretary of the university, John Bannister, responded with a breakdown of the funds, and with his view of the constraints on their use. The principal sums were in two trust funds: the first, worth $267,524, could be used for 'new residence purposes'; the second, valued at $119,731.39, was only for 'new residence construction.' Bannister added two cautionary notes: first, it would 'be unfortunate to tie up these funds for any new purpose in perpetuity.' Second, there might be 'some objection to limiting scholarships to women students'[37] – a point that Jean was 'not inclined to take seriously.'[38] No evidence suggests that she accepted any of the other constraints outlined in his letter.

Six weeks after assuming the chair, Jean wrote Evelyn Reid, the Dean of Women and member of her committee, lamenting that nothing had yet happened aside from 'conferences by letter and some conversations with people in this bailiwick.' In her letter, 'as basis for discussion,' she offered two proposals for the funds. The first was 'to establish a Centre which should not be called a Women's Centre but, rather, a Centre or Foundation for Continuing Education – in Radcliffe parlance.' She took three pages to outline this proposal, sparing only a paragraph for the second, namely, the setting up of a scholarship plan. She reported that so far, she and Helen Anderson liked 'the first suggestion though we may not be able to afford it,' and that she didn't know where other committee members stood. She had also consulted the former Dean of Women, Bea Bryce, 'who has a special interest in the way the money is used but she would not commit herself.' Jean thought – and this was 'pure supposition' – that Bryce 'would prefer a Scholarship Program,' and urged Evelyn to cancel a competing engagement in order to attend the first meeting 'because frankly we need you here.'[39]

'From its inception,' Jean recounted in the *Review*, 'the Subcommittee agreed that the funds should be invested in people rather than bricks and mortar.'[40] This put the committee on a collision course with the terms of the trusts as the university interpreted them. In the course of its deliberations, the subcommittee resisted an attempt by the university to sink the money into a general university centre for continuing education, and wisely recommended that 'the capital of the funds be left intact and the expenses of the project be kept within the limits of the income.' The decades of 'stern pruning' continued. People who did not know the history of women's struggle with the university argued for spending the capital, assuming that Queen's would continue to fund a successful project. Others suggested that the need for the foundation would 'disappear in time,' so why not blow the bundle – or not start at all? 'But members of the sub-committee,' Jean wrote, 'believed firmly that continuing education is not a passing phase.'[41] An interim report defined the foundation as 'an opportunity for mature Queen's women [currently] deterred [by] lack of encouragement' to return to university 'to continue their creative and professional development.'[42]

The project attracted great interest. 'You would not believe,' Jean wrote to Marion in September, 'how many women want to have a say in the spending. My mail is full of suggestions, many of which are sound. The majority opinion seems to be a project in continuing education but a large group want to put the money into bursaries.'[43] Some objections questioned the establishment of a centre for women only, but Jean was able to inform her sister at the end of January that 'we got through at the BR Board a plan for a project in continuing education for Queen's women. I shall now have to work up all the material for presentation to the Board of Trustees.'[44]

At the trustees' meeting, the proposal carried, with only the former Dean of Women raising objections to 'this form of segregation.'[45] In response, Jean assured members that there was 'no intention to segregate the sexes.' Women would 'be free to invite their friends, both men and women.' She reiterated that women faced specific challenges 'returning to university whether they are young or old.'[46]

Five years later, in her last, and barely legible, letter to Marion, Jean restated her concern about the potential impact of Bryce's opposition. 'As you possibly know, Bea Bryce has been vocal in her criticisms of using the special funds as a means of starting an experiment in Continuing Education.'[47] Marion understood, and put the problem bluntly: 'I hope the Bryce woman does not poison [people's minds] about the Foundation but, in any case, as you suggest, it surely has justified its existence.'[48]

Jean had been determined that it would. In February 1974, with the approval of the Board of Trustees still to come, she had swung into action on the naming of the first director. 'I am thinking of Helen Mathers (Donald's wife),' she informed Marion, '[although] I have not mentioned it to her as yet.' As Marion knew, Donald Mathers, Principal of Queen's Theological College, had died eighteen months earlier. 'Helen's two older boys are in College and the youngest of the family, also a boy, is well up in school. I think she might enjoy the job and certainly she would have a great deal to give to it. Added to that she knows the university in a very special way.'[49] Indeed she did. Helen accompanied Donald when he came to Queen's in 1953. 'Helen is a very good person,' Jean told her sister. 'She does not have the academic status of some of the other candidates but she does have a sound background of work at Occidental College followed by two years of graduate work at Union Theological Seminary under John Bennett, Reinhold Niebuhr, Paul Tillich and so on.' There she had met Donald. After his doctoral studies, 'they went to England to a job with the British Student Christian Movement.'[50] Jean held both Mathers in high esteem. Though much younger, both were SCMers, with something of a shared history and set of values. They were her kind of people. Their old SCM colleague – and hers – Martyn Estall had presented the university tribute to Donald. 'Written with great feeling, [it indicated] Donald's universal appeal. He was well liked and admired by everybody and with it all he always maintained his integrity.'[51]

Jean ruminated over other candidates with her sister, but even before advertising the position she agreed with Marion that Helen was 'the best choice if we can get her.'[52] A month later, Jean announced that 'if she decides to try it, we shall certainly appoint her.' By then, there were other applicants and the committee, according to Jean, had decided to advertise – not for the usual reason but rather 'in order that the public at large will know about the plan and the opening.'[53]

This Old Girls network equalled anything Queen's men routinely deployed. The committee made a gesture at an open competition, even interviewing twice one highly qualified candidate (who greatly impressed Jean). Though Helen believed that her appointment resulted from her status as Donald's wife,[54] others believe it was more complicated than that. Helen was an insider, untainted by any suspicion of (feminist) radicalism. Jean divined that a candidate acceptable to the powers-that-be at Queen's would alleviate criticism of this 'radical' venture, and ensure the centre a fighting chance.[55]

During those years, Jean was seeing close-up how difficult life could be for an outsider who marched to a different drummer, who had the winds of change at her back. Evelyn Reid assumed the position of Dean of Women in late October 1971. Less than a month later, Jean expressed 'amazement at her quick grasp of things; she has already noted the tendency to keep women in subordinate positions and the bias against women applying to professional faculties in spite of the pious comments by the University Council.'[56] An instant fan, Jean soon became a good friend. Two years into Evelyn's term, she wrote that 'she has a perceptive understanding of today's students, a happy rapport with them and a stimulating and imaginative approach. [But] her job here is uphill; Queen's draws too much from the Establishment to be an entirely satisfactory centre for her.'[57] Nothing that happened later changed Jean's mind about Evelyn's abilities, her difficulties at Queen's, or the reasons for them.

In June 1975, Evelyn visited Japan, thereby missing the fiftieth anniversary of Ban Righ Hall – 'a strategically unwise' move, Jean thought. Many alumnae attended, and the first rule of politics strongly suggests that Evelyn should have been there to 'combat the antagonistic forces who represent a largish group.' Though Evelyn enjoyed some strong support, 'an influential corps of both students and staff' and alumni still hankered after a 'matriarchal dean.' Evelyn often faced 'offensive' criticism from this 'articulate' group. 'If only alumnae had the chance to meet Evelyn who is her own best advocate, [they would have welcomed] a person who can help the students test their own experience and their new ideas about the society of the seventies.' Evelyn, Jean wrote, 'was as well equipped to do this as anyone we've got.'[58]

This account of Evelyn's attributes came in response to a letter from

Marion seeking applicants for the Office of Dean of Women at the University of British Columbia. A year later, Marion was scouting for a person to fill a senior position with the International YWCA. Once again, Jean extolled Evelyn's virtues: 'her philosophy, her understanding and powers of absorption enriched by her originality, fair practice and strong sense of fun.' By then, Jean thought she had 'earned the respect of her associates. Working under constant pressure she defeats the snobbery of the confirmed academic meeting him or her with her own quick perception.'

In response to Marion, Jean also assessed Helen Mather's qualifications for the YWCA position. She was full of praise for Helen, 'who is such a good person, but not so far ranging in her interests [and with] no administrative expertise.' By then, Helen had turned out to be 'exactly the right person for the Ban Righ Centre. She is doing a superb job, at her best working directly with people in her own constituency [maintaining] the personal connection.'[59]

At the formal opening, Jean presented 'a history of *The House That Grew* with quotes and pictures from the 1925 Ban Righ accommodation for 100 girls [to the current residence] for 1475. The photographs came from Montreal and Toronto and little towns all over the country.'[60] Two years later, at a gathering at the centre, Jean chatted with several women, some 'taking advanced degrees, others beginning programs, and all were enthusiastic about their work.' In one of her last letters, Jean enclosed the fall program for the BRF, adding that 'the way Helen spins out her tiny budget – [including] some special money gifts from interested friends – is almost miraculous.'[61]

Jean was canny. Once the foundation was set up, as she told Marion, 'I deliberately refrained from going on the board but I am sitting in with the group at this phase as a resource person.'[62] She knew she wouldn't be around forever. But she chose the members – and did the next best thing to being there by delivering the person she most trusted, her friend Margaret, to whom she wrote a formal confirmation of appointment.[63]

Jean's active involvement with the Marty Scholarship and the BRF locates her within the mainstream of 1970s feminist activism. Her comments about a Queen's conference on women, organized by Evelyn Reid in 1973, indicate at the same time her own line in the sand with regard to the substance and style of feminist radicalism. On the question of style, she could be scathing. 'Humans in the mass (there were several hundred women at the Conference) can be overwhelming and distasteful,' she wrote Marion. 'Strident females punctuating their utterances with four letter words, swarming around in bare feet that were not clean, smoking and coughing incessantly or chewing gum with machine-like precision, effaced the civilized among them. At one point [when a woman I know] exasperated by the vulgar expletives of the group around her, asked why they found it necessary to use such distasteful language she was told that it was for *emphasis*.'

At the other end of the conference's political spectrum, Jean was 'charmed' with Sister Catherine Wallace, who 'spoke of equality as a personal thing depending on the way the individual feels – if you feel equal you are equal, you become an existential being.' Sister Catherine had the added blessing of reminding Jean 'in so many ways' of her sister, who had died six months earlier: 'her mannerisms, her gestures, her way of speaking and her overlying objectivity.' She was 'equally charmed' with Jill Ker Conway, then a vice-president at the University of Toronto, because of her 'quickness of mind, background of knowledge and generally sound approach.'

Her reaction to the speech of Queen's alumna Gail Stewart reveals to us her sympathy with those who presented a radical critique that did not speak specifically to the position of women. Gail in her 'thoughtful paper ... analyzed the present state of society revealing a dark age which to her mind drained our spirits, our natural curiousity, our energies, our hopes and our health, gives us licence to manipulate, coerce and threaten each other, rapes our natural environment in pursuit of disconnected things. She feels that we are being forced to support and serve our institutions rather than the reverse.' Although she was 'too categorical,' her paper did provide 'room for discussion,' though at this conference – lamentably, in Jean's opinion – no discussion followed. 'Some half-dozen of the conferees simply took the floor after she finished and railed against the subservient position of women and the discriminatory forces at play against them.' For those women, in the heyday of second-wave feminism, Gail was a spoiler, analyzing the state of the world rather than honing in on the centrality of women's oppression. For Jean, Gail's rhetoric was more familiar, more in tune with some versions of 1930s SCM talk. It helped that she had known Gail 'for years, respected her fears and admired her ability.' She had become a 'confirmed revolutionary,' but she had 'spoken from the heart.'

Jean admired Gail. But Marion would have understood Jean's one-liner, about another conferee who 'took a large part of the time to introduce herself,' as at once dismissive and amusing.[64] Others, more in tune with second-wave feminism, would have approved: 'the personal is political' encapsulated the new perspective. At times, Jean did see the link between a woman's private and public life. In research she did on early Queen's women in medicine, she concluded that Elizabeth Smith 'made a very good marriage; her husband Adam Shortt must have been enlightened in his attitude to women.'[65] Certainly the personal could be fascinating, though she displayed some ambivalence. For Jean, the 'great value' of the memoirs of Dutch ecumenicist Visser T'Horft resided in their not amounting to an 'I' book: 'He did not dwell on his own achievements [but I] should have liked more comment on his wife and family and the process of living in Geneva through strenuous years.' The second volume of Virginia Woolf's biography was 'even more interesting [than the first] probably because it is based largely on unpublished material, it has a particularly personal quality.'[66] But these were literary works.

Overall, Jean held with the distinction between private and public; for example, she urged that 'in setting up courses on women that they have strong academic content, and are not just emotional in tone.'[67] The early women doctors 'seemed to surmount their difficulties with a lightness of touch,'[68] and this you may be sure was a compliment. As a 'junior lecturer,' Pauline Jewett remembered 'talking to Jean about my anxieties, and there were many and she would talk in that marvellously penetrating way. [But then] she would stop that conversation about me and my problems and tell about some trip she had just been on. And she was such a shrewd observer. And she was such a student of literature, that when she went away and she did sort of one country at a time and came back and told you about it, it was spell binding and she would stretch your own imagination beyond the day to day things.'[69]

Jean's letter to Marion about the women's conference reflects this calibration astonishingly well. At the time, Marion was recuperating in hospital from an operation on her foot (an unsuccessful one, as it would turn out). Jean acknowledged her sister's travails only in the last paragraph of her long letter, when she asked Marion to tell her when she would be released. 'I will come up at that time,' she promised.[70] In fact, she didn't. When Marion arrived home, Jean was busy; soon afterward, her sister was 'making progress' so there seemed no point.[71] Two weeks later, however, with Marion still immobilized, Jean wrote, 'I thought of asking you to come down here but I find that I prefer to be in my own house when I am under the weather and assume you do too.'[72] Marion should be forgiven if she couldn't quite countenance this statement of preference: Jean's habit of convalescing at Margaret's was by then well established. Jean found Marion's company stressful, and as she grew older she became less willing – or able – to manage her sister's presence. Perhaps her long and frequent letters were a form of compensation. The two sisters shared many interests, and because of these letters we know much about Jean's views on her favourite projects and about her political and social leanings. From these letters we also glean that Jean's irritation with various (mostly stylistic) attributes of early-1970s feminist radicalism never tarnished her commitment to the Marty and the BRF.

Jean also understood the effects of lack of recognition for women's accomplishments. At the conference, Lin Good, who had chaired a committee at Queen's on the Status of Women, gave a 'brilliant report.' But she did not touch 'on the subtle discriminations that do exist, particularly the failure to recognize the part women are playing without much recognition, and it may be that these stem from attitudes that are almost impossible to overcome.'[73] Yet there was also overt discrimination: a candidate for the directorship of the BRF was poised to receive a doctorate, but 'the chances of a lectureship in History for a woman are pretty slim with so many men seeking posts.'[74] And when 'Mrs. [Anne] MacDermott [was] appointed Acting Archivist formally,' Jean felt certain that 'had she been a man she would have been appointed to the job without delay.'[75] When crafting citations for honorary graduands, some of whom she recommended,[76] she worked on them assiduously. In writing a citation for Sylva Gelber, Marion's successor at the Women's Bureau, Jean found it 'easy enough to enumerate her activities in government service to Palestine and Canada and the Bureau but more difficult to get across her natural spontaneity and joie de vivre. Her ready wit, her histrionic ability, her compassion and her profound knowledge of music illuminate and give spirit to her achievements – but I am struggling over how to say this.'[77]

Jean pondered a good deal over honorary degrees. But tellingly, when Marion was awarded an honorary degree from Acadia, Jean explained to her that students, parents, and faculty were somewhat impatient with this part of Convocation. Indeed, she assured Marion that many faculty members 'are vehemently opposed to the whole idea of Honorary Degrees. George Rawlyk, an import from Dalhousie, a very articulate Professor of History with positive views, is almost emotional on the question; probably he feels he has to attend in fairness to his students and he begrudges extra items on the program.'[78] In an earlier letter she suggested that 'the business of a [honorary] degree seems a mixed blessing. Perhaps Pauline [Jewett] has found the best solution. Queen's offered her an LLD this spring and she refused in a very gracious way saying she wanted to prove herself in her new job before accepting special recognition.'[79]

During these years, many of Jean's university activities were a function of her membership on the Board of Trustees: that had been her route onto the Ban Righ Residence Board. But she also served on the advisory committee to set up the Faculty of Education, at the request of its first dean, Vernon Ready, who had been one of her favourite students.[80] After attending some policy meetings there, she concluded that it was 'a busy, happy place built on the affluence of the early sixties,' and standing therefore 'in sharp contrast' to the Opportunity Shop, where she did volunteer work and came up against 'quite a different group of people. I was struck [this morning] with the number of men buying clothes for their small children, worrying about size and style. I wondered several times if they had broken marriages behind them. The women shoppers are less intriguing because they are very sure of themselves and jealously eager to get bargains.'[81] She was a bargain hunter herself, and quite aware of rising prices. 'I do notice that more men are shopping with their wives,' she wrote, 'and I suspect that this is a device of the women to make their husbands realize how prices are affecting the food budget. I have noticed how carefully the Chinese students buy. [They] are economical and appear to watch nutritive values. They do not pick up yesterday's baking from the low-cost table (ghastly stuff with heavy sugar content) but always have greens and the cheaper yellow vegetables such as turnips.'[82]

At Queen's Jean sat on the Campus Planning Committee, the Board of *Queen's Quarterly*, and the Bookstore Committee, which she contemplated shaking up by urging the appointment of Bob Miller from the SCM Bookstore in Toronto. 'I had rather hoped that we might inveigle [him] into coming to Queen's,' she wrote, 'but that was just a thought at the back of my mind.' Although the bookstore had a competent manager, 'a goodly number of people would like to have the services expanded (there is no really good bookstore in Kingston). Unfortunately the politics of the situation [make] it difficult to do anything.' The bookstore had been 'established originally by the Faculty of Applied Science, and their representatives have a tight grip on it.'

Some students wanted a more general bookstore, but 'the engineers are content if the budget balances each year.'

As we saw with the directorship of the BRF, Jean was something of a head hunter. In early October 1974, she and Margaret were in Gananoque, 'beautiful beyond words with the autumn colouring. The swans were idling in the river and all the world seemed out of doors. We ran into Agnes Benidickson and the Senator en route to Kingston [who were] impelled by the scene to stop for a while.' Marion knew Agnes, who was the daughter of James Richardson, who served Queen's as chancellor from 1929 to 1939.[83] Jean said nice things about her and then added: 'We were on the Search Committee for the Principal last winter and I got to know her very well. I think she might well be our next Chancellor when the present incumbent drops out. I think she could do the job very gracefully.'[84]

Given that former governor general Roland Michener had been installed as chancellor only six months earlier, Jean's point was prescient.[85] She took the opportunity to leapfrog from Chancellor Stirling over Michener to the hoped-for Agnes Benidickson. 'Dr Stirling,' she wrote, 'had done a magnificent job. Every member of the university feels that he is a personal friend. His graciousness and personal charm and knowledge of the financial world made [John Deutsch's] path easier than it might have been.'[86]

For Stirling's successor, 'I should have preferred a younger man,' Jean admitted.[87] Yet the reasons for her tepid response to Michener – age and sex – seem disingenuous, given that she went on to extol the virtues of his predecessor, then 'well up in his eighties,' and that the entire discussion had been sparked by her chance meeting with Agnes Benidickson. Clearly neither 'younger' nor 'man' matched her criteria. More to the point, she did not seem to take the 'Honourable Roland' seriously, though she enjoyed telling Marion that 'garbed in his jogging dress he came second to the Dean of Arts and Science in a bicycle race around the football field, leaving the new principal far to the rear.' On that visit she had 'only a brief conversation' with him; neither she nor anyone else heard about his recent trip to China: 'Most of his free time here was given to athletic events.'[88]

Jean was heavily involved in Michener's installation, and relished all the finer points of protocol surrounding a person of his stature. His installation was a great occasion, 'entailing a great deal of planning and research,' including the ceremony and 'the invitation list. This latter seems a small thing but a great many decisions have to be made.'

Afterwards, she extolled the 'really beautiful Convocation. Grant Hall had been furbished up and the red carpet was out. The staff was colourful in academic dress [and] the chancellors from the universities of all of Canada looked regal in their elegant gowns.' How *all* the chancellors came to be invited provides an endearing comment on one of the most austere of public men.[89] 'In the beginning we agreed to invite the Chancellors of the Ontario Universities only but Trent Chancellor Eugene Forsey mentioned in passing to Stanley Knowles that he was coming to the Michener Installation and Mr. Knowles asked immediately why he had not been invited to represent Brandon University.' As a result, they invited the whole phalanx, 'and we had as distinguished a group of Canadians as it was possible to get – everyone from Bora Laskin to Gerhard Herzberg.'[90]

Less than two months later, in the wake of John Deutsch's resignation, Jean found herself 'in the thick of' another installation. 'You will be amused,' she wrote Marion, 'that I am again involved in the process here. The chancellors affair went so well that everybody urged the same committee to do the job again. Whether we were flattered by so much appreciation I can not decide.'[91] This ceremony would be 'perforce purely a Queen's affair,'[92] but five months in advance they were 'mulling over invitations, planning program, making decision on numbers, deciding on Honorary Degrees, [and] discussing student participation.'[93]

John Deutsch had 'broken the news' of his resignation at a board meeting the previous October. 'He will be difficult to replace,' Jean thought, 'but he insists that the time is ripe for him to go. Many of the projects on which he has been working are coming to a conclusion; he feels that the university is in a sound financial position and he wants relief from the tremendous pressures.'[94]

Following the board meeting where Deutsch announced his resignation, hallway talk began immediately on the question of his successor. Jean took exception to a 'brief conversation' she overheard and wrote to Chancellor Stirling: 'The suggestion came up that the search for a Principal might not be too arduous in view of the number of able men on the staff who could fill the position.' In support of her contrary argument that they should, instead, seek an 'outside' candidate, she cited a 'strong feeling among many members of staff and graduates [as well as] a desire to break the economics-political science tradition and to bring in a fresh point of view.'[95]

In making her case, she noted that the 'outside activities of the retiring Principal had brought great prestige to Queen's,'[96] as well as robust student registrations. Additionally, 'Dr. Deutsch's contributions to the local community brought town and gown together in an unprecedented way ... This kind of repute is essential in these days when universities are looked upon as public institutions.' Tactfully, she went on to explain why 'the men who had been here a long time' would not fit the bill. 'Long years in one Faculty may have the effect of producing a lack of interest in the essential needs of the rest of the university [while the] demands of a heavy post [may] not allow more than a minimum of opportunity for taking part in outside affairs.' Put bluntly, the men she knew they had in mind were too parochial.

She urged instead 'a man of considerable renown with connections that give him access to local, provincial and national circles; a man with quick perceptions who can listen as well as talk and can synthesize into a connected whole; a man interested in the student and his place in the scheme of things; a man capable of striking a delicate balance between academic awareness and administration.'[97] The only internal candidate she named was 'a young man,' Duncan Sinclair, who was currently a professor of physiology. (As a boy, he had awoken her on Saturday mornings by ringing the wrong doorbell.) She assured Stirling that he had 'great potential.' Jean's concern was that the search committee – to which she had been appointed – would 'force things by too much haste.' The following day she was leaving the country for six weeks, and should she not be back for the first meeting, she wanted her 'views ... communicated to the Committee.'[98]

Jean copied her letter to Chancellor Stirling to the board's chairman, Douglas Gibson, who, recognizing himself as the hallway gossip, wrote a reply. His response is curious. Part correction, part admonition, larded with condescension, it commented both on her promotion of external candidates and on the location of the internal talent. 'I think,' he began, that 'you are referring to the comments which I made on the way out of the board meeting on October 12th. Let me say in making those comments that I had no preconceptions about who should be our new principal or from where he should come.' Yet in offering this clarification, he inadvertently suggested that Jean understood quite well the implications of his remarks for a brisk set of deliberations. For 'it happened to be a fact that we have some very good candidates on our staff at Queen's' though (and on this point in agreement with Jean) 'none of them is really in the economics or political science tradition of our recent principals.' As an aside, but not irrelevant for students of organizations, Gibson's remark suggests that search committees create rather than discover 'very good candidates.' As the universe was to unfold, the principal-elect, Ronald Watts, had been firmly ensconced in the Department of Political Studies since 1955, and *his* successor, David Smith, at the time headed the Economics Department.[99]

Seven months later, Jean informed Marion that 'the new Principal is an inside man, the present Dean of Arts and Science; interestingly enough the grandson of Archibald Lampman. He is a political scientist, a former Rhodes Scholar, and he had a tight core of people on the Committee supporting him.'[100]

Perhaps Gibson and Jean were on the same page about the dearth of candidates in political science and economics. But her main point, stressed the importance of casting the net widely. On this point Gibson's letter conceded: 'It is good to have some resources of your own, and in this regard we are fortunate compared with other universities, but I agree entirely that we should look at all possibilities.' All members of the committee should engage in 'similar application of thought, avoid attaching themselves to particular candidates [and] look at the whole picture with open minds and try, [as you have], to visualize the characteristics of the person most suitable for the job.'

But on the onion-skin version of his letter that Gibson copied to the chancellor, he penned an additional – and telling – postscript: '*You may think this is too tactful Doug*.' This evidence of old boy talk indicates that Gibson's response to Jean's letter was, in fact, contrived. He prefaced his letter to Jean by noting that her 'letter addressed to the Chancellor was sent to [him] by mistake' though he had first 'thought it was a copy' for him.[101] In a breach of protocol, if not courtesy, he had then himself replied to Jean. The two men must have decided that an answer was required and that Gibson – whose comments were the target of Jean's letter – would do the job. Jean was an annoyance, but she couldn't be ignored. She already had been appointed to the search committee that would meet until the white smoke rose above Richardson Hall.

If Stirling was party to this venal subterfuge and shared Gibson's assumption that Jean needed stickhandling, Robert's Legget's expectation that, with Stirling, he could have saved her from Corry and Conn seems to be a pipe dream. But the question is, why was Jean considered such an annoyance? In this particular case, what was so outrageous about her letter – a letter that sounds for all the world like the work of a reasonable (wo)man? Clearly, there were differing opinions about the former registrar and her continuing presence in the corridors of power.

If Gibson and Stirling had had enough of Jean Royce, it was no doubt doubly irksome that John Deutsch held her in high esteem and ensured that she sat on many important committees, including the one to choose his successor.[102] During his regime, not only was she everywhere and on everything, but her name found a permanent place on the campus. Acting on Vernon Ready's proposal,[103] Deutsch announced at one of his last board meetings that the new west campus residence complex was to be named the Jean Royce Complex. 'I am not sure that complex is to be in the title,' Jean wrote Marion, 'and I was too abashed to ask any questions.'[104] She was mentioning the honour lest news of it reach Marion second-hand.

Gibson's condescension is interesting and begs comment. Mary Wilson Carpenter has coined the word 'sexagism' to capture the combination of sexism and ageism in academia,[105] which, she argues persuasively, has been so injurious to older women. Jean would hate such a neologism, but that makes it no less likely that she was on the receiving end of this common prejudice. That no board member matched her knowledge about Queen's, and about universities more generally, would not have spared her; no doubt, for some, her knowledge would have made her all the more irritating.

Two years earlier, Jean had responded to a letter from Gibson seeking advice about possible reforms to the Board of Trustees. In her letter she noted 'how much [she had] enjoyed [her] association with the board under [his] able chairmanship.' This experience had given her 'a new perspective on the university which academic administration did not afford. There is an aspect of reality and a sense of responsibility for final action.' But she had some thoughts. First, she wondered whether the board was overly freighted with alumni now that the university was 'so largely dependent on government aid. [It might be] foolish to tamper [with this] since we partially derive from the present situation what is known as the "Queen's Spirit."' [Nonetheless] in the climate of the times, it would be sounder [to appoint more] able men in public or private life who are not necessarily Queen's men. [In particular, there] should probably be more representatives from education (teaching), labour and local people.' Her list reveals that the contemporary corporate mentality had not yet made its influence felt.[106]

On another matter, she endorsed Gibson's recommendation for 'a maximum age limit' but suggested seventy-five rather than seventy-two. She herself had been enriched by her association with men of 'ripe wisdom [who were] well up in the seventies or early eighties.'[107] Jean's exclusionary language is striking today: Did she consider women part of this group of wise people?

Her letter to Stirling urging an outside appointment for principal sheds light on this question. After listing the potential men for principal, she observed that 'one of the most desirable qualities is a largeness of mind. If there is any chance of a woman being appointed, Dr. Jill Conway or possibly Dr. Pauline Jewett of Carleton University are both outstanding.' A year earlier, she had described Conway's appointment as 'Vice President, Internal Relations of the University of Toronto [as] an exciting step – (although it is a pity to take away such a productive person from her academic pursuits).'[108] Three years later, Conway was president of Smith College. Jewett became president of Simon Fraser University during the search for Deutsch's replacement. Chancellor Stirling regaled some of his colleagues with news of the Jewett appointment, noting incredulously that the university would be paying her $50,000 a year.[109]

Simon Fraser was still labouring under a 1968 censure from the Canadian Association of Universities and Colleges stemming from its dismissal of radical social scientists,[110] and Jean predicted that Pauline 'would have some difficult years ahead.'[111] A few months later, Jean spent 'an amusing evening with Pauline [who] ranges from great enthusiasm to cold fright. She says that she frequently wakes up at night in a state of clammy perspiration and wonders what she has done.' Jean thought that she should be 'all right: she is going into the job with a strong sense of purpose, good academic and practical experience, and I hope a lightness of touch.' Pauline was looking for 'a lady housekeeper,' and Jean found it amusing that 'her board presented some difficulties here. The chairman said that they had never had that kind of arrangement and when she pointed out that most presidents had wives to oversee the domestic side of life, the members recognized that this was not a conventional appointment.' After the visit, Jean received a note from Pauline: 'You are good for my anxieties. I could have gone on chatting with you for hours.' Jean was pleased: 'I think,' she wrote Marion, 'that I succeeded in opening up all kinds of situations of which she had not thought. I am always amazed at how little even high officials of the university know about its internal workings.'[112]

Jean remained alarmingly well informed about universities and their 'internal workings.' She spent the six weeks following Deutsch's resignation with Margaret, who had won a Commonwealth Fellowship to study academic administrative structures in England.[113] They sailed on the *Queen Elizabeth* from New York, and it was from on board ship that Jean informed Marion of Deutsch's resignation. Just before leaving, she was also 'saddened by the news that Hilda Neatby [was] dying of cancer.' As Jean reminded Marion, she had been at Queen's for three years writing the history of the university. Her plan was to spend the winter writing in Oxford, and she had invited Jean to visit.

She was writing to Marion on 'a glorious day at sea. Brilliant sun and blue skies, fresh but not penetrating winds.' The ship was 'comfortable [but] without the charm of the Canadian Pacific Empresses,' for the renovations had 'discarded some of the original splendour, while the lounges were garish and might have been decorated by Simpsons' cheaper services.' But these were small complaints: they 'had enjoyed every minute.'[114] Margaret needed a break from work, family, and personal pressures. Jean was in her element, and provided for Marion a snapshot of the English university scene. 'We have run the full gamut from the sleepy elegance of Exeter, the brisk purpose and efficiency of Bristol, highly influential people at Manchester, the Orwellian horrors of Leeds which for some impenetrable reason is being built up to be the great university of North England, [to] the obvious hopelessness of the future of Keele.' Jean provided an intriguing comparison between 'the new universities of Sussex and Kent. Sussex is self-conscious and inclined to take credit for all educational progress in England.' Sociologist David Lockwood headed Sussex, 'and is generally conceded to be the man in England who knows most about the running of universities; he is an attractive person, quite unassuming but obviously the director of the cult of constant evaluation of effort.' Those of us now labouring, some thirty years later, under notions of 'accountability' and the endless merry-go-round of reciprocal assessment, will be interested in the origins of this orgy of academic navel gazing. 'Planning is constant,' Jean noted, 'and one is left with the feeling that before the plan is implemented another is emerging.'

She had good things to say about Kent, which 'is not the traditional ivory tower [and] makes no boasts. [But] sound thinking is done there and the whole place has a quietude that encourages the mind to ponder. More than any other university we visited interdisciplinary courses are being worked out and there is good staff cooperation. Probably the rigors of adversity – [scarcity of funds and fewer students than expected] – are helping to bring teachers and students together.'[115]

Her letters do not fasten simply on university commentary; they reflect all manner of thought and observation. Though the autumn leaves had been 'falling slowly in the last few days high winds have brought many of them down and the oaks particularly are showing the full beauty of their contours. The various shapes have a kind of magic. I saw a little girl this morning tracing with her fingers the trunks and branches of a gnarled old tree and delighting in her play. I saw the same kind of delight in a child in a shop in Cheltenham, when she discovered the hands and feet of a model baby displaying a very pretty dress.' Here in North England she thought 'the birth rate must be rising; there are children everywhere with young mothers who look scarcely grown themselves.'[116]

Jean loved travelling, and from the late 1960s she and Margaret took several major trips and countless shorter excursions together. Aside from visits to her family, Jean – the inveterate solo traveller – now always travelled in tandem.

A trip to Scotland in 1968 'whetted [her] appetite for more of this lovely land.' In Inverness they 'were very lucky in coinciding [their] visit with the Scottish National Orchestra. While just so-so, [it presented a] really superb playing of the Mendelsohn Concerto in E,' which she had always thought of 'as part of Catherine's repertoire. The violinist was a young girl, probably 22 or 23, and she played as if inspired.' Her letter was written from a 'small hotel on the edge of the Loch at Kyle Lochalsh looking over at Skye,' and she was enchanted by almost everything.

Still, part of her letter drifts to education – this time in France, where the events of May '68 were sparking calls for reform. She knew, however, that the solution to France's problems 'cannot be in half measures.' As an example, she relayed the 'marvellous tale of the Dean of Nanterre unable to put through a simple time change to meet a local problem until it had been approved in Paris' – an unlikely event, she thought, in any case. The French, she observed, 'outbureaucrat the bureaucrats.'[117]

Two years later, they sailed on the Empress of Canada for England, Norway, and Amsterdam. On this trip, too, they left 'each place reluctantly, promising to return.' York was 'especially beguiling, a city for all time and all people. At every corner there is evidence of the Romans, the Saxons and Danes. ... William of Normandy spent his first English Christmas there.' 'Like gawking colonials' they had watched a 'fashionable wedding, a marvellous bit of pageantry.'[118] Bergen, Norway, reminded Jean of Lisbon 'built up on hills [appearing] in the distance as a mosaic of colour ranging from cream to brown to deep bright red. It was a delightful place; [I] could stand for hours watching the busy market, [yet] the charm of the town is in its people, friendly and curious and courteous with a special kind of well-being.'[119] All this would provide great cocktail conversation for Marion.

She compared the German North-West Express to Amsterdam, ('an excellent train, new and clean and modern in design') with the Dutch train that ran 'like some of our own trains in a clickety clackety fashion.' Sharing their compartment was a professor of English, 'a Wellesley woman [and] ardent admirer of Gene McCarthy.' She had worked in his 1968 campaign and 'like all his advocates thought that he had given a new interpretation to politics.'[120]

From a 'tea place' in Amsterdam she described an 'amazing scene: hippies singly and in groups, some sitting on the pavement with their knees drawn up to their chins and gazing drearily into space, some playing cards right in the middle of the thoroughfare, others in group singing to the accompaniment of a guitar, still others sauntering along.' They shared the street with 'neat Dutch couples of every vintage, families out for a Sunday stroll, groups of small girls and boys staring at the antics of older fry.'[121]

Hippies in Amsterdam were one thing, a nephew at home was something else. In the same letter, she despaired of Ian. 'Like a goodly number of his generation he has imbibed the idea that a university degree is an important accessory for a job without realizing its demands. He is quick-witted and he likes to talk and therefore he might take a course in business practice with the idea of getting some training in a lawyer's office before studying law or do you think he has thought of banking. The banks still give their young men sound training and if the manager is a good disciplinarian, this can be very good.' But Jean added, more wisely than she knew, he would probably think 'both of these suggestions tedious and boring.' She had 'great sympathy for him' but felt that he needed 'rigorous application at something that will demand everything he has.'[122]

As Ian recounts, he had become a sixties kid. 'When I first went into business at Western in 1968, I was pretty conservative, but within a year

I'd grown my hair, replaced my wardrobe with jeans, and didn't return to school' until later. Jean must have thought twice about banking and law, and decided that a sixties kid needed a sixties college. 'She gave me an introduction to the executive director of Frontier College. She said, "Go speak to these people. I'll phone them – it's a wonderful place." And I said, "Yeah, right," and I went [to talk to them].' But Frontier College was 'a very scholarly sixties place,' not at all what Ian had in mind. 'My aunts tried to do the right thing, expose me to the right influences,' Ian remembered. 'Usually, it just resulted in a lot of guilt because I was really oriented to the path of least resistance. I just hung out, I was just an ordinary kid.'[123] Jean seemed a bit crotchety about Ian.[124] When he graduated, he sent his graduation photograph, on which she commented gratuitously, 'I take no pleasure.' Style mattered, yet more important, she noted, 'He feels he has gained a great deal from his years at Western; he is happy and has a sense of fulfillment.'[125]

Her quarrel with Ian, she reflected some years later, was 'with his indifference to opportunity.'[126] She and Marion must have been quite a pair in their efforts to strew precious opportunity across the paths of their nieces and nephews. Jean could see humour in this. 'I am intrigued to learn,' she wrote Marion, 'that you have given your Spanish Grammar to Shelagh because when I learned that Spanish was one of her subjects, I sent her mine.' Although Shelagh had not acknowledged receipt, she had written a 'charming little note' after Jean had sent her *The Young Person's Larousse*. 'Perhaps she thought me over zealous in sending two grammars in one year. In any case she is a darling child. If only she could get into some kind of program that has genuine values. SEED seems to provide some kind of therapy but the range of subjects and the approach can hardly lead anywhere.'[127]

Her attitude toward her youngest nephew was quite different. Once again, Marion and Jean had been on the mark. 'I am amused,' Jean wrote Marion, 'that you also sent information about the Military Colleges to David. He must have been besieged with Literature.' Marion's lifelong interest in women's peace movements made her less sanguine about this prospect for her nephew. Her unease provoked a mini-essay from Jean:

> I have a very high regard for the program at R.M.C. and do not feel disturbed by the life there. Drilling and marching are good for posture. If a boy can take both the academic and physical demands of the course, he gets as good training as is offered in Canada; the College has an excellent

> staff in the humanities, the social sciences, and mathematics, and pure and applied science; the training is bi-lingual and the cost is minimal. David's passion for military history and his precise mind seem to give him rather special qualities for success (the attitudes of the students are as various as they are at the universities) and the staff are largely open-minded. In any case, he is not making a final decision; he has a long way to go. In view of Lyn's uncertainty about what she wants, it is refreshing to have a child whose thinking suggests some positive direction.[128]

A year after engaging hippies in Amsterdam, while Margaret and Jean were training home from Chicago after taking a freighter up the Great Lakes to Chicago, Jean had Ian's sister, Brenda, on her mind. Brenda was travelling at the time with Marion, first to a YWCA conference in Ghana and then 'all through Kenya, Ethiopia, Tanzania and Zambia.'[129] Jean addressed her letters to both. She appreciated Brenda's artistic talents, but fretted about her possible lack of focus. After recounting her visit to the Art Institute of Chicago, where she saw 'an exhibition of textiles designed by young people,' she announced that 'the Institute was a place that Brenda will have to get to know.'[130] That summer, however, as Brenda recalled vividly, Aunt Marion attended to her education: 'Did my mother tell you that [my other aunts] were dead set against [Marion taking me]? I guess they thought I was too young, and it would be a waste of time, and why waste this money on this kid? Aunt Catherine asked me, "Do you think this is a good idea?" Maybe she was appalled at my behaviour during my teenage years. Maybe she knew more than my Aunt Marion knew. We were pretty wild, running away, not listening to anybody. My parents were quite lost. In fact, I wasn't all that excited myself about the trip. I was cool about it. When you're fifteen going somewhere with your aunt ...'

However little Marion knew about the lives of Don's children, Jean knew less. As she herself noted, she saw them '*en famille*' very rarely. 'Usually Ian goes about his own affairs and Brenda has something of her own in hand, but Sunday night was unique in that we remained a family party till the end.'[131] Mostly Jean wasn't around, and no one would have thought to tell her what was going on, least of all her brother. 'My dad was a real loner,' Brenda recounted. 'He kept a lot to himself. After he met my mother and we were all little that was probably the happiest time. Then we turned into "rotten" teenagers, and he didn't know what to do with us. He just couldn't deal with it. He hid. In fact, he never said a word.'

Despite Brenda's initial coolness, and the dismay of her aunts, the trip to Africa made a deep impression on her:

> I was fifteen years old and I met all these amazing women from all over the world. We were guests of the wife of the President of Ghana in her home. And we had lunch with Haile Selassie's daughter in Addis Ababa. There was a complete welcoming party for the delegates – music, dancing, a dinner spread. We were also honoured guests at a procession of the Ashanti kings. I remember going to the house of an Ashanti king, and he was dressed in his Kenji [cloth] and all his gold jewellery, and he was so charming, and I thought, 'Well, everybody does this when they go to Africa.' We went to Treetop near Nairobi in Kenya [and] saw Haile Selassie's horses that had been given him by people all over the world.
>
> I drove my aunt crazy: There was another young girl from Quebec and we would run off, and Aunt Marion was just moved to tears – she was really quite frantic. And actually she fell and broke her arm, but she wasn't going to let it interrupt her trip. Until then she was trying to make sure I didn't run around with wet hair, yelling at me for not wearing my shoes. I mean she had no experience with kids.
>
> Near the end of the trip Marion loosened up. I went horseback riding, I guess without telling her. I had forgotten the time. The whole bus was loaded and I was [off] gallivanting. As soon as I saw the bus, I said, 'Oh no! Am I going to catch it!' But Aunt Marion was just beaming, and she said: 'Boy that horse is beautiful! You must have had a great time.' And everyone else stared daggers at me – and Marion. It was like she was secretly proud that I'd gone off and had a great morning.
>
> I think [Marion] was lonely; she really loved Shelagh and I, and she had strong feelings about our development. We were closer to Aunt Marion than I think she even knew.

Jean had gone to see Marion and Brenda off, armed with a bottle of liquor, a wallet for Marion, and a purse for Brenda.[132] Any opposition she had felt to the trip was based on projection: *she* didn't want to spend a month in Africa with Marion, and she had trouble imagining how it would all work. But Brenda was the niece, not the sister, and as a fifteen-year-old teenager set almost loose in Africa, she did as she pleased, laying the basis for a relationship that lasted until Marion's death.[133]

Brenda and Jean scarcely knew each other. Even so, over the next few years Jean often lamented her niece's non-linear trajectory. In 1974, on hearing that Brenda 'never succeeded in getting to classes on time' at the College of Art, she declared: 'If I were Don I would simply have her withdraw and get some kind of job.' Jean felt 'sorry for Celia and worried about Don.'[134] Perhaps, she thought, Gordon was right: 'Celia's children do impose on her.'[135] If true, they were hardly different from most of their peers; indeed, being 'imposed on' by one's children seems so much part of contemporary definitions of parenting as to render Jean's comment redundant. Celia's children sound for all the world like 'normal' teenagers, but this is as close up as Jean got to the species in their domestic habitat. Certainly the young of her generation and class were never teenagers in this sense.

Yet Jean also grasped for any hopeful signs. 'I am so glad,' she wrote Marion, 'that you succeeded in extracting from Brenda some information about her work at the college. It sounds as if she enjoyed talking about it and it may be that she has not found an opportunity previously.'[136] Late in 1976, just after Jean's second bout of cerebral vascular disease, Brenda considered returning to high school, and Jean sent some material on university entrance. Jean wrote a letter to Marion at two sittings. In the morning she declared: What an undisciplined youngster [Brenda] is and what a waste of potential.' Then in the afternoon she confessed, in a shaky hand: 'From afar I find myself engaged by Brenda. No doubt she will find herself later; I hope so.'[137] Two years later, when Brenda studied art in Mexico, Jean noted: 'She writes with great skill and no doubt she is making sketches as well as observing everything around her. I wish it would be possible to send her powdered milk and other food to improve her diet.'[138]

Of her brothers' children, only Stewart's daughter Lyn enrolled at Queen's. This occasioned more sightings of the 'Barrie Royces' than before – or after. In 1970 and 1971 Jean took a bus to Barrie for Christmas dinner.[139] Two years later,[140] she and Margaret dropped in en route to Sudbury.[141] Sixteen-year-old Lyn visited her for a few days in 1973. 'I had an ingenuous letter from her,' Jean wrote Marion, 'saying that it would be "fantastic" if she could come to Kingston. She will find life here very quiet but she can see the city in the midst of tricentenary activity and of course there is always the lake.'[142] Clearly, Jean didn't have a clue what they would do together: the effusive niece who could use words like 'fantastic' and the reserved aunt. But after the visit Jean was upbeat: 'Lyn is a nice youngster: she fitted in very well and was very helpful.' Jean enlisted Marie-Jeanne Coleman in the entertainment brigade, and Lyn pronounced her '"neat." It was a new descriptive term to

Marie-Jeanne and not particularly appropriate, but in the idiom of Lyn's generation probably conveys admiration.' Lyn shopped exhaustively, buying presents for herself and her whole family. On Lyn's suggestion, Jean sent Stewart 'a set of prints of old locomotives.' In his thank you letter, he reminded her 'that he had always been "somewhat of a steam-railway bug."' 'As a boy in St. Thomas he was able to identify the different railroads by the sound of the train whistle.'[143]

Earlier that summer, on the basis of Marion's letters, Jean observed that 'as a family they seem to be something out of a storybook with consistent honours in their school work, Lyn with a job, Evelyn supporting her by driving her in from the cottage each morning, [and] the boys prolonging their childhood with a summer free from commerce. They must take after the [other] side; thinking back I can't find anything so idyllic in the Royce experience.'[144]

Lyn's arrival at Queen's didn't tarnish the image, but it did entitle Jean to some observations of her own. Some months earlier Jean had expressed her generation's attitude toward long-distance telephone calls: 'I am amused at Lyn using the telephone to try to get in touch with me. This seems gross extravagance since she *can* write.' Lyn had called for information on becoming an *au pair* girl in Paris in order to learn French. Jean surmised that she would like 'to learn the language by the osmotic method.'[145]

Jean provided Marion an amusing account of Lyn's arrival. She called Lyn at Elrond College – Kingston's version of Toronto's Rochdale – to see if they had arrived. 'Her mother came to the phone and said at once: "I hope you are calling to let us know that there is a room in residence for Lyn. Elrond is quite impossible; it is filthy and I do not feel that I can have 'my daughter' in such a place."' On questioning, Jean informed Marion, Evelyn admitted that 'Lyn's room was not so bad and that the washrooms were clean.'

'I do not think,' Jean (the mistress of understatement) continued, that Evelyn 'has a clear understanding of a cooperative. Throughout the summer people come and go, and always the house management is slow in putting things in order. Some people are very careless about the way they leave their accommodation: our general standards of cleanliness have gone down everywhere and one has to make some allowances.' All in all, Jean thought it 'would be better if parents would let their young fry adjust' on their own. 'Parents always want perfection even when they are themselves somewhat slovenly in their habits. Ev has very high standards and she was really disturbed.'[146]

Once the mama was gone, Jean discovered that Lyn had 'developed greatly since [her visit]. She has embarked on two courses in Drama, one course in each of English and Latin, and Beginners' Greek. She is worried about her mother's reaction to this, but I advised it both because of her interest in theatre and in anthropology. Evelyn wants her to take French but Queen's is not a place to read French: the department is constantly at sixes and sevens, demands standards far beyond Grade XIII background, and is disinterested in the student who does not want to give all her time to French.'

Lyn's mother had 'taught her the rudiments of housekeeping, and at school she seems to have learned to sew. She is a dear child, obsessive with her own activities [but with] abundant health, high spirits and good ability.'[147] Jean followed her career in Drama with great enthusiasm, praising her 'very real triumph in carrying out the costuming of *The Cherry Orchard*'[148] and her acting ability, which for Jean conjured up 'a potential Barbara Hamilton.'[149]

Jean punctuated her comments about nieces and nephews with the phrase 'darling child.' But only with Gail, whom she saw so much more often after her mother's death, is there a sense of responsibility and complicity. It is an attachment of a different sort, provoking concern rather than criticism. With the others there was an edge in her voice, rooted in her deeper anxieties about her brothers. As she saw it, Don worked too hard, lived with too much stress, and was often ill. His kids should shape up, take responsibility, and give him a break.[150] She was 'stunned at the thought of Don shovelling. This is one thing that he should *not* do. Did you talk to Celia about it, and point out the dangers.'[151] Similarly, she had been 'saddened' to find that Lyn's mother was 'the great force in her life. Everything stems back to her authority and her achievements. Her father seems to be a figure in the mists with no part in the college adventure.' Yet Stewart had written to tell Jean 'of his pleasure' that his daughter had come to Queen's 'and his hopes for her success.' Though Lyn had expressed regret 'that her Mother's job was taking her away from her music, there was no [expressed] concern for Stewart.'[152]

Jean loved Stewart and felt protective toward him. The day Jean received the Montreal Medal,[153] in 1965, Margaret found her sobbing in her office. It was hard to imagine what could reduce this woman to a paroxysm of tears in this semipublic place. She managed to convey that she had just heard that Stewart was very ill. Although Margaret urged her to cancel her trip, she went off, reporting later that 'everybody said [she] gave a good speech which was kind.' But she was 'stunned,' she wrote, on returning, 'by Stewart's condition. There seem to be so many involvements and he needs freedom from worry.'[154] Whenever she faced a choice between her brothers and their children or wives, Jean's sympathies lay with her brothers. They were the team, albeit one with no practices and without a coach.

Jean's greatest and least cluttered familial commitment was to Catherine, whom she loved and admired. Only Catherine could keep her close to home. In January 1972, Jean put down a deposit for a cruise. Less than a month later, Catherine was hospitalized with a malignancy. Until her sister's death eight months later, Jean spent more time in Toronto, and travelling to and fro, than she had since her mother lived there nearly thirty years earlier.[155] During those months they wrote often to each other. 'Catherine dear,' Jean wrote on one occasion, 'thank you for the lovely pot of tulips with its little sprigs of pussy willow as an extra decoration. I am overwhelmed that you should have thought of a 68th birthday in the midst of all your personal worries.'

The letter is chatty, an account of 'Home,' a 'superb' television play with Ralph Richardson and John Gielgud, and news of a blackout that left her writing by 'inadequate candlelight.' But she also negotiated the arduous path that lent support without displaying false optimism. She applauded 'the quick action of Dr. Hahn in getting [her] into the right hands,' as well as Marion's news that Catherine had 'a very good physician. [Surely] her inheritance of [Dr.] Marion Hilliard's office bespeaks a high reputation in her specialty.' Such are the bits of intelligence that permit hopeful thoughts. She signed off, 'Love to you, darling.'[156]

In fact, over the course of Catherine's illness the family grew very unhappy about 'the apparent indifference' of her doctors. Jean told Marion that Catherine was 'amazing about all this,' in a letter that provided the gist of Catherine's 'second last letter.'[157] On 24 September she saw her sister for the last time. After that, her own medical problems kept her home. On 2 October Jean had her gall bladder removed. She was convalescing at Margaret's, where she remained for nearly two months,[158] when Catherine died on 16 October at Women's College Hospital.[159]

'We are all ever so thankful,' Marion wrote, 'that you have Margaret's love and support but it's hard to have you so far away. We missed you terribly, especially yesterday.'[160] She provided an account of the service, an account 'so vivid,' Jean wrote, that 'I feel I was there – as indeed I was in spirit and in thought.' Not surprisingly, for only time sees to this, Jean did not 'feel at all that she has gone. She will always be with us. We have so many memories.' (She had first written, '*I* have so many memories,' and then made the alteration.) Jean conjured up Catherine first as a child, 'a winsome little girl,' and then 'as a mature, creative woman who educated all of us. I look back on weekends with her full of music and talk and ideas and if the season allowed it at all, fires in the hearth.' Jean agreed that 'a service of commemoration would be a painful experience. None of us could bear it: it would be a kind of self-torture.'[161]

Catherine's letters from hospital revealed her humour and perceptiveness. Writing 'from the deck of this luxury cruise,' she was pleased that Margaret had taken Jean 'under her wing,' driving her, planning for her comfort. 'It is good,' she added, 'that you can lean on each other tho' I know she does most of the leaning.'[162]

Catherine was an accomplished violinist and teacher, and, on hearing the plan for a memorial to her in the music section of Lenox Library, Jean was 'moved to tears.' 'I don't think,' she wrote, 'anything would have pleased her more. As you know she revelled in the Library. I shall never forget the first day she took me there. It was almost as if we were treading on holy ground.' The memorial had begun, Jean thought, with Nancy Woods, 'who was sensitively aware of Catherine's quality,[163] and almost the daughter she would like to have had.'[164] Having Jules Eskin 'as one of the sponsors would be a great joy to her. I shall never forget her ecstasy after hearing his solo part in a concerto one afternoon at Tanglewood.'[165]

It was Marion who had experienced the 'full strain of [Catherine's last] terrible months.'[166] She had ministered to Catherine, displaying the essence of familial devotion. At one point during Catherine's illness, Jean implored Marion to take a vacation. 'I am sorry that you have decided not to go to St. Pierre and Miquelon. I think you would have enjoyed it and that the sea air would have been a benison. I hope *you will change* your mind.'[167] Instead, Marion decided on a local trip, starting in St Thomas, which, as Jean editorialized, 'you will find interesting and nostalgic but hardly a rest. You will have to be prepared to be lionized.'[168]

Jean was not only looking to give Marion a break. Catherine herself found Marion's constant presence wearying.[169] Certainly Jean did not want Marion's attention in the wake of her operation: 'I have been to the Doctor and I am having the operation on Monday morning. I am in good shape generally, and this is a good basis on which to have surgery done. *Margaret will ring when it is over.*'[170]

Immediately after Catherine's death, Jean felt 'troubled' that Gordon would be visiting. She was not up to it. 'He rang up the other night to say that he wanted to come down next weekend and proposed to bring you with him. Firstly, I question the wisdom of him driving on a weekend and secondly even while I am doing well, I should find it difficult to cope. Accommodation alone would present a genuine problem.'[171] Clearly, the same held for Marion, though Jean would 'enjoy' having her 'later in the fall' should she want a change.[172] Recuperating at Margaret's suited Jean well; it also provided a perfectly good way to ward off family.

Jean cared about Gordon, and she never tried to banish him from her life. They kept in touch, paid short visits, wrote letters. But his way of dealing with adversity tried her patience. In deteriorating health and prone to depression, he travelled, and sojourned with friends, but he never really recovered from Catherine's death.[173] Jean followed his mood swings, ever hopeful,[174] but she was honorary president of the 'get on with it' school of life. Two weeks after Catherine died, Jean wrote Gordon and 'challenged him to some hard walking'[175] when she came to Toronto to see Michael Redgrave in *Sounder*. After seeing the play, she 'suggested to Gordon that he take Shelagh. He was intrigued by the idea, but afraid she would refuse the invitation.' Jean thought they 'would enjoy knowing each other and he could give her some new interests [given his] really rich library.' She noted: 'Shelagh should be reading widely these days.' And how were *these* days, one might ask, different from all other days? But this was a perfect plan, weaving together, as it did, three of her themes: keep going, keep reading, and never give up.

Jean practised what she preached. Less than a month after her operation, less than two weeks after Catherine's death, Margaret drove her to and from the 'first meeting of a Committee on the new university bookstore so things were made very easy for me. The Quarterly Board meets tomorrow and Saturday morning I have the Ban Righ Board. This kind of thing gets one into the swing of activities and I find it stimulating.'[176]

'I am sorry for Gordon,' she wrote while on a Caribbean cruise in March 1976, but 'everybody has aches and pains and the only way to forget them is to interest oneself in some activity.' Mostly, she stayed on the 'amused' side of irritation, as she did during his brief visit two months later. 'He arrived in the early evening and immediately told me about his expected operation. Later, Margaret dropped in and his first word after greeting her was: "Jean will not have had a chance to tell you about me" – and then he retold the story.' Jean wasn't wild about hearing the story of an operation once – but twice! 'His concentration on himself is frightening,' she told her sister. 'He is the supreme egoist.' Jean could be pretty amusing too. After Gordon's visit, the lady who until six years earlier smoked with the best of them 'was trying vainly to get the smoke out of the house. I really have no patience with smoking; it is a filthy habit and the aftermath permeates every corner of the house.'[177]

Although Marion had coined the 'epithet – gentleman invalid' for Gordon (which Jean thought 'delicious'),[178] as his condition deteriorated she lavished attention on him. On one occasion he gave her 'a proper dressing down for interfering in his life.' Marion attributed this to his medication, 'for it was very unlike him. He is naturally very kind and he apologized the next day.'[179] And it was she who joined Celia and Brenda to empty his apartment after he leapt on 6 July from the window of his twenty-third-floor apartment.[180] At that time, Jean was recovering from depression and was judged too unwell to know the circumstances of her brother-in-law's death.

Gordon was part of her human landscape, and even in these last difficult years she appreciated his kindnesses. For her seventy-first birthday he gave her a subscription to *The New York Review of Books*, 'a joy to have though far too expensive a gift.'[181] She cheered whenever he showed signs of progress. '[At last] he has realized,' she wrote, some months before his death, 'that he has to put some effort into his recovery and he is working very hard at it.'[182] And Gordon, as she knew, had 'a great many kind friends [who appeared] to be faithful visitors in times of illnesses.'[183] After his death, she was 'amazed' to receive a $5,000 bequest. 'Like you,'she wrote Marion, 'I had no idea that Gordon had accumulated so much money; he did say confidentially the last time I stayed with him that he had done well with his investments but I did not pay much attention to him.'[184]

Marion and Gordon were both lonely. They had friends and family, but still they rattled about in their lives, Marion a dominant but touching figure who provided aid and sustenance to many, Gordon at sea once unanchored from his marital moorings. Both of them wanted more from Jean than she wanted from them, which was very little. Like them, she had many friends; like Marion, she had many projects. If Jean's friendship with Margaret had not developed as it did, it would be possible to think that at least in her later life she preferred people in moderate doses. Lunch, dinner, the occasional weekend, company at plays and concerts, committee meetings (lots of them): all this suited her well.

Margaret was perhaps her alter ego. It was as easy for her to be with Margaret as it was for her to be alone, and increasingly she opted for the together option. Margaret might well tell the story of an operation once, but never twice. She never earned the label egoist from Jean. Though reserved, Margaret did not shun the personal, and her interests were wide-ranging. She enjoyed theatre, and loved music – playing and listening – and revelled in good conversation. After Jean's retirement, their lives became asymmetrical, Margaret possessing far less discretionary time. Jean was a good sounding board when consulted, and helpful domestically when asked. Most important, she understood implicitly Margaret's multiple commitments. She had lived that life and knew it well. No one spent more time with them together than Dawn Cannon, who reflected that they were not as 'bound by patterns as most people'; they 'functioned independently but came to enjoy each other's mind.' They shared 'a vision of the university'; they also 'mentored each other,' sharing their love and knowledge of art, music, and literature.'[185]

Margaret and Jean discovered that they could be together without getting in each other's way. In one of those happy meetings of temperament, both thrived on companionship without control. Margaret found Jean non-judgmental, and about her, she clearly was. Anything Margaret did – or didn't do – suited Jean. At the heart of their friendship was a quiet, sustaining reciprocity and a buoyant sense of adventure. Their relationship seems remarkably unfreighted. Mother, daughter, sister, lover: to each other they were none of these, nor are any thorny projections and displacements visible. Their relationships with others provoked no jealousy or resentments; their own friendship was free of the jangle of unmet expectations, desires, and obligations.

Central to Margaret's conversation with me about Jean is the notion of trust. She trusted Jean not to want control, trusted her judgment, trusted her not to ever be boring. 'Jean was intellectually so exciting, original, and adventurous, and she really respected me.'[186] Their domestic plans were easily arranged. When Jean was convalescing, she stayed at Margaret's; when Margaret's back went out, she might stay at

Jean's. During the long illnesses of Margaret's parents – her father died in November 1974, her mother nine months later – Jean minded her house, kept up routines, paid bills.[187]

Jean still lived above Phyllis Knight, as she had since 1947.[188] Phyllis, some fifteen years her senior, relied on her presence. As Phyllis grew frailer, Jean ran errands, kept tabs, helped entertain Phyllis's niece when she visited. 'I have been shopping for Phyllis today. She can scarcely get out these days and has been wanting a new dressing gown and has hoped to get the advantage of the January sales. I found quite by chance a very pretty blue brushed nylon gown this morning and took it up on approval and she was delighted with it. The colour is becoming, it fits as if tailored for her and is warm and comfortable. At 85 she is like a little girl with a pretty new dress. The happiest part of the story is that the price was marked down from $30 to $15.'[189] At some point, they had stopped Miss Knight-ing and Miss Royce-ing each other.

Cats – Phyllis's cats – were an issue. 'Phyllis has just come out of the hospital. Sammy bit her hand, and a bad infection developed. The swelling was alarming.' Jean and Margaret rushed her to the emergency department. 'The sensible result is that Sammy has gone back to the Humane Society.'[190] Three months later there was Cindy: 'Margaret and I came in to find her with this quite enchanting little Siamese kitten in her arms. She was aglow with delight and it is a dear little thing, beautiful to look at and gentle in its disposition. It has none of Sammy's aggressiveness: it's just a quiet little householder. It followed me upstairs yesterday and inspected the house thoroughly. Someone had given me a single rose and Cindy walked around the vase in the most careful fashion and without mishap. I watched with bated breath and great admiration of the beautiful control of the body.'[191]

Then Phyllis acquired a pal for the gentle puss. After Jean's operation, the cats became a hurdle. 'I have been coming home in the mornings for some time now and gradually things are getting into shape,' Jean wrote. She felt no rush to move back. It was pleasant at Margaret's 'so close to the Lake,' and besides, the two cats were 'like an army. Every time I come in I have to make a mad dash for my door and fend them off while I get it unlocked and on to my stairway. They are a "bloody" nuisance to say the least but so important to her that I hesitate to make a fuss.'[192]

In 1977, Phyllis became 'part of an experiment' that provided care in the home for elderly people. Ever alert to her sister's circumstances,

Jean wondered whether Marion would 'consider taking advantage of "Meals on Wheels."' By way of encouragement, Jean described in minute detail a sample lunch. 'The portions are enormous. Phyllis can use hers for two days or even three but of course she *does eat like* a bird.' By then, Jean clearly felt some obligation to stay. She herself was rising seventy-four and in precarious health, and she was coping in a matter-of-fact way with a great deal. 'The ceiling of my living room is leaking: I have pots and pans littered about the hall and in the stairwell, and so far as possible have assembled the furniture towards the window at the far end of the room.' Because of this, she was staying at Margaret's, but 'Phyllis sleeps like a top and is quite safe alone as long as she is not aware of it.'[193] For some years, Jean had gone to Margaret's when Phyllis was away.[194] Perhaps it was Phyllis who kept her so long at '140,' as she referred to their home on Stuart Street.

Until May 1978, when she had a succession of small strokes, Jean moved easily and often between her cozy second floor (when the roof wasn't leaking) and Margaret's. She saw new friends and old, at her home and at theirs, sometimes at the Faculty Club or in restaurants. She entertained often – 'my invariable dish these days is spinach souffle with salad,'[195] she informed Marion while offering advice about what to serve guests. The 1973 Learneds provided a special occasion: she 'dispensed sherry and biscuits daily' and lunched each day with someone, including Robert and Mary Legget.[196] The Faculty Women's Club tea was 'always a fun occasion because we see people from the past who are old friends but seldom attend the same functions.'[197] A wintery day in January 1976 made 'walking hazardous but fortunately three buses per hour pass the house and it is relatively easy to get down town for grocery-shopping, necessary banking and visits to the Library. At mid-morning the bus is rather fun – a good many companionable people of older vintage travel at that time and it is possible to have en route a good visit with friends of long standing.'[198]

After Connie Martens retired to Capetown, South Africa, Jean saw her often when she visited, especially in the summer of 1975 when she was house sitting for Margaret, then in Sudbury while 'her mother [was] slowly dying.'[199] Margaret had a new colour TV, and Connie came over several times to watch edifying programs: *England at War*, Bill Moyers on Japan, and 'a wonderful film of Renoir's paintings.'[200]

Jean's oldest friend, Mary White, visited, and Jean's reactions were mixed. 'She was here for about two hours. She talked continuously chiefly about a recent find of Greek coins, her paper to be given in

Oxford in July, visits with friends in England to be followed by a trip to Greece.' A story Jean 'did manage to get to started her off on a diatribe against militant feminists and what she had done as a scholar to enhance the position of women.' That was not all: she gave an account of 'Pauline [Jewett's] rather pleasant arrangement for ushering in the Women's International Year' at Simon Fraser, but failed to attribute it to Zena Cherry in the *Globe and Mail*, leaving 'the impression that Pauline had consulted her. She talked about the weaknesses of the Robarts Library, the Corporation of Trinity College, the jealous manoeuverings of U.C. [University College] and Victoria, and Trinity's role of peacemaker.[201] I was getting over an attack of phlebitis, and she exhausted me completely.'[202]

Two months earlier, Jean had encouraged Marion to invite Mary to tea to help entertain some young, transplanted Oxfordians.[203] This had gone well: 'The fact that [your guest] had read Greats[204] and was aware of one of her articles would please her no end. I always got the impression that she feels she is not fully recognized in spite of all the honours that have come to her.'[205]

Undoubtedly, Mary had cause for her resentment. With more amusement than sympathy, Jean provided one story. Only one 'of the many people from Queen's who, over the years, have gone to Oxford came down with a First but Mary White always explains that she was "vivad" for a First but she was given a Second. I well remember Sir William Fyfe commenting at the time that it was pretty good for a girl and he accepted his daughter Margaret's Second as the natural result.'[206] Part of Jean's impatient response to Mary might have stemmed from what she described as 'rife academic snobbery' and the 'low tolerance' of some female academics for 'women in administrative posts.'[207]

Jean was always happy to hear from Anna Wright Robinson, who taught history at Queen's from 1943 to 1945, and then – despite a doctorate from U of T – was not renewed. With Anna there is no edge to Jean's voice, only interest, respect, and empathy.[208] Widowed with one son, her home base was Shropshire, where her husband had been principal of a boy's school. In the 1970s she went to Nigeria to teach but 'had to cut short her contract because of ill health. She has had two good years in Benin City, made a great many friends [and] become very fond of her Nigerian students and is particularly attached to her "House Steward." When she bade him "Good Bye" she felt she was leaving a son. He has been faithful and kind and a ready help during bouts of malaria. She is only 65 and wants to go back, perhaps to Zambia to a place in the mountains where the climate is more bearable.' Instead, Anna stayed in England, near her sòn – 'a likely lad who has a delightful relationship with his mother: he looks after her unobtrusively. He went out to Nigeria for some weeks last Christmas and they covered a great deal of the country on his motor bike.'[209] The next summer Anna visited, 'and was nostalgic about many things' in Nigeria. 'She would like to teach English to the many foreign women who have settled in Birmingham. They are tied to their homes. Their children and husbands are learning English at school and in business but the women are isolated.' Anna, Jean reported, 'could do this kind of thing superlatively: she is a born teacher with the gift of exposition and she always has a happy relationship with people.'[210]

Two years later, Anna wrote to say that she had remarried, 'an old friend who teaches at the University of California.' Jean's explanation for the marriage is sympathetic and revealing: 'She has been unsettled since her return from her school in Northern Nigeria, and although she is a person who gets a good deal of fun from living, she has reached a time when she needs support.'[211]

Here we might surmise that marrying at sixty-six makes a lot more sense than tying the knot at some more impressionable age – thirty or forty, for example. Jean felt happy for her friend and thought her marriage a good idea. Similarly, when her friend Eleanor Tett decided to marry, Jean declared the match 'eminently satisfactory and a happy solution to a number of problems,' chief among them Eleanor's ninety-two-year-old father, whom she was planning to look after now that she was retiring. 'The dear old man' lived in Newboro, so it was 'rather a grim prospect to think of being incarcerated' in that tiny village that did not even have benefit of a library. Bob was going to be 'a great boon.'[212] Jean enjoyed the wedding celebrations of her friends and their children, and chose their gifts carefully.[213]

But Jean never entertained the idea of marriage for *herself*, and so when Margaret, her true equal, seriously contemplated marrying, Jean asked rhetorically: 'Now why would anyone want to marry?'[214] This curiosity didn't translate into objection: that wasn't the point – she just wondered. In the arena of personal life, including affairs of the heart, Jean remained non-judgmental – and kind. How else to explain that she found herself 'sick at heart' on hearing that Margaret Shortliffe's fiancé had died suddenly? Margaret Shortliffe was an old friend, the widow of a French professor.[215] 'She and Doug had a long happy winter planning and every minute was fun. Neither of them dreamed of heart failure.'[216] If people wanted to marry, it was tragic when the fates intervened.

Jean was an adventurous traveller, and Margaret the Younger often felt the need to keep up. Their shorter trips during the 1970s – more than twenty – took them to Niagara-on-the-Lake and the Shaw Festival, the Eastern Townships and the Lennoxville Festival, and by various convoluted routes to Margaret's home in Sudbury, to Philadelphia, to Colonial Williamsburg and New York, and, of course, to Tanglewood. Their last trip was to Margaret's alma mater, Bryn Mawr, a favourite haunt.[217] In January 1975 the Guest House, built nearly three centuries earlier, served as their launching pad for a 'wonderful day in the Art Museum in Philadelphia, another day exploring Germantown and a trip to the city to see Eric Segal's 'Odyssey' with Yul Brynner and Joan Dierner, a play that follows closely the story of Odysseus after the Trojan War: the music is delightful and the choreography very good indeed.' On their last evening, 'a young American poetess, Adrienne Rich, came over from Brandeis where she is Poet in Residence. She is a talented woman and very charming.' And – home or away – 'most of all, [she] enjoyed the time in the new Library, a very satisfying building with a wonderful periodicals room and a quietness that makes for uninterrupted work. We went over practically every evening between tea and dinner.'[218]

On their last major trip, a Caribbean cruise in March 1976, 'a horrendous storm' in St Thomas forced them to take shelter in the Lutheran Church on Emancipation Square:

> a beautiful old church dating back to the early 16th century. The local mahogany of the Chancel and pulpit is rubbed to a warm glow by much use and the Communion vessels given by the original Danish Company are still in use. There is a beautiful golden cross on the chancel wall and it is like a glowing symbol. There was quite a large congregation of practically every colour from the darkest black to the sandy complexion of the vicar who has retired here from Minnesota. We were taken about by a serious black vestryman who told us the history of the church and the part it played in the political and religious life of the island. One of the early pastors of the church was the first to proclaim freedom to the slaves and the islanders are proud that this was done a good deal earlier than Lincoln's Proclamation.

Jean took great interest in the passengers. Most of them were American, but there were also 'two hundred aliens ... British, Canadians, French, Brazilians, and Venezuelans [ranging from] big business to small people enjoying a holiday.' On the whole, she judged them 'reactionary or certainly conservative in their thinking. We are both shaken at the prejudices of the Virginians, probably because we share a table with two of them – a man and his wife, pleasant people but biased on a great many questions.' She was especially shocked because they 'travelled a great deal on obviously very little, but their experiences have not opened their minds; their attitude to the negroes is incredibly stupid and yet they are charming, well-read and cultivated in other aspects.'[219] That they retained their prejudices belied her sturdy expectation that seeing the world provided the best way to break parochial and regional prejudices. For example, when a young friend from 'a singularly arid background' had gone to Guyana with Projects Overseas, her eyes had been opened 'to an entirely new world' and she had discovered 'several new dimensions of living. In helping the Guyanese professionally' she herself became 'a better teacher and an infinitely more interesting person.'[220] The way it was supposed to happen underpinned all her exhortations to the young to see the world, and her great admiration for those, like Allie Douglas, who as octogenarians travelled to China, Japan, and Africa.[221]

But however one travelled, one's mindset mattered most. 'I should say that the islands of the Caribbean are very tourist conscious: even small boys and girls are at the docks offering themselves as guides and/or entertainers. The only place where I noted overt dislike was at Martinique, but I expect there are strong undercurrents of feeling everywhere and to anyone taking pride in his particular island, it must be demeaning to have crowds from a big ship coming ashore eager to spend and expecting to be greeted warmly. Americans particularly seem to find it difficult to put themselves in the position of a well-meaning stranger.'[222]

The phrase, 'a well-meaning stranger,' is arresting, and not only as a description for what we can take to be her preferred stance when travelling abroad. More generally, she assumed that others had much to tell her, one way or another, and she observed and listened acutely, yet with no presumptions that she would achieve intimacy or acquire insider knowledge. People and places were fascinating, but outsiders only ever learn so much.

Like Anna Wright Robinson, her old friends Joe and Shirley Brooks spent several years in Nigeria. Jean was well informed about political developments there. On returning to Canada, the Brooks felt 'very strange and nostalgic about North Central Nigeria.'[223] Unable to find work in Canada, and despite Shirley's 'recurrent malaria,'[224] they returned, but 'obviously the situation had worsened since the coup.'[225] Earlier, Jean had decried the inevitable effects of oil production in Nigeria: 'I can well believe that Nigeria is ridden with corruption, the development of oil production will have brought the scum of the earth to the country and every man-jack of them will be fortune hunting. In a situation like this the ordinary people become like characters in a Kafka novel, living in a world of hints and allusions and nameless terrors.'[226] Here she was unfortunately prescient, though she didn't imagine the 'scum of the earth' packaged as a giant multinational corporation.[227]

Two years later she watched the 'Sadat proposal before the Knesset and was profoundly moved. *We seemed to be making history,*' she told Marion. 'Did you notice Golda Meir looking very regal in her purple dress and listening with great intentness to the proposal. I liked the fact that Sadat recognized what she had been advocating for some time and their brief meeting to exchange gifts to the youngest grandchild.' But she was also fearful, and again prescient: 'I hope Sadat has a strong bodyguard to protect him from foul play. [His decision to break off] diplomatic relationships with so many of the Arab states portended dire consequences.'[228]

Jean admired Golda Meir, and when she found (reading a *Maclean's* interview) that René Lévesque had just read and declared Meir's biography a 'wonderful book,' she began to 'enjoy [him] very much indeed.' Not surprisingly, she found Lévesque's 'passion for reading very appealing. Obviously it is an essential part of his life. Also his genuine concern for the development of the French Canadian is heart-warming.' She identified with 'his absorbed interest in history and his capacity for reading far into the night.'[229]

Jean was no lifelong Liberal – that's not how her loyalties played out – but she did support Lévesque's federal nemesis, Pierre Trudeau. For this reason, a visit to the Parliamentary Gallery for the opening of debate on the Throne Speech in January 1973 proved disappointing: 'Unfortunately Mr. Trudeau's speech was not good. [He spoke] in a dead sort of way like a penitent youngster apologizing for the misdeeds and lack of action of his Party. He was interrupted constantly in the most insolent way and made the great mistake of trying to reply to his hecklers.' Robert Stanfield, for his part, 'really had nothing to say,' and as she gazed down at the Conservative opposition she had 'seldom seen so sorry a collection of people. My chief reaction is that we must keep the present government at all costs.' At various times, she probably supported the CCF/NDP, and the day she attended really belonged to David Lewis. 'He made it clear that the fate of the government was in the hands of his party. ... He spoke with great assurance, his speech was well prepared, witty and direct.'[230] But Lewis was no contender, and eighteen months later she summoned Marion and her fellow Canadians to action: 'Trudeau's speech at Duke is being broadcast as I write this. We *must* return him to the Prime Ministership.'[231]

Two years later, Jean was somewhat dismayed to find that 'solid citizens [such as her friend] Robert Legget and his ilk are eager for change.' She thought they were supporting 'John Turner rather than Joe Clark,' but she had 'no knowledge of Turner's interest in the Headship of the P.C. Party.'[232] A month later, she wrote that 'the hate campaign against Trudeau is progressing and Robert is in the middle of the fray and entirely in sympathy with it. [While Robert] envisages Mr. Trudeau's dismissal early in the new year, the press recently seems to be a little more understanding [of Trudeau's motives], and certainly there is wide support of the values that he represents. An interesting coincidence,' she mused, 'Mr. Davis is having almost the same treatment in Ontario as Trudeau in Ottawa.'[233] Davis and Trudeau, incidentally, were her fellow honorary graduands. Jean's letters are replete with political commentary,[234] and there was no part of the world that couldn't catch her attention.

She also continued to reflect on the university's history, and on the politics and motivations of the men with whom she had worked. After the internment of Japanese Canadians in early 1942, there was a move to block their admission to universities in eastern Canada. In one of Jean's last long letters to Marion, she recalled the situation at Queen's, her memory having been provoked by Frederick Gibson, who 'had been asked to finish the history of Queen's after Hilda Neatby's death.' In response to Gibson's request, Jean reviewed the Senate minutes and settled into remembering. 'A liberal policy was urged by practically every member of Senate,' she reported, quoting directly from the minutes. But though the minutes read that 'discussion revealed strong feeling against race discrimination,' she added the words 'of any sort' in her letter to Marion.

Yet in retrospect (or was it at the time as well?), she found herself 'taken back' by the wording of a motion by her friends Reg Trotter and

Herman Tracy that 'a *limited* number' of Japanese Canadians should be admitted (she underlined the word 'limited' in the letter). Why limited, she asked, since in the words of the minutes, 'all Japanese students are passed by the R.C.M.P. before they are permitted to apply and, therefore there can be no reason for excluding [them on grounds of] disaffection'?

In trying to explain the use of the word 'limited,' she 'realized that R.G.T. was always inclined to smooth over any possible trouble and it may have been that the dissenter was pretty difficult to handle.'

'Several people from that Japanese Canadian group graduated,' she recalled, 'and one particularly showed exceptional promise. Unfortunately he had great difficulty in getting a job and finally took something much below his competence. On one occasion he wrote to me telling of the enmity he came up against in his job. I shall try one of these days to track him down.'

Her days for tracking were over. Even so, she continued to make political connections. After conferring with her, Gibson spoke 'to Mr. Corry who at the time of the Senate's decision was a relatively new member of staff. Corry said that he had not known of the matter at the time but that he would have been one of the first to champion the cause.'

Jean didn't put much stock in this easy posture of retrospective courage. 'It is not possible,' she wrote, 'to recreate the climate of the times. Prejudices with working groups can be very strong and the men are frequently quite ruthless in dealing with someone who is a victim of circumstance.' For an example, she pointed to Corry himself, who had 'oddly enough hedged a long time' before agreeing that Dr Edgar Brooke be asked to give the 1965 Dunning Trust Lecture.

Dr Brooke, Jean explained, 'was a political refugee from South Africa who had to leave his post and the country because of his sympathy for black people. [Corry had] complained that he was not a scholar, had no particular field except as a theologian and might cause problems with the Governments of both Canada and R.S.A.' But things went well. 'His series of lectures were superb.'[235]

During these years, Jean continued to bury herself in books. In January 1976 she was 'frantically busy writing a paper on Mavis Gallant – a writer I admire greatly but a very private person who does not reveal much of herself except in her stories.' The paper was for 'the Kingston Public Library venture into adult education.'[236] Unlike most of Gallant's readers, Jean had followed her work since 1951, when it first appeared in *The New Yorker.*[237] Jean enjoyed playing detective. 'By reading her one novel and short stories carefully,' she told Marion, 'it is possible to glean a good deal of information about her, but there is always the question as to whether she is writing of things personal to herself. It is a fascinating hunt on which I must concentrate closely for a time.'[238] In her presentation, Jean asked rhetorically, 'Who is this woman who delineates her characters so subtly and with so rare an understanding of human nature?' In the end, she declined to speculate, and refused to read art as an imitation of life, telling her listeners that we don't know Mavis Gallant because she is 'a person of deep reserve who does not like to talk about herself.' With this, Jean had every sympathy. 'Mrs. Gallant's genius is that she recognizes every nuance, she scorns the vulgarity of those who try to keep up the pretense of well-being, she is aware of indifference and hostility. She is critical of bad manners, approves the niceties of living but abhors overacting. She perceives the false but feels deep compassion for those caught in a web of uncertainty and forced to carry on against powerful odds.' Jean's portrait of Gallant carries the ring of autobiography.

For Jean, reading – not passive reading but an active engagement with text – was a life-long avocation. But as she grew older, music also became a vital source of pleasure. She went to many concerts, and they didn't have to be grand. She belonged to the Kingston Symphony Society, went to the concerts at Queen's, and hovered around the School of Music. There was even the occasional living-room concert. 'I was at a pleasant musicale at the Colemans the other night,' she wrote Marion. 'The wife of a visiting professor in mathematics is a graduate of Julliard and she played a program of Beethoven and Chopin for us. She is giving a public concert early in February and wanted to try it. Characteristically Marie-Jeanne got people together, had her piano tuned, and made the occasion into a preliminary party.' But Jean also tarried over Marie-Jeanne's preoccupation with family problems that evening, observing that she seemed 'heartened' when one of her guests, a Japanese woman who spoke little English, 'moved over, admired her dress and said "Eyes-sick" in the kindest way, so quietly that I think I was the only person who heard.'[239]

Jean read reviews and then made up her own mind. However, she took a modest view of her assessments: 'In spite of the *Globe & Mail*'s denigration [of the conductor],' she wrote on one occasion, 'we all found the London Philharmonic delightful. Oddly enough, Graham George [the Head of the School of Music] took the same position as the

G&M critic. I suspect that he talked to some of the orchestra members before the concerts and based his criticism on their hearsay: to the more unsophisticated listener it was beautiful music, played beautifully and conducted satisfactorily.'[240]

After reading 'Kragland's wonderful review of the Ashkenazy concert,' she confessed to Marion that she envied the Torontonians. 'I first heard him in Tanglewood [playing] the "Emperor Concerto" and we were entranced. I am sorry that you and Catherine don't have tickets. By the way, have you noticed lately that the students in the Faculty of Music at U. of T. are giving excellent recitals and concerts for a mere pittance and on some occasions free of charge.'[241]

Mostly she went to hear classical music, classically arranged. But not always. 'I was at a marvellous concert last night,' she told Marion, 'a re-interpretation of Bach in the jazz idiom. The musicianship of the three artists was magnificent – Jacques Loussier at the piano, Christian Garros with a battery of percussion instruments (cymbals of various sorts, drums and triangle played with sticks, knobs and wires) and Pierre Michalat, string bass. The concert was a remarkable feat. Yet, I suppose one might say that Bach still stands best on his own two feet.'[242]

'Mountains of snow, wicked winds,' and hazardous footing didn't keep her, in mid-January 1976, from 'a delightful noon-time concert at the Music Building – a solo and chamber ensemble performance ranging from Bach and Beethoven to Handel, Schubert, Faure and *Crawley*. The last is a member of the staff and his music is full of dissonance. He labelled it *Four Inventions for Piano* and the young pianist came through it triumphantly. There were two very promising sopranos, one of them a French Canadian had a particularly charming voice, the other showed promise but she has a lot of work ahead.'[243]

Jean's love for music was thoroughly intertwined with sentiment for Catherine. As much before as after her death, Jean listened for both of them, in a way that delicately transformed wonderful events into deeply moving experiences. 'We had an expected bonus in Music in Williamsburg, two gifted young people and their mutual admiration was charming to watch. As I tucked the program in my purse my mind went to Catherine and I thought I must tell her.'[244] A particular piece of music, the way a soloist played, the pilgrimages to Tanglewood, Jean's attraction to Leonard Bernstein: all of these gathered up Catherine's abilities, desires, and fascinations. Margaret's passion for music (and her car) made it possible for Jean to visit Tanglewood long after she could have gone on her own, and they went each year at least once.

'Leonard Bernstein conducted Friday night and it was a magnificent concert. The orchestra responds to him in a very special way, partly, I think because he is to some degree a Tanglewood product, trained entirely in America at Harvard and the Curtis Institute, but mostly because of his wonderful musicianship. [That night] he conducted and simultaneously played the piano part of the Mozart Concerto K453, using his left knee and foot during the piano interludes and standing up from the keyboard in the demanding orchestral parts. It is a beautiful concerto, and he was supported by two Haydn symphonies. His range is enormous, when you think of the music for "West Side Story" to Mahler.'[245]

A year later, Jean noted,

> Bernstein conducted with his usual verve, but there is an indefinable change in him, something foreboding, heightened by his black turtle-necked sweater under his white coat and a black handkerchief in his pocket. His face showed the ravages of ill-health and I had the feeling that he would not be with us for long. There seemed to be a sense of another world about him and yet he carried the orchestra through triumphantly. Liszt's 'Faust Symphony' is a lengthy piece of music, not really a symphony in classical form with restatements from one movement to another: each movement is a statement by itself and the finale is a version of a single verse with a chord [*sic*] accompaniment.
>
> All things corruptible
> Are but a reflection
> Earth's insufficiency here finds perfection
> Here the ineffable
> Wrought is with love
> the Eternal womanly
> Draws us above
>
> The Tanglewood Male Chorus sang as with one voice: only the tenor stood out and his voice floated over the audience into the night. At the final curtain Bernstein called him forward and hugged him as they took the applause – for the moment he was the old Bernstein.[246]

Just over a year later, Bernstein's name arose during a considerable dust-up between Jean and Marion. After they spent Thanksgiving weekend together in Toronto, Marion wrote:

> Your comments on my arrogance in insisting on being 'right' weigh heavily. Don't let me do it. As I think about it, I seem to allow myself to fall victim to a kind of madness of tenacity. In the case of Catherine and the photograph, the really significant thing was evidence of Catherine's endearing eagerness to meet and talk to people whom she admired. That was one of her deepest satisfactions at Lenox – she sought out people like Bernstein and how she blossomed in such meetings – exchanges – because she did have a kind of enchantment and always individuals responded to her. And I let that lovely quality be submerged in irrelevant argument. Do forgive me, if you can and if ever I do it again simply say 'Stop!' and insist that I do. I'll remember, I think. ... It was ever so good to have you come. Do come again and again whenever you have strength to endure my horrid bitchiness.[247]

Throughout her life, Jean was not one for argument, certainly not of the domestic sort. She stated her opinion, and she could launch some one-liner zingers, but she didn't go for the jugular, and winning wasn't the point. But in criticizing Catherine – especially her attachments to anything or anyone musical – Marion had trespassed on sacred ground. This argument reveals the subterranean tensions in their relationship that would begin to surface as Jean's health failed.

After her serious depression in 1976, Jean's social life overlapped increasingly with Margaret's: she saw friends and family, but Margaret was quietly organizing the visits, seeing to the food, keeping the show on the road.[248] Like many women with senior posts, she was a superb juggler. Her life was well-decked with people who mattered, as much before and after as during her friendship with Jean. She also ran a remarkably open house, including nightly dinners with Dawn and Bill Cannon and others. Her nephews and niece lived with her at various times, and students were often invited. Jean fit in with all this, and happily so. 'This is a doozer of a day. I do not remember so all pervasive a storm – wind, snow and bitter cold which seems to increase all the time. I am house-sitting for Margaret who is having some plumbing done. She has provided a half-way house for people stranded in the city because of the storm which as the day wore on developed almost hurricane proportions. It was an evening unparalleled in my experience.'[249]

Jean gave precious little ink to her health – and by all accounts, little air space – but her body was now giving her a real run for her money. She had taken several nasty falls, her heart was unreliable, and she had to cope with stroke-induced depression, especially between October 1976 and April 1977. In late 1977 and early 1978 she suffered another series of small strokes. A letter from Marion to Margaret in February expressed the hope that 'Jean is as well as she protests,' and recalled the 'agonizing uncertainty of this time a year ago,' when Jean had undergone shock therapy. 'Can you even guess,' Marion asked, 'how grateful I feel for and to you?'[250]

By April, Margaret noted, Jean had 'recognized that it was not wise to be entirely alone.'[251] Whether by accident or design, Margaret had just added on a small apartment in the upstairs of her house. In May 1978, Jean gave up her apartment on Stuart Street and moved in with Margaret and her nephew Mark, then a Queen's student. As Margaret remembered, the move happened rather slowly, but as soon as Jean's desk arrived, so did she. There she was, and there she stayed.

Don and Marion were perplexed. After Don visited in June, Marion wrote to Margaret that 'both of us are concerned lest you have too great a burden of responsibility.' Don was also 'worried lest Jean feel "stuck" upstairs.' However, Marion had reminded him that not only was Jean 'used to living upstairs but that she may, under the very wise house rules, go down if she wishes.' This was an odd comment, perhaps betraying how little Don and Marion understood about Jean and Margaret, both of whom saw the arrangement as 'house sharing.' For the first year, Jean was still able, much of the time, to roam the house as she pleased, making porridge and muffins, receiving visitors. 'It was reassuring to know,' Marion continued, 'that she enjoys life despite such unpredictable handicaps and we know that the enjoyment is in large part – in fact almost wholly due to your constant and loving concern. Our appreciation and gratitude to you beggar our power for expression – not that it is difficult to love her. She is a very special person.'[252]

Only on this last point – that Jean was a very special person – was Margaret in agreement. She found that the 'appreciation' coming from Jean's family and friends missed the nature of their friendship, which until Jean's death continued to be reciprocal and mutually sustaining. Jean's interests never flagged. For example, there is a note from Jean to Margaret from that time to pick up three books from the library: *Death Comes to the Archbishop* by Willa Cather, *The Diviners* by Margaret Laurence, and Chaim Potok's *The Chosen*. And Jean wasn't at all disturbed by her maladies. The first year, when Jean was 'stroking out,' Margaret went upstairs one day to say good morning. 'I couldn't see her so I called her name, and heard this little voice come back, cheerful little voice. She was on the floor beside her chair' and she wasn't the least bit concerned. No panic, you know.'[253] At Christmas 'she was quite active though wobbly. As both Mark and I were going away Dawn and Bill [Cannon] decided to sleep over. They didn't have a fireplace [so] slept in the living room so they could watch the fire. Each morning Jean would come down and quietly knock on the inside of the door – they were charmed by her tact – to let them know she was coming through. She had got into the habit of coming down and making a large thing of porridge for the household though I doubt the Cannons would ever touch the stuff.'[254]

Starting in April 1979, however, Jean suffered a series of critical illnesses, any one of which, Margaret wrote later to Jean's friends, 'most people would not have survived.' Margaret and Dawn recall that although the 'essence' of Jean was there for the duration, her old stamina, her capacity for give and take, and her ability to tolerate stress all declined. A major casualty of these developments was her relationship with Marion. Perhaps Jean had always needed to gird herself for Marion's visits, but now she fended them off. 'The calendar shows Easter approaching,' Marion wrote at the end of March. 'Any chance of you coming or will Marg not be driving this way? I'd like to have you and I know that Don and Celia would too. If you cannot come, perhaps I'll invade you at the week-end after Easter.'[255] When these proposals weren't taken up, Marion tried another tack. 'By the way,' she began, with studied casualness, 'I'd really like to go to see you if you do not go to Greece, before I leave for England.' She then provided three weekends to choose.[256] If the trip to Greece had been on, there would have been, for the moment, a reprieve. Jean longed to go to Greece, and Ian Vorres, the Queen's student whom she had befriended at the end of the Second World War stood ready to host her.[257] 'I do hope you will be able to bring off the Greek trip,' Marion added. 'You've always wanted to see that country and the offer of such rare hospitality comes seldom.'[258] But Jean wasn't well enough to travel. Shirley Brooks remembered helping produce a compensation prize for Jean, 'a most magnificent Middle Eastern dinner.'[259]

So the ruse was up. Jean could dream of a trip to Greece, but not contemplate a visit from her sister. Sooner war, sooner peace. She wrote Marion, in her now spindly, fragile hand – the unprecedented spelling error in one of the drafts bearing witness to her struggle to get words, any words, onto a page: 'I am sorry to tell you that I cannot have you. I have been ill, and although I have recovered I do not think we can find a sound basis for seeing each other. It may be a matter of temperament, and I am sure it is not your fault. We argue continuously, and neither of us seems able to break this pattern. I hope you will enjoy your visit in England.'[260]

Margaret and Dawn went into gatekeeping mode with an accompanying letter that stiffened the message. 'Even your letter indicating a planned visit resulted in a depressed state. It would be impossible to predict how serious the consequences might be if you arrived now.' Invoking the doctor's warning that 'emotional stress could be damaging,' they assured Marion of their own distress at having to deliver this message: 'It is so hard to be kept at bay by the ones to whom we most want to be close.'[261]

Marion was devastated. In Celia's words, 'it nearly broke her heart.' Perhaps, Celia mused, Jean had flashbacked to their childhood. 'Jean always felt that Marion was doing everything right and she was doing everything wrong and that Marion was too hard on her.' Donald reiterated that 'Jean did everything on her own, no support whatever financially while Marion got some help.' Perhaps old resentments surfaced during this time.[262] Celia and Don urged Marion to realize that 'it had more to do with Jean's mental state near the end than anything.'

Others, including Jean's physician, also thought that she was never the same after the electric convulsive treatments. But there was no softening the blow to Marion, who wanted to look after Jean, as she had Catherine and Gordon. Unlike Jean's friends, who found Marion intimidating, Celia felt that Jean was 'a harder person than Marion.'[263] 'Jean expected you to live up to your potential,' Donald added, 'and very few people do.'[264] According to Jean's brother and his wife, Marion's attitude toward nearly everyone was 'motherly.'[265] And if Stewart was the family's 'most relaxed' member, Jean was the 'most tense.' Celia explained: 'I feel that this is a reserve she had. Inside she wasn't that way. I really liked her, she was a really loving person.[266] But 'she couldn't break out of the mould she set for herself.'[267]

'When Jean lived upstairs from Marg Hooey,' Donald recalled, 'we went out fairly frequently, but she couldn't communicate. You could feel that she was dying to say something but she couldn't.'[268] Marion was granted the occasional short visit, and once she stayed with Helen Mathers and had 'several visits.'[269] To Margaret she wrote: 'Thank you for your usual warm hospitality. Like the Monsignor [Hanley, a priest-friend of Jean's] I would thank you for what you do for Jean – I have done and continue always to do so. Somehow I'd like to thank you, too, for her sake. Your loving care is the most precious gift within human capacity. It blesses you both.'[270] She continued to write long, newsy letters to Jean, about people Jean knew and didn't know, about books she was reading, about the book she was writing,[271] about plays she had seen. One night after seeing Brenda and Shelagh, Marion wrote that 'they both have innate dignity or some indefinable quality' – an observation not to be attributed to 'auntly prejudice.'[272] Margaret took pains to keep her in the loop, and entertained her at her cottage the summer after Jean died.

Just a month after Jean's letter to Marion, Margaret informed Don that 'Jean arranged for her to have power of attorney on her behalf.' They had just started a night nurse, and they had 'some day help too.' Now it was necessary to spend some of Jean's 'own resources,' and while Jean was 'extremely generous to others, she is not inclined to spend money on herself.' Margaret insisted that she was not 'carrying a particularly heavy burden. Our friends [the Cannons] are very much involved with Dawn taking responsibility in consultation with Jean in getting health care personnel, while Bill is setting up an accounting system. Jean is much loved as you know and friends have been coming in and wanting do what they could. We are all happy doing it.'[273] Jean had found – created – an extended family, and until she died enjoyed 'more personal intimacy than she had shared except for brief periods in her earlier life.'[274]

Four months later, while Jean was in hospital for a pulmonary embolism, she suffered 'a major stroke which paralysed her left side.' Doctors felt 'she could survive only a few hours.' Mark, self-described as the 'last student Jean counselled,'[275] arrived for the vigil, but she roused herself from her coma, 'greeted him warmly, chatted for a while,' assuming he was back in Kingston to start classes. Afterwards, Jean advised Margaret, 'I think Mark really would like to talk over his course selection with you.' After the doctors agreed that nothing more could be done, Jean wanted to go home, and from then on she had full-time nursing care in her second-floor flat at Margaret's. She rallied for some months, walked short distances, spent two or three weekends by a lake, watched television, and listened avidly when people read to her. 'Her spirit really is indomitable,' Margaret wrote to Jean's friends in September 1980. She encouraged them to check with her nurse before visiting: 'She responds more easily sometimes than others but I know from many conversations that she is missing her old friends.'[276]

Near the end, when Jean was completely incapacitated, some people thought that Margaret was having a gruelling time, becoming perhaps a martyr to their friendship. Margaret denied it. 'Even in the last couple of years, when half the time she really couldn't express herself very well, there continued to be a really good line of communication.'[277] As a remarkable example, she told the story of a conversation with Jean, a few months before she died, when Margaret decided to deal with her one great regret about their history.

'I had terrible personal guilt to deal with,' Margaret remembered, 'after everything that did transpire and she was ditched and then tried to take her own life.' She had never discussed this with Jean, and knew that for her 'own self' she 'had to have it out with her.' So she resurrected the moment – from nearly twenty years earlier – when she had told Principal Corry that working with Jean Royce was proving to be heavy weather. As Margaret gained experience running her own busy office, she noted how her own staff so often had to wait to talk with her. More especially, her respect for Jean's competence, knowledge, and vision – thrown into ever greater relief through comparisons with her detractors, and coloured by growing affection – had converted her earlier rather inchoate distress into a profound feeling of complicity.

As it transpired, 'Jean remembered it all really clearly. She remembered my discontent. I told her my feelings about my part and at certain times I was absolutely speechless. I couldn't say things, and she who had lost her speech nine-tenths of the time was filling in the words for me. I remember, in particular, that I had these terrible regrets that I hadn't been more supportive at an earlier stage, and I couldn't think of the word "supportive," and she filled it in for me. She and I both wept.'[278]

The other memories of Jean's last months are gentle – remarkably so, given the difficulties she had breathing, swallowing, and talking. One of her nurses wrote that 'working with Jean taught me more about dignity and quality of life than 8 years of hospital experience ever did. It was Jean who showed me how to accept life as presented and not "grumble" about it.'[279] Margaret had long observed Jean's apparent obliviousness to bodily distress – despite contemporary scepticism, she seemed to have managed the Cartesian mind-body separation. Once, when an ambulance had to be called because she was having trouble breathing, Jean insisted that the nurse 'read to her in the ambulance.'[280] And she continued to be transported by music. 'Shortly before she died,' Dawn remembered, 'we came home and she had watched a symphony on television and she was just exhausted by it.'[281] One night she told Margaret that 'Beethoven's music is very comforting,' and went on to tell her 'how well our house sharing had turned out – that we did things simply didn't we?'[282]

Certainly that's how it seemed to her, and to the observer coming to the evidence some twenty years later. She died at home on 16 April 1982. Those closest to her say she was with them to the end, and they felt bereft. 'Margaret doesn't cry, doesn't readily break down,' Dawn told me. 'It may be that the only time that she wept with me was sometime after Jean died, not immediately – several weeks later, maybe. And her voice became strangled, and I made her repeat it because I wanted to hear, and she said, "I miss Jean so much."'[283]

There are two discrete stories about those who were left to mourn. The official obituary and the news stories mentioned her surviving siblings. Some friends addressed their letters of sympathy to Marion, including Allie Douglas. 'Jean was a remarkable woman,' she wrote, 'as scores of letters to you must have said – able, gifted and large of heart and mind. I valued her friendship very greatly.'[284] Those who spoke at the memorial service told the story of the created family. Pauline Jewett acknowledged Margaret, 'who has been with her so many of these last years.' Chancellor Emeritus Stirling wrote to Margaret: 'I know you were very close to her and just wanted to extend my deepest sympathy on the occasion of your great loss.'[285] Evelyn McLeod – 'my dear Evelyn McLeod,'[286] as Jean referred to her – remembered 'all the happy times she and Jean had together during the Kingston years. We really did enjoy one another's company, and I felt it a great honour to be counted among her friends. I loved the summer letters she wrote from all over the map, full of such keen and humorous observations. I will always miss her. She was my dear friend.'[287]

Margaret was co-executor of Jean's will. In a letter acknowledging his bequest, Jean's nephew Ian also acknowledged Margaret, 'Jean's friend and companion who had preserved her memory when she died. Our whole family thanks you so much.'[288] Jean would have been touched and amused by a similar letter to Margaret from Shelagh, which was much more effusive: 'I would like to extend my heartfelt thanks to *you* who was such a dear, *dear* friend. After experiencing such a close relationship with her for all those years – it is probably *you* whom the loss of such a magnificent lady as Jean Royce touches most deeply.'[289]

Jean's last will and testament, signed on 3 October 1973, belongs – and doesn't belong – to the conventional family story. Her great concern was for the welfare of Marion, whose important jobs and splendid achievements ironically left her without a pension. Jean directed her executors 'to keep invested the residue of [her] estate and to pay the interest [to] her sister during her lifetime.'[290] This sum made all the difference to Marion, who advised Margaret that these payments would 'adequately supplement my income at the current rate of inflation and allow me both to indulge in some luxuries and also give more to needy causes and other people.' Having observed her mother's struggles in penury, Jean couldn't bear to think of her sister in similar straits – and without children to offer help.

But Jean's main beneficiary was Queen's University, which was to receive the residue of her estate on Marion's death. On the surface, this makes her will unconventional in terms of a family story. But Jean loved Queen's, and her attachment to the university was the longest and deepest of her life. When she was dismissed, she felt jilted as surely as anyone whose spouse walks out after thirty-five years of marriage. But Jean did not cede 'ownership' of the university to anyone, nor in her view had the university done her wrong. Even more strikingly, as Margaret wrote Robert Legget, 'Jean spoke highly of Mr. Corry until the end of her life having separated her respect for him from his personal injury to her.'[291]

Though Jean's bequest had no strings attached, two things influenced its destination. Just before she died, the Marty Committee was exploring the idea of a second scholarship, this time in Jean's name. The Marty fund seemed sufficiently robust to carry a second award, and the need was clear. Margaret discussed the idea with Jean, who was 'deeply moved and, as usual, genuinely surprised that such an honour should have been thought of for her.'[292]

After Marion died in September 1987, Margaret wrote to the Board of Trustees reporting that the bequest, some $113,000, was now available. Though 'Jean did not suggest a specific use for her bequest,' both the Royce family and Margaret as executrix hoped it would be directed to the Jean Royce Fellowship 'to ensure sufficient capital to support a substantial award.' The value of this bequest had been ensured, Margaret added, by the 'ingenious administration of Professor William Cannon who refusing any fee managed all administrative aspects of arranging the interest payments, tax submissions and investment decisions.'[293] The board obliged. Jean's memory, as her nephew Ian had noted better than he knew, was as well served by her friends as she herself had been.

Two services honoured Jean: a family service on 16 April, and a memorial service in Grant Hall on 28 April. Jean had given no thought to a service – as Margaret wrote to me, 'her instructions to us were to stick her in a garbage bag, etc.'[294] But she had allowed that the principal of the Theological College represented the legitimate voice of things religious on campus, so it was Principal Robert Bater who conducted the service.

Among the eulogists was Robert Legget, close friend and admirer for forty-six years. Until the end of her life he phoned Jean and visited her. 'Memories of sitting there holding her tightly will ever be with me,' he wrote a decade after her death.[295] Much has been written about romantic friendships between women 'who had no hope of actually spending their lives together.'[296] Perhaps there is something to be said also about romantic heterosexual friendships. Such friendships may well have flourished, especially before serial (marital) monogamy became a respectable option. Perhaps this concept captures a certain reality better than, for example, that of the 'affair,' which offers sexual intimacy as the marker for beginning and end. The idea of romantic friendship permits the question: Would she have married him, had he been free? One tends to think not. Even within their friendship, Jean noted Robert's possessiveness.[297] She showed no interest in being possessed; indeed, she may have seen possessiveness as the problematic *sine qua non* of marriage.

In the words of the *Alumni Review*, the service was 'as unique as the lady it honoured,'[298] and featured excerpts from Jean's writing. Here she is from a paper written in 1969:

> I opened my door the other morning on a painted world. It had rained during the night and everything had a newly washed look. The limestone sparkled and the green of the lower campus shimmered in the sun. The daffodils were in full bloom and the tulips were bursting their buds; the trees had the lovely feathered look of May. It was a quiet morning. For once the curb was free of parked cars, most of the students had gone down for the Summer. Instructors were incarcerated in their offices and studies, assessing the work of the year. The street was practically empty ...
>
> The hands of the south face of the clock in Grant Hall Tower stood at 10:45 and by craning my neck, I could see that the west face registered 10:30. The north and east were not within my range of vision but I knew quite well that they would show a similar divergence. It seemed for the moment as if time were standing still, but this was only a delusion.[299]

Jean would have been pleased to know that Duncan Sinclair, the boy who woke her by mistake on Saturday mornings, the young man with 'potential' at the time of the search for principal in 1973, read the tribute to her in the university's Senate. She was, he said, 'the last member of a small group of able and dedicated people who literally ran the university before, during and after the Second World War – the symbol of a past era fondly remembered by many thousands of graduates.'[300]

With the exception of George Grant, no one in Queen's history came more to symbolize the university, and no one for so long. Yet Sinclair's nostalgic characterization belies Jean Royce's steadfast and creative sponsorship of those values which many still believe should define the mission of the university. Certainly she knew that time did not stand still, and she did not wish it to. But just because she grew old, just because she retired, she should not be relegated to symbol, however fond. For then we would be retiring those values which animated her and which still provide the best argument for the defense of the university.

Notes

Most of Jean Royce's papers and letters are currently in the possession of the author or Margaret Hooey. Most of this material will be deposited in the Queen's University Archives after the publication of this book, as will all the material – letters and interview transcriptions – collected by the author.

Abbreviations

BLC	Minutes of Board of Library Curators, Queen's University, Library fonds, QUA
BT	Queen's University Board of Trustees, Minutes and Proceedings, QUA
CFUW	Kingston Branch, Canadian Federation of University Women, QUA
DR	Donald Royce
FAS	Faculty of Arts and Science, Minutes and Proceedings, QUA
HV	*Hidden Voices: The Life Experiences of Women Who Have Worked and Studied at Queen's University* (oral history project, 1975–80)
JH	Jill Harris
JIR	Jean Isabel Royce fonds, QUA
JR	Jean Royce
JRP	Jean Royce Personnel File, Department of Human Resources, fond, QUA
MH	Margaret Hooey
MR	Marion Royce
PR	*Report of the Principal of Queen's University to the Board of Trustees*, QUA
QJ	*Queen's Journal*
QUA	Queen's University Archives
STTJ	*St Thomas Times-Journal*

Introduction

1 Robert Legget, 'Jean Royce,' 23 September 1993.
2 *Report of the Principal of Queen's University to the Board of Trustees* (PR), 1933–34.
3 Frederick W. Gibson, *Queen's University*, vol. 2, *1917–1961* (Montreal and Kingston: Queen's University Press, 1983), 114.
4 For a mesmerizing story of a woman who *did* seek recognition for her accomplishment see Brian McKillop's *The Spinster and the Prophet*: *Florence Deeks, H.G. Wells and the Mystery of the Purloined Past* (Toronto: Macfarlane Walter and Ross, 2000).
5 Letter from Jean Royce (JR) to Dean R.L. Watts, 29 May 1970.
6 As recalled by Margaret Hooey (MH), 16 April 1993.
7 Corry confirmed this discussion by letter, 23 February 1968. JRP.
8 This was later published as 'The Secret Anguish of Jean Royce' in *Kingston Whig-Standard Magazine*, 6 June 1992.
9 Royce MacGillivray, Review of *Queen's University*, volume 2, by Frederick Gibson, *Ontario History* 76 (1984), 93.
10 *Making a Middle Class: Student Life in English Canada during the Thirties* (Montreal and Kingston: McGill-Queen's University Press, 1990). Axelrod draws on statistics from select universities, which show that only 8 per cent of the students had fathers classified as skilled workers, while 5 per cent had fathers classified as semiskilled or unskilled (23). In 1930, the year Jean graduated, just under one-quarter of university students were female (21). Extrapolating, then, no more than – and probably far fewer than – 5 per cent of students were the *daughters* of men classified as semiskilled or unskilled labourers. In 1930, fewer than 3 per cent of Canadians between twenty and twenty-four were enrolled in institutions of higher education (22).
11 For an earlier Canadian example, by a woman whose career presaged Jean's, see Margaret Addison's *Diary of a European Tour: 1900*, ed. Jean O'Grady (Montreal and Kingston: McGill-Queen's University Press, 1999). Addison returned from her 'tour' to become the first dean of Annesley Hall of Victoria University (later Victoria College of the University of Toronto) in 1903. For a broader picture, see Cindy S. Aron, *Working at Play: A History of Vacations in the United States* (New York: Oxford University Press, 1999).
12 For a synopsis of this history, see Alison Prentice et al., *Canadian Women: A History*, 2nd ed. (Toronto: Harcourt Brace, 1996), 313–29. For discussions of feminism in the 1930s, see Veronica Strong-Boag, *The New Day Recalled: Lives of Girls and Women in English Canada, 1919–1939* (Toronto: Clark Copp Pitman, 1988). See also Mary Kinnear's *Margaret McWilliams: An Interwar*

Feminist (Montreal and Kingston: McGill-Queen's University Press, 1991) for a biography of one of the founders of the Canadian Federation of University Women.

13 Gibson, *Queen's*, xvi.

14 For elaboration, see Philip Abrams, *Historical Sociology* (Somerset, U.K.: Open Books, 1982).

15 Muriel received her BA from Queen's in 1942, and her MA the following year.

16 Memoir dated 4 August 1993. Also see Bader's autobiography *Adventures of a Chemist Collector* (London: Weidenfeld and Nicolson, 1995), especially 37–41. For a detailed account of the history of the internment camps, see Eric Koch, *Deemed Suspect: A Wartime Blunder* (Toronto: Methuen, 1980).

17 I owe this insight to Marion Campbell.

18 For a cogent treatment of these processes, see Maryann Neely Ayim, *The Moral Parameters of Good Talk* (Waterloo, ON: Wilfrid Laurier University Press, 1997).

19 See, for example, J.L. Granatstein, *The Ottawa Men: The Civil Service Mandarins, 1935–1957* (Toronto: University of Toronto Press, 1998).

20 See, for example, M.A. Reimer, 'The Social Organization of the Labour Process: A Case Study of Documentary Management of Clerical Labour in the Public Service' (PhD diss., Ontario Institute for Studies in Education, 1987).

21 In Principal Mackintosh's words, the success of the Soviet Union's Sputnik I 'alerted the western countries to the dangerous lag in scientific and technological education and research.' Accordingly, the Faculty of Arts at Queen's – 'moving briskly with the times,' as Frederick Gibson put it without a trace of sarcasm – 'became the Faculty of Arts and Science' (316–17).

22 Ibid., 109.

23 Ibid., 161.

24 Here again I take my cue from feminist scholars who have revealed connections between apparently disparate categories of social life. Even the prototypically isolated nuclear family of the 1950s has been interrogated for its links with the class- and gender-based economies of modern capitalist societies. See, for example, Pat Armstrong and Hugh Armstrong, *The Double Ghetto*, 3rd ed. (Toronto: McClelland and Stewart, 1994) and Meg Luxton, *More Than a Labour of Love* (Toronto: Women's Press, 1980). In the case of Jean Royce, the links are not only visible but seamless.

25 Interview with Lyn Royce, 9 June 1995.

26 Marion, for example, earns two mentions in Prentice et al., *Canadian Women*.

27 Marion Royce, *Eunice Dyke, Health Care Pioneer: From Pioneer Public Health Nurse to Advocate for the Aged* (Toronto: Dundurn Press, 1983).

28 Legget, 'Jean Royce.'

29 For a sustained and persuasive theoretical analysis of this position, see Judith Butler, *Bodies That Matter: On the Discursive Limits of 'Sex'* (New York: Routledge, 1993).

1: 'The Girls Got All the Charisma'

1 MR to JR, 25 October 1972.

2 Primarily he is listed as cooper. The mill 'had the capacity to produce 300 barrels of flour a day which was later raised to 800. All barrels were constructed in the cooper shop which measured 30′ × 50′.' Wayne Paddon, George Thorman, Don Cosans, and Brian Sim, *St. Thomas: A Hundred Years a City: 1881–1991* (St. Thomas Centennial Committee, 1991), 44. In this 30′ × 50′ space, David Royce would have spent most of his days from 1891 to 1928.

3 Telephone interview with Hazel Charleton, 14 September 1997. Hazel Charleton was a friend of Catherine's, a 'quiet friendly girl' whom she would pick up on the way to school. The Royce house has been torn down to permit the widening of the cross street.

4 Telephone interview with Florence (Billingsley) Snell, 14 September 1997.

5 Interview with Helen (Babe) Bythell, January 1994.

6 Letter from MR to MH, 30 May 1982.

7 The notice identifying James Henry as the youngest son of Mr and Mrs David T. Royee [*sic*], thereby acknowledging his brother Stewart, but not his sisters Marion and Jean (as alternative wording 'youngest child' would have), suggests a gendered ordering of recognition – though by whom it is not clear. Later in life, Jean would have been unlikely to be critical of this language, although it is certain that she would have red-pencilled 'youngest.' At that time the Royces only had one other son! Alone among his siblings – all of whom lived beyond middle age – Harry's marked gravestone stands beside those of his mother and father in St Thomas Cemetery.

8 All the interviews with Jean Royce were conducted as part of an oral history project, *Hidden Voices: The Life Experiences of Women Who Have Worked and Studied at Queen's University* (henceforth cited as *HV*), undertaken by the Office of the Dean of Women at Queen's, 1975–80. Excerpts from these interviews were published under the name above in 1980. The tapes are housed in the Queen's University Archives. Jean was interviewed on six occasions: 17 June 1977 and 24 August 1977 (by Susan Jackson); 31 October 1977, 24 November 1977, and 18 February 1978 (by Diane Gordon); and 5 March 1978 (by Margaret Hooey).

9 According to the *St Thomas Daily Times*, 5 June 1908, Rev. Munro was billeted with Mrs D. Royce, Rev Stephens with Mrs David Royce, and Ida Royce with D. Royce. Had the Royces consulted one another about their invitations?
10 From an introduction to *The Letters of Josiah Royce* (Chicago: University of Chicago Press, 1970). This Josiah taught philosophy at Harvard and was Josiah's grandson.
11 Reuben Butchart, *The Disciples of Christ in Canada since 1830* (Toronto: Canadian Headquarters Publications, Churches of Christ (Disciples), 1949), xiii.
12 Willard Thompson, 'Gold Didn't Make This the Golden State,' *Sacramento Bee*, 27 July 1896.
13 At the point of unification there were some 10,000 Christians and 12,000 Disciples.
14 As B.A. Abbott wrote, there is 'no written authoritative statement of doctrine.' Though the New Testament 'sometimes needs to be explained ... this is better done by the living voice than by the dogmatic utterance of any church council or the stereotyped statement of any creed.' *The Disciples* (1924, reprint, Bethany Press for Abbott Books, 1964), 55.
15 Lester G. McAllister and William E. Tucker, *Journey in Faith: A History of the Christian Church (Disciples of Christ)* (Saint Louis, MI: Bethany Press, 1975), 23ff.
16 Unless indicated, all the information about the Royces's church membership comes from the records of the St Thomas Church of Christ (Disciples), courtesy of the Rev. and Mrs Wallace Howlett, who lent them to me on June 5, 1996.
17 JR, *HV*, 24 November 1977.
18 Donald Royce (DR), in an interview with Dawn Cannon, 19 March 1993.
19 *St Thomas Times-Journal* (*STTJ*), 21 July 1928.
20 Now Princess Street.
21 Butchart, *Disciples*, 486.
22 *St Thomas: A Hundred Years a City*, 74.
23 Butchart, *Disciples*.
24 *Old Everton and the Pioneer Movement amongst the Disciples of Christ in Eramosa Township, Upper Canada from 1830* (Everton, ON: Church of Christ (Disciples), 1941).
25 JR, *HV*, 24 November 1977.
26 DR interview, 19 March 1993.
27 JR, *HV*, 24 November 1977.
28 Bythell interview, January 1994.
29 Ibid.

30 Butchart, *Disciples*, 486.

31 As Warren Miller has written, 'On Saturday mornings when there was no school, the bucksaw was brought out and some unfortunate member of the family began his stint of cutting the long wood into stove lengths. The school boy was usually the victim as father was years away from the five day week.' *Vignettes of Early St. Thomas: An Anthology of the Life and Times of Its First Century* (St Thomas, ON: Sutherland Press, 1968), 291.

32 As noted in David's obituary, *STTJ*, 21 July 1928.

33 Stewart Royce Jr interview, 6 June 1996.

34 DR interview, 19 March 1993.

35 Bythell interview, January 1994.

36 Stewart Royce Jr interview, 7 June 1996.

37 Lionell Rinn and Jean Royce both received graduation diplomas in spring 1922.

38 *The Collegian*, December 1916, 4–8.

39 JR, *HV*, 24 November 1977.

40 DR interview, 3 March 1994.

41 Conversation, 5 June 1996. Dorothy Marion Scram is not Marion's only namesake. Lucy (Chute) Goldsmith's father, also an elder at the Church of Christ (Disciples) in St Thomas, named his younger daughter, born in 1921, after Marion 'except [he] got the spelling wrong and called her Marian.' Marion, Lucy Goldsmith recalled, 'was my idol ... a lovely person ... my favourite in the family.' Telephone interview, 23 November 1997.

42 17 August 1918. In April 1919 (33), *The Collegian* ran the *STTJ* picture and story. But, strangely, here Marion is identified as Jean Royce, both under the picture and in the accompanying list of winners. How could such a mistake be made in a small high school, especially given that Marion had been editor the year before and Jean was still a student? It's hard to believe that it was an innocent mistake – one wonders how the two sisters felt about it.

43 The school records were available at the Elgin Board of Education (public school) and Parkside Collegiate Institute. *The Collegian*, December 1922, reports that in the upper school that year 168 papers were written and 80.1 per cent were successful. By today's standards this is a very low success rate. Moreover, there were 1,061 papers written in middle school with 72.5 per cent successful. Making it through high school proved quite a hurdle in 1922.

44 JR, *HV*, 24 November 1977.

45 *STTJ*, 21 July 1922. This is less than scientific, but Catherine was one of twenty-three graduating from Scott Street, so just over 4 per cent graduated with honours from this working-class school. There were, in contrast, sixty

students graduating from Wellington Street, where the doctors and lawyers sent their children, and sixteen, or just over one-quarter of these, graduated with honours.

46 DR interview, 19 March 1993.

47 Donald's wife, Celia, believed that Katherine 'thought it was really important that [the children] – especially the girls – went to university. Don and Stewart didn't go to university. I think they're all quite brilliant. I was always sorry that Don didn't go to university because he had a great mind.' Interview, 25 November 1996.

48 Florence Campbell to JR, 8 November 1968, JIR.

49 DR interview, 19 March 1993.

50 Bythell interview, January 1994.

51 DR and Celia Royce (CR) interview, 19 March 1993.

52 As Lyn Royce commented about her father, 'You don't become corporate secretary on a grade eight education if you don't have some smarts.' Interview, 9 June 1996.

53 For a summary of the literature explaining gendered differences in school performance, see Peter J. Burke, 'Gender Identity, Sex, and School Performance' in *Social Psychology Quarterly* 52 (June 1989): 159–69.

54 Stewart Royce Jr interview, 7 June 1996.

55 CR interview, 25 November 1996.

56 DR interview, 19 March 1993.

57 Stewart Royce Jr interview, 7 June 1996.

58 JR in *HV*, 24 November 1977.

59 CR interview, 25 November 1996.

60 DR and CR interview, 3 March 1994.

61 Lyn Royce interview, 9 June 1996.

62 DR interview, 9 March 1993.

63 JR in *HV*, 24 November 1977.

64 According to McAllister and Tucker: 'No religious body was thought to hold more conservative views than the Disciples in regard to the participation of women in the work or services of the church.' But women led the way in regard to missionary work, though they had trouble getting recognition. The first woman was ordained in the 1890s. 'Ordination of women as a theological issue was never discussed,' and by the first decade of the twentieth century a number of women were ordained (*Journey in Faith*, 259).

65 In a conversation among fifteen women, all members of the Church of Christ (Disciples), Nancy remembers that 'My mother was a "deaconess," so many times after church we would help her wash the trays and the little cups.' Rita Nakashima Brock, Claudia Camp, and Serene Jones, *Setting the*

Table: Women in Theological Conversation (St Louis, MI: Chalice Press, 1995), 251.

66 Jessie (Mackinnon) Reid was born 'on Jean's grandfather's farm' and grew up near Guelph. She attended summer sessions from 1935 to 1941, graduating in spring 1942, but this meeting would have taken place in the mid-1930s. Jessie added, 'Jean suggested that I apply to be warden because she knew that money was tight and I did that for two summers.' Telephone interview, 27 April 1998.

67 During her final illness, in 1946, Katherine came to Jean's to live; six months later she died in Kingston.

68 I am indebted to Muriel G. Luton, archivist for the Ontario Assembly of the Christian Church (Disciples of Christ) from 1974 to 1985, for providing me with a copy of this announcement.

69 As revealed on the letterhead of the All-Canada Committee.

70 Soon after graduation Marion had taken a position with the All Canada Movement of the Church of Christ (Disciples) as 'children's specialist and educational worker.' Butchart, *Disciples*, 185. (In 1928 her father's obituary proclaimed – perhaps rather extravagantly – that Marion was 'known from end to end of Canada and in many of the United States as field secretary of the Churches of Christ.') Marion was also the first graduate – in 1924 – of the college that selected Katherine for residence mother. Ibid., 159.

71 Of course, David was the family's wage earner. Katherine must have managed the family's finances, hence to her the credit for the financial help.

72 DR interview, 19 March 1993.

73 MH's handwritten note to the author, September 1979.

74 Bythell interview, January 1994.

75 22 May 1922, 18.

76 Ibid., 59.

77 JR, *HV*, 24 November 1977.

78 May 1915, 29.

79 December 1916, 17, 19.

80 1921, 60.

81 In 1977 (on 24 November) Jean mentioned a 'legacy' – presumably offered by the St Thomas Public Library, which must have helped finance her year at OLS. She started work in the library before going to the school, and had secured a position to which to return (HV).

82 Telephone conversation with Florence (Billingsley) Snell, 14 September 1997.

83 'The ex-students of the St Thomas Collegiate Institute continue to place themselves in very desirable positions in all parts of the continent, in fact, in all parts of the world, so it would almost be an impossibility to include

all the ex-students in our list,' *The Collegian* announced grandly in May 1923 (46). Other than three students at school in the United States and Bruce Shaw 'of rugby fame' who is 'upon the high seas ... somewhere on the Pacific ... and whose whereabouts aren't exactly known,' all the others mentioned are pretty close to home, most of them right in St Thomas.

84 Jean recalled, in *HV*, 31 October 1977: 'In that summer I couldn't get any accommodation in the old red house at the top of the Earl Street – it was called the Hen Coop and there was a second residence, the Avonmore. But that summer I hadn't applied early enough to get a place and I lived across from Chalmers Church, at that time a very nice house where they took students – women students – down close to William Street; it may not be there now.'

85 JR, *HV*, 31 October 1977.

86 *Tricolour*, 1929, 82. Although she graduated in 1930, her graduation photograph and write-up appear in 1929.

87 25 November 1927.

88 For an account of the strike and its resolution, see Frederick W. Gibson, *Queen's University*, vol. 2, *1917–1961* (Montreal and Kingston: McGill-Queen's University Press, 1983), 76–81.

89 13 May 1972, at an Alumnae Luncheon. She recalled, 'On one occasion that the strikers pushed their way into Professor McArthur's lecture room but were quickly dispersed by him with a sharp anger that none of us had witnessed before in that phlegmatic man.' (Untitled, [Queens in the 1920s])

90 Arthur L. Davies, *Sketches, Scholars and Scandals of a Quiet College Town* (Toronto: J.M. Dent & Sons, 1975), 59.

91 *QJ*, 4 October 1929.

92 Ibid., 4 November 1927.

93 Letter, JR to MR, 4 September 1974.

94 *Tricolour*, 1929, 82.

95 Ibid., 1929, 89.

96 JIR, 3 December 1933. Pooh Bear added, 'You certainly have done very well ... I hope you are most happy.' I have not identified Pooh, who was at the time 'appalled' at the 'enormity of the task of finishing her thesis.' Another university friend was Sarah Common, who by 1933 was Dr Sarah Common.

97 JR, *HV*, 31 October 1977.

2: Did She Run the Place?

1 Frederick W. Gibson, *Queen's University*, vol. 2, *1917–1961* (Montreal and Kingston: McGill-Queen's University Press, 1983), 114.

2 In historian Brian McKillop's assessment, *Matters of Mind: The University in Ontario, 1791–1951* (Toronto: University of Toronto Press, 1994), during the 1930s 'the University of Toronto had flourished under [President Robert] Falconer [and] McMaster and Western were renewed institutions on new sites. But the golden age of Queen's seemed to lie in its past' (440). Queen's principal Hamilton Fyfe probably agreed but he also 'spoke to the problems of all in charge of universities in the Depression[,] ... classes were too large for effective teaching; assistants were too few in number; serious research was all but impossible,' 437.

3 *Hidden Voices* (*HV*), 17 June 1977 and 24 August 1977 (Susan Jackson); 31 October 1977, 24 November 1977, and 18 February 1978 (Diane Gordon); and 5 March 1978 (Margaret Hooey).

4 This is how Jean referred to Miss Rayson in *HV*, 5 March 1978.

5 Minutes of Board of Library Curators (BLC), 6 October 1930. As university librarian, Mr Kyte prepared and signed the minutes.

6 JR, *HV*, 24 August 1977. Jean's appointment at OLC depended on her background in religious education gained as a girl and young woman from her activities with the Church of Christ (Disciples). She attended courses at the L.C. Lumsley College and at young people's camps, which the church had initiated in the late 1920s. As she told Diane Gordon (*HV*, 31 October 1977), 'in those days also at camps we had courses in religious knowledge.'

7 As recalled by MR in an undated letter to MH.

8 Letter from Alice (Carscallen) Griffiths to MR, expressing sympathy on Jean's death, 19 April 1982, JIR.

9 JR, *HV*, 24 November 1977.

10 JR, *HV*, 24 August 1977. Jean added that 'meanwhile my friends went elsewhere; my greatest friend at college [Mary White] had won a Canadian Federation [of University Women] Scholarship and was at Oxford.' (Perhaps from here Jean began to say to students she respected: 'My dear, you should go to Oxford.') Some were at OCE and various other places, 'just as a group finds its way after graduation.'

11 Report of the Executive Committee of the Board of Trustees (BT), 6 May 1931.

12 JR, *HV*, 5 March 1978.

13 1931.

14 JR, *HV*, 5 March 1978.

15 JR, *HV*, 24 November 1977; *HV*, 5 March 1978.

16 JR, *HV*, 24 November 1977.

17 BT, 5 July 1930.

18 Gibson, *Queen's*, 101. Indeed, at the end of his term, Principal Fyfe argued

strenuously that McNeill should succeed him as he was doing all the work in any case, and 'doing it admirably' (134).

19 JR, *HV*, 24 August 1977.

20 JR, *HV*, 5 March 1978.

21 JR, *HV*, 24 November 1977.

22 That the registrar – even one in good health – *needed* an assistant had not yet dawned on anyone. Alice King's successor would not be granted such a person until 1939.

23 *Alumnae News*, December 1933.

24 *PR*, 1933–4.

25 Letter to JR, 11 May 1933, JRP.

26 JR, *HV*, 24 November 1977.

27 Dr Wilhelmina Gordon graduated 'from Queen's with a master of arts degree and the university medal in 1905.' *Kingston Whig-Standard*, 11 November 1968, 15.

28 JR, *HV*, 24 November 1977. 'They couldn't get out fast enough,' Jean continued, 'and I heard someone say' that he didn't want to fail English.

29 This is an obvious point, but it is worth noting that in 1933 – the year Jean became registrar – an editor of the *Queen's Journal* signalled the 'real tragedy in the failure of university students to secure positions upon graduation.' Gibson, *Queen's*, 103. He was convinced, however, 'that there will always be openings in every line of endeavour for young men who are honest and who are willing to take an interest in whatever they are doing.' It is an interesting question whether the Jean Royces fell within the editor's purview. See Paul Axelrod, *Making a Middle Class: Student Life in English Canada during the Thirties* (Montreal and Kingston: McGill-Queen's University Press, 1990), 149–50, for a discussion of the problems of employment for students and graduates during these years.

30 The proportion of female students at Queen's dropped sharply in the early years of the Depression. The Dean of Women, Hilda Laird, reported that 'a young man unable to find employment is sent to the university; a young woman is kept at home to help with domestic work.' Quoted in Gibson, *Queen's*, 102–3.

31 Hilda Laird, a Queen's graduate, was hired in 1925 as the second Dean of Women and as a lecturer in the Department of German. She resigned the deanship in 1933. Twenty-five years after joining the Department of German she was appointed head. Aside from the director of the School of Nursing, until 1970 she was the only female head of department at Queen's (Gibson, *Queen's*, 103, 104, 344). After that year they came sporadically – in ones.

32 Hilda Neatby, *Queen's University*, vol. 1, *1841–1917*, ed. Frederick W. Gibson and Roger Graham (Montreal and Kingston: McGill-Queen's University Press, 1978), 303.

33 In Brian McKillop's summation, 'in this way through the back door and the principal's office female academics found a place at Queen's.' Although other Canadian universities had few women on academic staff at this time, Queen's lagged significantly behind its counterparts. *Matters of Mind*, 277. By 1931, women's participation in the academic workforce in Canada was 19.19 per cent. See McKillop's assessment of the record, 274–9 and 622, n. 68, as well as Alison Prentice, 'Bluestockings, Feminists, or Women Workers? A Preliminary Look at Women's Early Employment – The University of Toronto,' *Journal of the Canadian Historical Association* 2 (1991): 231–61.

34 Gibson, *Queen's*, 114.

35 From a letter dated 29 November 1984 enclosing a donation to the Royce Fellowship by Muriel E. Smith (BA Hon. 1933). The full sentence reads: 'It pleases me to be able to give this small amount toward the Royce Fellowship; small compared to the wonderful, warm, helpful spirit of our Jean Royce.'

36 The *Queen's Journal* proudly announced that 'although she might well have owed her election to the dearth of men during the Second World War,' she was well qualified for the post. She was 'educated at McGill University and lectured there in physics and astronomy for 16 years previous to assuming' the position at Queen's. 'She was on the staff of the British war office and ministry of national service during the last war [and] for her services was invested in the Order of the British Empire [*sic* – Douglas was awarded the MBE]. She worked in collaboration with Sir Arthur Eddington at the Cavendish Laboratory and the Cambridge observatory in England. During this time she has had numerous scientific papers published on the results of her original research in the fields of stellar motions and spectoroscopic work.' *QJ*, 19 January 1943.

37 According to the Dominion Bureau of Statistics, in 1931 women held only 4.8 per cent of positions classified as 'managerial,' rising to 7.2 per cent in 1941. Cited in Axelrod, *Making a Middle Class*, 8–9.

38 11 May 1933, JRP. As secretary to the Board of Trustees, the letter was undoubtedly written by William McNeill, but the existing copy is unsigned.

39 BT, 28 October 1933.

40 Later on, Eleanor Smith 'thought it would be kind of fun to run the jewellery store but I never got very far with that.' Interview, 30 October 1996. It wasn't just at the university that the opportunities for women were circumscribed.

41 The Alumni Association was formed in 1927 (Gibson, *Queen's*, 62), 'financed from a small annual grant from the trustees' (444, n9). Certainly the salary Gordon Smith gleaned here would have been more in the nature of an honorarium. It is worth signalling, however, that the Queen's Alumnae Association had begun in 1909, without a grant (27). The Alumnae Association offered to raise half the money for a women's residence if the board would match it. In 1923, to the board's astonishment, the alumnae had raised $80,000, and Ban Righ was opened in the fall of 1925 (40).

42 Gordon Smith wrote a formal letter of application to Principal Fyfe, citing his 'close connection with Queen's' for over twenty-five years, 17 April 1933. Smith held a BA in mineralogy and geology and a BSc (Honours) from Queen's. Gordon Smith Personnel File, QUA.

43 Eleanor Smith interview, 30 October 1996. Mrs Douglas Chown (née Mary MacPhail) graduated in 1917.

44 This was in accordance with the Scottish system. Almost all of Charlotte's classmates interviewed sixty years later for *Hidden Voices* (1980) volunteered memories about their most illustrious classmate.

45 Frederick Gibson includes a detailed description of the search committees and their procedures. 'On May 9, 1929, after receiving Principal Taylor's resignation, the Board of Trustees struck a committee, under the chairmanship of W.F. Nickle, to find a new principal. It was a large committee – thirteen men and Charlotte Whitton – which represented Queen's only in a geographic sense. Made up of trustees, it contained only one scientist, Mackintosh Bell and only one member, Adam Shortt, who had ever taught at a university' (*Queen's*, 83). On the search process for Principal Wallace, see 133ff. Charlotte was a great critic of her fellow trustees and especially of the arbitrary and secretive back-room practices from which most of them – including her – were excluded (88–9 and 139–40). She served as a member of the board until 1940.

46 See her biography by Patricia T. Rooke and R.L. Schnell, *No Bleeding Heart: Charlotte Whitton, A Feminist on the Right* (Vancouver: UBC Press, 1987).

47 Whitton to William McNeill, 5 September 1946. Charlotte Whitton Papers, QUA.

48 Clara Brook interview, 4 January 1999.

49 *Queen's Review* 49, 2 (1975), 26.

50 Note by MH, 10 August 1981. In a letter to Chancellor Richardson, Principal Fyfe described 'the lady member ... [as] particularly poisonous' after a rambunctious meeting of the board, but not all the men took this view. Richardson replied that he admired 'her zeal and energy' and wanted her on the search committee for the new principal. Gibson, *Queen's*, 134.

51 For example, Winnifred Kydd, Dean of Women from 1934 to 1939, wrote to Jean as follows: 'Put the enclosed in a safe place for me. But did you ever??' She signed 'love,' and an illegible nickname (undated). This is the only evidence that I have found for a friendship between them, but it certainly bespeaks intimacy and trust (JIR). For an account of Kydd's career, see Maureen Garvie and Jennifer L. Johnson, eds., *Their Leaven of Influence: Deans of Women at Queen's University, 1916–1996* (Kingston: Queen's Alumni Association on Women's Affairs, 1999), 41–50.

52 This was first formulated as a Joint Recommendation of the Principal and Vice-Principal to the Executive Committee of the Board, and was subsequently passed by the Board of Trustees on 28 October 1933.

53 *PR*, 1933–4.

54 Undated, Sunday, JIR. Mary White had graduated from Oxford the previous summer and was teaching at the Riverbed School for Girls in Winnipeg.

55 Gibson, *Queen's*, 17.

56 Neatby, *Queen's*, 176.

57 Ibid., 169.

58 Ibid., 4–5.

59 Ibid., 175. As Neatby wrote, in 1902 'when Principal Grant died the only full-time administrator was the secretary-treasurer of the board, J.B. McIver. George Bell, the late registrar, had been on the teaching staff, as was Grant himself' (286).

60 Ibid., 169.

61 James Cappon was also appointed the first Dean of Arts in 1906. Ibid., 288.

62 McNeill's letter to Whitton was dated 20 July 1946, Charlotte Whitton Papers, QUA. For a fuller account of the succession crisis in the Department of English, see Gibson, *Queen's*, 52–5. Gibson points out: 'Before order was eventually restored, an assorted procession of six heads and acting heads had passed in and out of the English Department in as many years.' He blames Principal Taylor for 'this imbroglio,' that is, for allowing the board to reject McNeill and then to involve itself thoroughly in the subsequent searches, thus 'turning the normal procedures of academic administration upside down' (55). Drawing on Gibson's version, McKillop refers to 'the comic opera proportions of the faculty struggle at Queen's in the 1920s' (*Matters of Mind*, 467).

63 8 September 1946, Charlotte Whitton Papers, QUA.

64 Neatby notes that public speaking was 'still highly regarded, particularly for the theological students' (Neatby, *Queen's*, 284).

65 JR, *HV*, 5 March 1978.

66 JR, *HV*, 24 November 1977.

67 Neatby, *Queen's*, 175.

68 A faithful paraphrase from Karl Marx's 'The 18th Brumaire of Louis Bonaparte' [1869] in Karl Marx and Friedrich Engels, *Selected Works*, vol. 1 (Moscow: Progress Publishers, 1969), 398.

69 Neatby, *Queen's*, 288.

70 For a discussion of the merger, see Elsie Watts '"Inevitable from the Beginning": Queen's University and Separation from the Presbyterian Church, 1900–12,' *Historical Papers 1996*, Canadian Society of Church History, 128–54.

71 Until the university legally secularized in 1912, it was not eligible for government grants or Carnegie money. The autonomy of the Faculty of Medicine and the School of Mining was a semifiction that allowed both to receive funding. Queen's parked all of her science departments in the School of Mining until 1916. Principal Grant is generally credited with these sleights of hand. Neatby, *Queen's*, 275–7; Gibson, *Queen's*, 6.

72 Most important decisions were in the hands of the Board of Trustees, which astonishingly had no special financial officer until 1913. Neatby, 289. G.Y. Chown was appointed the board's secretary in 1903 and acted as an informal financial advisor. According to Neatby, Chown 'contrived to annoy and anger and even to alarm senior and responsible members of the faculties and of the Board of Trustees' (*Queen's*, 288), mainly because the university's 'now considerable endowment was not entrusted to independent, professional management' (334 n 56). John Watson, named vice-principal in 1901, stated later that 'only the sustained efforts of himself and other stalwarts on the arts faculty had saved the university from ruin.' Gibson, *Queen's*, 11, 15; on the issue of the vice-principalship, see also Neatby, *Queen's*, 245.

73 Gibson, *Queen's*, 9.

74 Neatby, *Queen's*, 288–9. According to Gibson, 'during the 1920s and for some time thereafter the Senate had only four standing committees: Arts and Public Lectures, Honorary Degrees, Medical Services for Students and Social Functions for Students' (*Queen's*, 445 n 27).

75 See Gibson's chapter on the last years of the Taylor principalship, 'A Spreading Disaffection' (59–82), which ends with two lines from Thomas Moore's *Sacred Songs*, which Clifford Clark in Economics sent by telegram to his friend Norman Miller, in Mathematics, on hearing that Taylor had submitted his resignation: 'Sound the loud timbrel o'er Egypt's dark sea! / Jehovah has triumph'd – his people are free.'

76 The members of the selection committee first looked for a Canadian but were turned down by their preferred candidate, O.D. Skelton, Queen's professor and Undersecretary of State for External Affairs – probably after

Mackenzie King made it perfectly clear that he intended Skelton to remain in the post. Gibson, *Queen's*, 86.

77 Gibson, *Queen's*, 88. Gibson adds: 'Since 1926 he had been headmaster at Christ's Hospital, the famous "Blue-Coat" school at Horsham, Sussex, where he had made a reputation by modernizing the curriculum.'

78 Letter, 18 October 1930, quoted in Gibson, *Queen's*, 89, from May Chown to Charlotte Whitton. 'Believe me,' May told Charlotte, 'you have no idea how high the feeling on this subject runs.'

79 JR, *HV*, 24 November 1977.

80 JR, *HV*, 5 March 1978.

81 As newly elected board member D.D. Calvin wrote to Professor T.R. Glover: 'I'll show it to you when you get here; and I think you will agree that while it has much profound truth in it, and is most suggestive, yet our constituency couldn't – well, there is the Ontario Govt grant, for one thing.' Quoted in Gibson, *Queen's*, 131. For an account of the Fyfe report and the decision to produce a substitute report, see ibid., 128–32.

82 But Fyfe was also critical of faculty salaries and student and faculty governance. Ibid., 128–32.

83 Quoted in ibid., 129.

84 Ibid., 130.

85 McKillop, *Matters of Mind*, 439–41. In these pages Brian McKillop refers to Hamilton Fyfe as a 'combination of Jeremiah and Job [who] happily returned to Scotland ... to become principal of the University of Aberdeen, where northern lights rather than city sights dominated the imaginative landscape.'

86 JR, *Queen's University*, Radio Address for CFRC, 1970–1. 'Under his leadership,' she continued, 'the Course took on a high degree of specialization in one field, similar in structure to the British degrees.'

87 Of course Fyfe also appointed her registrar – and when she was ill on one occasion, brought her home so that he and his wife could care for her (as she told MH).

88 Gordon Dunn, e-mail, 7 August 1996.

89 See Hilda Neatby's account of the Gordon years, Frederick Gibson's brief account of the same period, and his full account of the Taylor and Fyfe regimes. Chancellor Richardson wrote that Fyfe had made 'a fine impression on the public mind and in the outside world has reflected some credit on the university. We never advertized to the outside world just how short he has fallen of our expectations in certain other directions' (131). But perhaps the job was a set-up for failure. Fyfe himself wrote after a defeat at the Board of Trustees: 'Principals don't carry weight at

Queen's. At least this one doesn't and the last one didn't.' Quoted in Gibson, *Queen's*, 127.

90 JR, *HV*, 24 November 1977.

91 Letter to President Sherwood Fox dated 12 September 1934. Quoted in Gibson, 451, fn. 8.

92 JR, *HV*, 5 March 1978. Jean didn't serve on the Faculty Board of Applied Science, only going to its meetings when 'it was something directly related to [her]' or medicine. She had little to do with the Faculty of Law after it was set up in 1957, 'but they did [invite her] to their meetings' until the appointment of their own registrar, Mary Alice Murray. Jean was, however, along with the principal, the vice-principal, Deans Matheson and Clark, and Professors Mackintosh, Knox, and P.G.C. Campbell, named to the committee to administer the commerce degree (within the Faculty of Arts) when it was set up. FAS, 15 May 1937.

93 JR, *HV*, 5 March 1978. See also Gibson, 162.

94 The Committee of Departments was spared when a majority supported the principal's motion that 'the Committee of Departments [remain a standing committee] for the purposes for which [it was] constituted and ... not make recommendations to the Faculty on matters outside [its] purview.' FAS, 15 March 1935.

95 In discussing the major campus controversy that erupted in 1961 when the Board of Trustees voted to put the new physics building on the lower campus, which would have destroyed the last large green space, Gibson wrote: 'Student protest, though it might be taken with a pinch of salt, was still to be noticed, both in its own right and because, as the rector pointed out, students were the alumni of the future' (*Queen's*, 402). But as Gibson concluded, it was the united opposition of faculty that caused the board to change its mind – as well as the solo act of the university's real estate agent, Graham Thomson, who quietly went about, in the month following the board's decision, buying property for an alternative site (393–403).

The only potential seller that Thomson failed to convince was Jean's landlady, Phyllis Knight, from whom she rented a 'lovely apartment' on the second floor. *HV*, 17 June 1977. Principal Mackintosh himself successfully negotiated the sale with Miss Knight, and Phyllis and Jean moved to a small house, also on the Queen's campus at the foot of University Avenue (Gibson, *Queen's*, 401), found for them by Morley Tillotson, the former University Treasurer, by then in charge of property acquisition (394). It now houses the Writing Centre.

96 FAS, 18 January 1962.

97 Harold Good letter, 7 February 1993.

98 Former Dean of Arts and Science (and Principal Emeritus) Ronald Watts recalled 'that she was not absolutely silent but she wasn't an obtrusive secretary. She wouldn't hesitate to draw relevant factors to the attention of Faculty Board but she didn't really try to dominate it.' Interview, 6 June 1997.

99 JR, *HV*, 5 March 1978.

100 The former student was her interviewer, Diane Gordon. *HV*, 24 November 1977.

101 JR, *HV*, 5 March 1978.

102 David Slater to JH, 8 February 1993.

103 Interview, 4 March 1999. Dr Eichner came to Queen's in 1950 and served as head of the Department of German from 1962 until 1967, when he resigned to become department head at the University of Toronto.

104 JR, *HV*, 5 March 1978.

105 JR, *Queen's University*.

106 Jean was not exaggerating. Mackintosh joined the Department of Economics and Political Science in 1920, became head in 1927, and despite his relative youth was seriously considered for principal in 1936. After distinguished wartime government service, he received very attractive offers to remain in Ottawa. Gibson, *Queen's*, 299–303. To provide a competitive financial offer, the university made him, in addition to the posts mentioned by Jean, W.E. McNeill's successor as vice-principal and 'agreed that he was to be free to devote part of his time' to government work. 'These unusual arrangements,' Gibson wrote, 'supplied final proof of how much the Queen's principal and trustees desired Mackintosh's return' (302).

107 JR, *HV*, 5 March 1978.

108 Judith Wedderspoon to JH, 16 February 1993. Perhaps it was such decisions that were responsible for the times that political science professor J.E. Hodgetts remembered 'when students would come to faculty with problems which derived from Miss Royce's sheer inability to keep up with the permutations and combinations of course offerings.' Letter, 27 February 1993.

109 JR, *HV*, 24 November 1977. Jean added, 'We're not [on tape]?' And then the tape went off.

110 JR, *HV*, 5 March 1978.

111 Gibson, *Queen's*, 98. This merger might have been the cause of an ongoing cold war in the department. 'There were two men in Classics who were not on speaking terms,' Jean told an alumnae luncheon (Untitled, [Queen's in the 1920s], 13 May 1972), 'and the third member has told me many times that in his first few years at Queen's he served as an errand boy carrying messages from one to the other.'

112 See the discussion in Gibson on the Senate debates on the admission of Japanese Canadians and Jewish students during the early 1940s (*Queen's*, 197–202), and pp. 252–3 this volume.

113 Professor Tracy reminds me of a well-known physics professor at Queen's who, on being told that there were insufficient spaces for students in the Drama courses, insisted – only partly in jest – that this was not a problem: they had plenty of room in physics.

114 JR, *HV*, 5 March 1978.

115 But this came later. During his first year teaching, Martyn Estall remembered that Jean – whom he had met at an SCM conference – 'more than anyone else [helped] me to find my feet and to learn such things as timetable requirements, keeping plausible attendance records, setting and marking exams, always remembering the needs and existence of an unseen cloud of witnesses enrolled extramurally.' At that time, as Estall noted, she was still assistant registrar. Letter, 2 March 1993.

116 JR, *HV*, 5 March 1978.

117 4 March 1948. The signature is illegible, but he must have been a senior professor to have negotiated successfully. JIR.

118 JIR. Rollo and his wife Olga became good friends.

119 23 January 1978, JIR. History professor Gerald Graham left Queen's in 1946 for the University of London, where he became Rhodes Professor of Imperial History at King's College.

120 Harold Good interview, 4 March 1999.

121 This was in no sense pejorative; Good went on to say that 'I don't rate myself very good at that either.' Interview, 20 September 1994.

122 JR, *HV*, 24 August 1977.

123 Elsie Curtis to JR, 7 October 1980.

124 Elsie Curtis interview, 16 September 1993.

125 Shirley Brooks interview, 28 May 1997.

126 JR, *HV*, 5 March 1978.

127 Letters to JH from A. John Coleman, 11 March 1993; W.B. Rice, 9 March 1993; David B. McLay, undated.

128 Vernon Ready to JH, received 6 April 1993.

129 Harold Good to JH, 7 February 1993.

130 Harold Good interview, 20 September 1994.

131 On May 12, 1943, the Chairman of the Board of Trustees [Dr J.M. Macdonnell] referred to the excellence of the organization of the Convocation exercises and gave credit to the principal, the vice-principal and the registrar. 'The Principal also spoke in high praise of Miss Royce.' Then, on the chairman's suggestion, the Board of Trustees passed a resolution 'in appreciation of the efficiency and ability with which she is discharging her

duties as Registrar.' By a letter of 17 May, the motion was conveyed to the registrar. JRP.

132 *The First Fifty Years: A History of the Applied Science Faculty at Queen's University, 1893–1943* (n.p., n.d.).

133 Arthur Clark to JR, 29 September 1943, JIR.

134 JR, *HV*, 24 August 1977.

135 Priscilla Galloway to author, March 1995.

136 'How many carbons did we have to make?' Priscilla mused. 'One of everything, certainly – but often it was more than one. That, no doubt, was one reason why accurate typing was important. It was difficult to make corrections on multiple carbon copies – the document might slip; if one was near the bottom of the page, the probability got higher – and then the carbons were not in alignment, and they looked messy.' E-mail to author, 27 November 1996.

137 Priscilla Galloway to author, March 1995.

138 Priscilla Galloway to author, 27 November 1996.

139 Priscilla Galloway to author, March 1995.

140 Eleanor Smith worked in the Registrar's Office after the Second World War for four years, and in the language departments for twenty years.

141 Interview, 29 August 1997. Mrs Wilkie worked in the Registrar's Office during the summer of 1956.

142 Eleanor Smith interview, 20 October 1996.

143 Magda Davey interview, 27 November 1998.

144 Eleanor Smith interview, 20 October 1996.

145 Quoted in Gibson, *Queen's*, 259.

146 See McKillop, *Matters of Mind*, 547–61, and Paul Axelrod, *Scholars and Dollars: Politics, Economics, and the Universities of Ontario 1945–1980* (Toronto: University of Toronto Press, 1982), 19.

147 McKillop, *Matters of Mind*, 545. McKillop draws his evidence about Queen's from Gibson, *Queen's*, 233–4.

148 JR, *Queen's University*, JIR.

149 In McKillop's words, 'Queen's administrators and staff were engaged in a sustained exercise in ... damage control' (*Matters of Mind*, 548).

150 JR, *HV*, 24 August 1977.

151 Gibson, *Queen's*, 98.

152 JR, *HV*, 24 November 1977.

153 Eleanor Smith interview, 30 October 1996.

154 Dawn Kiell to JH, 31 May 1993.

155 Jean Richardson in an interview with MH and Dawn Cannon, August 1995.

156 Eleanor Smith interview, 30 October 1996.
157 *Leaven of Malice* (London: Penguin Books, 1980), 313, 335.
158 Jean Richardson interview, August 1995.
159 JR, *HV*, 24 November 1977.
160 JR, *HV*, 24 August 1977; *HV*, 24 November 1977.
161 Interview, 30 October 1996. Eleanor added: 'I was going out with a professor for a while and he always said that he thought Roycie was mean with Jean. Jean will never say that of course.'
162 Jean Richardson interview, August 1997.
163 Gibson, *Queen's*, 373. 'The splendour of the administration building is the topic of gossip,' McNeill wrote. 'Two rooms have broadloom carpets from wall to wall; all offices have rugs and drapes.' Nor was he alone in his dismay; history professor Arthur Lower claimed it was 'monstrous' and 'disgraceful,' and Principal Mackintosh, 'whose interest in buildings was altogether limited to what went on inside them,' was said to be 'not a little uncomfortable in the panelled and carpeted elegance of his new office' (371).
164 Shirley Brooks interview, 28 May 1997.
165 This lack of concern for the physical also registered in her distance from her own body and any pain or discomfort that it might be experiencing. But it did not extend to her apartment, as we see in Chapter 5.
166 In a 1970 CFRC Radio talk, Jean noted that 'Richardson Hall (Administration) was opened in 1955 and this made extra space for the Library,' clearly a worthy enterprise. JR, *Queen's University*.
167 Eleanor Smith interview, 20 October 1996
168 Jean Richardson interview, August 1997.
169 Dawn Kiell, letter, 31 May 1993.
170 Rona Wilkie interview, 29 August 1997.
171 Ruth Bialek, letter, 16 February 1993.
172 Connie Martens, letter, 15 February 1993.
173 And perhaps, Magda speculated, it helped that the registrar at York was a Queen's alumni, and knew what a recommendation from Jean Royce meant. Interview, 27 November 1998.
174 Ibid.
175 Connie Martens Memoir, 15 February 1993.
176 'Some Notes about Jean Royce' by Jean Richardson. Undated.
177 Rona Wilkie interview, 29 August 1997.
178 Ruth Bialek to JH, letter, 16 February 1993.
179 Connie Martens to JH, 15 February 1993.
180 Connie Martens interview, 27 August 1994.

181 JR, *HV*, 24 November 1977.
182 Magda Davey interview, 27 November 1998.
183 Jim Whitley conversation, 1 August 1997.
184 Ralfe Clench to JH, letter received 1 February 1993.
185 Jean Richardson had decided to work part-time, and moved into the job of recorder, which she held until 1965. At that time she resigned, citing the desire 'to live, whatever that may mean,' as Jean wrote to her sister Marion. '[She] has been with me for many years [since 1939], first as assistant registrar, and subsequently as recorder. [She will] replenish her pocket book with odd jobs, and live. [She] plans to spend September with a group of naturalists banding birds.' Dated 'Saturday' – written in July 1965.
186 JR, *HV*, 24 August 1977.
187 JR, *HV*, 24 November 1977.
188 MH's Tribute. JIR.
189 Jean Richardson interview, August 1997.
190 Connie Martens to JH, 15 February 1993.
191 JR, *HV*, 24 November 1977.
192 Jean Richardson would have them all 'over to her cottage and Jean Royce would always come over,' as Magda Davey remembered. And she especially remembers a lunch Jean Royce had at her apartment. Everything was served 'so daintily, she prepared it all herself ... it was very special.' Interview, 27 November 1998.
193 John Porter's summary of the Dominion Bureau of Statistics reports on Higher Education indicates that between 1946 and 1958, 9 per cent of the student-age population entered university. In 1961, the figure was similar, and only 40 per cent were girls, although in Porter's words, 'on the average girls are better performers than boys.' *The Vertical Mosaic* (Toronto: University of Toronto Press, 1965), 178.
194 JR Untitled, [University Education] 1950s.
195 JR 'Population Explosion and Standards of Admission,' *Queen's Review* 39, September–October (1965): 116.
196 Ed Funke, letter, 3 May 1993.
197 Mary-Louise (Funke) Campbell, letter, 13 February 1993. With reference to this course, Mary-Louise wrote: 'I still possess [the copy of] H.W. Fowler's *The King's English* she gave me ... when I gloriously failed an English exam.' She and her siblings 'still occasionally have good laughs when we think back to how Miss Royce tried to correct our typically old-fashioned Old-World mannerisms and thus helped to make us more comfortably Canadian.'

198 Ed Funke to JH, 3 May 1993.
199 In this sentence, I rather think that the phrase 'it was felt' is a bit like the 'it' that populates the minutes of meetings that she took. 'It' means I, though not in any direct substitution sense; undoubtedly others thought the same. But no registrar had gone on the hustings before.
200 JR, *HV*, 17 June 1977.
201 As recalled in a letter, 31 July 1996, from the Reverend James Scanlon. He was a Queen's graduate and remembered that several years later, 'when I lived at Moose Factory as rector of old St Thomas Church and Archdeacon of James Bay, she came up on the tourist train, the Polar Bear Express, with Miss [Melva] Eagleson from the Library.'
202 JR, *HV*, 5 March 1978.
203 JR, *HV*, 17 June 1977.
204 Douglas McCall, 9 July 1996.
205 JR, *HV*, 5 March 1978.
206 Bernard Champagne, telephone interview, 19 September 1996; Benjamin Scott, letter dated 10 July 1996; Bob McLarty, e-mail, 1997, undated.
207 JR, *HV*, 5 March 1978.
208 JR, *Guidance Dialogue*, Ottawa University, August 1968. JIR.
209 Her partner in organizing these weekends was Monica McQueen, the principal's special assistant. *HV*, 17 June 1977.
210 This speech, 'An Excursion in Ideas,' was a description of the Teachers Weekend of 1955. JIR.
211 Or in Jean's more respectful words: 'In the brief span possible in a visit of an hour or so, a student only gets an external view and can have little more than a pleasant time.' *Guidance Dialogue*.
212 She went on to say that these were 'the values the teachers of Queen's' had in mind in their invitation to their secondary school colleagues. 'Excursion in Ideas.'
213 'An Excursion in Ideas,' written during the late 1950s and in *Guidance Dialogue*, 1968.
214 *Guidance Dialogue*, 10–11.

3: Keeping a 'Watching Brief'

1 Dr Scott to Jo-Anne (Bechthold) Brady, 24 March 1996.
2 Dr Scott to author, 10 July 1996.
3 Philosophy professor Martyn Estall also wrote to JH that 'Jean cared about students (some said she had her pets) [but I] had better not start on anecdotal review of this claim' (2 March 1993).

4 Jane D. declined my request for details.

5 Paul Axelrod, *Making a Middle Class: Student Life in English Canada during the Thirties* (Montreal and Kingston: McGill-Queen's University Press, 1990), notes that after the mid-1920s, McGill 'led the way' in limiting and reducing the number of Jewish students. By the end of the 1930s, Jewish students needed a 75 per cent average from high school to gain admission, in contrast to gentile students 'who were permitted to enrol in the Faculty of Arts' with 60 per cent (33).

6 JR, *HV*, 17 June 1977.

7 Bernard Champagne, telephone conversation, 19 September 1996.

8 JR, *HV*, 17 June 1977.

9 John Matheson to author, 25 January 1998.

10 The Honorable John Matheson's military, judicial, and parliamentary career earned him many honours, including an honorary degree from Queen's. See *Canadian Who's Who* 1999.

11 Phyllis (Nunn) Bray to author, 10 March 1998. To Shirley (Ayres) Brooks, who registered at Queen's in 1937, Jean was 'very severe, hair back in a bun' (interview, 28 May 1997). And Evangeline (Phillips) Murray remembered that 'her hair style was a surprise to me. It seemed very severe (to author, 17 July 1997).

12 Evangeline (Phillips) Murray to author, 17 July 1997.

13 To author, 6 September 1996. Doris Burns was in first year in 1938.

14 Letter from Mariam Fletcher dated 28 December 1984, accompanying a donation to the JR Fellowship Fund.

15 Letter from Lester Anthes, 31 March 1984, accompanying 'a small contribution ... for the fellowship in her memory.'

16 Letter from Douglas Smith, 14 April 1984, accompanying contribution to JR fellowship.

17 'We were winners of the Eastern Ontario Drama Festival,' he added. See also Frederick W. Gibson, *Queen's University*, vol. 2, *1917–1961* (Montreal and Kingston: McGill-Queen's University Press, 1983), 147.

18 Telephone conversation, 29 October 1999. Judge Gold received an honorary degree from Queen's in 1982. He also did the essays for Minnie Gordon.

19 John Hanna to author, 9 July 1996.

20 Registration, 1937. Jake Warren to JH, 16 March 1993.

21 At the time of Kathleen's graduation, Jean received a letter from her father. 'Mrs Butcher and I have long been grateful to you for the guidance and inspiration that you gave Kathleen. We understand that she owes much to a certain interview that you had with her after the Xmas exams of her first year.' C. Ward Butcher to JR, 19 April 1943. JIR.

22 Letter to JH, 1 March 1993. See also Dr Kathleen (Butcher) Whitehead's

reminiscence 'Dilemmas of a Part-Time Professor' in Joy Parr, ed., *Still Running* (Kingston: Queen's University Alumnae Association,1987), 55–63.

23 Dr Mary Elizabeth (Jeffery) Collier to JH, 12 February 1993. Both women earned the PhD and went on to careers in university teaching.

24 James Courtright to JH, 2 February 1993.

25 Apparently Miss Royce was undeterred by the knowledge that Raymond was just at Queen's awaiting another birthday – his seventeenth so that he could replace his father in the Navy. Phone interview, 3 July 1997.

26 John Matheson to author, 25 January 1998.

27 Shirley (Ayres) Brooks interview, 28 May 1997.

28 Like the nursing students, Dr Ross came from Kingston Collegiate Vocational Institute. He confirmed that Miss Royce's conclusion about inadequate preparation in chemistry had been 'perfectly correct.' Letter to author, 30 November 1996.

29 Gibson, *Queen's*, 194. 'In 1942 the Senate, at the initiative of Principal Wallace and to meet a growing demand for trained nurses capable of holding executive positions, introduced a five-year degree course in nursing science.'

30 Anne (Constantine) Ginn to author, 3 January 1998.

31 Jake Warren to JH, 16 April 1993.

32 The Honourable Mr Justice Binks graduated in 1948, and his four children all subsequently graduated from Queen's. Letter to author, 4 October 1996.

33 Letter to author, 14 January 1997.

34 E-mail to author, 6 September 1996, from Mike Lafratta (BA '45). In a letter, dated 8 April 1984, accompanying a contribution to the JR Fellowship, Robert D. Hendry wrote: 'In memory of a notable lady. In her work and actions, Jean truly exemplified the spirit of Queen's.'

35 Frank Ritchie telephone conversation, fall 1999. Like Jean, Frank found a job in Douglas Library the next year, and he was a tutor – at $1.00 an hour.

36 Letter to author, 8 July 1996, from Margaret (Cutten) Boyce, who 'did achieve an undistinguished B.A. eventually, and the fact that I didn't come a cropper completely I ascribe at least partly to her efforts above and beyond the call of duty.'

37 Vernon Ready to JH, 6 April 1993.

38 Brooks interview, 28 May 1997.

39 Kay Mein to MH, 15 June 1992.

40 Mary Elizabeth (Jeffery) Collier to JH, 12 February 1993.

41 Joyce Hemlow letter, 25 May 1984.

42 This fall 1942 visit was 'to let her know that one of my final marks in Grade 13 had been upgraded in case she wanted her records to be dead accurate.

She did – and proceeded to berate me roundly for all of 10 seconds for not notifying her during the summer.' Donald Gormley to author, 7 January 1997.

43 David Moyer to Alfred Bader, 12 August 1993.
44 Undated letter (c. January 1999) from Elizabeth (Marsh) Kennedy (Arts '48) to author. Her older brother graduated in 1948, her younger sister (who 'took a sisterly delight' in the story) in 1954.
45 David Sweezey to author, 22 October 1996.
46 Kate (Macdonnell) Lawson to JH, 2 February 1993.
47 Lawson, telephone interview, 31 March 1998.
48 Annette Wolff, telephone conversation, 30 March 1998.
49 Letter to JH, 4 August 1993. Alfred Bader recorded these events in *Alfred Bader: Adventures of a Chemist Collector* (London: Weidenfeld and Nicholson, 1995).
50 For an account of the committee's work and the participants, see Thomas Socknatt, *Witness against War* (Toronto: University of Toronto Press, 1987), 260–7. Also see Eric Koch, *Deemed Suspect* (Toronto: Methuen, 1980) for a detailed history of the internment camps.
51 Socknat, *Witness against War*, 265.
52 Vernon Ready to JH, 6 April 1993.
53 Letter to JH, 9 February 1993. James Martin writes that although he took Jean Royce 'a bouquet of roses in Sept. 1945 and should have again in 1967,' he did not know her personally, except across her desk. Nor was James – at least until after the war – a noteworthy student. There seems no explanation for why she acted so often on his behalf, except that when possible, that's what she did.
54 Sylvia (Mackenzie) Mercer to JH, 15 March 1993.
55 Kathleen R. (Barclay) Bowley to author, 21 November 1996. Kathleen Bowley later wrote that on her first day 'Jean Royce threw me into such a frenzy of fear of failure (that was not her intention, I know), that I did very little socializing.' Letter to author, 17 April 1998.
56 George Jewett to author, 30 September 1996.
57 Fred Moote to author, 22 March 1993.
58 David Slater to JH, 8 February 1993. In 1970, David wrote to Jean thanking her for her letter of 'good wishes' upon his appointment as president of York University. 17 June 1970, JIR.
59 Later renamed the Ryerson School of Technology.
60 During the postwar years there were two entrance (and two graduating) classes a year.
61 John Collins to author, 19 August 1997.

62 The Reverend James Scanlon to author, 31 July 1996.
63 Hartwell Illsey to author, 1 May 1998. I am grateful to the Reverend Glenn H. Wilms for alerting me to this story. Letter, 13 November 1996.
64 Major (Ret'd) J.B. Kelly to author, 14 July 1996.
65 Ready to JH, 6 April 1993. And in 1951, 'Jean Royce was instrumental in granting [Howard Manchester] two credits from the year [he] spent in Engineering.' Howard was a teacher who was pursuing his degree extramurally. Letter to author, 23 September 1996.
66 Bill Craig interview, 2 June 1997.
67 Dr Carmichael interview, 21 December 1998.
68 Wilms to author, 10 October 1996.
69 Frederick Gibson provides the data. In Canada some 50,000 veterans took 'advantage of the financial help available to them through the Department of Veterans Affairs.' At Queen's 'the registrar informed a startled Senate that, of the 2,242 intramural students who had registered for the 1945–46 winter session, a total of 1,030, nearly half, were veterans. When there were added the veterans who enrolled in the special summer sessions of 1945 and 1946, the grand total of veteran registrations in the twelve months following the end of the European war rose to 1,962, a figure which exceeded the entire intramural student body in any of the prewar years' *Queen's*, (243).
70 David Slater to JH, 8 February 1993.
71 Ian Vorres to JH, 1 April 1993.
72 Ready to JH, 6 April 1993.
73 Stewart Fyfe to JH, 1 March 1993.
74 Galloway, *Memories of Jean Royce*, March 1995.
75 Confidential conversation with a former staff member in Applied Science.
76 As told by his classmate, James Courtright, letter, 2 February 1993, to JH. Captain Lynch died 1 July 1993, so I was unable to hear his own story. He did, however, write to Jean on 16 October 1968: 'I was encouraged by the personal interest you took in this problem, and in my family. [T]o be frank,' he ad-ded, 'I had counted on this because you always did take a personal interest in everyone' JIR.
77 A. Chiperzak to author, 2 October 1996.
78 Chiperzak to author, 6 July 1996.
79 Chiperzak to author, 2 October 1996.
80 Chiperzak to author, 6 July 1996. For an administrative account of the stresses on Applied Science during these years, see Gibson, *Queen's*, 232–3.
81 Neil Black to author, 17 November 1997.

82 Al Hyland conversation, 30 May 1997.
83 Michael Humpheries phone interview, 12 September 1996.
84 Pauline Jewett interview with Ann Hargreaves, *HV*, 11 January 1980.
85 The professor was Dr Alec Corry. *Tribute to JR*, 28 April 1982. In Pauline's interview two years earlier (ibid.), she said that Jean called her in as a result of her Christmas exam grades, and that Corry's encouragement came later, when he urged her to go to graduate school.
86 JR in *HV*, 11 January 1980.
87 Pauline Jewett, *Tribute to Jean Royce*, 28 April 1982.
88 Elspeth (Wallace) Baugh to JH, 25 February 1993.
89 Sylvia (Mackenzie) Mercer to JH, 15 March 1993.
90 Elspeth Baugh to JH, 25 February 1993.
91 JR, CFRC Radio interview, 1970.
92 Ed Funke to JH, 3 May 1993.
93 Douglas Ross to author, 16 September 1996.
94 Ann Saddlemyer, 'In memoriam Jean Royce,' 28 April 1982.
95 Michael Humpheries phone interview, 12 September 1996. This farewell conversation took place in 1953, after Michael had successfully completed a BA and an MA in Industrial Relations.
96 John Ashley to JH, 1 February 1993.
97 Quoted in Gibson, *Queen's*, 129.
98 John Matheson to author, 25 January 1998.
99 Glenn Wilms to author, 10 October 1996.
100 Letter undated (c. January 1999), Elizabeth (Marsh) Kennedy to author.
101 Principal Fyfe titled a section of his final report with these words. Gibson, *Queen's*, 129.
102 Jenny Weir to author, 29 March 1998.
103 John Ashley to JH, 1 February 1993.
104 Douglas Slack to MH, 3 August 1992, 'following [her] disclosure of the treatment of Jean Royce by Queen's administration.'
105 Kristian Palda to author, 10 March 1993. Professor Palda returned to Queen's as full professor in 1970.
106 Tom Fahidy to author, 5 July 1996. Dr Fahidy added, 'I gained admission to Canada in December 1956 as a refugee upon the Hungarian revolution (Oct. 23/1956) and was interviewed by Padre Laverty in Montreal ... I arrived in Kingston (in April, if my memory serves me right) with about 15–20 other Hungarian students to take an intensive English course ... and was admitted to the third year in Applied Science.'
107 'To appreciate that remark,' Eugene Cherniak wrote, 'you would have to

discover all you can about the history of the Slovaks.' To JH, 5 March 1993.

108 See, for example, Michelle LeDoeuff, 'Women and Philosophy' in *French Feminist Thought*, ed. Toril Moi (Oxford: Blackwell, 1987), 181–209.

109 Stewart Fyfe to JH, 1 March 1993.

110 Letter from Margaret (McKenzie) Atack to JH, 11 March 1993.

111 Diane (Polson) Duerkop, 'Blood Is Thicker Than Water,' *Queen's Journal*, 18 October 1996, 5. Diane came to Queen's in 1959.

112 Catherine Eddy to JH, 29 June 1992, and to author, 4 July 1997.

113 Frances Macdonnell to author, 9 September 1996.

114 Bob McLarty to author, undated.

115 'The chance she had taken on me,' Catherine Harland continued, 'paid off in the sense that I had won the Medal in English.' To JH, 26 February 1993.

116 Bruce Hamilton (Queen's Science '43) to author, 21 September 1996.

117 Later it was disclosed that 'students in the early part of the alphabet marked by a particular examiner went from very good grades to very bad grades,' whereas those going into the exam with very bad grades did well. Jo-Anne Hawley phone interview, 29 March 1998.

118 Jo-Anne's mother worked for Miss Royce, and of course Jean would have checked out Jo-Anne's record with Vernon Ready. There is no reason to believe, however, that she wouldn't have done the same for any student in a similar predicament. Certainly Jean would not have had occasion to regret this judgment call. Jo-Anne went on to teach English in high school. As she put it: 'The supreme irony is that I now produce English literature festivals in London.' Her whole life 'would have been completely different' she declared, had not Jean Royce admitted her into Queen's. Ibid.

119 Steven Leikin to author, 4 September 1996.

120 'From that moment on,' Dr Simon continued, 'she knew who I was and followed how I was doing because I kept winning prizes. I got my MD when I was twenty-two. I think I was the youngest in the class.' Interview 1 August 1996.

121 Rona Wilkie interview, 29 August 1997.

122 Dr Mabel Corlett to JH, 11 April 1993.

123 Dr James Shute, Director, Centre for International Programs, University of Guelph to author, E-mail, 29 July 1997.

124 Shute to author, 15 August 1997.

125 Zander Dunn phone interview, 23 October 1999.

126 Brian Mosgrove BA '58, BSc '59; Neil McNeill BCom '60; Lionel Lawrence BA (Hons) '62; Cornelis Keyzers BA (Hons) '69.

127 Brian Mosgrove to author, 9 September 1996.

128 Fax, 5 September 1996 to author. Neil McNeill began by writing that 'the way she handled the correspondence, was one of the reasons I went to Queen's.'

129 Lionel Lawrence to author, 16 September 1997.

130 C. Keyzers to author, received 22 July 1996.

131 John Olsen's parents were Canadians; his father worked in Cuba. John was in Cuba visiting when 'Castro took over. We had to be evacuated. I had my moment of fame, my picture with another guy holding up the revolutionary flag just before we were evacuated' (interview, 28 August 1997).

132 Ibid.

133 Esther R. (Jamieson) Magathan to JH, 25 February 1993.

134 This is one of two stories mentioning tears, but the presence of the tissue box – when Jean always carried a handkerchief for her own use suggests that this was not unusual. In 1948, Jean Lawson came to Queen's from Thunder Bay, and at the ripe age of seventeen fell in love, 'the courtship and my marks proceeding in inverse order.' She lost her scholarship, switched from an honours to a pass degree, and in April 1951 arrived in tears at Jean's office to request a supplemental exam form. 'On that particular day,' Jean recalled, 'she took time to listen and gently probe, as I told her about my wedding plans and what this would mean if I didn't graduate.' In 2001, Jean (Lawson) MacLean (BA '51) celebrated her fiftieth wedding anniversary, and recalled: 'Jeannie Royce – a wise counsellor and friend.' E-mail to author, 14 February 2001.

135 Sandra passed one of her supplementals, so she was able to continue without penalty. On 'June 27, 1996, [she] retired after 33 wonderful years of teaching math. I often thought that she might have appreciated knowing how well I was doing and how grateful I was for her kindness and help. Perhaps if you can use this anecdote in some small way to help show the softer side of Jean Royce, then I will have finally repaid her.' Sandra (French) Sinclair to author, 14 July 1996.

136 Confidential conversation.

137 In those days, after two years of premed, students went directly into the first of four years of medicine. 'We were all young kids,' he says with some amazement, 'about to find ourselves doctors.' Dr Jerry Simon interview, 1 August 1996.

138 Ibid.

139 Dr Barbara (Excell) Hawgood to JH, 25 February 1993.

140 Denzil Doyle to JH, 15 February 1993.

141 'A meeting,' Esther adds, 'never to be forgotten.' As with others, Jean's support for Esther continued after she left Queen's. Jean encouraged her to apply for the Marty Fellowship and later the CFUW Fellowship – aid that made it possible for her to complete the PhD in geology. 'Memories of Jean Royce,' Esther R. (Jamieson) Magathan, 25 February 1993.

142 'On a project suggested by my father,' noted Dr Corlett, 'not by anybody in the department.' Letter, 11 April 1993.

143 Lin Good to JH, 15 March 1993.

144 Esther Magathan to JH, 25 February 1993.

145 Pauline Jewett, *HV*, 11 January 1980.

146 Cheryl (Elliott) Creatore interview, 23 October 1996. This is a reference to Levana's annual ceremony to welcome first-year female students. For many years, each student was given a candle decorated with a ribbon, the colour of the ribbon indicating her future husband's faculty.

147 Magathan to JH, 25 February 1993.

148 For a sociological explanation, see William Goode, 'Why Men Resist' in *Rethinking the Family: Some Feminist Questions*, ed. Barrie Thorne, (New York, Longman, 1982), 131–50. In Goode's words, 'Men view even small losses of deference, advantages, or opportunities as large threats' (137).

149 Esther Magathan's words, letter dated 25 February 1993: 'She was most encouraging to students she perceived to be serious and gifted.'

150 Dr Jackson wrote: 'As the years passed I began to be more successful academically and went on to graduate work at Princeton and the University of London, and I have taught at the University of Toronto for almost thirty years' in the Department of English. Letter to JH, 10 February 1993. Wallace Muir, a student from the 1930s, wrote to Jean in 1968 (24 June, JIR) with a similar message: over the years, he wrote, 'you have encouraged me to have more faith in my own abilities than in fact I had, with the result that on occasion I have struggled ... to merit the more generous view.'

151 Professor Corry assumed the principalship in September 1961; Jean must have expected him to reduce his teaching load.

152 'For those whose averages fell below 75%, the floor of the A range, [Doug McCalla] suspected that Jean Royce decided where it lay, based on individual circumstances.' E-mail to author, 16 September 1996.

153 Dr Wilson wrote: 'I went on to earn my PhD and become a member of the faculties of the University of Texas and Harvard.' E-mail to author, 8 July 1996.

154 E-mail to author, 15 August 1997. Dr Taylor told a slightly different ver-

sion of this story fifteen years earlier at Jean's memorial service. In that version Jean said: 'I was disappointed with the B in English, Mr Taylor. That was the one subject I hoped you would do well in.' I am sure that every story I have been told might be somewhat different if told earlier or later or later again. The social scientist's nightmare, the postmodernist's dream.

155 Douglas Patriquin to JH, 14 March 1993.

156 A comment attributed to Abbie Hoffman when he spoke at Queen's in the 1980s.

157 Interview, 18 October 1996, with Cheryl (Elliott) Creatore.

158 JR, letter to Dean R.L. Watts, 29 May 1970.

159 George de Hueck earned the BA (Gen) in 1946. He died 2 May 1991.

160 Robin Jackson to JH, 10 February 1993.

161 Judith Lave to author, 15 July 1996. Dr Lave wrote that 'in retrospect, it is strange that it was Miss Royce and not my professors who encouraged me to go on to graduate work.' Earlier when she changed majors from commerce to economics and history, she discussed this beforehand with Miss Royce, who was 'very supportive and encouraged me to go ahead. (In retrospect, it is surprising that I did not think to discuss these plans with either the head of the Commerce program or the chair of the economics department.)'

162 Judith (Plumptre) Wedderspoon to JH, 16 February 1993.

163 Speaking of her year, 1963, Judith wrote, 'Queen's did very well that year – won several Woodrow Wilson Fellowships, thanks not least to Jean's initiative.' Ibid.

164 Gibson calculated that Queen's students made up 2.8 per cent of the students in all Canadian universities and had received 9.4 per cent of the Woodrow Wilsons (*Queen's*, 414).

165 Gordon Dowsley to author, 16 September 1996. George Kelman Murray, BA (Gen), graduated in 1967. He died 23 June 1991, so I was unable to hear his account. But when I reported George's death to Gordon, he had this to add: 'I have a vague recollection that he told me [the story] more than once – one time on University Avenue and another around a table in the coffee shop at the union. I do remember someone laughing at the outrageousness of her comments.' E-mail, 19 March 1998.

166 26 February 1993.

4: The Prime of Miss Jean Royce

1 David Sweezey to author, September 1996.

2 Sponsored by the National Association of Universities and Colleges, following a recommendation from the Canadian Association of University Teachers, the commission was better known as the Duff-Berdahl Commission after the two commissioners, Sir James Duff, Vice-Chancellor Emeritus of the University of Durham, and Robert O. Berdahl of San Francisco State College. The commissioners submitted their report in August 1965, and it was published in 1966 by the University of Toronto Press.

3Three years later, in a convocation speech at the University of New Brunswick, J.A. Corry, 'for convenience of reference,' referred to the 'sizeable operating staff that keeps up a flow of essential services for students and scholars' as 'housekeepers.' He offered a critique of student radicals who insisted that the university should be a political democracy. 'If students and teaching staff have a democratic right to sit on the governing bodies ... surely the housekeepers who have an interest in finance as well as housekeeping should be there too.' Corry, University Government,' in *Farewell the Ivory Tower: Universities in Transition* (Montreal and Kingston: McGill-Queen's University Press, 1970), 115. His intention was to reveal the absurdity of such a state of affairs.

4 JR, *HV*, 5 March 1978. But Jean was never involved in the finances of the university. Nor did she share McNeill's apparently pathological penuriousness. (A pencil stub had to be exchanged for a pencil, one story goes.) You also will remember that Jean reported trying to get higher wages for those in her office, without success. Later, in 1962, she asked Margaret Hooey to name her salary expectations. 'I gave a figure that represented some improvement over what I had been getting at the government. Jean replied, "Margaret, you've got to say something better than this," and she stroked it out and inserted a higher figure. "If you go with this," said the voice of experience, "it will follow you forever."' Interview with MH, 7 August 1997.

5 10 September 1956. John Orr, a bacteriologist, was longtime secretary of the medical faculty and a friend of Jean.

6 Eleanor Smith interview, 30 October 1996.

7 MH interview, 30 July 1996; note by MH, 10 August 1981.

8 Or in Bernard Trotter's words, 'until 1930 MacNeill was registrar and treasurer. So then the power was divided and Jean really looked after the academic side of things and MacNeill kept the screws on the purse.' Interview, 5 August 1997. Bernard's father, Reginald G. Trotter, was head of the Department of History from 1934 until his death in 1951. The McNeill Royce division of labour was part of his family history, as it was for Duncan Sinclair, whose father was head of Biochemistry from 1937 to 1949. 'At that

time it seemed to me the University was run by four people: the Principal who was the leader; Mr McNeill, who looked after the money; Ralph. "Old Man Hinton," who ran the plant; and Miss Royce, who looked after all the rest.' Letter, 15 February 1993.

9 Sharing their educational experience 'with [these] mature students who had such strong motivation was a privilege for the young people from the schools,' Jean continued. This was one of her continuing themes – that taking time out from studies to do other things made for better students and a more vibrant intellectual environment. (*Queen's University.* Radio address CFRC, 1970–1.)

10 Frederick W. Gibson, *Queen's University*, vol. 2, 1917–1961. (Montreal and Kingston: McGill-Queen's University Press, 1983), 262. Gibson took a dim view of McNeill's 'inextinguishable [financial] pessimism' and role as 'all-too-successful disseminator of anxiety on the Board,' 271.

11 Quoted in ibid., 307.

12 Sydney Smith, letter, 31 May 1951. Quoted in ibid., 307.

13 Confidential conversation.

14 *Queen's University*, 6. Gibson wrote that Mackintosh's 'successors were to look back on that decade as a kind of golden age of progress and serenity in the affairs of Queen's University' (*Queen's*, 311).

15 McNeill's vice-principalship went in 1947 to W.A. Mackintosh, who had added this honorific to his responsibilities as dean, department head, and Ottawa mandarin (ibid., 303).

16 Ibid., 262.

17 Quoted in ibid., 309.

18 If so, it is worth noting that no Tillotson-like memo clutters the registrar's files during those years. Moreover, Mackintosh's letters informing Jean of salary increases (21 May 1955; 21 May 1957) expressed his 'own and the Board's appreciation' of her 'great service to the University' (JRP). Jean told Margaret Hooey that Mackintosh was very fair to her about salary – more so than the others.

19 Gibson, *Queen's*, 340–1.

20 Ibid., 338; 417–21.

21 Bill Craig interview, 2 June 1997.

22 Bernard Trotter interview with Ronald and Donna Watts, 6 June 1997.

23 Hale Trotter to JH, 5 February 1993.

24 Bernard Trotter, interview, 5 August 1997.

25 JR, *HV*, 5 March 1978.

26 Confidential conversation.

27 Gibson, *Queen's*, 338.

28 Confidential conversation.
29 W.B. Rice to JH, 9 March 1993.
30 Gibson, *Queen's*, 315 and 475 n.77.
31 For J.A. Corry's public lectures on the state of the university during the 1960s, see his collection *Farewell the Ivory Tower.*
32 Trotter interview, 5 August 1997.
33 Bingham had been one of a cluster of senior men 'handpicked by Principal Wallace' to be department heads. Gibson, *Queen's*, 245.
34 Jenny Weir to author, 24 March 1998.
35 Trotter interview, 5 August 1997.
36 Interview with Ronald and Donna Watts, 6 June 1997.
37 MH interview, 24 February 1994.
38 MH interview, 7 August 1997.
39 MH interview, 24 February 1994.
40 The report is dated 27 October 1964.
41 Eleanor Smith's phrase in an interview, 30 October 1996.
42 Draft memo, 30 April 1965.
43 Connie Martens to JH, 15 February 1993.
44 MH interview, 15 September 1997.
45 'Memorandum on Appointment of an Admissions Officer,' 7 April 1966.
46 MH to Robert Legget, 22 June 1982.
47 MH interview, 24 February 1994.
48 Memo dated 28 April 1966.
49 Memo dated 11 April 1966.
50 'Report on the Office of the Registrar, Queen's University,' 15 July 1966.
51 'The purpose of this report,' he added, 'is *not* to look into detailed staffing and work procedures for the office, except so far as these have a bearing on general and organizational questions.'
52 MH, e-mail, 25 September 1997.
53 Dean Harrower's announcement at Faculty Board. Minutes, 17 March 1967, FAS. It is worth noting that there is no evidence that the registrar ever considered these duties 'burdensome.' She just wanted more assistance.
54 W.C. Lougheed to JH, 16 February 1993.
55 Political Studies Professor Stewart Fyfe heard that Jean Royce was dismissed because she would not computerize the office. Letter to JH, 1 March 1993.
56 Letter to author, 7 October 1997. I am very grateful to Elspeth Ross for responding to my letter, particularly so soon after her husband's death.
57 Robin Ross wrote about his disillusionment with the University of Toronto

during this period in *The Short Road Down: A University Changes* (Toronto: University of Toronto Press, 1984).

58 JR to MR, 17 November 1974.

59 For an account of Robin Ross's career, see his account in *The Short Road Down*, 1–3. In 1958, at the age of forty, he was appointed assistant registrar at the University of Toronto, his first university position. Recruited to the university from the federal agency Central Mortgage and Housing, he had previously served in the Indian Civil Service and the Commonwealth Relations Office of the United Kingdom.

60 Confidential conversation.

61 MR to MH, 29 June 1966.

62 MR to MH, 14 August 1966.

63 Ronald Watts interview, 6 June 1997.

64 MH to RL, 22 June 1982.

65 MH interview, 15 September 1997.

66 Bernard Trotter interview, 5 August 1997.

67 Watts interview, 6 June 1997.

68 'Memorandum on the Appointment of an Admissions Officer,' 7 April 1966, 3. Given her respected role in the National Association of Registrars, what she was really saying was that she needed more time and support so that she could play a leading role.

69 *University Government in Canada: Report of a Commission Sponsored by the Canadian Association of University Teachers and the Association of Universities and Colleges* (University of Toronto Press: 1966), 3.

70 For example, Robert Wallace, was the last external appointment as principal until William Leggett's appointment in 1994.

71 Watts interview, 6 June 1997.

72 Josiah was a first cousin of Jean's grandfather, also Josiah.

73 Jean Royce continued to attend Faculty Board meetings as registrar until she retired. At her last meeting, on 19 July 1968, the dean thanked the chairman, Martyn Estall, and the secretary, H.R. Wynne-Edwards, for their able work on their retirement from these offices. FAS. My research assistant Marion Campbell, who read the Faculty Board minutes, added this comment: 'Well it seems Jean Royce was sent off from her long years of service with this board without a whisper. No goodbye to her and no introduction of the new registrar. No wonder it nearly put her over the edge. Shame shame.'

74 Watts interview, 6 June 1997.

75 Dated 13 January 1967.

76 Commission Report, 32.

77 She mentions residences and athletic facilities for students and staff as examples.

78 She added that the secretariat would require a 'well-qualified person capable of doing the necessary research, collecting and co-ordinating material and disseminating it in proper form.' By then she had Margaret Hooey tagged for this position.

79 In support of her view, she cited the 'relatively new departure' in the Faculty of Arts and Science, where, with an appointed chairman in place, the dean now had 'more opportunity to give guidance to his Faculty.' She assured the principal: 'His new role [had not] in any way lessened his effectiveness as spokesman for his Faculty.'

80 13 January 1967.

81 As one instance, Macintosh cited her 'capricious' admission policy. 'If you wanted a student in who played football you had to hide the fact that he played the game.' Conversation, 12 September 1993.

82 Ronald and Donna Watt interview, 6 June 1997.

83 Vernon Ready to JH, David McLay, 6 April 1993.

84 Undated reminiscence.

85 Judith (Plumptre) Wedderspoon to JH, 16 February 1993.

86 Wedderspoon, phone interview, 7 April 1998.

87 JR, *Queen's University.*

88 MH e-mail, 25 January 1998.

89 JR to Dean Watts, 29 May 1970. As Dean of the Faculty of Arts and Science, Ronald Watts was chairing a Committee on Grievance, Discipline and Related Matters. It was in that connection that Jean responded to a letter from him.

90 Confidential conversation with a senior administrator.

91 MH to Robert Legget, 22 June 1982.

92 Eleanor Smith interview, 30 October 1996.

93 27 January 1967.

94 MH interview, 24 February 1994. Jean mentioned this incident in her interview of 24 November 1977 (HV). 'After Mr Leech came I went abroad for quite a long time. I went to a meeting of Commonwealth universities. He left his minutes for me to finish. I don't know what he did when I ... left. He must have had some other arrangement for taking the minutes.'

95 Mr Leech outlined her proposed responsibilities in a letter to Principal Corry, 24 April 1968.

96 MH, e-mail, 25 September 1997.

97 She is referring here to the abolition of the provincially set exams at the end of grade 13.

98 'Admission Procedures and S.A.C.U.' Delivered to the Annual Meeting of Service for Admission to College and University, 28–9 March 1968.
99 *Guidance Dialogue*, Ottawa University, August 1968.
100 Or as Robert Taylor wrote for the *Kingston Whig-Standard*, 'Miss Jean I. Royce was the only woman [and] the only recipient to receive a standing – long and loud – ovation' (9 November 1968).
101 JR to MR, 14 November 1968.

5: More Than a Registrar

1 Priscilla Galloway, 'Memories of Jean Royce,' March 1995.
2 Robert Legget, 'Jean Royce,' 23 November 1993.
3 Carolyn Heilbrun, *The Last Gift of Time* (New York: Dial Press, 1997), 50.
4 David Riesman, *The Lonely Crowd* (New Haven: Yale University Press, 1950). Jean's account book reveals that she purchased the book in March 1961 soon after the paperback version was published.
5 Celia Royce interview, 25 November 1996.
6 Ian Royce interview, 8 June 1996.
7 Heilbrun, *Last Gift of Time*, 50.
8 In 'Together they go into the dark night' by Sally Lyall, *Globe and Mail*, 31 December 1998, D2. See Bayley's memoir, *Elegy for Iris* (New York: St Martin's Press, 1999).
9 Nathaniel Micklem, *The Box and the Puppets* (London: Geoffrey Bles, 1957).
10 JR to MR, 4 September 1974.
11 Micklem, *Box and Puppets*, p. 13.
12 JR in *The New Outlook*, 9 October 1929, 1023.
13 Marie-Jeanne Coleman to JH, 1 March 1993.
14 John Coleman to JH, 11 March 1993.
15 JR *HV*, 24 November 1977.
16 Moira Cartwright to MH, 19 July 1982.
17 Cultural capital – a concept developed by French sociologist Pierre Boudieu – refers to 'types of knowledge, typically taught in family settings, but also in schools and other institutional settings, that give certain persons an ad-vantage in social life or mark them as members of a distinctive social status or class group.' In Karen Anderson, *Sociology* (Scarborough, ON: Nelson, 1996), 471.
18 It is possible that Jean had a companion on her first trip, according to Margaret Hooey, but she never used 'we' in referring to that trip.
19 JR to MR, 11 March 1973
20 JR to MR, 2 July 1961.

21 JR to MR, 11 April 1974.

22 Harvey Cushing, *William Osler: The Man* (New York: Hoeber, c.1920).

23 JR to MR, 16 September 1975. She stated precisely in this letter that she was in Oxford forty-three years ago, which would put her there in 1932. Perhaps she was one year off, or perhaps she travelled to England before 1933 as well. I think this unlikely.

24 14 February 1933, JIR. The letter is signed only 'Sarah,' but the *Alumnae News* (1934) reports that Dr Sarah Common resided in London and married Dr Harley Stevenson on August 7, 1933. By then Jean was back in Canada, but she saw Sarah and Harley whenever she visited London. Letter to MR, 20 July 1961.

25 Her paper 'France' is undated, but she referred to the recent resignation of Gaston Doumergue, who resigned on 9 November 1934.

26 This is the only comment I have found in Jean's writings that makes this suggestion.

27 Along with other right-wing leagues, François de la Roque's Croix de Feu was disbanded by the Popular Front government. La Rocque then transformed his 'army' into a political party, the Parti Social Français (PSF), in 1936. Jean's paper was clearly written before the dissolution.

28 William L. Shirer, *The Collapse of the Third Republic* (New York: Simon and Shuster, 1969), 213–23.

29 Lovat Dickson, n.d. The preface was signed HD.

30 William D. Irivine, 'Fascism in France and the Strange Case of the Croix de Feu,' *Journal of Modern History* 63 (June 1991): 294.

31 'Fallen Bastions,' book review for Study Group. Undated, but clearly written in 1939.

32 G.E.R. Gedye, *Fallen Bastions* (London: Victor Gollanz, 1939). From the foreword.

33 'Social and Economic Japan.' She provided her listeners with the obligatory history lesson: how the 'medieval empire ... came out of her seclusion' after 1867 and 'opened her ports to foreign traders and her mind to modern economic and political ideas.' She then posited that Japan's turn from feudalism to industrialization and capitalism could only be understood by considering the complex intertwining of old power elites revamped for the new age, the heady mixture of religious and political power, the lack of material resources at a time of population expansion, and the machinations of other imperial powers.

34 See Catherine Gidney, 'Poisoning the Student Mind? The Student Christian Movement at the University of Toronto, 1920–65,' *Journal of the Canadian*

Historical Association 8 (1997): 147–62. See also Paul Axelrod, 'The Student Movement of the 1930s,' in *Youth, University and Canadian Society* (Montreal and Kingston: McGill-Queen's University Press, 1989), 216–46.

35 Richard Allen, *The Social Passion: Religion and Social Reform in Canada, 1914–28* (Toronto: University of Toronto Press, 1971), 222–3. According to Allen, 'The social gospel rested on the premise that Christianity was a social religion, concerned, when the misunderstanding of the ages was stripped away, with the quality of human relations on this earth. Put in more dramatic terms, it was a call for men to find the meaning of their lives in seeking to realize the Kingdom of God in the very fabric of society' (4).

36 Quoted in Margaret Beattie, *A Brief History of the Student Christian Movement in Canada, 1921–74* (Toronto: SCM, 1975), 52. The SCM was among the groups that protested the Canadian government's treatment of Japanese Canadians and Aboriginal peoples, and that put an early version of 'deux nations' on the table (48).

37 Ibid.,15.

38 Ibid., 84–93. As historian Thomas Socknat writes: 'In their attempt to raise the peace consciousness of Canadians SCM members adopted the radical critique linking war with capitalism and argued that as long as that connection existed there would be a continuous de facto war.' *Witness against War: Pacifism in Canada, 1900–1945* (Toronto: University of Toronto Press, 1987), 157.

39 Gidney, 'Poisoning,' 150, notes that this fear was 'reinforced by continued RCMP surveillance of the movement' – a distinction that it shared with many other 'left-wing groups on Canadian campuses during the interwar years.'

40 Jean is in the group photograph of the Student Christian Association's 'cabinet' at Queen's in *The Tricolour*, 1929.

41 JR to MR, 28 January 1971. Nor was Marjorie the only friend from SCM days invoked in Jean's letters to Marion in the 1970s. On 8 April 1973, she wrote: 'I was saddened to hear of Eleanor French's death. It feels as if something productive and good has gone out of the world. Actually I knew Eleanor very little but a few meetings made her seem like a friend. I met her first at an American-British-Canadian conference in New Hampshire and subsequently she came to Kingston from time to time to stay with the Estalls to do a job at the YWCA. She and Martyn and Mollie [Estall] were very good friends; they spent a long summer during their undergraduate days at a Sharman Seminar in Algonquin Park, and became very close to each other.' And on 27 June 1973, she asked, 'Is Mary Rowell Jackman as beautiful as ever?' She was secretary of the University of Toronto SCM from

1927 to 31. Ernest A. Dale, *Twenty-One Years A-Building: A Short Account of the Student Christian Movement of Canada, 1920–1941* (SCM, n.d.), 44. On 27 June 1973 she was 'shaken that Harriet Christie has been given a prognosis of cancer. I knew that she was ill. Marie-Jeanne went up last week to see her. The surgeon has removed a lymph gland and that Harriet was not aware of how serious her condition is.' She was secretary of SCM at Western from 1936 to 1938. Dale, 44. And after Harriet's death she wrote: 'I am glad that she was able to carry on until the end. What a fruitful life she had!' 28 January 1975.

42 Beattie, *Brief History*, 21; Socknat, *Witness against War*, 156.

43 Part of a statement of the Central Area (Ontario) Conference in September 1938. Quoted in Beattie, 37–8.

44 But that year was the last time she gave a donation, though her use of the word 'annual' in 1966 indicates that this was not her intention. Donations to the SCM: February 1935, $5.00; January 1936, $25.00; April 1958, $10.00; March 1959, $10.00; November 1960, $10.00; February 1963, $100.00; March 1964, $100.00; August 1965, $100.00; June 1966, $100.00 (annual gift).

45 Gidney, 'Poisoning,' 158–63.

46 Doug Owram, *Born at the Right Time: A History of the Baby Boom Generation* (Toronto: University of Toronto Press, 1996), 225.

47 Gidney, 'Poisoning,' 163.

48 Her travelling was curtailed by the war, as she noted in passing in another paper, 'Canadian Mosaic.' 'If, in these days when we stay at home perforce, we seek to assuage our nostalgia for New York by looking at magazines, such as *The New Yorker* and checking on theatres and places to eat, we are quite likely to see "Polish ham" listed as a speciality, but few of us realize that Polish ham is now imported from Saskatoon instead of from the ancient town of Recklinghausen.'

49 'To Be Young, Gifted, and Black: A Portrait of Lorraine Hansberry in Her Own Words,' adapted by Robert Nemiroff (New York: S. French, 1971), 14. Five years later, while her second play, *The Sign in Sidney Brustein's Window*, was running on Broadway, Hansberry died of cancer at the age of thirty-four.

50 JR to MR, dated Sunday, early 1960.

51 'JR', 23 September 1993. As he explained in an aside, 'There was still thought that Norway might have to be invaded, in winter!'

52 Celia Royce interview, 3 March 1994.

53 MH interview, 16 April 1993.

54 'JR,' 23 September 1993.

55 Richard Wright's fictional heroine Clara Callan, a public school teacher in the 1930s in a small town north of Toronto, is fired when she becomes pregnant and decides to keep her baby. Clara and her sister Nora – the adventurous one who goes to New York to seek a career in radio – were born in the same years as Marion and Jean. Clara and Nora also had a baby brother who died as a toddler. Wright's book is a brilliant evocation of the era. His genre allows for a moving depiction of Clara's innermost thoughts and desires that I can only beckon towards in this biography.
56 JR to MR, 27 September 1976.
57 Donald did not cite Marion's public accomplishments to bolster this claim, but rather the many things that she did for people who needed help. The minister who presided at her funeral emphasized this. Interview, 19 March 1993.
58 See Carolyn Heilbrun, *Writing a Woman's Life* (New York: Norton, 1988), for an account of the available scripts women draw on to 'write their lives.'
59 Jean may have regretted that Marion chose to write the biography of Eunice Dyke instead of her own autobiography.
60 Jean provided a list: 'Advisor to Canadian Delegations to International Labour conferences, Canada's Representative to the United Nations Commission on the Status of Women, Meeting of Experts at the Organization for Economic Cooperation and Development, and so on – not to mention the enormous amount of research on health, welfare, [and] employment.'
61 JR to MR, 4 January 1974.
62 At the meeting of the University Women's Club on 10 April 1946, 'Miss Chown moved that flowers be sent to Miss Royce ($5.00 from the treasury).' Jean was president that year (CFUW).
63 JR to MR, 12 July 1975.
64 Here Donald met Celia. He managed to return for his mother's funeral – and to make arrangements to keep her apartment, housing being in such short supply. Interview with Donald and Celia Royce, 3 March 1994.
65 JR to MR, 11 April 1974.
66 Gail Royce interview, 1 September 1996, and JR's letters to Marion, 5 July 1974, 3 June 1976.
67 JR to MR, 2 July 1961.
68 Ian Royce interview, 8 June 1996.
69 Robert Legget, 23 September 1993.
70 On this date, Japan bombed Pearl Harbor, thus bringing the United States into the war.
71 Mary (Krotkov) Finegold to author, 16 September 1996. Jean must have been fond of Mary also, and records purchasing a wedding gift for her on 22 December 1964.

72 Elizabeth Harkness phone interview, June 1999.
73 Duncan Sinclair to JH, 15 February 1993.
74 Twenty years on, Jean jogged Marion's memory about one occasion when she was 'down with Ian' for the weekend. 'I recall telling him when he objected to going to bed that he had had a little party in the afternoon and we were now having a party for you' (letter, 2 June 1974).
75 JR to MR, 10 July 1959.
76 JR to MR, 24 July 1959. When I told Ian about his aunt's feelings, he expressed surprise, not with her sentiments but that – given her reserve – she had shared them, and thought perhaps it was easier for her in writing than in conversation.
77 JR to MR, 11 July 1962.
78 Lyn Royce interview, 9 June 1995.
79 JR to MR, 29 December 1962.
80 Mabel Corlett to JH, 11 April 1993.
81 Ann Saddlemyer, Memorial Service, 28 April 1982.
82 JR to MR, 10 March 1976.
83 Minutes, 13 October 1948, CFUW.
84 JR to MR, 18 July 1954.
85 Years later, when Marion was in Amsterdam, Jean asked her 'to salute the Dutch School' in that gallery and 'the paintings in the Stedelijk. Do see the Puppet Show in Dam Square' and have 'an East Indian Meal; there used to be a good restaurant in Leidsestraat but actually they abound' (3 October 1969).
86 As reported in the CFUW Chronicle (1954–5), Marion was to assume her duties on 1 September 1954, CFUW.
87 JR to MR, 18 July 1954.
88 *History of Canadian Federation of University Women, 1919–1949* (CFUW, n.d.).
89 I should point out that Betty Phillips's lamented absence is this history's good fortune, yielding as it did our protagonist's version of events.
90 Biéler spoke in April 1946, Hilda Hay in January 1944. The clothing drive was held early in 1946. Minutes of UWC April 1946; 6 January 1944; 16 January 1945; and 10 January 1946, CFUW.
91 Minutes, 15 September 1948, CFUW.
92 Years later she lamented the 'mismanagement' of Reid Hall, where she had 'two delightful periods. I feel a genuine affection for the place' (letter to MR, 12 September 1974).
93 She gave a report on the Paris conference to the UWC (Minutes, 20 September 1946, CFUW).
94 Ibid., 20 September 1956. Perhaps Jean was even more engaged with 'the fine arts group she joined' to study the Sculpture Gallery of the Louvre.

95 As reported in the Minutes of the CFUW 13th Triennial Conference, University of Alberta, August 16–20, 1955. Ibid.

96 International Federation of University Women Newsletter 12(3), November 1956. CFUW.

97 Jeanne was a voting delegate (each nation had two); Jean was one of many Canadian member-observers who attended. Chaton was listed on the 1947 program as Professor of History and Geography at the Lycee Lamartine, Paris. CFUW.

98 History of Canadian Federation of University Women, pp. 5, 15. In Canada 'in 1949 a campaign to augment the Crosby Hall Endowment Fund raised $3,743.50.' CFUW.

99 JR to MR, 20 November 1972.

100 JR to MR, 28 July 1959.

101 Under the date of her last letter – 28 July – Marion had written: 'Letter of July 31 from Helsinki forwarded to C. + G.'

102 Jean gave the talk on 21 January 1960.

103 JR to MR, 15 September 1969.

104 '* [DuBois asked] whether women are inherently conservative for biological reasons [and/or] whether women are inclined to operate with traditional stereotypes, that as products of their culture, they tend to accept.'

'** [Althea Hollet was very keen about this.] At dinner she bearded Blanche Dow (the fellowship committee's chairman) on the question of setting up a team of *men* and women' to study '(1) the differences between men and women that are relatively inflexible and (2) the differences that are essentially malleable because they are conditioned socially.'

105 JR to MR, 2 July 1961.

106 According to her account book, and a coat as well.

107 JR to MR, 20 July 1961.

108 The castle stop was on the return journey from a trip to Innsbruck and the Brenner Pass. JR to MR, 1 August 1961.

109 'Merebeth Cameron who was to have been the Speaker was unable to come and I pinch-hitted for her.' JR to MR, 22 August 1961.

110 JR to MR, 22 August 1961. Mary Winspear, her debating opponent from 1927, 'had dropped in for lunch the other day on her way to Montreal to give [her] a report on the rest of the Conference.'

111 JR to MR, 20 June 1965.

112 JR to MR, 1 November 1974.

113 JR to MR, 25 March 1967.

114 JR to MR, 29 December 1967.

115 JR to MR, 11 July 1962.

116 JR to MR, dated Thursday [August 1962].
117 Marion and Jean visited Mexico City, Christmas 1961. JR to MR, 1 January 1962.
118 JR to MR, dated August 1962. Mexico City was Jean's last IFUW conference. She considered going to Australia in 1965 but the trip was 'very expensive' and the timing wasn't good for her. JR to MR, July 1965.
119 A 'thank-you speech' at a dinner inaugurating the Eliza Gordon Dining Hall in Adelaide Hall at Queen's in the 1950s.
120 By the Saskatoon Women's Calendar Collective, which has published the calendar every year since except for 1983 and 1984.
121 JR to MR, 26 May 1974.
122 Allie could never have financed this herself, her Queen's pension being so scanty that it was only through the good offices of her beloved brother that she lived out her years in an attractive and convenient condominium. Interview with Evelyn Reid, 7 January 1999.
123 Mary-Louise (Funke) Campbell to JH, 13 February 1993.
124 Pauline Jewett, 'Tribute to Jean Royce,' 28 April 1982.
125 See Judith Mackenzie, *Pauline Jewett* (Montreal and Kingston: McGill-Queen's University Press, 1999), 33–5.
126 Mrs Saunders is listed in Jean's account book in January 1949, when she is paid $10.00. But there are no earlier records, and she was probably coming before this.
127 Culled from Jean's account books, Mrs Saunders earned $10.00 a month until 1954, $20.00 a month until 1957, $35.00 a month from 1957, $25.00 twice a month from March 1962, and $30.00 twice a month from December 1964.
128 After Mrs Saunders left, she contracted with cleaning companies until December 1967, when she hired Lena Jaworksi, who came weekly as long as she had her own apartment.
129 After the arrangement ceased, Jean and Phyllis Knight often came to Cooke's together. Ada Terry, who worked there all her life until retiring in 1977, remembered Jean as 'very very lovely, a special kind of person, always very polite, a real kind customer.' Telephone conversation, 8 August 1999.
130 Note, MH, August 1997.
131 Note, MH, 19 August 1997.
132 JR to MR, 8 February 1975.
133 JR to MR, 5 June 1973.
134 JR to MR, 2 June 1974.
135 JR to MR, 14 October 1963.

136 Elsie Curtis interview, 16 September 1993.

137 JR to MR, 17 November 1974.

138 Ibid. Her itals. She is refering to *Mike: The Memoirs of the Right Honourable Lester Pearson* (Toronto: University of Toronto Press, 1972). Jean credited both Day and Douglas LePan with writing Pearson's speeches.

139 Ibid. Jean recalled Archie Day's career for Marion after several conversations with him, in 1975, when he was having tests at Kingston General Hospital. His roommates were 'not particularly congenial [and she and Archie] found chairs in a comfortable little ante-room to the Lounge' whenever she went to visit, 'and chatted without interruption' (13 June 1975).

140 As with her other Kingston friends, she was interested in their children, was invited to their weddings, and purchased gifts.

141 The letter from Jean to Marion is simply dated 'Wednesday,' but Kennedy's announcement that the Soviet Union had missiles in Cuba came on 22 October 1962.

142 JR to MR, 14 October 1963.

143 JR to MR, 1 November 1974.

144 After listening to two long interviews with Katharine Hepburn, she concluded that 'Spenser [Tracy] and she had a marriage of minds that must be unique' (JR to MR, 8 October 1973).

145 JR to MR, 8 April 1973.

146 One of Jean's younger friends lamented that she had been dropped from the social calendar of many of her friends after the death of her husband, and that was in the 1980s.

147 JR to MR, 20 September 1968.

148 JR to MR, 31 January 1960. Jean continued: 'Our radio-astronomer, George Harrower, and his wife went out to meet him and Mrs H. said she thought he was wearing rather an unusual coat when he got off the train. He explained that when he was leaving home, he realized suddenly that he was coming to a place with a more rigorous climate than that of Princeton and that his overcoat was too light. He had not time to buy a heavier coat. His wife solved the problem. She said, "Take my heavy topcoat," and that is what he did.'

149 She went to Stratford in 1957, 1958, and 1960 (Account Books).

150 JR, *HV*, 24 November 1977.

151 MH, conversation, 26 July 1999.

152 JR to MR, 25 March 1967.

153 JR to MR, 25 March 1967.

6: Ranging the Universe

1 JR to MR, 10 March 1969.

2 JR to MR, 30 April 1969. 'I have been elected to the Board of Trustees; my first meeting is at the end of next week, and the Council meets later in the month.'

3 Kenneth Draayer, 'Jean Royce Leaves Queen's,' *Kingston Whig-Standard,* 6 September 1968, 5.

4 JR to MR, 30 April 1969. Stanley Gray, a political radical and lecturer at McGill charged, in Douglas Owram's words, that the university was 'an English fortress in the middle of a French nation' (286) and led a 'McGill en Français' movement in the late 1960s. *Born at the Right Time: A History of the Baby-Boom Generation* (Toronto: University of Toronto Press, 1996).

5 JR to MR, 6 June 1969. Jean's source was John Bovey, Provincial Archivist of Manitoba, who had been told by President Tom Symons, who 'has constant police protection.' Previously, Bovey had met Marion, and referred to her in his conversation with Jean as 'another Eleanor Roosevelt' – a comment that Jean was happy to pass on, knowing how appreciative her sister would be.

6 JR to MR, 6 June 1969.

7 Connie Martens interview, 15 August 1994.

8 Carolyn Heilbrun, *The Last Gift of Time* (New York: Dial Press 1997), 7–9.

9 JR to MR, 9 February 1974. In such views, she told Marion, she was 'like Catherine.' Marion, on the other hand, as Jean noted, had 'a special feeling about birthdays.' 18 January 1975. Her first comment may just have been a way of
lining up the sides.

10 Heilbrun, *Last Gift*, 9.

11 Her account books and savings attest to her careful planning. Her friend William Cannon managed her finances during the last years of her life as well as her bequest, and confirmed this assessment. Telephone conversation, 5 September 2001.

12 MH, 'The Secret Anguish of Jean Royce,' *Whig-Standard Magazine*, 6 June 1992.

13 May had taught classics for thirty-two years at York Mills Collegiate.

14 May Hambly, phone interview, 26 March 2000.

15 Alisha Berger, 'When Silent Strokes Evoke Depression,' *New York Times,* 5 October 1999. Margaret Hooey provided me with this article.

16 MH, 'Secret Anguish.'

17 MH to Robert Legget, 22 June 1982.

18 Roland Nadeau to JR, 27 February 1969, JIR.

19 Connie Martens interview, 27 August 1994.

20 Note from MH, 10 June 1996. 'It was part of the conversation I had with Jean after the suicide attempt. She said she would not have attempted it, had she thought of Catherine first, because Catherine would have been "devastated." And it was her realization of this, more than her promise to her doctor, that would deter her in the future.'

21 Marion's 167-page report, *Continuing Education for Women in Canada*, was published by the Ontario Institute of Higher Education in 1969.

22 JR to MR, letter dated 'Saturday,' after returning from the cottage.

23 Ibid.

24 JR to MR, 13 May 1971.

25 JR, dated April 1976.

26 JR to MR, 9 May 1976. See also Barbara Excell Hawgood's account, 'Go East Young Woman,' in *Still Running*, ed. Joy Parr (Kingston: Queen's University Alumnae Association, 1987), 88–94.

27 JR to MR, 11 May 1977.

28 JR to MR, 9 May 1976.

29 JR to MR, 23 September 1973.

30 JR, April 1976.

31 JR to MR, 4 March 1971.

32 Charlotte Whitton to William McNeill, 8 September 1946: 'The prospect of a very definite and heavy undertaking again seemed to spur the Alumnae this spring ... That has simply collapsed with the attitude and spirit of that resolution after all these years ... I see no hope of any of the really solid core of the Alumnae ever getting into real service in the next decade. I myself cannot get back my enthusiasm even if I actually pray to be made less bitterly resentful.' Charlotte Whitton Papers, QUA.

33 JR to MR, 14 September 1973.

34 For an excellent analysis of this 'takeover' that emphasizes the political climate of bureaucratization and rationalization, see Marion Campbell, 'Separation or Integration, A Case Study: The Ban Righ Board of Queen's University' (MA thesis, Queen's University, 1995).

35 JR, 'Foundation for Continuing Education for Women,' *Alumni Review* (1974), 6–7.

36 'The Ban Righ Building Fund and the Ban Righ Board Building Fund.' Submission to the Board of Trustees, 22/23 February 1974. See also Campbell, 'Separation.'

37 John W. Bannister to JR, 26 March 1973.

38 JR, 'confidential' to Evelyn Reid, 1 April 1973.

39 Ibid.
40 JR, 'Foundation' (1974).
41 JR, 'Establishment of Foundation for Continuing Education for Women at Queen's University.' 14 May 1974.
42 Jean I. Royce, 'Report of the Special Committee on the Use of Accumulated Ban Righ Funds,' 12 October 1973.
43 JR to MR, 14 September 1973.
44 JR to MR, 29 January 1974.
45 BT, 22/23 February 1974. In fact, the centre was not housed in the residence but at 32 Queen's Crescent in the home of the former vice-principal, William Everett McNeill, and his wife, Caroline, the first Dean of Women. There it remains.
46 Ibid. She also noted that there was 'provision ... for a constant review of the Foundation's effectiveness.' Jean then seconded a motion, moved by Principal Deutsch, that the foundation be established.
47 JR to MR, 28 February 1979.
48 MR to JR, 11 March 1979.
49 JR to MR, 2 February 1974.
50 JR to MR, 2 June 1974.
51 JR to MR, 29 September 1972.
52 JR to MR, 20 February 1974.
53 JR to MR, 18 March 1974.
54 Conversation with Helen Mathers, 19 December 1998.
55 Evelyn Reid interview, 7 January 1999.
56 JR to MR, 24 November 1971.
57 JR to MR, 21 July 1973.
58 JR to MR, 13 June 1975. Three months earlier, after a request from Principal Watts, Jean wrote recommending that the Office of the Dean of Women be retained, and that Evelyn's appointment be renewed. Jean described the dean's transition from 'mother figure' to a person who 'provides the wisdom of an experienced person to help them weigh the values of University life [and] explore the new ideas that are crowding in on them as they take part in a diverse intellectual scene.' She then enumerated Evelyn's many qualifications for the job, especially her ability to help 'all who come in contact with her to recognize the inevitability of change and the need to adjust to it.' In conclusion, she disputed the view that would prevail three years later, that an 'academic' dean was needed. As Jean put it: 'I have a fairly wide acquaintance with Canadian women who seem to have the necessary qualities for a Deanship but ... the true academician is no longer interested in posts of this kind. It distracts her creative work to too great a degree and limits her movements. The

alternative is likely to be someone with a doctrinaire approach who is really nothing more than a limited administrator. Therefore ... we should be well advised to keep what we have and give her as much support as the budget allows.' 13 March 1975.

Interestingly, two years earlier, Jean had told Marion: 'Frankly I think the title outdated – it should probably be Dean of Students or Dean of Student Affairs. Students are not now interested in being divided by sex: men and women like to do things together. So far as I can see, there is only one advantage in being labelled a "Dean" and that is to have entree to the Dean's Committee. I am not speaking for Queen's here but generalizing from most of the Ontario universities.' 21 July 1973. Her change of mind probably stemmed from seeing how Evelyn Reid had redefined the job, and also from the fact that her friend needed a job. For an account of Evelyn Reid's renewal and later non-renewal, see Maureen McCallum Garvie and Jennifer L. Johnson, *Their Leaven of Influence: Deans of Women at Queen's University, 1916–1996* (Queen's Alumni Association Committee on Women's Affairs, 1999), 93–6.

59 JR to MR, 15 June 1976.

60 JR to MR, 9 November 1974. See also the accounts by Charlotte Whitton and others in Mary Chown, Melva Eaglson and Thelma Boucher, *A Generous Loyalty: The Queen's Alumnae Memory Book*, ed. Margaret Gibson (Kingston: Queen's University Alumnae Association, [1962] 1992).

61 JR to MR, 26 November 1977.

62 JR to MR, 16 June 1974.

63 JR to MH, 2 May 1974.

64 JR to MH, 2 June 1973.

65 JR to MR, 16 July 1974.

66 JR to MR, 25 August 1973.

67 JR to MR, 25 October 1976.

68 JR to MR, 16 July 1974.

69 Pauline Jewett, tribute to Jean Royce, 28 April 1982.

70 JR to MR, 2 June 1973.

71 JR to MR, 6 June 1973.

72 JR to MR, 20 June 1973.

73 JR to MR, 2 June 1973.

74 JR to MR, 18 March 1974.

75 JR to MR, 25 October 1976.

76 'I am enclosing a copy of the statement I sent in on behalf of Allie Douglas,' she wrote to Marion, 'with a recommendation that she be given an honorary degree.' 15 February 1975.

77 JR to MR, 1 October 1975. And on 11 May 1977, she wrote that she was

'working on a draft citation for Ann Saddlemyer the Director of the Graduate Centre for the study of Drama at U. of T. and Professor of English Language and Literature at Victoria. She is an authority on Anglo-Irish Literature and has had national and international acclaim. She has given great strength to the theatre in Canada.'

78 JR to MR, 20 April 1975. The late George Rawlyk accepted an honorary degree from Acadia on 14 October 1995.

79 JR to MR, 8 February 1975. Jean must have known that Pauline remained unforgiving about her treatment at Queen's in the late 1940s, when her teaching position was not renewed. She considered this a 'betrayal' by her mentor, A.C. Corry. See Judith Mackenzie, *Pauline Jewett* (Montreal and Kingston: McGill-Queen's University Press, 1999), 32–4. Chances are good that this is the reason she refused the degree.

80 JR to MR, 24 October 1970 and 11 November 1970.

81 JR to MR, 29 October 1971.

82 JR to MR, 13 June 1975.

83 Jean knew Agnes as a Queen's alumna (BA 1941). At the time of this meeting, Agnes was a fellow member of the Board of Trustees and was just finishing a term as president of the Canadian Council of Social Development. *Queen's Encyclopedia* (Kingston: Queen's University, 1994).

84 JR to MR, 5 October 1974.

85 Agnes Benidickson served as Queen's chancellor from 1980 to 1996.

86 JR to MR, 2 June 1973.

87 JR to MR, 23 September 1973.

88 JR to MR, 24 October 1973.

89 See Susan Mann Trofimenkoff's *Stanley Knowles: The Man from Winnipeg North Centre* (Saskatoon: Western Producer Prairie Books,1982).

90 JR to MR, 11 April 1974.

91 JR to MR, 16 June 1974.

92 JR to MR, 24 October 1974.

93 JR to MR, 16 June 1974.

94 JR to MR, 23 October 1973.

95 She went on to elaborate that the new principal should come 'from another kind of discipline (Medicine or Law, or Science or Engineering).' Though the 'last three appointments [Mackintosh, Corry, and Deutsch] had been self-evident and it [was] not likely that other persons would have brought equal skill and wisdom to the post, this sequence [had] unfortunately [ended].' JR to J.B. Stirling, 17 October 1973.

96 She mentioned Deutsch's work 'with Government, Business, Industry and [his] International affiliations.' Ibid.

97 She had lofty thoughts on the matter, citing as examples Bora Laskin, Tuzo

Wilson, Maurice Strong, and John Coleman – 'a Canadian by birth [and] the President of Haverford College in Pennsylvania [and] J.F. Mustard – the Vice President Academic (Health Sciences) at McMaster.' Ibid.

98 Ibid.

99 The late David Chadwick Smith came to Queen's in 1960. He headed the Department of Economics from 1969 to 1981 and served as principal from 1984 to 1994.

100 JR to MR, 12 May 1974.

101 As a result, he had 'read it carefully and found it most interesting.' Douglas Gibson to JR, 24 October 1973.

102 Although John Deutsch endorsed the university takeover of the women's residences, the women believed that 'it was due to his intervention that the Ban Righ Foundation existed at all.' He supported their claims to the surplus funds and 'appeared to stand as a buffer between his administrative officials and the Ban Righ Board women.' Campbell, 'Separation,' 77.

103 Margaret Hooey recalled that Vernon Ready relayed his embryonic idea to her.

104 JR to MR, 12 May 1974.

105 Mary Wilson Carpenter, 'Female Grotesques in Academia: Ageism, Antifeminism and Feminists on the Faculty,' in *Anti-feminism in the Academy*, ed. Vévé Clark, Shirley Nelson Garner, Margaret Higonnet, and Ketu Katrak (New York: Routledge, 1996), 142.

106 On another issue – whether the reappointment of members should depend on their contribution – she cautioned that in 1968 the Committee of Government had 'found that if there were a design for dropping inactive members [there] might be [a] danger of losing members with special expertise in [areas such as] finance [and] management.' JR to Douglas Gibson, 3 September 1971.

107 Ibid.

108 JR to Stirling, 17 October 1973; JR to MR, 20 November 1972. Jean provided Marion with a description of Conway's work: the doctoral dissertation in history and her subsequent books and research plans.

109 Phone interview with MH, 30 May 2000.

110 For a brief summary of these events as they pertain to Pauline Jewett's presidency, see Mackenzie, *Pauline Jewett*, 92–7.

111 JR to MR, 19 January 1974.

112 JR to MR, 16 June 1974.

113 They went to Manchester, Leeds, York, Exeter, Keele, Open University, Sussex, Kent, and Bristol.

114 JR to MR, 23 October 1973.

115 JR to MR, 25 November 1973.
116 JR to MR, 6 November 1973.
117 JR to MR, 20 September 1968.
118 JR to MR, 8 August 1970.
119 And to Marion, she exclaims, somewhat incongruously, as she signs off: 'How was Moosenee!' Her sister was no slouch; she was travelling the country, 'preparing to write a report.' 8 August 1970.
120 JR to MR, 15 September 1970. 'Young, lively and highly intelligent,' she was travelling with a Dutch friend, 'a highly sophisticated Hotel employee with a multitude of languages.'
121 JR to MR, Ibid.
122 Ibid.
123 Ian Royce interview, 8 June 1996.
124 Even when Ian went on a 'real adventure,' travelling for months, she 'shudder[ed] at the cost.' JR to MR, 27 January 1977. She expressed concern when she learned that he had been seriously ill while travelling. 'Did Ian's medical examination put him on a rigorous program of rest and protein?' she asked MR, 4 October 1977.
125 JR to MR, 5 June 1973. She contrasted this with the experience of a friend's son, who was 'questioning the value of his university degree [and] presumably [had] *not* found fulfilment.'
126 JR to MR, 8 February 1975.
127 JR to MR, 16 September 1975. SEED was the first alternative school opened by the Toronto District School Board. Founded by students in 1968 as a summer school, it was authorized by the board in 1970 for high school students from grade ten. In 2000–1, it had an enrolment of 125.
128 JR to MR, 28 January 1975.
129 Interview with Brenda Royce, 23 November 1996.
130 JR to MR, 25/26 August 1971.
131 JR to MR, 12 November 1971.
132 Jean's account book and daybook.
133 Brenda Royce interview, 23 November 1996.
134 JR to MR, 14 September 1974.
135 JR to MR, 15 January 1973.
136 JR to MR, 8 February 1975.
137 JR to MR, 10 October 1976.
138 JR to MR, 9 April 1978.
139 Daybooks and account books.
140 JR to MR, 9 February 1974.
141 'They are a delightful family ... I found David particularly interesting. He

showed me some of his drawings and the little figures he paints – he has wonderful hands and is obviously very bright.' JR to MR, 16 June 1974.

142 JR to MR, 21 July 1973.
143 JR to MR, 25 August 1973.
144 JR to MR, 9 July 1973.
145 JR to MR, 15 February 1975.
146 JR to MR, 6 September 1975.
147 JR to MR, 16 September 1975.
148 JR to MR, 21 November 1976.
149 JR to MR, 7 November 1977.
150 JR to MR, 12 June 1973.
151 JR to MR, 21 January 1977.
152 JR to MR, 16 September 1975.
153 Jean was the second woman to receive The Montreal Medal (then in its twenty-fourth year), an award of the Montreal Alumni Association for 'meritorious contribution to the honor of Queen's University.' Charlotte Whitton was the first.
154 JR to MR, 7 May 1965.
155 Her daybook and account book record two trips in February, the second for ten days. She bought a gown for Catherine at the Greek Shop, paying far more than her custom. Each month thereafter, she spent another week, in July two. At some point she arranged and paid for home care. After a week at Tanglewood with Margaret, in July, she was back in Toronto at the end of the month. By then, Catherine was back in hospital and Jean was not well herself. She returned to Toronto for two shorter visits in September, and bought her books.
156 JR to Catherine Royce, 22 February 1972. Hilliard was well known as the author of *A Woman Doctor Looks at Life and Love* (Garden City, NY: Doubleday), 1957.
157 JR to MR, 20 October 1972.
158 She moved back home on November 27.
159 In a postscript to a letter to Marion on 27 October 1972, Jean wrote that 'the last two letters that I wrote to Catherine were returned today.' The letters are dated 15 and 16 October 1972. JIR.
160 MR to JR, 19 October 1972, JIR. Catherine had been 'alive in her mind and spirit to the very end,' Marion wrote, 'and concerned about you.'
161 JR to MR, 20 October 1972. Jean wrote that she regretted having been 'deterred by Gordon's statement that there would be no flowers,' but was pleased that Marion had sent some. 'I don't think I would have thought of white carnations,' she wrote, '[yet] they seem to have been the perfect

choice. In a sense, I should have liked her to have her "treasures": she told me about them in her last letter.' What the treasures were, I don't know, but it is a sweet comment from someone who believed only in this world.

162 Catherine Royce to JR. The letter is undated. JIR.

163 JR to MR, 1 November 1972. Nancy was the daughter of Catherine's close friend, Bernice.

164 JR to MR, 27 October 1972.

165 JR to MR, 1 November 1972. Eskin was the principal cello in the Boston Symphony Orchestra.

166 JR to MR, 20 October 1972.

167 JR to MR, 15 August 1972.

168 JR to MR, 18 August 1972.

169 Comment from MH's conversations with Jean.

170 JR to MR, 29 September 1972.

171 JR to MR, 20 October 1972; also 1 November 1972.

172 JR to MR, 27 October 1972.

173 JR to MR, 21 July 1973. Celia Royce confirmed this. Interview, 25 November 1996.

174 'A letter from Gordon [sojourning in Panama], says that he seems less depressed than he was.' JR to MR, 27 February 1973. A few months later, he seemed 'to be flourishing.' He hosted a dinner party and 'was particularly glad to do something for Celia who has been very kind to him [with] dinner invitations, afternoons by the pool, and so on.' JR to MR, 21 July 1973.

175 JR to MR, 1 November 1972.

176 Ibid.

177 JR to MR, 18 May 1976.

178 JR to MR, 12 April 1976.

179 MR to JR, 17 June 1977.

180 Interview with Brenda, 25 November 1996, and with Celia, 25 November 1996.

181 Letter to MR, 25 February 1975.

182 JR to MR, 28 September 1976.

183 JR to MR, 10 October 1976.

184 JR to MR, 7 November 1977.

185 Dawn Cannon interview, 27 August 1997.

186 MH interview, 7 August 1997.

187 Letter from Jean to Margaret (after her father died), 18 November 1974.

188 From 1947 to 1962 at 52 Queen's Crescent, afterwards at 140 Stuart Street, now the Writing Centre.

189 JR to MR, 28 January 1975.
190 JR to MR, 29 October 1970.
191 JR to MR, 28 January 1971.
192 JR to MR, 1 November 1972.
193 JR to MR, 14 December 1977.
194 JR to MR, 21 July 1973.
195 JR to MR, 24 October 1974.
196 JR to MR, 6 June 1973.
197 JR to MR, 27 November 1974.
198 JR to MR, 14 January 1976.
199 JR to MR, 13 June 1975.
200 Daybook.
201 First appointed at Trinity College (University of Toronto) in 1940, Mary White was named head of the Department of Classics in 1965, the first woman to be a departmental head in Arts and Science at the university. *Globe and Mail*, 26 June 1965. She died on 7 January 1977.
202 JR to MR, 20 January 1975.
203 JR to MR, 24 October 1974.
204 The popular designation for the honours course in classics and philosophy at Oxford.
205 JR to MR, 9 November 1974.
206 JR to MR, 28 March 1975. In fact, he was William Fyfe when he made this comment. He was knighted in 1942.
207 JR to MR, 27 November 1977.
208 She was on one of Jean's bedtime lists of 'good people,' a pastime she engaged in with Margaret during the last year of her life.
209 JR to MR, 12 September 1974.
210 JR to MR, 2 June 1975. Anna was not happy with Thatcher, whose 'knowledge of world affairs is nil. [Her] dislike of her really stems from her scurrilous public utterances against members of the Labour Party, particularly Mr Wilson. Her opinion is an interesting contrast to that of John Deutsch by whom I sat at Allie's luncheon on Saturday. He was very taken with Mrs T.: found her a delightful person in a group, quick-witted with apt phrasing and very pleasant to look at.' Also, letter of 25 February 1975.
211 JR to MR, 11 May 1977. 'Her son John is a fine chap,' Jean added, 'but he is taken up with his own work and responsibilities ... She will be living in Los Angeles and should have a very pleasant life.' Two years later, Anna wrote: 'I never forget your kindness to me and feel that all my wonderful

years in England as student, wife and mother sprang from the help you gave when I applied for the scholarship.' Letter dated Christmas 1979, JIR.

212 JR to MR, 29 March 1969.

213 JR to MR, 12 August 1973.

214 Interview with MH, 7 August 1997.

215 For a revealing discussion of the career of Margaret's husband, Glen, see Gibson's 'The Cold War and the University: The Cases of Israel Halperin and Glen Shortliffe' in *Queen's University*, vol. 2, *1917–1961* (Kingston and Montreal: McGill-Queen's University Press, 1983).

216 JR to MR, 9 September 1973.

217 In April 1978.

218 JR to MR, 8 February 1975.

219 JR to MR, 10 March 1976.

220 JR to MR, 12 November 1971.

221 'Allie Douglas left for China on Friday,' Jean wrote Marion. 'When she rang up to say Good-Bye she was almost incoherent. She has waited so long for a visa. She has just reached her eightieth birthday and had practically given up all hope of going.' 12 May 1974.

222 JR to MR, 17 March 1976.

223 JR to MR, 20 February 1974.

224 JR to MR, 10 March 1974.

225 JR to MR, 12 February 1976.

226 JR to MR, 28 March 1975. She provided a similar assessment on 18 March 1973.

227 See Ken Wiwa, *In the Shadow of a Saint* (Toronto: Alfred A. Knopf, 2000), for a devastating account of the role of Shell Oil in Nigeria.

228 JR to MR, 26 November 1977.

229 JR to MR, 14 December 1977. A note on a scrap of paper from this time asks Margaret if she would 'mind also to track down the Golda Meir book: is it in the Douglas Library?'

230 JR to MR, 15 January 1973.

231 JR to MR, 12 May 1974.

232 JR to MR, 31 October 1976.

233 JR to MR, 21 November 1976.

234 On Vietnam, 3 March 1973; 11 March 1973. On Rosemary Brown, 8 July 1975; on Trudeau hosting Gandhi in Niagara-on-the-Lake, 20 June 1973. She took a great interest in John Kenneth Galbraith, another graduate of the St Thomas Collegiate Institute. When he came to Queen's she reported that at 'a formal private dinner party the only person who could engage

him in dialogue was David Smith, the Head of the Department of Economics and the son-in-law of Kenneth Taylor, the former Deputy Minister of Finance. Amusingly, the Rt. Hon. Roland Michener had only one question: had Professor Galbraith ever returned to India; whereupon Galbraith said "no." I gather that the table conversation was largely a tête a tête between the two professors. I believe David is a Harvard man.' 18 October 1976. She had enjoyed *The Affluent Society* and especially Galbraith's account of his work in India as U.S. ambassador, where he 'revealed his hypochondriacal tendencies, and his weakness for pretty women'; however, this did not suggest 'unfaithfulness to his wife who is a New England aristocrat, or lack of affection for his sons' (31 October 1976). Letters to MR.

235 JR to MR, 14 December 1977. 'At the end of his visit,' she added, 'the Senate was unanimous in awarding him an honorary degree.'

236 JR to MR, 16 January 1976.

237 'Mrs Mavis Gallant,' undated. '*The New Yorker*,' she wrote, is 'one of the pleasures of our reading society.'

238 JR to MR, 16 January 1976.

239 JR to MR, 28 January 1971.

240 JR to MR, 29 October 1971.

241 JR to MR, 24 November 1971.

242 JR to MR, 3 November 1971.

243 JR to MR, 14 January 1976.

244 JR to MR, 9 March 1973.

245 JR to MR, 8 July 1975. This visit to Tanglewood was a brief respite for Margaret: 'A few hours after our return [she] had a call from Sudbury that her mother was failing even more rapidly and she left immediately for the north.'

246 JR to MR, 28 July 1976.

247 MR to JR, 10 October 1977.

248 JR to MR, 2 July 1977. 'We enjoyed Lyn and Gail last week. They came to supper at "204." 11 May 1977, 'Mona Mulligan dropped into "204" the other weekend ...' 204 was Margaret's street number.

249 JR to MR, 27/29 January 1977.

250 MR to MH, 16 February 1978.

251 MH to Jean's friends. Undated, ca September 1980.

252 MR to MH, 11 June 1978. As if not sure of the answer, Marion asks, 'You will call on me in case of need, won't you?'

253 MH interview, 24 February 1994.

254 MH, 25 January 1998.

255 MR to JR, 27 March 1979.
256 MR to JR, 22 April 79.
257 As Vorres wrote in his memoire dated 1 April 1993: 'Informed of her failing health, and to lift her sagging spirits, I urged her to come to Greece to enjoy the warmer climate. I offered to act as her private guide, showing her not only Athens, but all the famous classical sites, such as Olympia, Delphi, Delos, Corinth, Mycenae that I knew interested her.'
258 MR to JR, 8 April 1979.
259 Shirley Brooks interview, 28 May 1997.
260 JR to MR undated.
261 Dawn Cannon and MH to MR, 2 May 1979.
262 Celia Royce and DR interview, 3 March 1994.
263 Celia Royce interview, 3 March 1994.
264 DR interview, 3 March 1994.
265 DR and Celia Royce interview with Dawn Cannon, March 19, 1993.
266 Celia Royce interview, 25 November 1996.
267 Celia Royce interview, 19 March 1993.
268 DR interview, 3 March 1994.
269 MR to JR, 8 March 1981.
270 MR to MH, 6 March 1981.
271 MR, Eunice Dyke. The book was published by Dundurn Press in Toronto in 1983.
272 MR to JR, 13 September 1980.
273 MH to DR, 22 May 1979.
274 MH to Robert Legget, 22 June 1982.
275 Mark Hooey, quoted in 'Former Students Remember Jean Royce's Kind Understanding,' *Kingston Whig-Standard*, 29 April 1982.
276 MH to Jean's friends, circa September 1980.
277 MH interview, 7 August 1997.
278 MH interview, 24 February 1994.
279 Irmigard Bollis to MH, 8 May 1982.
280 MH interview, February 24, 1994. E-mail, 24 April 1998.
281 Dawn Cannon interview, 27 August 1997.
282 MH's note, 22 October 1981.
283 Dawn Cannon interview, 27 August 1997.
284 Marion received many letters of sympathy available in JIR.
285 Undated. Stirling went on to say: 'Jean was a great person – a fine officer of the university and a constructive member of the Board of Trustees.'
286 JR to MR, 24 July 1974.

287 To MH, 7 May 1982. Evelyn McLeod worked at Queen's for many years, and is one of Jean's many friends who hasn't appeared in this book, simply for reasons of space.

288 Jan Royce to MH, 23 July 1982.

289 Shelagh Royce to MH, September 1982.

290 After expenses, taxes, and $1,000 bequests to her nieces and nephews, the Kingston Symphony Association, and the Kingston Public Library (which also received first choice of any of her personal books).

291 MH to Robert Legget, 22 June 1982.

292 MH to John Bannister, Secretary, Board of Trustees, 11 June 1982.

293 MH to Alison Morgan, Secretary, Board of Trustees, 29 December 1987.

294 MH e-mail, 26 March 1998.

295 'JR' by Robert Legget, 23 November 1993. In a letter to Principal David Smith, Legget urged that 'the University do something about having Jean Royce's life story written up, while so many of her friends are still around.' In the letter he wrote that 'even in our short stay [at Queen's – from 1936 to 38] Queen's gave much to my dear wife and me, perhaps above all the treasured friendship of Jean Royce, who became one of the dearest and closest friends we ever had.' 6 November 1992.

296 Lillian Faderman, *Surpassing the Love of Men: Romantic Friendship between Women from the Renaissance to the Present* (New York: Morrow, 1981), 413. Also see Carroll Smith-Rosenberg, 'The Female World of Love and Ritual: Relationships between Women in Nineteenth Century America,' *Signs* 1(1) (1975): 1–29.

297 Telephone conversation with MH, 2 December 1996.

298 'The Memorial Service,' *Queen's Alumni Review*, July–August 1982, 7.

299 Untitled paper [University Education] dated 26 May 1969.

300 Duncan Sinclair, Senate Minutes, 22 April 1982.

Select Bibliography

Papers Written by Jean Royce

'Books.' Mid-1930s

'Canadian Mosaic.' Early 1940s

'Czechoslovakia: The Constitution.' 1930s

'Entrance Scholarships and Bursaries.' 1963

'Excursion in Ideas.' 1955

'Fallen Bastions (book review).' 1939

'France.' 1935

'France-Constitution.' 1930s

'Glimpses at the Letters of Charles Lamb.' *New Outlook,* 9 October 1929, 1023

'Guidance Dialogue.' August 1968

'Marked for Riposte.' Second World War

'Mrs Mavis Gallant.' January 1976

'Mexico.' January 1941

'Population Explosion.' 1963

'Population Explosion and Standards of Admission.' *Queen's Review* 39 (September–October 1965), 116–17

Proceedings Annual Meeting Service for Admission to College and University, March 1968

'Queen's University.' Radio Address for CFRC, 1970–1

'Rival Canadian Craftsman.' Radio Lecture for CFRC, *QJ*, 27 February 1942

'Social and Economic Japan.' 1942–3

'Some London Byways.' Fall 1934?

'T.E. Lawrence 1882–.' 1933–4

'University Women's Club of Kingston.' 9 October 1968

Untitled (Queen's in the 1920s). Alumnae Luncheon, 13 May 1972
Untitled (University Education). 1950s
Untitled (University Education). 26 May 1969
'University of the Sixties.' 19 January 1966

Secondary Sources

Abbott, B.A. *The Disciples*. 1924. Reprint, Bethany Press for Abbott Books, 1964.

Allen, Richard. *The Social Passion: Religion and Social Reform in Canada 1914–1928*. Toronto: University of Toronto Press, 1971.

Anderson, Karen. *Sociology.* Scarborough, ON: Nelson, 1996.

Armstrong, Pat and Hugh Armstrong. *The Double Ghetto: Canadian Women and Their Segregated work*. 3rd ed. Toronto: McClelland and Stewart, 1994.

Aron, Cindy S. *Working at Play: A History of Vacations in the United States*. New York: Oxford University Press, 1999.

Axelrod, Paul. *Scholars and Dollars: Politics, Economics, and the Universities of Ontario, 1945–1980*. Toronto: University of Toronto Press, 1982.

– 'The Student Movement of the 1930s.' Pp. 216–46 in *Youth, University and Canadian Society,* ed. Paul Axelrod and John G. Reid. Montreal and Kingston: McGill-Queen's University Press, 1989.

– *Making a Middle Class: Student Life in English Canada during the Thirties*. Montreal and Kingston: McGill-Queen's University Press, 1990.

Bader, Alfred. *Adventures of a Chemist Collector.* London: Weidenfeld and Nicholson, 1995.

Beattie, Margaret. *A Brief History of the Student Christian Movement in Canada 1921–1974*. Toronto: SCM, 1975.

Brock, Rita Nakashima, Claudia Camp, and Serene Jones. *Setting the Table: Women in Theological Conversation*. St Louis, MI: Chalice Press, 1995.

Butchart, Reuben. *The Disciples of Christ in Canada since 1830*. Toronto: Canadian Headquarters Publications. Churches of Christ (Disciples), 1949.

Carpenter, Mary Wilson. 'Female Grotesques in Academia: Ageism, Antifeminism and Feminists on the Faculty.' Pp. 141–65 in *Anti-feminism in the Academy,* ed. Vévé Clark, Shirley Nelson Garner, Margaret Higonnet, and Ketu Katrak. New York: Routledge, 1996.

Chown, Mary, Melva Eagleson, and Thelma Boucher. *A Generous Loyalty: The Queen's Alumnae Memory Book*. 1962. Reprint ed. Margaret Gibson. Kingston: Queen's University Alumnae Association, 1992.

Corry, J.A. *Farewell the Ivory Tower: Universities in Transition*. Montreal and Kingston: McGill-Queen's University Press, 1970.

Cushing, Harvey. *The Life of Sir William Osler.* 1925. Reprint, London: Oxford University Press, 1940.

Dale, Ernest A. *Twenty-One Years A-Building: A Short Account of the Student Christian Movement of Canada, 1920–1941*. Toronto: Student Christian Movement of Canada, n.d.

Davies, Arthur L. *Sketches, Scholars and Scandals of a Quiet College Town.* J.W. Dent, 1975.

Davies, Robertson. *The Salterton Trilogy.* London: Penguin Books, 1980.

Duff, James, and Robert O. Berdahl. 'University Government in Canada.' Toronto: University of Toronto Press, 1966.

Faderman, Lillian. *Surpassing the Love of Men: Romantic Friendship between Women from the Renaissance to the Present*. New York: Morrow, 1981.

Garvie, Maureen McCallum, and Jennifer L. Johnson. *Their Heaven of Influence: Deans of Women at Queen's University, 1916–1996*. Kingston: Committee on Women's Affairs of the Alumni Association of Queen's University, 1999.

Gedye, G.E.R. *Fallen Bastions: The Central European Tragedy.* London: Victor Gollancz, 1939.

Gibson, Frederick W. *Queen's University.* Volume 2. *1917–1961*. Montreal and Kingston: McGill-Queen's University Press, 1983.

Gidney, Catherine. 'Poisoning the Student Mind? The Student Christian Movement at the University of Toronto, 1920–65.' *Journal of the Canadian Historical Association* 8 (1997): 147–62.

Heilbrun, Carolyn. *The Last Gift of Time*. New York: Dial Press 1997.

– *Writing a Woman's Life*. New York: Norton, 1988.

Hilliard, Marion. *A Woman Doctor Looks at Love and Life*. Garden City, NY: Doubleday, 1957.

Hooey, Margaret. 'Sisters in the Old Boys Network.' *Kingston Whig-Standard Magazine*, 6 June 1992.

Irvine, William D. 'Fascism in France and the Strange Case of the Croix de Feu.' *Journal of Modern History* 63 (June 1991): 271–95.

Kinnear, Mary. *Margaret McWilliams: An Interwar Feminist*. Montreal and Kingston: McGill-Queen's University Press, 1991.

Koch, Eric. *Deemed Suspect*. Toronto: Methuen, 1980.

La Rocque, Lt.-Col. Casimir de. *The Fiery Cross*. London: Lovat Dickson, n.d.

LeDoeuff, Michelle. 'Women and Philosophy.' Pp. 181–209 in *French Feminist Thought*, ed. Toril Moi. Oxford: Blackwell, 1987.

Low, David. *St. Thomas, Ontario Canada: A Centre of Influence in Elgin County.* St Thomas, ON: *St Thomas Times-Journal*, 1960.

Luxton, Meg. *More Than a Labour of Love: Three Generations of Women's Work in the Home*. Toronto: Women's Press, 1980.

MacGillivray, Royce. Review of *Queen's University,* Volume 2, by Frederick Gibson. *Ontario History* 76 (1984): 91–4.

Mackenzie, Judith. *Pauline Jewett*. Montreal and Kingston: McGill-Queen's University Press, 1999.

McAllister, Lester G., and William E. Tucker. *Journey in Faith: A History of the Christian Church (Disciples of Christ).* Saint Louis, MI: Bethany Press, 1975.

McKillop, A.B. *Matters of Mind: The University in Ontario, 1791–1951*. Toronto: University of Toronto Press, 1994.

– *The Spinster and the Prophet: Florence Deeks, H.G. Wells and the Mystery of the Purloined Past*. Toronto: Macfarlane Walter and Ross, 2000.

Micklem, Nathaniel. *The Box and the Puppets*. London: Geoffrey Bles, 1957.

Miller, Warren Cron. *Vignettes of Early St. Thomas: An Anthology of the Life and Times of Its First Century.* St Thomas, ON: Sutherland Press, 1968.

Neatby, Hilda. *Queen's University.* Volume 1, *1841–1917*. Ed. Frederick W. Gibson and Roger Graham. Montreal and Kingston: McGill-Queen's University Press, 1978.

Nemiroff, Robert (adapted by). *To Be Young, Gifted, and Black: A Portrait of Lorraine Hansberry in Her Own Words*. New York: S. French, 1971.

O'Grady, Jean. *Margaret Addison*. Montreal and Kingston: McGill-Queen's University Press, 2001.

– ed. *Diary of a European Tour by Margaret Addison*. Montreal and Kingston: McGill-Queen's University Press, 1999.

Owram, Doug. *Born at the Right Time: A History of the Baby Boom Generation*. Toronto: University of Toronto Press, 1996.

Paddon, Wayne. *'Steam and Petticoats,' 1840–1890: The Early Railway Era in Southwestern Ontario*. London, ON: Murray Kelly, 1977.

Parr, Joy, ed. *Still Running*. Kingston: Queen's University Alumnae Association, 1987.

Porter, John: *The Vertical Mosaic: An Analysis of Social Class and Power in Canada.* Toronto: University of Toronto Press, 1965.

Prentice, Alison. 'Bluestockings, Feminists or Women Workers? A Preliminary Look at Women's Early Employment – The University of Toronto.' *Journal of the Canadian Historical Association* 2 (1991): 231–61.

Prentice, Alison, Paula Bourne, Gail Cuthbert Brandt, Beth Light, Wendy Mitchinson, and Naomi Black. *Canadian Women: A History.* 2nd ed. Toronto: Harcourt Brace, 1996.

Reimer, M.A. 'The Social Organization of the Labour Process: A Case Study of Documentary Management of Clerical Labour in the Public Service.' PhD thesis, Ontario Institute for Studies in Education, 1987.

Rooke, Patricia T., and R.L. Schnell. *No Bleeding Heart: Charlotte Whitton, A Feminist on the Right*. Vancouver: UBC Press, 1987.

Ross, Robin. *The Short Road Down: A University Changes*. Toronto: University of Toronto Press, 1984.

Royce, Josiah. *The Letters of Josiah Royce*. Intro. John Glendenning. Chicago: University of Chicago Press, 1970.

Royce, Marion. *Continuing Education for Women in Canada: Trends and Opportunities*. Toronto: Ontario Institute for Studies in Education, 1969.

– *Eunice Dyke, Health Care Pioneer: From Pioneer Public Health Nurse to Advocate for the Aged*. Toronto: Dundurn Press, 1983.

Shirer, William L. *The Collapse of the Third Republic*. New York: Simon and Shuster, 1969.

Smith-Rosenberg, Carroll. 'The Female World of Love and Ritual: Relationships between Women in Nineteenth Century America.' *Signs* 1(1) (1975): 1–29.

Socknat, Thomas Paul. *Witness against War: Pacifism in Canada, 1900–45*. Toronto: University of Toronto Press, 1987.

Strong-Boag, Veronica. *The New Day Recalled: Lives of Girls and Women in English Canada, 1919–1939*. Toronto: Clark Copp Pitman, 1988.

Watts, Elsie. '"Inevitable from the Beginning": Queen's University and Separation from the Presbyterian Church, 1900–12.' *Historical Papers 1996: Canadian Society of Church History*: 128–54.

Wright, Richard. *Clara Callan*. Toronto: HarperFlamingoCanada, 2001.

Acknowledgments

Nine years after Jean Royce's death, Phyllis Bray, Dawn Cannon, Jill Harris, Margaret Hooey, and Joy Hosleton decided to record her contributions to Queen's University. When I became the biographer, they provided me with the material they had collected – and a free hand. I am very grateful to them for their confidence and assistance.

During the subsequent eight years, I spent more time in Jean Royce's company than anyone in her adult life, save perhaps two or three of her closest friends. Total immersion in another's life – or what one takes to be another's life – makes for strange times. One night I announced that Jean Royce had quit smoking in late 1969. The laughter was deafening. Who was I? Who was Jean Royce? What was the nature of our relationship? The lines between fiction and biography – and between biography and autobiography – must be continuously scrutinized.

One receives help in this endeavour. A hypothesis, a speculation, an assumption bumps against the evidence, virtually thousands of bits and pieces, letters written at the time, stories recollected later, documents convened for a different purpose. I am immensely grateful to the many people who helped me. They made sure that this would not be primarily a work of fiction, and that even if it was, it would be a fiction collectively recalled, and no less 'true' for that.

I am grateful to those who helped me with Jean's early life in St Thomas, Ontario. Duncan Mckillop educated me about the Church of Christ (Disciples) and lent me his books. Howard Mills answered my notice in the *St Thomas Times-Journal*, invited me into his home, and shared his extensive collection of St Thomas history, including City Directories and *The Collegian*, the St Thomas Collegiate and Vocational

Institute's yearbook. Muriel G. Luton, archivist for the Ontario Assembly of the Christian Church (Disciples of Christ), also answered my notice, referring me to 'older members of the Princess Avenue congregation' and sending me clippings from *The Canadian Disciple*. Mary Jane Edwards provided me with the names of the Royce's neighbours. Hazel Charleton, Lucy (Shute) Goldsmith, Florence (Billingsley) Snell, and Myrtle (Richards) Fyle all kindly spoke to me on the phone, culling memories from eighty or ninety years ago. Helen (Babe) Bythell invited me to her home in Toronto and offered me her childhood memories of the Royce family. Jessie (Mackinnon) Reid knew the Royce family through the church, and as a Queen's student in the 1930s met Jean and her mother again. Jessie's Queen's friend, Rosetta (Wolff) Elkin, provided her name, and we met on the phone and by letter.

I am especially grateful to the Reverend Wallace Howlett and Mrs Elaine Howlett for lending me the records of the Church of Christ (Disciples) in St Thomas. On 5 June 1996, they opened the cupboard in the new church on Wellington Street, pulled down some boxes, and gave them to me for the night. I was thrilled, and thank them for their confidence. I am also grateful to Nancy Millman and Judy Regan of Parkside Collegiate for providing me with the high school records of the Royce children, and to Carolyn Blewett of the Elgin Board of Education for providing access to their records in the public schools. The staff at the St Thomas Public Library were also very helpful.

Writing Jean's life at Queen's involved help from many people, and I am grateful to everyone who spoke to me, sometimes at street corners, in taxis, and in stores and restaurants. Jean Royce was well known in Kingston, and such casual conversations often confirmed other evidence or set me off in new directions. Their names are not all here, but their memories helped.

In January 1993 the group that initiated this project wrote to alumni, faculty, and staff who had known Jean Royce. The following people responded to their letter – signed by Jill Harris – either with their own memories or with the names of others: John Ashley, Margaret Atack, Alfred Bader, Elspeth (Wallace) Baugh, Anne Bodnarchuk, Mary-Louise (Funke) Campbell, Eugene A. Cherniak, Ralfe J. Clench, A. John Coleman, Marie-Jeanne Coleman, Mary Elizabeth (Jeffery) Collier, Mabel Corlett, Denzil Doyle, Martyn Estall, Ed Funke, James Courtright, Stewart Fyfe, Lin Good, Catherine R. Harland, Joan Eichner, Albert Fell, Eric Harrison, Barbara (Excell) Hawgood, J.E. Hodgetts, Robin Jackson, Jane Kaduck, Dawn Kiell, A.M. Laverty, W.C.

Lougheed, Esther R. Magathan, Kate (Macdonnell) Lawson, Connie Martens, James E. Martin, David B. McLay, Sylvia (Mackenzie) Mercer, Fred G. Moote, Gladys R. Munnings, Jacqueline Neatby, Kristian Palda, Douglas Patriquin, Judith (Plumptre) Wedderspoon, Chris Redmond, W.B. Rice, Vernon Ready, Ann Saddlemyer, P.A. Scrivener, Duncan Sinclair, David W. Slater, Gail Stewart, Hale Trotter, Ian Vorres, Jake Warren, and Kathleen B. Whitehead. I am very grateful to all of them.

Many people responded to my notices in the *Alumni Review*, or to my letters, with stories of their own or names of others whom they thought could help. I am very grateful to the following people: George Ashman, Ruth Bialek, Justice Kenneth C. Binks, N.H. Black, Kathleen (Barclay) Bowley, Margaret Boyce, Konrad Brenner, Doris Burns, A. Chiperzak, J.H. Collins, the Honourable John C. Crosbie, F. Gordon Dunn, T.S. Durham, Catherine I. Eddy, T.Z. Fahidy, Mary (Krotkov) Finegold, Doug Frayne, Priscilla Galloway, Anne Ginn, Donald J. Gormley, Hardy Grant, Bruce M. Hamilton, J.E. Hanna, the Reverend Hartwell B. Illsey, G.A. Jewett, Major (Ret'd) J.B. Kelly, Elizabeth Kennedy, C. Keyzers, Mike Lafratta, Judith Rice Lave, Lionel Lawrence, Steven M. Leikin, Frances Macdonnell, Jean MacLean, Howard Manchester, John Ross Matheson, Douglas McCalla, William E. McDowell, Bob McLarty, Neil McNeill, T. Brian Mosgrove, David Moyer, Evangeline Murray, Arthur E. Ross, Douglas H. Ross, Elspeth Ross, James P. Scanlon, Jim Shute, Sandra K. Sinclair, David Sweezey, Peter Taylor, Jenny M. Weir, Glenn Wilms, and David Wilson.

Several people kindly spoke to me on the phone: Bernard Champagne, William Cannon, James Courtright, Zander Dunn, Judge Alan B. Gold, May Hambly, Elizabeth Harkness, Jo-Anne Hawley, A.J. Michael Humphries, Kate (Macdonnell) Lawson, Raymond Phillips, Frank Ritchie, Ada Terry, Jerry Tulchinsky, E.E. Watson, Judith Wedderspoon, and Annette Woolf.

I interviewed Magda Davey in Toronto, Ann Hall in London England, and the following people in Kingston, and I am very grateful to all of them for their time and candour: Olive Blainie, Clara Brooke, Shirley Brooks, Dawn Cannon, John Carmichael, Bill Craig, Cheryl Creatore, Elsie Curtis, Gordon Dowsley, Hans Eichner, Rosetta Wolff Elkin, Harold Good, Connie Martens, John Olsen, Evelyn Reid, Dr Jerry Simon, Eleanor Smith, Frances K. Smith, Bernard Trotter, Ronald Watts, Donna Watts, and Rona Wilkie. The following people talked to me more informally: Elspeth (Wallace) Baugh, Donna Ede, Stewart

Goodings, J.A.W. Gunn, George Henderson, Al Hyland, Donald Macintosh, Helen Mathers, and Jim Whitley.

Queen's alumnus Dr Benjamin Scott, (BA '38, MD '43), helped me more than he knows. Not only did he write letters and speak to me several times on the phone, but he read an early draft of every chapter and provided thoughtful commentary. Dr Scott inspired me with his stories and his courage, and I am forever grateful to him. I am grateful to Jean Richardson, Jean Royce's assistant from 1939 to 1962, for talking to Margaret Hooey and Dawn Cannon, and later to me, and for writing some of her memories. I want to thank Phyllis and Lucinda Bray for reading several chapters, Dawn Cannon for reading the first chapter, and Karen Dubinsky for reading the entire manuscript and giving me excellent commentary.

My greatest debt is to Margaret Hooey, who answered more questions – by e-mail, phone, letter, and in person – than anyone had a right to ask. She read several drafts of the manuscript, often confirming, sometimes questioning, occasionally taking exception. As Jean Royce's assistant for the last six years of her registrarship, and her closest friend in the last twenty years of her life, she was well placed to facilitate this project, and she did, in many ways. Most of Jean Royce's letters and papers are in Margaret's possession, and she made everything available to me. I appreciate her support and assistance very much.

I owe a special debt to Jean's brother Donald and his wife Celia. They spoke to Dawn Cannon at their home in Toronto in March 1993, and again to me a year later. After Donald's untimely death, Celia gave me yet another interview. Without their help, the material on Jean's childhood and on the Royce family ethos would be even more speculative than it is, and I am touched by their generosity. Jean's nephews Ian and Stewart and her nieces Brenda, Gail, and Lyn all spoke to me at length, Ian in London, Ontario, Stewart in St Thomas, Brenda in Toronto, Gail in Kingston, and Lyn in Niagara-on-the-Lake. Ian also provided me with the Royce family tree and answered questions by e-mail throughout the project. Brenda painted a moving portrait of Jean's sister, Marion, which helped in considering the complex relationship between the two sisters. Lyn provided many memories from her father, Jean's older brother Stewart, as well as her own stories, all of which enlivened my sense of the Royce family. Gail provided a picture of her Aunt Jean, the person who played a nurturing role in her life after the death of her mother. Stewart took me to the St Thomas cemetery where his grandparents are buried along with their infant son Harry.

I am pleased to acknowledge support from several quarters at Queen's University. The late David C. Smith, Principal Emeritus of Queen's University, the Advisory Research Council, and Alison Morgan, Secretary Emeritus of the University Senate, provided funding at different stages of the project. A sabbatical in 1997–98 gave me time to write the first chapters. I am very grateful to those at the Katherine Ryan Archives at Queen's University for their patient assistance at all stages. In particular, the associate university archivist Paul Banfield saw the project through from beginning to end. He shared my enthusiasm, and with his consummate professionalism helped me solve many mysteries. Holly Papi in the Office of Advancement responded to innumerable requests for information on alumni, and always so quickly.

Three graduate students in the Department of Sociology at Queen's worked as research assistants on this project. Marion Campbell did a lot of work in the early stages and provided some important insights. Also, her MA thesis on the origins of the Ban Righ Foundation made an important contribution to this book. Shelley Reuter continued this archival work, becoming in the process a good historical detective. Krista Robson compiled the index. I am grateful to all of them. Jessica Hamilton discovered through *The Queen's Journal* that Jean Royce had an active extra-curricular life as a student, and also selected relevant stories over the decades.

Natalie Forknall in the Faculty of Arts and Science, and June Pilfold, Lynn Wagar, and Joan Westenhaefer in the Department of Sociology, assisted me with this project at different stages, not least by being so encouraging. Without Joan's work in the final stages, I am not sure when this manuscript would have been delivered. Her careful attention to matters big and small – as well as her willingness to disappear her weekends and evenings – helped immeasurably.

I am pleased to acknowledge that this book has been published with the help of a grant from the Humanities and Social Sciences Federation of Canada, using funds provided by the Social Sciences and Humanities Research Council of Canada. I also extend my appreciation to the two anonymous reviewers for their warm encouragement and good advice, to the series editors Karen Dubinsky and Franca Iacovetta for supporting the project, to Matthew Kudelka for his fine copy editing, and to my editors Jill McConkey, Frances Mundy, and Len Husband. Special thanks to Len for inventing the title. My working title 'Is This the Best You Can Do?' summed up Jean Royce for me, but 'Setting the

Agenda' draws attention to her day-to-day work, as well as to her influence in the development of the university.

As always, I have been heartened by many friends and colleagues. In particular, for being there, I thank Beverley Baines, Michèle Barrett, Duncan Barrett, my youngest friend – Jordi Belyea-Dubinsky – and his parents Karen and Susan, Jane Errington, Philip Goldman, Olga Kits (also my computer guru), Susan Lederman, Colin Leys, Leslie Monkman, Vincent Sacco and Pamela Dickey Young.

My family is loving and helpful. My mother, Elizabeth Russell, read drafts of all the chapters and advised me to keep going. (I said I would if she would.) Thanks to my children and their partners – Joe and Michelle, Susan, and Jessica and Jay – for keeping me light, and continuing to give the impression that they need me.

My partner, Geoffrey Smith, was my in-house editor for the completed manuscript. Following others, I discovered his fine editorial eye, and ruthless interest in economy of language, active verbs, and eliminating block quotes. Just as it seemed the household might come apart along with the manuscript, he completed his work, making my final revisions infinitely easier and more satisfying. I am very grateful to him for this, and much else. In truth, he was more interested in the movie version than the book, and entertained me by choosing appropriate actors for all the parts: Meryl Streep as Jean Royce was my favourite. For several summers he left me and Tuborg the Dog on his island by day, and brought provisions by night. Tuborg was my constant companion, and I shall never remember writing this book without thinking of him, and of Geoff who provided perfect conditions for writing – and not writing.

My final acknowledgment must be to Jean Royce. She lived a life that kept me engaged, sometimes obsessed, for several years, thus warding off all manner of existential crises in my own life. Until recently, I remained uncertain about her stance to this project. Now I think that she would have been interested in her biography, as indeed she was in so many others. She might find the scholarship 'sound,' while noting that she left so much beyond the biographer's purview. That is as it should be.

Illustration Credits

Margaret Hooey: Margaret Hooey, 1968; Jean with Phyllis Knight; Jean receiving honorary degree; Jean and Margaret, embarking; Jean in Margaret's garden, summer 1980; Jean in front of Margaret's house.

Queen's University Archives: Levana Executive; Katherine's birthday, 1937; Jean with her niece, Gail, 1937; Jean with friends; Jean at her desk, early 1940s; Students registering in Douglas Library; Jean in Florence; Jean in Switzerland; IFUW, Helsinki; Robert Legget after honorary degree; Jean on eve of retirement.

Lyn Royce: Royce family picture, 1909; Marion Royce, high school graduation; Jean Royce, Queen's University graduation.

Index

STUDIES IN GENDER AND HISTORY

General editors: Franca Iacovetta and Karen Dubinsky

1 Suzanne Morton, *Ideal Surroundings: Domestic Life in a Working-Class Suburb in the 1920s*
2 Joan Sangster, *Earning Respect: The Lives of Working Women in Small-Town Ontario, 1920–1960*
3 Carolyn Strange, *Toronto's Girl Problem: The Perils and Pleasures of the City, 1880–1930*
4 Sara Z. Burke, *Seeking the Highest Good: Social Service and Gender at the University of Toronto, 1888–1937*
5 Lynne Marks, *Revivals and Roller Rinks: Religion, Leisure, and Identity in Late-Nineteenth-Century Small-Town Ontario*
6 Cecilia Morgan, *Public Men and Virtuous Women: The Gendered Languages of Religion and Politics in Upper Canada, 1791–1850*
7 Mary Louise Adams, *The Trouble with Normal: Postwar Youth and the Making of Heterosexuality*
8 Linda Kealey, *Enlisting Women for the Cause: Women, Labour, and the Left in Canada, 1890–1920*
9 Christina Burr, *Spreading the Light: Work and Labour Reform in Late-Nineteenth-Century Toronto*
10 Mona Gleason, *Normalizing the Ideal: Psychology, Schooling, and the Family in Postwar Canada*
11 Deborah Gorham, *Vera Brittain: A Feminist Life*
12 Marlene Epp, *Women without Men: Mennonite Refugees of the Second World War*
13 Shirley Tillotson, *The Public at Play: Gender and the Politics of Recreation in Post-War Ontario*
14 Veronica Strong-Boag and Carole Gerson, *Paddling Her Own Canoe: The Times and Texts of E. Pauline Johnson (Tekahionwake)*
15 Stephen Heathorn, *For Home, Country, and Race: Constructing Gender, Class, and Englishness in the Elementary School, 1880–1914*
16 Valerie J. Korinek, *Roughing It in the Suburbs: Reading* Chatelaine *Magazine in the Fifties and Sixties*
17 Adele Perry, *On the Edge of Empire: Gender, Race, and the Making of British Columbia, 1849–1871*

18 Robert A. Campbell, *Sit Down and Drink Your Beer: Regulating Vancouver's Beer Parlours, 1925–1954*

19 Wendy Mitchinson, *Giving Birth in Canada, 1900–1950*

20 Roberta Hamilton, *Setting the Agenda: Jean Royce and the Shaping of Queen's University*